THE UNITED STATES AND

LATIN AMERICA IN THE 1990S

1

2

A

4

THE UNITED

Edited by

Jonathan Hartlyn,

Lars Schoultz, and

Augusto Varas

STATES AND

LATIN AMERICA

IN THE 1990S:

BEYOND THE

COLD WAR

The University of North Carolina Press

Chapel Hill and London

Library of Congress Cataloging-in-Publication Data
The United States and Latin America in the 1990s :
    beyond the Cold War / edited by Jonathan Hartlyn,
    Lars Schoultz, and Augusto Varas.
        p.   cm.
    Includes bibliographical references and index.
    ISBN 0-8078-2070-9 (cloth : alk. paper). —
ISBN 0-8078-4402-0 (pbk. : alk. paper)
    1. Latin America—Relations—United States.
2. United States—Relations—Latin America.   3. United
States—Foreign relations—1989–   4. Latin America—
Foreign relations—1948–   I. Hartlyn, Jonathan.
II. Schoultz, Lars.   III. Varas, Augusto.
F1418.U652   1992
303.48′27308—dc20   92-29400
                                                         CIP

The paper in this book meets the guidelines for
permanence and durability of the Committee on
Production Guidelines for Book Longevity of the
Council on Library Resources.
96   95   94   93   92   5   4   3   2   1

To · *Javiera, Karina, Liza,*
María Elena, Nils,
Trinidad, and Zachary

CONTENTS

· TABLES

· ACKNOWLEDGMENTS

This volume represents a collaborative project of the Facultad Latinoamericana de Ciencias Sociales (FLACSO)–Programa Chile, the Institute of Latin American Studies at the University of North Carolina (UNC), and the Duke–UNC Program in Latin American Studies. Nearly all of its chapters were first presented for critical comment at a conference on inter-American relations, cosponsored by these three institutions and held in Chapel Hill in April 1990. Now, several revisions later, we believe that they represent a comprehensive analysis of U.S.–Latin American relations in the 1990s.

The principal funding for this project was provided by the Z. Smith Reynolds Foundation, whose president, Smith Bagley, and executive director, Thomas Lambeth, were instrumental in initiating our interest in a collaborative effort. Indeed, at a luncheon in Paraguay in 1986 Smith Bagley suggested to one of the editors that we needed to begin preparing then to understand the forces that would shape inter-American relations outside the cold war framework that dominated everyone's thinking at the time. Bagley also gently suggested that U.S. and Latin American specialists should consider working together on such a project, a suggestion we took seriously, as the following chapters indicate.

Although it is only with Tom Lambeth's and Smith Bagley's assistance that the Chapel Hill conference became a reality, we gratefully acknowledge the receipt of additional financial support from the provost, the dean of the College of Arts and Sciences, the Curriculum of Peace, War, and Defense, and the Institute for Research in Social Science—all of the University of North Carolina at Chapel Hill. Partial funding for this project from the Ford Foundation is also gratefully acknowledged. The foundation's support to the International Relations and Security Studies Area of FLACSO-Chile has facilitated the development of an intellectual and research capability enabling collaborative research with U.S. academic institutions on topics such as the future of hemispheric relations.

This volume represents the work of many more people than the editors and the authors of the individual chapters. Several colleagues from Duke and UNC, and others, including Manuel Alcántara, Heraldo Muñoz, Patricia Pessar, Carlos Rico, and Gustavo Vega, helped focus the discourse and challenge the authors to rethink their positions on a variety of issues. Constructive comments by the anonymous reviewers for the University of North Carolina Press were very helpful. We are also indebted to the professional staff of the Institute of Latin American Studies at the University of North Carolina, especially to Josie McNeil and Sharon Mújica, who not only handled the million-and-one details of an international conference but also made it look effortless. Several UNC graduate students helped with various aspects of the conference and the manuscripts that resulted from it, but we are especially indebted to Pamela Erwin, who struggled mightily to generate a master bibliography and produce a manuscript in a single coherent style, and to Eduardo Feldman, whose job it was to track down errant citations.

Finally, we wish to express our appreciation for the assistance of David Perry of the University of North Carolina Press, who has been the ideal editor: supportive, helpful, and unwilling to accept even the most imaginative excuses.

THE UNITED STATES AND

LATIN AMERICA IN THE 1990S

UNITED STATES

Bermuda (U.K.)

ATLANTIC OCEAN

MEXICO

Gulf of Mexico

Mexico

CUBA
Havana

See inset below

GUATEMALA
Guatemala
EL SALVADOR
San Salvador
HONDURAS
Tegucigalpa
NICARAGUA
Managua
COSTA RICA
San José
PANAMA
Panama

BELIZE
Belmopan

Caribbean Sea

Canal Area

Quito

ECUADOR

GUYANA
Georgetown
SURINAME
Paramaribo
FRENCH GUIANA
Cayenne

Caracas
VENEZUELA

Bogotá
COLOMBIA

PERU

BRAZIL

Lima

Brasília

BOLIVIA
La Paz
Sucre

PACIFIC OCEAN

PARAGUAY

Asunción

ARGENTINA

URUGUAY
Montevideo

Santiago

CHILE

Buenos Aires

Falkland Islands
(Islas Malvinas)

THE BAHAMAS

DOMINICAN REPUBLIC
Santo Domingo

HAITI
Port-au-Prince

PUERTO RICO (U.S.)

VIRGIN ISLANDS
(U.S., U.K.)

CUBA

Guadaloupe (Fr)

JAMAICA

Dominica (U.K.)
Martinique (Fr)
St. Lucia (U.K.)
St. Vincent (U.K.)
Barbados
Grenada

Netherlands Antilles

Curaçao

Trinidad and Tobago

Introduction · *Jonathan Hartlyn,*

· *Lars Schoultz, and*

· *Augusto Varas*

On October 27, 1983, President Ronald Reagan went before the television cameras to explain the U.S. invasion of Grenada. Although he cited several reasons for the action, including threats to the safety of U.S. citizens, his focus was on the need to contain communist adventurism. Grenada, he said, "was a Soviet-Cuban colony, being readied as a major military bastion to export terror and undermine democracy. We got there just in time." In his ten-minute discussion of Grenada, Reagan mentioned the Soviet Union and Cuba fourteen times.[1]

Seven years later, on December 20, 1989, President George Bush went before the television cameras to explain the U.S. invasion of Panama. Although he, too, cited several reasons for the action, he centered on threats to the safety of U.S. citizens by a single individual, General Manuel Antonio Noriega: "As President, I have no higher obligation than to safeguard the lives of American citizens. And that is why I directed our Armed Forces to protect the lives of American citizens in Panama and to bring General Noriega to justice in the United States." In his brief speech, Bush never mentioned the Soviet Union or Cuba.[2]

What happened during the seven years that separated the invasions of Grenada and Panama? In international relations, these were the years of glasnost and perestroika, the years of Soviet withdrawal from Afghanistan, the years of communist breakdown in Central Europe and, soon thereafter, of the dissolution of the Soviet Union itself. They were also the years of the continuing economic emergence of Japan and the European Community, as well as of dramatic changes in the global economy. In Latin America, they were the years of violent turmoil in Central America, of severe economic decline followed by economic restructuring elsewhere in the region, as well as of a continuing turn away both from military governments and state-centered development models. These were also years of dramatic ideological evolution of parts of both the Latin American Right and the Latin American Left. In the United States, they were the years of intense debate over the appropriate policy for Washington to follow in Latin America—years when much of the public and many of its elected officials concluded either that U.S. security concerns in Latin America could best be served by focusing on nontraditional threats such as drug trafficking, environmental degradation, and migration rather than on communist adventurism, or that these had been largely superseded by economic issues of debt and trade. And they were years of an emerging bipartisan consensus that the promotion of democracy and the protection of human rights should be goals of U.S. policy in Latin America, although differences remained regarding the nature and appropriate means of implementing these goals.

This is a book about the implication of these changes for U.S.–Latin American relations in the 1990s. New actors, new issues, and new international realities have altered the form and substance of U.S. policy toward Latin America. In a post–cold war era, it will no longer be possible for the United States to organize its policy toward the region around the goal of seeking to exclude extrahemispheric rivals from the region. Different and more varied political, social, and economic relationships among the peoples and states of the Western Hemisphere are being forged even as Latin American states have more sophisticated and complex foreign policies. In combination, these new actors, issues, and relationships appear to require a substantial adjustment in the traditional inter-American system, in U.S. policy toward Latin America, and in the ways Latin American states formulate and implement their foreign policies.

The emergence of more varied links among the United States and different Latin American countries and subregions, as well as among the nations of Latin America, points to a more complex reality than is captured by the single term, *U.S.–Latin American relations*. Will Latin America as a region, or certain parts of it, become increasingly marginalized on the fringe of international relations and U.S. foreign policy concerns, as some have forecast? Will we see the hegemonic presumption of the United States toward Latin America find expression in new ways and through new issues, or will a new consensus and a new international regime of greater cooperation be at least partially realized? The chapters that follow provide benchmarks for evaluation and tentative answers to these difficult questions. They suggest that it is highly unlikely that the region as a whole will become marginalized, although some parts of it might move more in that direction as a greater differentiation in U.S. attention to Latin America takes place. For many issues, such as trade, drug trafficking, and migration, geography and markets will play pivotal roles, although individual Latin American countries may well counteract or reinforce trends by their choice of policies. Most difficult to predict is whether a new era of unilateral U.S. actions or of increased hemispheric cooperation is upon us, as indicators of both trends are present. What is certain now is that previous bedrock security concerns, economic patterns, and expectations of political solidarity in U.S.–Latin American relations are being replaced by a variety of other issues related to finance, trade, democracy and human rights, narcotics, the environment, and migration. And, in this context, new ideological divisions and restructured political coalitions within the United States and across all nations of the continent are likely to emerge during the 1990s.

The United States and the Traditional Inter-American System

For the 180-year period prior to the late 1980s, U.S. policymakers had a special way of thinking about Latin America. It was developed early in the nineteenth century, when England, allied with Spain in Europe and on the verge of war with the United States, threatened to seize Spanish Florida and use it as a base to attack the United States. As an act of national defense, Congress responded in 1811 by adopting the No-Transfer Resolution, the first substantial statement of U.S. policy toward Latin America. Noting "the influence which the destiny of the territory adjoining the southern border of the United States may have upon their security, tranquility, and commerce," the No-Transfer Resolution asserted that the United States "cannot without serious inquietude see any part of the said territory pass into the hands of any foreign Power [i.e., England]; and that a due regard to their own safety compels them to provide . . . for the temporary occupation of the said territory."

The die was cast with the No-Transfer Resolution. Although other goals have emerged over time, since the early nineteenth century the fundamental goal of U.S. policy toward Latin America has been to exclude extrahemispheric rivals from the region. What began as an effort to keep the British out of Florida (and Cuba) soon expanded when, in the early 1820s, the Holy Alliance authorized France to assist Spain in recovering its American colonies. This led to the Monroe Doctrine, the cognitive bedrock of U.S. policy toward Latin America. Since 1823, most premeditated acts of significance by the United States in Latin America have been based on six sentences written by President James Monroe and his secretary of state, John Quincy Adams:

> The citizens of the United States cherish sentiments the most friendly in favor of the liberty and happiness of their fellow men on that side of the Atlantic. In the wars of the European powers, in matters relating to themselves, we have

never taken any part, nor does it comport with our policy, to do so. It is only when our rights are invaded, or seriously menaced, that we resent injuries, or make preparation for our defense. With the movements in this Hemisphere we are of necessity more immediately concerned, and by causes which must be obvious to all enlightened and impartial observers. The political system of the allied powers, is essentially different in this respect from that of America. . . . We owe it, therefore, to candor and to the amicable relations existing between the United States and those powers, to declare that we should consider any attempt on their part to extend their system to any portion of this hemisphere as dangerous to our peace and safety.

From early in the nineteenth century, then, U.S. policy toward Latin America has been guided by a conceptual framework that we can call *strategic denial*. The specific threats that have been processed within this framework have varied over time. After the change in focus from England in 1811 to the Holy Alliance in the 1820s, there were major shifts back to Great Britain in the years preceding the U.S. Civil War, to France immediately after the Civil War, to Germany and (in the case of Mexico's Magdalena Bay) Japan around the turn of the century, to fascists in the 1930s and 1940s, and finally to communists in 1945.

Conceptually, these shifts in focus were not especially significant, although in terms of their impact on particular Latin American countries they may have been. The important point is that for the 180 years prior to the late 1980s, U.S. policy toward Latin America had as its primary goal the exclusion of extrahemispheric rivals from Latin America. As the United States emerged as an economic power, complementary subgoals such as the drive for economic advantage, the protection of private U.S. interests, and the promotion of "good government" or democracy also emerged in different periods and with different intensities. Yet the objective of exclusion remained. The Monroe Doctrine has become a political anachronism, but its underlying meaning is related to a tangible national security concern: prudent people keep potential adversaries as far away as possible. Indeed, the history of warfare can be written as a continuous adjustment between technological change, on the one hand, and the significance of geographic proximity, on the other. In the 1820s, the United States was vulnerable to attack from Latin America and it made good sense for Washington's defensive posture to include a warning that European powers should not attempt to regain their colonies. At that historical moment, strategic denial earned its status by providing policymakers with a framework to address a problem they considered acute. Over two centuries, however, the changing nature of warfare has slowly but inexorably rendered less compelling the significance of geographic proximity and, hence, the rationale behind the Monroe Doctrine. And more recently, with the dissolution of the Soviet

Union, Washington's fears about the most recent of its extrahemispheric rivals have disappeared.

With the end of strategic denial as an organizing principle for U.S. foreign policy toward Latin America, some analysts and policymakers have predicted the marginalization of the region from U.S. foreign policy concerns. This view is challenged by the authors of the first three chapters of this book, Alberto van Klaveren, Augusto Varas, and Abraham F. Lowenthal. As they note, other goals and issues—some old ones that are being redefined and some new ones—have become increasingly prominent. Moreover, they argue, the region's economic potential and possible impact on the United States should not be underestimated. These three chapters paint a complex, evolving picture over the past two decades of an apparent international economic ascendancy on the part of Latin America in the 1970s, followed by decline in the 1980s, and increasing regional differentiation as we move into the 1990s. As van Klaveren (chapter 1) notes, a major difference between the Latin American debt crisis of the 1980s and the earlier crisis of the 1930s is that the more recent one has affected mainly the region and not the entire world. At the same time, he contends, negative short-term trends in the 1980s should not obscure brighter long-term prospects for the region's economies in the 1990s or its security ties and political significance to the United States. Van Klaveren also provides an appraisal of the earlier, exaggerated (and currently more realistic) view of the significance of the European Community and of Japan and the Pacific Basin for Latin America and for U.S.–Latin American relations.

For Varas (chapter 2), one critical consequence of the recent global and regional shifts has been a change in the very concept of Latin America. The old view of an inter-American system organized as a single actor around regional institutions—itself an incompletely realized aspiration—is now being substituted by a more complex, regionally diverse vision and reality. As the predominant power in the region, the United States continues to seek to create a hemispheric order; historically, this has been realized in either a hegemonic or a coercive fashion. Although Varas sees many coercive continuities in U.S. behavior toward Latin America, particularly related to unilateral actions such as the invasion of Panama, drug trafficking, and the continuation of covert action, he also notes the existence of new realities that suggest the possibility for effective hemispheric cooperation. These new realities include support on the part of the United States for political democracy as well as condemnation of political instability encouraged by the Right as well as the Left, a shift toward a clear condemnation of military coups, and support for the reduction in levels of military forces. Varas then examines how the potential for greater cooperation through the development of novel security regimes in the region might be more fully realized.

If van Klaveren and Varas focus on changing international structures, issues, and actors from an international and a Latin American perspective, Lowenthal (chapter 3) does so from the perspective of the United States. Lowenthal reviews five major recent global changes that have had an impact on inter-American relations: the collapse of the Soviet Union, the end of the cold war, the validation of political democracy and of free markets, the diffusion of economic power from the United States to the European Community and to Japan, and the restructuring of the world economy. He also examines how the past decade has represented "years of political gain and of economic disaster" for Latin America and why the ways in which the United States addresses its domestic problems will likely have a major effect on the region.

Lowenthal then explains why he believes Latin America will continue to be important to the United States. The reasons he gives include the region's economic impact and potential (in terms of exports, energy, and finance, not primarily imports and investment as before), massive and sustained migration, U.S. domestic problems such as narcotics and environmental protection, and core U.S. values such as human rights and democracy. These various issues, some of them reformulated versions of older ones, all suggest that the United States may become even more concerned with the internal affairs of Latin American countries than in prior decades.

In sum, all three of these chapters indicate that the traditional era of the post–World War II inter-American system, centered around U.S. concerns for strategic denial of the Soviet Union, is over. As we move beyond the cold war, new issues are now the focus of the regional agenda. At the same time, other profound changes have occurred in the inter-American system. Of these, two of the most important relate to actors: within the United States there has been a "democratization" of the policy-making process, and within Latin American countries there have also been profound changes in the range of actors involved in their foreign policy processes.

Changes in U.S. Foreign Policy-making toward Latin America

In the United States, foreign policy-making has traditionally been the task of a handful of elites. Until World War II, U.S. policy toward Latin America was made by no more than two dozen men, and on most issues the number of policymakers was less than half that size. Not only were they few in number, but they also tended to agree with one another. This was especially true in the early postwar era, when a broad consensus existed on the central goals of U.S. foreign policy. Like all major crises, World War II served to consolidate public opinion around the single objective of military victory, ending the bitter interwar dispute between isolationists and internationalists. After the war, when a normal fragmentation of opinion might have been expected to reemerge, McCarthyism exerted a stultifying effect on political debates.[3] Fed by the fear of Soviet aggression in the new nuclear age, a siege mentality—cold war internationalism—dominated early postwar U.S. foreign policy.

It was only in the 1960s that sufficient space existed in public opinion for critics to initiate a normal debate over the content of U.S. foreign policy. Specifically, a steadily growing number of disaffected citizens and policy analysts began to criticize the tendency of Washington policymakers to interpret instability anywhere in the Third World as an example of communist adventurism. Opposition to the Vietnam War, which the cold war internationalists could not resolve satisfactorily, became the principal manifestation of this disaffection, but the erosion of support for containment was also evident elsewhere—especially in U.S. policy toward Latin America. From Jacobo Arbenz's Guatemala to Fidel Castro's Cuba to Salvador Allende's Chile, the Latin American component of the cold war consensus slowly disintegrated. By the late 1970s it was irreparably damaged, and when the storm clouds of instability unleashed their fury in Central America, partisan politics once more surged over the water's edge.[4]

One important reason why the Reagan administration's policy toward Central America generated such partisan debate in Washington is that although the debate built on these disputes of the 1960s and 1970s, it was not primarily the product of dissent among existing elites; instead, it was produced to a large extent by the incorporation of new groups of U.S. citizens into the policy-making process, groups that had never before played a role in foreign policy-making. These groups represented the "democratization" of the U.S. foreign policy-making process. Today, the democratized process stands in stark contrast to the policy-making process that existed only a few decades ago, when a few officials in Washington were the only relevant participants. This is true of practically any issue in U.S.–Latin American relations. Even relatively minor policy questions are likely to involve both a bewildering array of official participants and a widespread number of nongovernmental interest groups and associations, each of which represents some interest in U.S. society. Major policy issues regularly inject the public at all levels of government, from public opinion polls to grass-roots organizations to highly organized lobbies to congressional pressure.

The critical phenomenon is not simply that there are more participants, but that there are different kinds of participants. During the 1970s and 1980s, many of these new participants—the liberal foreign policy community of human rights organizations, church groups, and university student bodies and faculties that emerged in the 1960s to anchor the left end of the U.S. political spectrum—refused to accept the cold war–strategic denial orientation of U.S. policy toward Latin America. Thus, their insertion infused a greater diversity of opinion among participants in the foreign policy process. These liberals lacked the raw numbers of their moderate and conservative adversaries, and they invariably lost any simple up-or-down vote on issues like the 1989 invasion of Panama.[5] When united on an issue and given sufficient time, however, liberals gradually developed the power to stymie virtually any major foreign policy initiative to which they were strongly opposed.

The inability of the Reagan administration to carry out its interventionist policies in Central America in the 1980s with the kind of freedom granted U.S. administrations in the past was evidence of this power. The liberal foreign policy community forced President Reagan to incur substantial opportunity costs—to make repeated pleas for support, often on national television, for example—in order to pursue his policy in Central America. It placed the administration on the defensive in Congress. It made life miserable for embassy personnel in Central America who were forced to host repeated visits from members of Congress and influential citizens seeking information on human rights conditions. It so devastated the administration's initial evidence of communist adventurism (the February 1981 white paper on El Salvador) that the Reagan State Department was forced to take the unprecedented step of creating an Office of Public Diplomacy for Latin America, and even then it never regained its credibility, as public opinion polls indicate throughout the 1981–89 period. Much as President Jimmy Carter in the 1970s found many of his initiatives blocked in Congress by opposing conservative forces, throughout the 1980s the liberal foreign policy community fought the administration tooth and nail over Central America, particularly in Congress. *Before* the collapse of the Soviet Union became evident, the high political cost of these battles in Congress had clearly made the incoming Bush administration wonder whether it might not be wiser to change course in Central America.

In the 1990s, however, policy debates over issues critical to Latin America are likely to occur in a very different fashion. Conservative isolationism may reemerge as the more powerful opponent to U.S. involvement in Latin America. And, as the irrelevance of strategic denial has become evident to citizens and policymakers across the entire political spectrum, coalitions of liberals and conservatives are beginning to form and re-form in complex and unexpected ways. As Lowenthal and the authors of several of the chapters examining specific issues emphasize, the new topics in U.S.–Latin American relations are complex "intermestic" ones that will divide people by region and by ideology in unconventional ways. This has been particularly evident in policy debates surrounding migration, drug trafficking, and trade. Thus, the U.S.-based allies of Latin Americans on issues related to drug trafficking or the treatment of refugees may bitterly oppose Latin Americans on many of the trade issues that Latin Americans now consider central to their interests. Concerned as they are with stability and economic growth, newly democratic Latin American governments may chafe at continuing criticisms from U.S. liberals and moderates regarding the lack of clarification about or judicial processing of human rights violators in past military governments or in ongoing conflicts with guerrillas. Similarly, congressional votes on free trade with Mexico or elsewhere in Latin America are likely to be determined as much or more by the expected regional and sectoral impacts of such an accord as by political party affiliation, ideological belief in free trade, or solidarity with U.S. unions.

Changes in Latin American States

The third change in the traditional inter-American system as we move beyond the cold war has been in the role played by Latin America. Since the early nineteenth century, Latin American states have slowly emerged as independent actors on the world stage. The principal response of the United States to this growing autonomy has been to establish an inter-American system to enlist the support of Latin Americans in preserving the paradigm of strategic denial—that is, to "multilateralize" not just U.S. policy but the framework upon which it is based. This multilateralization has required the creation of a structure to facilitate interaction between the United States and Latin America. The initial steps were taken in the final quarter of the nineteenth century and led to the formation of the Pan American Union, to U.S. participation in a series of inter-American conferences,[6] to expanded diplomatic representation throughout the hemisphere, and, by the late 1920s, to acceptance of the need to be a good neighbor, which implied a recognition of the sovereignty of Latin American states.

The experience of World War II was especially influential in convincing U.S. policymakers of the need for the cooperation of Latin Americans to exclude extrahemispheric rivals. In January 1942, little more than a month after the Japanese attack on Pearl Harbor, the United States called an emergency meeting of Latin America's ministers of foreign relations in Rio de Janeiro and sent the administration's chief Latin Americanist, Sumner Welles, to convince the nations of the region to declare war on the Axis powers. Rebuffed by Argentina and given lukewarm support by several other governments of the region, the Rio conference produced a document that merely recommended a break in relations with the Axis. The resolution was interpreted at the time as an indicator of the fascist sympathies of Argentina's leaders, but it was also a signal that the United States would need to pay more attention to the growing autonomy of the region if strategic denial was to be preserved in the postwar era.

It was within this context that Latin America became a principal initial focus of U.S. postwar concerns and that the inter-American system, currently in redefinition, emerged. At the very pinnacle of its power, the United States invited the countries of the region to another meeting in Rio de Janeiro, and this time Washington had its way: the first formal U.S. peacetime mutual security alliance—the 1947 Inter-American Treaty of Reciprocal Assistance—committed all the signatories to the principle that "an armed attack by any State against an American State shall be considered as an attack against all the American States and, consequently, each one of the said Contracting Parties undertakes to assist in meeting the attack."[7]

In the context of a rapidly emerging rigid bipolar world, the Rio treaty firmly attached Latin America to the U.S. pole. That is what the United States wanted. But in return for their nominal allegiance, Latin Americans extracted from the United States (1) a formal pledge of nonintervention building on often-cited (but commonly violated) norms of international law, and (2) consent to the creation of institutions to regulate the inter-American system. Foremost among these institutions was the Organization of American States (OAS), created in 1948 by the Act of Bogotá to replace the amorphous Pan American Union. Other spinoff organizations, ranging from the rejuvenated Pan American Health Organization to the Inter-American Commission on Human Rights, have also contributed to the creation of an institutionalized inter-American system.

These concessions have strengthened Latin Americans somewhat when conflicts have arisen with the United States. This may not be immediately evident to observers who correctly recognize that the United States has continued to intervene regularly in Latin America, that the OAS and its ancillary organizations have generally been weak, and that Latin American states have been able to work together only in limited fashion. Nonetheless, the U.S. concessions are important because they have led to a new mental environment for inter-American relations. They have redefined how members *should* act. This has made deviations from expected behavior increasingly costly, because deviations have served as the justification for Latin American resistance when the rules of the inter-American system are violated.

The obsolescence of the institutions of the post–World War II inter-American system was particularly evident to Latin American states in the context of the 1982 Malvinas-Falklands war, when the United States ultimately sided with its NATO ally, Great Britain. At the same time, the ability of Latin American states to establish new institutions through which to channel their dissatisfaction has been constrained. In spite of several efforts, Latin American states were largely not unified regarding their response to the continent's debt crisis during the 1980s. However, in the face of blatant intervention at odds with international law and with the OAS charter, such as U.S. support for the contras in Nicaragua, a number of Latin American states were able to establish ad hoc institutions in an effort to resist U.S.

policy. In this way, first Contadora (and subsequently the Contadora Support Group) and then the Esquipulas peace process were formed.

It appears, then, that Latin Americans have learned how to use international law, multilateral forums, and ad hoc institutional channels, as well as the broader international system, as a weapon of the weak to seek to limit U.S. influence in their countries. Although the structural space enabling Latin American states to act more autonomously has waxed and waned over the past several decades, their administrative capabilities and technical expertise to do so appear to have grown steadily.

In the early 1990s, however, Latin American interest in the development of openly confrontational institutions was in decline, while efforts to revive traditional multilateral institutions with U.S. cooperation, like the OAS, were apparent in such consensual activities as opposition to the overthrow of the civilian regime in Haiti and attempts to reinstate constitutional government in that country. This new emphasis upon cooperation was at least in part a result of the fact that ideologies and mentalities among Latin American elites have also experienced transformations over the past decade. Although the origins of these changes are many, two of the principal ones have been reflection on the causes for the emergence of repressive military governments throughout the continent, on the one hand, and the evident need to recast economic strategies in the face of the continent's economic crisis and the ongoing global economic restructuring, on the other. As is evident in two chapters of this volume, one by Rosario Espinal (chapter 4) on the Right and the New Right in Latin America and the other by Marcelo Cavarozzi (chapter 5) on the region's New Left, the reasons for the emergence of new kinds of thinking on either side of the political spectrum vary considerably, as does their likely political impact.

As Espinal notes, the meaning of the Right in Latin America has always been diverse. However, the most recent connotation—that of the "New Right" as propounder of free markets—is sharply opposed to the views as well as to the interests of some traditional conservative elements in Latin America. As she also observes, the belief in free markets throughout Latin America emerged much more as a consequence of pressure from abroad than as an autochthonous societal project. As a consequence, rightist groups advocating these views have tended to be both politically and electorally weak, and thus the extent of their commitment to political democracy will be tested repeatedly in electoral contests throughout the region during the final decade of the twentieth century.

Changes within the Left in Latin America may ultimately be broader, deeper, and of greater significance. As Marcelo Cavarozzi's chapter indicates, the Left in Latin America has become transformed from a movement of relative homogeneity on the continent to one of extreme diversity. In addition to proponents of millenaristic violence and guerrilla movements, there are also a grass-roots Left and a political Left. Particularly within the political Left in Latin America there is now a widespread, though not universal, acceptance of political democracy. There is also a recognition that more purely national development strategies have become less and less viable, and that greater integration into world markets, with its concomitant social dislocations, may well be an inevitable cost of economic growth.

Latin American state structures are undergoing vast changes as a result of past political and economic legacies and of current economic pressures. In many countries, previous authoritarian regimes strengthened certain nondemocratic institutions or practices, and these will present continuing challenges to the consolidation or the deepening of democratic politics in the region. Similarly, in combination with changes in the global economy, the economic crisis of the 1980s—the oft-discussed "lost decade"—has led to an economic restructuring in nearly all countries of the region. Economic policies such as the opening of these economies to international commerce, the privatization of state-owned enterprises, and the development of dynamic export-oriented sectors (referred to confusingly as either neoconservative or neoliberal strategies) have been espoused and implemented to differing degrees with the hope of strengthening national economies and international competitiveness.

The combined effect of authoritarian experiences, the debt crisis, and economic restructuring has been the emergence or continued existence of restricted or semicompetitive democratic regimes throughout much of the continent. Thus, in the 1990s Latin American countries are being confronted by three challenges: (1) how to democratize their semicompetitive political regimes without destabilizing them and risking authoritarian regressions, (2) how to restructure their economies without fueling social unrest, and (3) if more democratic political institutions evolve and are consolidated and higher levels of economic development are achieved, how to provide greater social equity, thus preventing future political instability.

At the same time, the very changes identified here will impose new challenges for Latin American states. Because of the importance of market mechanisms in current international relations, and because of the emergence of new actors, hemispheric governments will face difficulties in managing the many interactions that will be carried out mainly through nongovernmental channels. An additional consequence of the growing importance of new governmental actors is the emergence of more complex types of bilateral international relations. The growing international dimensions of the work of many governmental agencies are thus producing a rapid diversification and internationalization of the activities of Latin American states. The international bilateral and multilateral linkages of governmental agencies will grow rapidly, and central governments will face increasing problems of coordination and coherence.

Conclusion

As we move through the last decade of the twentieth century and into the twenty-first century, there is little question that we are entering a new era of U.S.–Latin American relations. What to date has been the bedrock of U.S. policy toward Latin America—strategic denial—is almost totally irrelevant. The foreign policy process in the United States now involves many more actors and organizations, both governmental and nongovernmental. Latin American governments also confront more complex internal processes even as many of them have also become increasingly more able to express their demands and concerns internationally.

In this dramatically different context, continental trends such as the democratization of the region, the enactment of market-oriented policies, and the reduction in the role and size of the state in Latin American economies all create possibilities for the emergence of a new consensus between the United States and Latin America. Ominously, they also point to the possibility of new and perhaps acrimonious conflicts. In addition, there is the likelihood of increased regional differentiation in relations with the United States with a potential for marginalization, at least for some subregions. These themes are analyzed in Part I of this book in the chapters by van Klaveren, Varas, Lowenthal, Espinal, and Cavarozzi. All five of these authors agree that old confrontations have now been superseded by new ones that reflect Latin America's autonomous ability to affect the United States. The ability of the United States to affect Latin America has never been in doubt. The implication now, however, is that domestic and international issues and politics, always somewhat blurred in Latin America, will become increasingly so within the United States.

The U.S.–Latin American policy agenda of the 1990s will consist of such issues as international debt; trade; democracy, human rights and the appropriate role for the armed forces; drug trafficking; environmental degradation; and migration. Each of these is the topic of a chapter in Part II of this book.

Riordan Roett (chapter 6) begins his essay on the complex relationships among Latin American debt, economic stabilization, and structural adjustment by summarizing the evolution of the debt crisis of the 1980s. The surge in international oil prices and the onset of the international economic crisis of 1980–82, with its high interest rates and reduced demand for Latin American exports, led to the suspension of debt payments by most Latin American governments in mid-1982. In response, commercial banks stopped lending to the region. The immediate consequence of the 1982–83 debt crisis was the inauguration of programs of economic stabilization and adjustment in almost every country in Latin America. These programs required considerable economic sacrifice from much of the population, as the quickest way to achieve the goals of IMF-monitored programs was for Latin

American governments to cut their "social" budgets. The poor were especially hard hit. As the dimensions of the international economic crisis became apparent to Latin American leaders, they attempted without success to develop a collective response. Roett analyzes the reasons behind this failure of collective action, concluding that the "divide-and-conquer" tactics of the developed countries (especially the United States) were especially important.

As the evidence mounted that Latin America would never generate sufficient income to pay (or in most cases even service) its foreign debt, the United States slowly began to reconsider its opposition to debt relief. First the Baker Plan (1987) and later the Brady Plan (1989) opened the door to creative responses from the U.S. public and private sectors, and the Bush administration's 1990 "Enterprise for the Americas Initiative" contained an explicit commitment by the U.S. government to consider substantial debt relief. The end of East-West tensions and the persistence of U.S. economic problems lead Roett to conclude that solutions to Latin America's debt crisis will receive a low priority among U.S. policymakers in the 1990s. Renewed economic growth and increased foreign investment have the potential to reduce the severity of the crisis, however.

Roberto Bouzas's (chapter 7) analysis of U.S.–Latin American trade relations begins by noting a continuation of a fundamental disequilibrium: while the United States is still the most important trading partner for nearly all of the countries in Latin America, the region's importance in U.S. foreign trade is relatively modest. Although there are marked differences in trade patterns among the countries, this overall disequilibrium has led to a common set of problems for Latin America's fragile economies: U.S. tariff and nontariff protection; the need for preferential tariff treatment for Latin American exports to the United States; discrimination (especially the proposed North American Free Trade Agreement, which disadvantages most of Latin America); and what Bouzas refers to as "procedural protectionism" in the form of countervailing duties and antidumping legislation. On the other side of the trading relationship, the United States has been concerned for many decades with the highly protective nature of Latin America's development strategy of import-substitution industrialization, but this concern is rapidly receding as economic restructuring continues throughout the region.

The second section of Bouzas's chapter underscores a cruel paradox. Even as Latin American economies are moving toward more open trade regimes, the United States has increasingly become more assertive and, to a certain extent, even protectionist. The most likely outcome of U.S.–Latin American trade relations over the 1990s is the stimulation of ongoing processes of economic differentiation within the region; a North American Free Trade Agreement and a partially implemented Western Hemisphere Free Trade Agreement are likely to augment such effects.

A country-by-country review of civil-military relations leads J. Samuel Fitch (chapter 8) to conclude that many of the conditions that favored past military interventions remain, although current democratic regimes clearly benefit from higher domestic and international legitimacy. Yet, in many countries the military lacks the necessary self-confidence or support to govern itself, while civilian political leadership remains fragmented and is unable to inspire confidence in a period of prolonged social and economic crisis. The outcome has been formal continuation of constitutional rule with the continued assertion of a military right to intervene as the "guardian" of national interests.

Fitch discusses the present state of civil-military relations on the continent in terms of a five-step typology ranging from full military dominance to institutionalized democratic control over the armed forces. Most Latin American countries fall somewhere between these two extremes. In this context, Fitch analyzes two critical problems for civilian governments: accountability for human rights violations by past military governments and for continuing violations in ongoing internal wars under democratic governments. He then considers what each Latin American country can do to seek to empower civilian institutions so they take more direct responsibility for internal security, determine the appropriate missions for the armed forces, and creatively manage civil-military tensions. His concluding section discusses how the various facets of U.S. policy—ranging from democracy promotion, to military assistance and training programs, to regional security agreements—could be modified to assist democratic consolidation as well as the institutionalization of democratic models of civil-military relations.

Bruce Bagley and Juan Tokatlian (chapter 9) analyze the shifts in drug diplomacy between the United States and various Latin American states over the past decade. Drug trafficking, like migration, is an issue in which market forces have often overwhelmed state policies. Bagley and Tokatlian first discuss how the drug issue became a major focus of policy concern in the United States in the 1980s, leading to progressively "tougher"—but not more effective—policies toward the producing countries.

By the end of the decade, however, leaders of Latin American countries had also come to believe that drug trafficking represented a national security threat, even as a progressive militarization of the war on drugs was occurring. This was a result of the increasing threats from powerful drug mafias in their own countries, continued pressure from the United States, and the failure to generate a regional alternative to the U.S. "national security" perspective with its logic of escalation. However, the authors argue that efforts by the United States to impose an antidrug "regime" have not met tests of legitimacy, credibility, or symmetry. For this reason, U.S. efforts are not likely to succeed. Bagley and Tokatlian call for a more realistic diagnosis of the complex and multifaceted aspects of the drug trade, a more multilateral and consensual approach, and more realistic criteria to measure "progress" given the limits to state action in this area.

Steven E. Sanderson (chapter 10) begins his essay on environmental issues by challenging the conventional wisdom of officials and analysts from the developed countries of Europe and North America. Rather than focus on the *global political structures* that must be changed in order to begin to arrest the alarming process of environmental deterioration—deforestation, poaching, animal smuggling, and high-impact frontier settlement—officials of the industrialized countries (that is, those of the Organization for Economic Cooperation and Development—OECD) search instead for policy "cures" for Latin America's domestic problems such as poverty. Sanderson argues that this approach is seriously flawed, for it diverts attention from the subject that environmentalists ought to emphasize: the complex relationship between OECD development and trade policy, on the one hand, and the future of resource conservation and use in Latin America, on the other. By ignoring the global dimensions of environmental politics, OECD prescriptions for environmental protection have led to a set of useless, often-harmful policies to "reform" Latin America. Sanderson recognizes that poverty alleviation and other social policies are involved in the issue of environmental protection, and therefore that some emphasis on national-level political economics is important, but he argues forcefully that the main focus of environmental policy should be on changing the nature of international development and trade.

"The history of the Western Hemisphere is a tale of migration," Robert L. Bach (chapter 11) reminds us at the beginning of his essay on hemispheric migration in the 1990s. The economic and political changes since the 1940s have altered the nature and enlarged the scale of this migration, however, and the 1990s will almost certainly see a continuation of the relatively new phenomenon of large-scale migration flows. Bach marshals a growing body of empirical data to indicate the forces behind these flows. "Little mystery remains in the search for under-standing the large-scale structural forces that underlie regional migration," he observes. Although regional conflicts have caused large flows of migrants (most recently from Central America), most migration is predominantly influenced by the regional demand for labor—workers of all types, from tennis stars to farm-hands, move from locales with relatively low demand for labor to sites with relatively high demand and relatively high wages. In practice, this most frequently means a movement from Latin America to the United States and Canada, though in recent years it has also meant a flow from Paraguay and Bolivia to Argentina, from Central America to Mexico, and from Colombia to Venezuela. Given the economic and, at times, the political incentives to migrate, efforts by the U.S. government to curb the flow of Latin American migration have been ineffectual, especially be-cause the strongest U.S. political forces in the current debate on immigration are those who support *expanded* levels of immigration. Bach concludes that the strength of market forces that underlie labor migrations is highly resistant to state intervention. This suggests that the 1990s will see an increased integration of the hemisphere's labor markets.

Latin America, of course, was never simply an inert piece of territory; today, however, as each of these chapters emphasizes, unlike in the early nineteenth century, the United States can no longer act as if it were. There are now four hundred million people in the region, and the continuing revolutions in communications and transportation mean that these people, their products, their cultures, their aspirations, their successes, and their tragedies will be in ever-more-intimate contact with U.S. citizens as they enter the twenty-first century. The chapters that follow describe a complex reality in flux, which combines the potential for increased cooperation in several areas with the renewal of patterns of conflict or of neglect in many others.

Notes

1. *Weekly Compilation of Presidential Documents* 19 (October 31, 1983).

2. *Weekly Compilation of Presidential Documents* 25 (December 25, 1989).

3. During the McCarthy era, about one-fifth of the U.S. work force (13 million out of 65 million workers) was affected by loyalty and security programs. See James L. Gibson, "Political Intolerance," esp. p. 514. Gibson's discussion of McCarthyism draws on Brown, *Loyalty and Security*.

4. Throughout the twentieth century, politicians have regularly used "water's edge" language to decry the intrusion of partisan politics into foreign policy matters, but they regularly have violated their own principle. Senator Arthur Vandenberg, for example, once urged his colleagues to join him in "a mutual effort . . . to unite our official voice at the water's edge," but his own career (especially his vehement opposition to Woodrow Wilson's League of Nations) exemplifies how partisan foreign policy can become. Thus, although there has always been a general consensus in Washington that the United States can only speak "with maximum authority against those who would divide and conquer us" if Washington has a single "official voice," in U.S. history there is nothing apolitical about foreign policy. For the full text from which the above quotations were taken and for Vandenberg's extended view of the relationship between foreign policy and partisan politics, see Vandenberg, *Private Papers*, pp. 552ff.

5. On February 7, 1990, for example, the House of Representatives voted 389–26 to approve a resolution praising President Bush for sending U.S. forces to invade Panama.

6. Prior to a structural change in 1970, there were ten major conferences, each identified by its number and location: the first (1889) in Washington, the second (1901) in Mexico City, the third (1906) in Rio de Janeiro, the fourth (1910) in Buenos Aires, the fifth (1923) in Santiago, the sixth (1928) in Havana, the seventh (1933) in Montevideo, the eighth

(1938) in Lima, the ninth (1948) in Bogotá, and the tenth (1954) in Caracas. Each of the first nine was called an International Conference of American States. After the 1948 OAS charter changed this name to the Inter-American Conference; only one meeting occurred (in Caracas in 1954). In 1970 the Inter-American Conference was replaced by the OAS General Assembly, which now meets annually. For detailed information on inter-American conferences (and on nearly every other aspect of inter-American relations), the best source is Atkins, *Latin America*, p. 206.

7. Article 3, Inter-American Treaty of Reciprocal Assistance.

Part One · STRUCTURES AND IDEAS

· *Alberto van Klaveren*
·

Chapter One · LATIN AMERICA AND THE
·
. INTERNATIONAL POLITICAL
·
· SYSTEM OF THE 1990S
·
·
·

he analysis of Latin American international relations seems prone to the
already-familiar cycles that can be observed in the study of the region's domes-
tic politics or economics. A cycle of remarkable optimism and, in a sense, of
triumphalism has given way to one of growing pessimism and even fatalism about
the prospects for the insertion of the region in the international system. The image
of a weakened and stagnant Latin America in a world in constant flux pervades
many debates and, what is worse, is fairly common among the region's leaders and
reflected by public opinion. Whereas the rest of the world—except for most of
Africa and parts of Asia—seems to be in the international limelight, Latin America
is viewed by its own politicians and experts as an increasingly marginalized and
abandoned region.

In the 1970s and at the beginning of the 1980s, perceptions about the international relations of the region were very different. Of course, because of the region's
distorted and peculiar development patterns, experts never ceased to talk about
the *crisis* of Latin America while tending to neglect its rather impressive economic
achievements.[1] Some of the rather gloomy analyses of those times were also
employed to draw attention to the perceived misfortunes of Latin America in an
unfair international system. Nevertheless, during those years nearly all Latin
American countries experienced rapid economic and social change. Their average
annual growth rate reached 5.9 percent between 1960 and 1973, slowing down to
a still-impressive 5.4 percent for the rest of the 1970s. Despite an enormous
demographic explosion, Latin America's real per capita gross domestic product
(GDP) rose by about 3.5 percent annually during the period 1960–70 and by
about 4.1 percent during 1970–80.[2]

Even though the region's growth process was characterized by significant limitations and inequalities, many of its social indicators changed significantly during the 1960s and the 1970s. Aggregate measures of public health, education, and housing showed considerable improvement. Although social contrasts remained and were even accentuated in several countries, an overall increase in social indicators meant there were more opportunities for even the poorest Latin Americans.

Several Latin American countries (for example, Brazil and Mexico) rose to the status of newly industrializing countries (NICs). At the same time, the region's vast natural resources assumed a new economic and strategic importance in the context of the oil crisis of 1973–74 and fears of exhaustion of other primary products that seemed essential for the economies of the United States, Japan, and Western Europe.

In the field of international relations, observers called attention to the decline of U.S. hegemony, the diversification of Latin America's external links, and what seemed an ascendant and unstoppable march toward the autonomy of the region. The idea of the Western Hemisphere, which had laid the basis for the establishment of the inter-American system, was replaced by the idea of the Third World as the international identity of the region. In turn, if until the 1960s Latin America's main international arena had been precisely the inter-American system, in the 1970s the region seemed to expand its external activities to the whole global system, forming new ties with Japan and the Soviet Union, resuming a strong relationship with its old European partners, and building coalitions with other developing areas. The new international assertiveness of Latin America was emphasized, and in most cases celebrated, in a growing number of studies that were published at the time.[3] In fact, the appearance of these works was a reflection of the region's new international role.

During the 1970s Latin America placed high expectations on the reform of an international system that was deemed profoundly biased in favor of the developed and rich countries. The region sought the redistribution of economic and political power by aligning itself with other developing countries and regions. At the United Nations, several Latin American countries promoted the adoption of a New International Economic Order. Several countries also joined the Nonaligned Movement, which seemed to express the political interests of the emerging countries of the Third World by formally rejecting traditional cold war divisions and promoting neutralism, decolonization, and the establishment of a more just world order. Latin America also became a promoter of the North-South dialogue, finding a generally positive reception in the more progressive and liberal political sectors of the Western, developed world.[4] To be sure, Latin America's support for the idea of a single Third World was not without ambiguity and doubt, but it provided a new dimension to the region's foreign relations and reinforced its drive for the reform of the international system.[5]

Latin American countries were able to play a significant role in the adoption of a new international regime for the law of the sea. The new assertiveness of the region was also expressed in the development of ambitious nuclear development programs, despite the misgivings and strong opposition of foreign powers such as the United States, which were interested in avoiding nuclear proliferation. Most Latin American countries were able to greatly diversify their arms supplies during that period, depending less and less on the United States for weapons. Indeed, Brazil and, to a lesser extent, Argentina became important arms exporters themselves, competing with, and in some cases displacing, their old suppliers in third markets.

Political regimes of a very different nature and varying persuasions developed innovative and dynamic foreign policies. Brazil, ruled at the time by a right-wing military dictatorship, established extensive economic relations in Africa and the Middle East. It also revised its relations with other Latin American countries, overcoming its relative historical isolation in the region and putting an end to its already-outdated perceptions of rivalry with Argentina. Mexico adopted a more active foreign policy, abandoning its customary introspection and moving toward the rest of Latin America through important albeit somewhat rhetorical foreign policy initiatives. Cuba consolidated its position as a central actor in the Non-aligned Movement, even challenging the traditional concepts of neutrality and equidistance between the blocs that had dominated the initial stage of the movement. Its revolutionary regime was able to dodge the blockade that had been erected against it by the rest of Latin America, acting at the request and under the pressure of Washington. Venezuela became a regional power in the Caribbean area and a donor country in terms of development aid.

In the early 1980s, just when the encouraging democratization processes that were taking place in many countries seemed to reinforce the new international role of the region, a severe economic crisis struck Latin America, significantly eroding the new self-confidence that had characterized its foreign policies in the 1970s. The most dramatic manifestation of the new cycle was the debt crisis that erupted in 1982 and rapidly threatened the region's economic and, by implication, political autonomy. Latin America had not faced a similar problem since the Great Depression. But, in contrast to that first traumatic experience, the 1982 crunch seemed to affect mainly the region, leaving most of the world economy relatively unscathed. Latin American economies and societies began to suffer serious dislocations, which were somehow amplified in a frustrated effort to appeal to the solidarity or the coresponsibility of the rich developed countries. The crisis seemed to confirm the external vulnerability of the region as well as its continued dependence on the United States, although on different terms than in the past.[6]

The drastic reduction of Latin American exports caused by the debt crisis reinforced the recent decline of the region's participation in world trade. Internal drops in production and consumption and the prospect of widespread economic, social, and even political instability left little immediate incentives for foreign investors and partners. On the other hand, the end of the oil crisis and the fact that pessimistic predictions concerning the exhaustion of the world's natural resources proved incorrect seemed to devalue Latin American potential in natural resource exports. In fact, the prices of most of the region's primary exports fell, aggravating its traditional terms-of-trade problem.

In the field of international political relations, the Malvinas-Falklands war, irresponsibly provoked by the Argentine military dictatorship but still actively supported by several Latin American countries, seemed to demonstrate that the region's increased autonomy could also have negative and even dangerous implications. Simultaneously, it exposed the ambiguities and difficulties for Latin American regional cooperation, as well as the vulnerability of the region with respect to its main foreign partners, including the United States and Western Europe.

Later in the 1980s Cuba, which had enjoyed the admiration of many political and intellectual sectors throughout the world, began to be perceived as a dogmatic and uncomfortable external actor, led by a rather typical caudillo, and incapable of adapting itself to the changes that were reshaping the polities and economies of its old socialist allies. For its part, Brazil—the most dynamic and powerful country in the region—plunged into a crisis of governance and lost a considerable part of its bargaining power to confront several major foreign policy issues, such as the protection of its infant computer industry. Mexico, despite its nationalistic foreign policy principles, appeared to be integrating its economy more and more with that of the United States, gradually disentangling itself from the Central American crisis. The Mexicans also seemed to be seeking to balance the growing attraction of the U.S. market by strengthening links with Japan and Western Europe, rather than with their weakened Latin American southern neighbors.

In this context of gradual but clear foreign policy changes in Latin America, the old hegemonic power in the region seemed to recover the initiative. Several governments began to adopt the market-oriented economic doctrines praised by the Reagan administration during the 1980s. U.S. influence in Central America seemed to be confirmed by electoral results in the area. The United States deployed a massive military force to occupy Panama, the country that had best symbolized U.S. imperialism at the beginning of the century. Contrary to many expectations, Latin American protests were confined to the diplomatic sphere and did not trigger any significant popular reaction regionwide or, for that matter, in the rest of the world. On the other hand, the only Latin American countries that seemed to adapt themselves to the changes that were occurring in the world economy were precisely those that had renounced the developmentalist creed of the 1960s and the 1970s, and that had accepted the solutions imposed on them by financial multilateral organizations dominated by rich countries.

At present, it is difficult to avoid the impression that the profound changes that are altering the structure of the international system are leaving Latin America by the wayside. In a clearly pessimistic and fatalistic mood, politicians and experts alike talk about marginalization and abandonment.[7] The notion of a region left behind by history predominates among Latin Americans and their foreign partners.

Despite the insistence with which Latin Americans propound this image, it appears to be another oversimplification of a rather complex reality. To begin with, it overlooks fundamental differences and even uniquenesses in the region. It ignores the impressive economic and political changes that are taking place in numerous countries. It confuses negative short-term trends with undoubtedly brighter long-term trends. And it neglects the tremendous resilience of Latin American economies and societies, which in the past—as now—have been able to overcome crises that in other areas of the world would probably have led to widespread social violence, open state repression, fascism, and aggressiveness abroad.

The great difficulties that Latin America has had to confront during the 1980s, appropriately termed the region's "lost decade," have not eliminated with a wave of the hand all its impressive achievements of previous decades. It is true that the roseate predictions about the capacity of the region to transform its international environment did not materialize. It is also true that the United States continues to be the principal external actor in the region, and that the search for alternative partners in Western Europe, Japan, and the former Soviet Union did not produce all the expected results. Undoubtedly, regional integration experiments attempted since the 1960s have ended in frustration if not in total failure. Nonetheless, the most dynamic sectors of the Latin American economies are still closely intertwined with the world economy. Foreign investment continues to flow to certain countries in Latin America. In contrast to the distressing case of the United States, Latin America's trade balance has improved dramatically over the last decade, not only as a consequence of the reduction of imports but also as a direct result of increased exports, which grew at an annual rate of 12 percent between 1987 and 1989 and at a still-impressive rate of 10 percent during 1990.[8]

Although the United States is still the main foreign actor in the region, its influence has declined in various sectors and the possibility that it will restore its traditional hegemony seems remote.[9] Also, even though the Western Europeans were incapable or merely unwilling to meet Latin American expectations, they remain important economic partners for the region and they have established a network of political relationships that in several countries surpasses that of the United States and one that is certainly less polemical. Japan's ascendancy in the world economy has had a clear impact on Latin America. And although Latin American economic integration is still distant, several countries in the region have engaged in exercises of external political cooperation, proving their value in the Central American crisis. Moreover, the region is attempting to innovate in the field of economic integration, adopting new models that tend to be more realistic and pragmatic than their predecessors of previous decades.[10]

Because of the contradictory evidence presented here, it seems appropriate to review the main factors contributing to the external importance of the region. These factors provide the long-term basis for Latin America's participation in the international system. On the other hand, the utilization and enhancement of these factors depend on the foreign policy capabilities of the different states and on the concrete strategies that they adopt to this end.

Latin America's External Significance

Despite its current problems, Latin American countries possess resources that are important for the rest of the world. Although the region is not a central actor in the world economy and any prospects in that direction seem rather remote, the **economic potential** of Latin America is considerable. Brazil retains its place as one of the ten most powerful economies of the world; Mexico ranks in the next group; and even though Argentina has a declining economy, it still ranks close to Taiwan or an oil power such as Nigeria. The aggregate value of Latin America's gross domestic product amounts to nearly 5 percent of the total world product. This figure is not particularly impressive compared to that of the rich developed countries, but it is significant for a developing area. Moreover, Latin American markets have expanded considerably over the last decades, partly as a consequence of the growth of the middle classes and partly as a result of the incorporation of new social sectors in the national economies. Even though this growth was halted during the 1980s, demographic as well as economic trends point toward a continuing expansion.

Several Latin American countries already possess diversified economies. Although the importance of the agricultural sector in the national economies has declined steadily during the last decades, the region is a notable exporter of agricultural raw materials and food. In fact, Latin America enjoys comparative advantages for several commodities in this sector; these benefits have been nullified by protectionist agricultural policies adopted by Western Europe, the United

States, and Japan. This comparative advantage could be partially recovered if the Uruguay Round succeeds. Certainly of value are the region's mineral resources, some of which are crucial for the industrialized nations. The importance of Latin America's oil reserves is obvious, especially from the perspective of a hypothetical new oil crisis and growing instability in a Middle East shaken by Islamic fundamentalism and other tensions.

The region's generous endowment of natural resources is complemented by a relatively developed industrial sector, which has grown at a more rapid pace than the economy as a whole. Although this sector has evolved irregularly and has suffered from serious limitations,[11] its prospects are less bleak than many would think. Indeed, as Gary Gereffi observes, Latin American NICs have developed a sophisticated array of exports on the basis of their earlier import-substituting industries. Mexico is producing state-of-the-art engines for the U.S. automobile industry. Brazil exports assorted capital goods and technologically advanced armaments, and its large car industry holds an important position in international supply networks. And even a stagnant economy like that of Argentina can boast of internationally competitive firms in the metallurgical and metalworking sectors. According to this analysis, Latin American industrial powers are adapting themselves to the logic of transnational integration based on geographic specialization and tightly linked international supply networks, while moving away from the national segmentation that characterized the import-substituting industrialization. Much like the East Asian NICs, which usually are offered as examples for Latin America, the region is starting to exploit its own export niches and seems to perform well in the fields of commodities exports, export-processing industries, and component supplies.[12]

As Raymond Vernon states, Latin America can benefit from the persistent decline in the costs of communication and transportation and the accompanying decline in the importance of scale in manufacturing due to preference for product differentiation. According to this analysis, the new structure of the productive process seems to require "a cadre of relatively well-trained technicians, capable of serving the receiving end of a technological flow, and of adapting what they learn to the local environment." At present, elements of such cadres are fairly common in Latin America. Moreover, several countries in the region have already developed a modern industrial core while retaining an ample supply of low-cost labor.[13] This supply seems especially valuable in light of the aging populations in Japan, the United States, and Western Europe, which will create new job opportunities in these markets as well as impel changes in the location of labor-intensive industries. The combination of these factors could allow Latin America to create its own comparative advantage profile. This potential is clouded by several major economic uncertainties in the short term. In essence, these derive from the persistence of the region's economic crisis during most of the 1980s. However, the commitment of most countries to liberalization, privatization, and increased openness to direct foreign investment is offering powerful incentives for the foreign partners of the region.

For better or worse, Latin America is not of primary strategic importance to the rest of the world. The relative physical isolation of most of the continent has placed it outside the mainstream of global power politics. Of course, it could be argued, as many geopoliticians of the Southern Cone do,[14] that the South Atlantic, the South Pacific, the Strait of Magellan, Easter Island, the Malvinas, and the Antarctic, not to speak of Panama, Mexico, the Caribbean, or the Brazilian bulge, are essential elements for world dominance, but the mere enumeration of these apparently highly strategic territories reveals the dubiousness of such a claim.

Despite all the rhetoric of successive U.S. administrations, the region was not, with the notable exception of Cuba, an important scenario of the East-West conflict. In any event, as this traditional international cleavage has been superseded, Latin America may be placed in an even lower priority, a fact that—ironically—has caused some concern in the region.[15]

Contrary to the popular view, Latin America has been relatively peaceful and stable in international terms. External conflicts have been rare since World War II.[16] Generally, military expenditures have been lower than what might be expected, although they still lack justification in view of the region's tremendous social needs. The Central American crisis, which during the 1980s represented the only long-term conflict in the region with potentially destabilizing international effects, now seems under control. Admittedly, the region has a history of internal violence, which continued into the early 1990s in such countries as Colombia, Guatemala, and Peru. But with the exception of Colombian drug-related violence, the international implications of this turbulence have tended to be limited.

No foreign power has grounds to fear a direct military threat from Latin America. Nor are there crucial military bases installed by third powers. The number of foreign soldiers in the region is low compared to the number in Europe, Asia, or even Africa. Only in 1961 did a conflict in Latin America—the Cuban missile crisis—become a world security concern. Since this exceptional event, world security preoccupations have not implicated the region in any meaningful way, especially in comparison to such hot spots as the Middle East, Korea, and Indochina. In this respect, the Central American crisis was a borderline case; nonetheless, internal conditions prevailed over external factors, and foreign powers, with the exception of the United States, were reluctant to get involved.

True as this may be, international relations are shaped more by perceptions than by facts. Thus, although Latin America represents a secondary security interest for the rest of the world, views of its strategic value tend to vary. And at least for the

United States, the northern areas of the region—Mexico and the Caribbean—do represent a legitimate security concern.[17]

Traditionally, security interests have had a military connotation. They have referred especially to constraints on the use of force, threat prevention, arms control, and force postures. Because security depends on specific resources, economic interests have also been a concern. Currently, however, the concept of security extends far beyond traditional military and economic considerations. Global interdependence and the emergence of new values and fears are leading to a redefinition of the concept of security, which has implications for Latin America. The cessation of the East-West conflict reinforces this tendency. In fact, the chapters in this volume reveal the emergence of **new security interests** with respect to Latin America.

The Bush administration has already defined the first new security interest concerning Latin America: the struggle against drug trafficking. Although it is often forgotten, Latin America is not the only region to respond to massive drug demand from the rich countries. Indeed, most drug addiction in Europe, which consists mainly of heroin, is nurtured from Asia. However, there can be little doubt about the relevance of Latin America in the "war on drugs" declared by the U.S. government but also seconded, albeit with different emphases and tactics, by European officials.

Environmental protection represents a second global security interest that has important repercussions for Latin America. Although it is profoundly hypocritical to single out the depletion of the Amazonian rain forest as the main cause of the greenhouse effect and other serious global ecological problems,[18] the importance of this immense reserve for the protection of the world environment is unquestionable. In fact, dealing with environmental issues is becoming one of the highest priorities of Brazilian foreign policy and is gradually involving other countries of the region as well. The new relevance of the region in this area provides an equally new rationale for its participation in the international system of the 1990s and beyond—despite the dismal record of environmental policies proposed for Latin America by the rich countries of the Organization for Economic Cooperation and Development.[19]

Although migration flows from Latin America or from any other region do not necessarily represent a security question, it is clear that policymakers in the United States and, to a much lesser extent, in certain European countries, sometimes tend to view them in those terms. As Abraham F. Lowenthal states, massive migration from a few Latin American countries—particularly Mexico, the Caribbean islands, and some countries in Central America—will directly affect life in the United States.[20] Although emigration from the developed countries has declined for obvious reasons, Japan still assigns a certain importance to its emigrants in Latin

America. (The Japanese are mainly concentrated in Brazil, which has received more Japanese immigrants than any other country in the world, and have a significant presence in Bolivia, Mexico, and Peru.) Other Asian countries such as South Korea and Taiwan continue to send emigrants to the region. Until recently, Latin America experienced a massive European emigration, which has contributed to making it the most Western part of the developing world.

Geographic, cultural, and political proximity between Latin America and the Western world could play a role in supplying specialized and nonspecialized labor to the increasingly aging societies of the United States and Europe. This likely development of the next century could cast a rather different light on migration originating from Latin America if it helped to alleviate a likely labor shortage in the North. However, it could also aggravate Latin America's traditional brain drain to the United States and Europe.

Latin America also enjoys a certain **political significance** from an international perspective. The fact that the increasingly rich and prosperous populations of the United States and Europe will have less and less demographic weight in an overwhelmingly poor and populous world may compel their governments to establish new links with those developing areas with which they have political and cultural affinities. The middle-income status already achieved by several Latin American countries, regardless of their tremendous social inequalities, tends to reinforce this possibility.[21]

Another aspect of Latin America's importance internationally has to do with the political values that it increasingly shares with Europe and the United States. Although democracy and the protection of human rights in Latin America are not irreversible trends and still exhibit enormous shortcomings, the region has made significant progress in strengthening these values. No one would have predicted the breadth of the democratic wave that has embraced Latin America despite the severe economic crisis it suffered during the 1980s.[22]

To be sure, massive human rights violations persist in several countries. Cuba still refuses to initiate a process of democratic transition, Peru has reverted to authoritarian rule, Haiti seems to have few possibilities for democratization, and democracy is more nominal than real in other areas of Latin America. But the idea of pluralist democracy is more cherished and legitimized in the region than in any other developing area. The thesis that a distinct political tradition sets Latin America apart from other areas of the Western world has been challenged not only in theoretical terms but also by recent experience.[23] In fact, Western democratic principles and human rights are supported by an increasing majority of the region's political elites.

Links between Latin American and European political parties constitute the core of Political Internationals—indeed, these organizations could transcend their

European origins only through the establishment of regular relationships with Latin America. The region is also linked to the rest of the world, and especially to the developed countries, through a dense network of nongovernmental relationships involving religious organizations, labor unions, solidarity groups, political foundations, charitable organizations, academic institutions, and so forth.

What is the relevance of these interests for the different external partners of Latin America? How did these interests combine in the 1980s, and what role will they play in the decade of the 1990s? Which interests tend to predominate? Obviously, the answers to these questions tend to vary from case to case, depending on the specific profiles of Latin America's major international relationships.

The United States: A Special Interest without a Special Relationship

The United States retains an obvious influence in Latin America. Economically, it is the main trading partner, an essential source of badly needed foreign investment, and the principal financial power in the region. Although it lost its predominant position in the field, it is still an important arms supplier, especially to the smaller countries. U.S. influence in the domestic politics of the region can never be discounted. And although the time has long since past when almost all Latin American foreign policy actions took place with reference to Washington, the United States continues to be an essential factor in the region's international relations.

The evident asymmetry of U.S.–Latin American relations should not obscure the fact that Latin America is also important to the United States. Although it is not as meaningful as Europe, the United States has a profound interest in the future of the region and in the evolution of its relations with it. Latin America is significant economically as a market for U.S. exports and investments, as a supplier of primary commodities, as an industrial partner in a productive process that tends to be global rather than national, and as an often-worrisome financial partner. Although some of these sectors have become less attractive during the last decades, they could grow again as the region's economic potential is developed over time. President George Bush's recent proposal for the establishment of a free trade area that would encompass the whole hemisphere underlines the perceived economic importance of Latin America in Washington.[24]

To a much greater extent than for any other major power, Latin America also represents a security interest for the United States. The Caribbean Basin is one of the principal foci of traditional U.S. security interests in the world. Owing to the growing interdependence between the two countries, the United States has vital interests in Mexico. Although Washington's almost obsessive attention to Cuba seems to stem more from ideological than security considerations, Cuba represented a major obstacle in relations with the former Soviet Union, even under Mikhail Gorbachev. A rather long list of Latin American issues has reached the U.S. National Security Council during the last decades, which usually deals on a regular basis with events in Central America, Cuba, and Mexico. Although it is true that Latin America's significance to the United States in the security area has been declining steadily, the region still tends to be perceived as important in this regard.

The Central American conflict and the Cuban issue have confirmed the critical ideological relevance that Washington attaches to political events in Latin America. Obviously, the end of the cold war could alter this perception, but there is need to exercise caution in drawing such a conclusion. First, some political sectors in Latin America may not have relinquished the hope of introducing orthodox models of socialism into the region. Second, as already noted, extrahemispheric actors have rarely played a major role in U.S. concerns about political developments in Latin America. Third, although the Panamanian invasion also had other connotations, it tended to confirm the importance attached by the U.S. establishment to ideological and political developments in the region, despite the absence of any serious foreign involvement in that case. Finally, as the February 1992 coup attempt in Venezuela demonstrated, authoritarian groups—often with nationalistic and populist inclinations—are still active in the region.

As Abraham Lowenthal argues in chapter 3 of this volume, Latin America could become increasingly significant for the United States in the context of new security interests derived from the region's proximity and the degree of Latin American–U.S. interpenetration. Complex issues such as migration, environmental protection, drug trafficking, and economic and political stability will require even more U.S. attention to Latin America in the coming decades.

The promotion of pluralist democracy and the protection of basic human rights in the hemisphere represent additional concerns of the United States. With different emphases and approaches, these issues have been particularly salient during the last decades, although it seems clear that the construction of strong, consolidated political systems and the observance of human rights largely depend on national conditions. Be this as it may, the United States has clearly singled out Latin America in this context, whereas many political actors in the region have subscribed to the need to promote these values with the support of foreign state and nonstate participants.

The issues at the heart of U.S.–Latin American relations in the 1990s will uphold or even increase the relevance of Latin America to the United States. At the same time, they will confirm the crucial nature of these relations from a Latin American perspective. For better or worse, no other foreign power has a similarly intense relationship with the region, nor a comparable combination of economic, political, and security interests.

The confirmation of the relevance of U.S.–Latin American relations for both partners does not imply that these relations have remained static over the last decades. As already noted, the agenda of hemispheric relations has gradually changed. New issues have been added, old ones have been redefined, and still others have been overtaken by events. The *nature* of the relationship has also been altered in the sense that analyses that part from the premise of an unchanged U.S. hegemony, not to speak of imperialism, do not account for the complexity of those relations during the last decade.[25]

Moreover, the actors in hemispheric relationships have changed. Latin American countries are no longer the passive and often-subservient partners of previous times. Their knowledge about the U.S. political system and the factors that shape its foreign policy has improved considerably. Their foreign interests and external relations have diversified significantly. And, what is often forgotten, the United States has also changed. Its declining international economic position has affected Latin America as well. Severe domestic problems constrain its ability to employ economic and financial assistance to support its foreign policy objectives in the region or, for that matter, in Eastern Europe. The diffusion of power, information, and access in the U.S. political system makes it extremely difficult for Washington to pursue consistent and coherent long-term policies with regard to Latin America. These factors also underscore the difficulty of introducing any "grand design" for the development of a special relationship between the partners. In fact, the concept of the special relationship itself belongs to the past.

Finally, the *context* of U.S.–Latin American relations is undergoing profound changes. The impact of the decline and then breakup of the Soviet Union, Japan's consolidation as an economic world power, and the likely emergence of an economically unified Europe all have yet to be defined. For instance, while the end of the cold war has removed one pretext for U.S. intervention in the region, it could have eliminated one of the few obstacles to overt intervention as well.[26]

The Role of Europe: From Illusion to Realism

Throughout the 1970s and at the beginning of the 1980s, Latin America placed great hope in its relations with Western Europe. Often encouraged by their European partners, Latin Americans saw in Europe an increasingly open market for their products, an alternative source of investments for the region, a generous provider of development assistance, a promising partner for technological cooperation and the establishment of joint ventures, and, since the eruption of the debt crisis, a more understanding partner in financial negotiations. In the political realm, Latin Americans viewed the Europeans as pillars of the democratization processes that were taking place in the region; they also looked to the highly successful southern European models of transition to democracy for inspiration. In the area of international relations, Latin America discovered similarities with European governments and political sectors, cherishing the idea of Europe as a third option to the superpowers and as a counterweight to the United States.[27]

To a large extent these expectations have not been met, in part because they were founded on a deep misunderstanding of the external realities of both regions. It is also clear that, in general, European–Latin American relations have not represented a first priority for either region. Nonetheless, the European presence in Latin America is still substantial and, more important, it is there to stay.

Although trade between the two regions has fallen significantly, Europe, and specifically the European Community, is still the second largest partner of Latin America. In several countries, Europe even surpasses the United States in this respect. In the financial sector, more than one-third of the Latin American debt is held by the major European banking systems. European direct investments in Latin America are still relevant for the region and during the last years have tended to grow and to produce better results than U.S. investments. Even though Latin America does not occupy a privileged position in most European development assistance programs, the sheer size of these programs makes Europe the main supplier of foreign aid to South America and the second largest supplier of aid to Central America. Europeans are developing new forms of cooperation with Latin America, directed mostly to the industrial, scientific, and technological sectors. Countries like Italy and Spain are endorsing new bilateral agreements with the largest nations of South America. The Europeans have also become the major arms suppliers for Latin America, displacing the United States in the 1970s from many regional markets.

If economic relations have not responded to Latin American expectations, political links between the two regions have intensified. After many decades of indifference to the political plight of Latin America, from the 1970s Western Europe has shown a strong interest in the protection of human rights and in the processes of democratization that have taken place in the region. Indeed, Bonn, Madrid, Paris, and Rome now compete with Washington as places that Latin American presidents and other authorities must visit.

Western Europe has also assumed a more active role in the Central American crisis. Although the European presence remains secondary in comparison to that of the United States, it is significant that Europe has decided to project a discrete influence in an area where it has no great economic or security interests.[28]

The relative importance of migration links between Europe and Latin America has already been stressed. It is by no mere chance that Italy is establishing association agreements with Argentina, Brazil, and Venezuela, the three most common destinations of the considerable Italian population immigrating to Latin America; or that Argentina, despite its recent economic and political difficulties, is one of the Latin American countries that receives the most attention from Spain; or that Germany has strong ties with Brazil and Chile and even shows some interest in a country as small as Paraguay. The United States's own experience shows the influence of these linkages in unifying two continents. Europe also received a significant number of Latin American political refugees, many of whom returned to their countries to occupy posts in politics and government. These often highly qualified and politically active people are also playing a role in maintaining contacts between the two regions.

Some European powers also have distinct security interests in the region. France considers its Caribbean and South American possessions as an integral part of its territory. The Kingdom of the Netherlands includes Caribbean territories as well. Great Britain clings to its South Atlantic fortress. And the Caribbean still contains strategic seaways for Europe.[29]

Although it is difficult to evaluate how the European Single Market will affect Latin America, it is likely that its impact will not be particularly strong, at least in the short term. There could be some trade diversion, but the idea of *Fortress Europe* seems to be more a reflection of U.S. apprehension than a real possibility. In the long term, the strength and dynamism of an economically unified Europe could be felt in Latin America, despite the rather marginal weight of the region in Europe's external economic relations.

Many Latin Americans fear that the political changes taking place in Eastern Europe threaten to relegate Latin America to an even lower priority in European foreign policies. These concerns have some justification, but precisely because Latin America has not been a priority for Europe, one should not overstate the possible effects that the changes in Europe are likely to have on relations with the region. On the other hand, with one or two exceptions, the economic prospects of Eastern Europe do not look brighter than those of Latin America, and many Latin American countries may well be closer to the goals of economic reconversion and modernization than their Eastern European counterparts. The economic strength of Brazil is far greater than that of any Eastern European country, with the obvious exception of Russia; Mexico can be favorably compared with Poland; Argentina's per capita income surpasses that of Hungary; and Chile has economically (and politically) little to envy in Romania.

Some new interests have emerged in Europe with regard to Latin America. The most important relate to the environment, which has become one of the most important issues in European domestic politics. Drug trafficking gradually has also become a concern of Europe.

For all of these reasons Europe will likely maintain its involvements in Latin America, although at a more modest level than in the 1970s and the 1980s. In the long term, a stronger economic and political Europe will inevitably seek a more salient role in a region with which it has historical and political affinities. But this possibility will depend more on economic conditions in Latin America than on mere political goodwill.

Japan and the Pacific Basin: The New Partners

The emergence of Japan as a new economic world power has also been visible in Latin America, despite the absence of important historical links and the geographic and cultural distances that separate the new partners. Following a familiar pattern, Japan's presence in Latin America has had an economic dimension. Japan already provides 7 percent of Latin America's imports and receives 5 percent of its exports. Although these figures are important, they do not approach those of the United States and Europe, which jointly account for approximately two-thirds of the region's foreign trade. On the other hand, Latin America accounts for only 4 percent of Japan's foreign trade. Nevertheless, it is an important source of raw materials for Japan, whereas Japan is already the second largest trading partner of Chile, Mexico, and Peru.[30]

Japanese investments in Latin America have increased significantly during the last decades, concentrating especially on the exploitation of Latin America's natural resources due to Japan's strong perceptions of vulnerability in that area. Recently, Japan also turned its attention to Mexican industries located near the U.S. border in an attempt to take advantage of facilities accessible to the U.S. market.

Since 1985 Japan has been Latin America's leading source of external finance. Japanese banks have continued to make private loans, while U.S. banks have been rapidly withdrawing funds. Latin America's foreign debt crisis has also affected Japan. The Asian country holds approximately 16 percent of the total Latin American debt; in turn, Latin America has received approximately 70 percent of Japanese loans to the developing countries.[31] Although the Japanese banking system was able to adopt provisions to counter the crisis, its vulnerability and the government's desire to become more involved in the stabilization of the international financial system led to the launching of the Mijazawa Plan, which apparently inspired the Brady Plan.

Japan is also playing a larger role in financing development projects in Latin America. Although its assistance programs are heavily concentrated in Asia, funds for Latin America are expected to increase in the next years. Japan is willing to lift its per capita ceilings in the case of Latin America; until recently, these ceilings made most countries in the region ineligible for official development assistance.

All specialists tend to agree that Japan's growing economic relevance will inevitably create new political responsibilities as well. Owing to its peculiar history, Japan has been reluctant to assume a more salient political role worldwide. This traditional dilemma for Japanese foreign policy also applies to its relations with Latin America. In fact, Japan has adopted an even lower political profile in the region than in other parts of the world, partly because it did not want to challenge its main ally—the United States—in what was perceived as its area of exclusive influence. Although the changes in Latin America's external relations did not pass unnoticed by Japanese diplomats, difficulties in adapting to the new international realities of the region and an obvious desire not to endanger growing economic interests led to Japan's passivity regarding the chief political issues of the 1980s in Latin America. Thus, Japan—unlike the United States and Western Europe—has not had a salient role in the promotion of democracy and human rights in Latin America, it did not adopt a clear position with respect to the Malvinas-Falklands war, and it opted for a passive role in the Panamanian crisis—despite its extensive economic involvement in that country.[32]

Latin American efforts to develop a closer relationship with Japan have been fairly limited. Mexico has had a diplomatic presence in Tokyo and is strengthening its ties with the Asian power. Brazil has also made some efforts in that direction, but one would have expected a more assertive role considering its large Japanese emigrant population. Not surprisingly, President Alberto Fujimori emphasized Japan's new importance for Peruvian foreign policy. Japan is still a little-known partner in the region, however, and the potential of this new relationship has yet to be explored by most Latin American countries.

Several Latin American nations have turned their attention to other countries in the Pacific Basin, a rather vague classification that generally includes, apart from Japan, the People's Republic of China, the member countries of the Association of Southeast Asian Nations (ASEAN), Australia, New Zealand, South Korea, Taiwan, and Hong Kong.[33] Although most of these countries have shown some reluctance to include Latin American members in the new Pacific regional groupings, their economic dynamism has led Latin American countries to seek ties with the region. Whereas Mexico has taken the lead in the North Pacific, Chile, Peru, and, to a lesser extent, Argentina have made some progress in the South Pacific.

The People's Republic of China has a limited presence in Latin America. China's very pragmatic approach to the region, which replaced its initial ideological activism, permitted good relationships with the dictatorships that ruled most of Latin America during the 1970s and at the beginning of the 1980s. Beijing has established modest but growing economic links with several countries and has supported Latin American positions on such important issues as the debt crisis and the Central American conflict.

The Soviet Union: Normalization and Perestroika

The relations of the former Soviet Union with Latin America did not develop until the late 1960s, when Moscow, after several failed attempts, began to consolidate its presence in the region. As Eusebio Mujal-León has written, initially Soviet policy toward Latin America operated along two tracks. The first one focused on expanding normal trade and diplomatic relations, with a certain emphasis on the region's major powers. The second one aimed at consolidating a more lasting, structural relationship with leftist and nationalist governments throughout the region.[34] The first track responded basically to economic and foreign policy interests; the second one addressed political and ideological interests but also had strategic connotations, especially with regard to Cuba. Despite critical setbacks, both tracks were maintained until the late 1980s. Following a clear division, the first track was applied especially to Mexico and South America, with the partial exception of Chile, where for historical and symbolic reasons Moscow maintained strong ideological interests. The second one was especially visible in the Caribbean and Central America, where Soviet policy focused less on economic and diplomatic relations and more on ideological affinities and the prospects in those countries for revolutionary change and extrication from the United States.

Soviet relations with specific Latin American countries tended to vary. Obviously, Moscow established the most intense relationship with Cuba. Its generous economic assistance to the Cuban revolutionary regime made the island increasingly dependent on, and vulnerable to, the USSR. Cuba also received important military support from its Soviet ally. The foreign policy implications of this vulnerability were more complex than might have appeared on the surface. Even though the external interests and actions of the two countries often coincided and overlapped, they were not identical.[35] On the other hand, just as traditional economic dependence on the United States has not been automatically equivalent to foreign policy compliance in Latin America, Cuban economic reliance on Moscow has not meant external (nor internal) subservience, as became evident in 1990. However, the question remains about the viability of Cuba's socialist economy after the loss of its former Soviet and Eastern European supporters.

The close ties that the USSR and its Eastern European allies developed with the Nicaraguan Sandinista government had economic and military components, although of a considerably lower scale than in the case of Cuba. During the 1980s, Moscow also followed with interest and sympathy the evolution of revolutionary warfare in other Central American countries, especially El Salvador, but was careful not to become directly involved in those basically endogenous conflicts. Recent developments in the region, particularly the Sandinistas' electoral defeat, and in the former Soviet Union are likely to decrease the Russian and Eastern European presence in the area in the coming years.

Soviet relations with most South American countries and Mexico were characterized by pragmatism and rather traditional national interests. They involved trade links, economic cooperation, arms supplies, and common positions on certain foreign policy issues. Moscow also showed interest in those countries' search for greater external autonomy. Moreover, from a Latin American perspective, stronger relations with the Soviet Union were an essential element in the region's efforts to diversify its external relations and in some cases fulfilled an internal policy function as well.[36]

It seems obvious that, in the short term, increasing upheaval within the former Soviet Union will lead to a significant decrease in the Russian political presence, not to speak of military involvement, in the region. Moscow's once-important economic relations with such countries as Argentina and Brazil will also be affected. Over the long term, however, the economic transformation and the changed ideological profile of Russia and Eastern Europe may facilitate the establishment of new links with the region.

The Prospects for Collective Action

Regional self-consciousness and subsystem cohesion have played an important role in Latin America's participation in the international system.[37] Relationships among the Latin American countries themselves have represented an obvious priority for their foreign policies. In political terms, intraregional relations have been marked by a dualist tendency. On the one hand, they have been characterized by a recurrent drive toward regional cooperation, derived from common history, geographic proximity, political and cultural affinities, and shared perceptions about the external context of the region. On the other hand, intraregional relations have been plagued by conflict and mutual distrust, owing to a long history of territorial disputes, ideological differences, economic and demographic pressures, and, especially, geopolitical perceptions and obsessions. The interplay of both tendencies has had a "push-pull" effect in Latin American relations, an ambivalent situation of mutual attraction and separation.[38] Although these contradictory forces are less evident at the external level, a certain ambiguity can also be observed with respect to the means for promoting the external interests of Latin American countries. To be sure, all countries invariably have paid lip service to the principle of collective regional action, but in practice there have been important differences between individual and collective players. Interestingly enough, these differences have tended to vary over time and from case to case. Thus, although there can be little doubt about Mexico's preference for individual action in the context of the debt issue, the same country acted as the moving force of the Contadora Support Group. Similarly, whereas historically Brazil has been a typical individual player, since the 1980s it has opted for a more collective approach in some of its foreign policy actions.

What are the prospects for concerted regional action on the part of Latin America in the 1990s? Will the region act as a bloc in the international political system, or will individual strategies prevail? Will the region look for coalitions with other developing regions, as it attempted in the 1970s, or will it opt for a singular strategy? There are no simple answers to these questions, but it may be useful to consider some possibilities.

Latin American regional integration did not make much progress during the 1980s and, despite familiar rhetoric, major global advances do not appear likely in the foreseeable future. The modest level of economic interaction and interdependence among most Latin American countries will probably continue to be a major obstacle to integration. Although this is true at the regional or even subregional levels, however, it is less true for specific areas and groups of countries. Thus, the 1980s witnessed the emergence of new forms of integration and regional cooperation in Latin America, which could continue to develop in the 1990s. These new forms tend to confirm the finding of neofunctionalist theory that an integration process is not necessarily a unilinear progression toward a concrete model, and that especially in Latin America integration is to a certain extent a "spill-around" process, whereby an impasse in one scheme typically leads to the creation of yet another scheme.[39] Be this as it may, integration in Latin America is evidencing a certain dose of pragmatism that has led to the superposition of instruments and strategies, including formal and informal mechanisms, bilateral and multilateral processes, restricted and broad initiatives. In this context of diversification and multiplication, groupings and instruments tend to vary from sector to sector and from issue to issue, covering such disparate topics as specific trade regimes, the development of physical infrastructure, the utilization of shared natural resources, technological development, nuclear energy, the coordination of economic international postures, and, of course, foreign policy cooperation.

Argentina, Brazil, Paraguay, and Uruguay are engaged in a process of subregional economic integration—the Common Market of the South (Mercosur)—that looks promising if and when Brazil overcomes its present economic difficulties and is able to open up its economy to the same extent as its partners have done.[40] Although the Central American Common Market virtually collapsed in the 1970s, its member countries were able to establish and sustain the Esquipulas peace process, which has played a crucial role in the lessening of tensions in the area. Also important in this respect has been the pioneering role of the Contadora

Support Group. Moreover, the countries of the Contadora Group and its Support Group laid the basis for the establishment of the Group of Rio, which includes eleven permanent member countries of the region and purports to increase foreign policy cooperation among their members.[41] Most of these schemes have displayed shortcomings, but they are establishing new interactions and linkages and new styles of external problem solving in Latin America. There does not seem to be much room for grand cooperation designs in the region, but the results of this rather piecemeal and untidy approach could well be more fruitful than the more ambitious but always frustrated initiatives of previous decades.

The external interests of the Latin American countries are not necessarily similar in all areas. Brazil and Colombia have held rather different positions with respect to the liberalization of the services' sector in the Uruguay Round. Only some Latin American countries have joined the Cairns Group of food exporters, which also includes several rich countries. The divergent and sometimes conflicting interests of oil exporters and oil importers in Latin America need not be explained. Brazil and Chile have developed very different alternatives to solve their debt crisis. In the political realm, the resolution of the Central American conflict was a much higher priority for Mexico and Venezuela than for Argentina and Brazil. Brazil may be interested in Africa and the Middle East, but it is doubtful that a small state like Uruguay can devote any foreign policy energies to such remote areas. Venezuela may have a stake in the future of the English Caribbean, but it is not clear whether Chile has any serious interest in that area.

This is not to imply that the prospects for collective action are dim in Latin America. Rather, the experience of the last decades indicates the need to base any new initiatives on concrete common interests, rather than on grandiose and all-embracing projects that invariably end in frustration.

The prospects for concerted action with other developing areas must be seen in the same light. There are specific areas in which coalition forming is possible, but even in those cases alignments will tend to vary from sector to sector. It also is likely that, at the symbolic level, Latin American countries will continue to vote with African and Asian countries on international economic issues brought before the United Nations General Assembly. However, increased differentiation within the Third World will probably limit the chances for a return to the activism shown by Latin America in this field during the 1970s.

Conclusion: The Challenges Ahead

Latin America will face important challenges during the 1990s. It is likely that its pleas for increased solidarity and a more just international order will continue to fall on deaf ears. It is also likely that most of the changes that are taking place in the international system will have only indirect and long-term effects on Latin America. Accordingly, the prospects for increasing the region's influence in the international system will depend on the specific strategies that Latin American countries adopt, as well as on the internal economic and political conditions on which those strategies can be based.

This obvious conclusion is sometimes overlooked by Latin American politicians and diplomats, who too often continue to plead for the understanding of the developed world, while at the same time portraying the region's present situation in the gloomiest terms. Unfortunately, there are grounds to sustain this approach. But it seems condemned to failure in an international system ruled by concrete and often crude interests and power relations, which reserves the little solidarity it can muster for the most desperate cases of the poorest nations of Africa, Asia, and Latin America. In the long term this approach is counterproductive as it inevitably tends to focus on the region's problems and misfortunes, rather than on its impressive potential.

The marginalization of Latin America is more a danger than a reality. To a certain extent, it is also a state of mind. The region possesses a considerable array of economic, political, and even strategic resources, which it can mobilize to enhance its participation in the international system. The utilization of these resources depends on the capabilities of its governments and on the quality of its foreign policies. If they fail to meet these challenges, Latin America will in effect be left alone, not because of the intrinsic perversity of an international system that obviously has not been shaped according to the region's interests, but because of its own failures.

Latin American foreign policies will have to rapidly adapt to the new international system that is emerging. In a world in flux, the possibilities for the diversification of external relations seem higher than ever. But an obvious scarcity of resources demands selective approaches, careful choices, and sound implementation. It also calls for highly professional foreign services and a good comprehension of international changes on the part of political leaders and public opinion.

Even the soundest and most brilliant external strategy is doomed to fail if it is not backed by satisfactory domestic conditions. Economic and political stabilization represent essential elements for a solid and coherent external strategy. Of course, it can be argued that those preconditions in turn depend on a more favorable external environment. This argument is undoubtedly correct in general terms, but it requires some further qualification, especially in order to determine the precise weight of external and internal factors in the crises that are affecting diverse Latin American countries. Although this analysis would be extremely useful in intellectual terms, its political relevance is less evident. Even in the unlikely event that external factors are responsible for the present crises in Latin

America, the countries of the region will have to rely mainly on their own efforts to overcome them. Indeed, the level of the region's participation in the international system of the 1990s will depend to a large extent on the ways in which they confront this challenge.

Notes

1. This point has been cogently made by one of the most perceptive analysts of Latin American economic development and political economy. See Hirschman, "Political Economy of Latin American Development."

2. These figures are drawn from Middlebrook and Rico, "The United States and Latin America in the 1980s."

3. A first wave of studies included Hellman and Rosenbaum, *Latin America*; Atkins, *Latin America*; and Treverton, *Latin America*. Soon following these studies were more specific analyses of Latin American foreign policies, such as Ferris and Lincoln's *Latin American Foreign Policies* and a vast collection of books published under the auspices of RIAL (The Joint Program for the Study of the International Relations of Latin America), mainly by the Grupo Editor Latinoamericano (GEL) of Buenos Aires. Especially representative of the latter works are Muñoz and Tulchin, *Latin American Nations in World Politics*; Drekonja and Tokatlian, *Teoría y práctica*; and Puig, *América Latina*.

4. For a representative Latin American evaluation of the North-South dialogue, see Tomassini, *El Diálogo Norte-Sur*.

5. For a positive evaluation of Latin American Third Worldism, see Briones, "El tercer mundo." See also Mansilla, "Latin America."

6. Whitehead, "Debt, Diversification, and Dependency," pp. 125–26.

7. One recent publication by a Colombian-Spanish foundation bears the eloquent title *América Latina se ha quedado sola* (Bogotá: Fundación Santillana para Iberoamérica, 1989). The title was inspired by that of Gabriel García Márquez's acceptance speech of the Nobel Prize, *La soledad de América Latina*. For a rather emotional view of the same subject, see Rubio, "La soledad de Iberoamérica." For a more systematic treatment of the marginalization of Latin America, see IRELA, *Europe and Latin America in the 1990s*, esp. chap. 1.

8. CEPAL, *Estudio económico de América Latina*, p. 80.

9. On this subject, see Lowenthal, *Partners in Conflict*, and Hirst, *Continuidad y cambio*.

10. On new forms of regional cooperation in Latin America, see van Klaveren, "Las nuevas formas de concertación política." For more discussion on issues of trade and economic integration, see chapter 7—by Roberto Bouzas—in this book.

11. Fajnzylber, "Democratization, Endogenous Modernization, and Integration," p. 144.

12. Gereffi, "New Patterns of Industrial Integration," pp. 8, 17–23.

13. Vernon, "Critical Factors," pp. 2–4.

14. For an overview of geopolitical thinking in the Southern Cone, see Child, "Geopolitical Thinking in Latin America," and Kelly and Child, *Geopolitics*.

15. Helio Jaguaribe, for one, warns against the dangers of superpower alliance in the case of Latin America. See his article, "América Latina dentro."

16. For a review of Latin American interstate conflicts, see Grabendorff, "Interstate

Conflict Behavior," and Child, "Inter-State Conflict." Carlos Portales concentrates on the South American case in "Sudamérica."

17. U.S. traditional security interests are analyzed in Hayes, *Latin America*. For a critical and very persuasive interpretation, see Schoultz, *National Security*.

18. Guimaraes, "Brasil vuelve al banquillo."

19. See chapter 10—by Steven E. Sanderson—in this volume.

20. Lowenthal, *Partners in Conflict*, p. 55.

21. Some authors tend to view Latin America as a middle-class region within a stratified international system. Although it is problematic to apply an already-difficult category of traditional sociological analysis to such a disparate field as international relations, there are some interesting facets in this parallel. See Orrego Vicuña, *América Latina*.

22. J. Samuel Fitch emphasizes this point in chapter 8 of this volume.

23. The most insistent proponent of this thesis is Howard J. Wiarda. See, for instance, the introduction to his edited volume, *Politics and Social Change*, and his "Corporatism and Development." I have attempted to critique this approach in my article, "Enfoques alternativos."

24. For a Latin American perspective on the Enterprise of the Americas, see "Análisis Regional sobre la Iniciativa de las Américas," *Capítulos del SELA*, no. 28, 1991.

25. For a good overview of the state of the debate on U.S. hegemony in Latin America during the 1980s, see Maira, *¿Una nueva era?*

26. This possibility was discussed at the workshop on "The Changing Global Context for U.S.–Latin American Relations," organized by the Inter-American Dialogue, Aspen Institute, Airlie House, Warrenton, Va., May 23–25, 1990. See the "Rapporteur's Report," prepared by Michael C. Desch, p. 5.

27. I have dealt with this subject in more detail in "Europa Occidental y América Latina." The next paragraphs draw on this work.

28. On the European role in Central America, see Grabendorff, "The Central American Crisis"; Pierre, *Third World Instability*; Insulza, "Europa, Centroamérica y la Alianza Atlántica"; and Abelardo Morales Gamboa, "El discreto encanto por Centroamérica en el Viejo Mundo," in Atilio Borón and Alberto van Klaveren, eds., *América Latina y Europa Occidental en el umbral del siglo XXI* (Santiago: PNUD/CEPAL, 1989).

29. Europe's strategic interests in Latin America are analyzed in Insulza, "Los temas estratégicos."

30. Stallings and Székely, "A Rising Sun," p. 1.

31. Ibid.; Anderson, "Las visiones japonesas," p. 204.

32. For a general overview of Japanese–Latin American political relations, see Matsushita, "La política japonesa."

33. On this subject, see Armanet, *América Latina*, and "Latin American Perceptions on the Pacific Basin." In some of the articles included in these publications, the concept of the Pacific Basin is so broad as to include the United States and the former Soviet Union. This seems questionable because Latin American relations with those powers formed their own singular subsystems and had little to do with the Pacific Basin.

34. Mujal-León, Introduction to his edited volume, *The USSR and Latin America*, p. xx. See also Varas, *América Latina*.

35. For a recent analysis on this subject, but prior to the last dramatic changes in Soviet foreign policy, see Domínguez, "The Nature and Uses of the Soviet-Cuban Connection."

36. Varas, "Soviet–Latin American Relations," p. 13.

37. On this subject, see Atkins, *Latin America*, pp. 23–50.

38. Ibid., p. 29.

39. Ferguson, "Cooperation in Latin America," p. 53.

40. On the origins of this integration scheme, see Hirst, "El programa de integración y cooperación"; Moneta, *El acercamiento Argentina-Brasil*; and Mármora, "Integración argentino-brasileña." For a preliminary appraisal of Mercosur, see IRELA, *A New Attempt at Regional Integration: The Southern Cone Common Market* (Madrid: IRELA Dossiers no. 30, 1991).

41. For a general overview of Latin American foreign policy cooperation, see Tomassini, *Nuevas formas de concertación regional* and IRELA, *El Grupo de los Ocho.*

Augusto Varas

Chapter Two · FROM COERCION TO PARTNERSHIP:

A NEW PARADIGM FOR

SECURITY COOPERATION IN

THE WESTERN HEMISPHERE?

I n April 1989 George Kennan told the Senate Committee on Foreign Relations that "whatever reasons there may once have been for regarding the Soviet Union primarily as a possible, if not probable, military opponent, the time for that sort of thing has clearly passed. [Soviet interests] are also not so seriously in conflict with ours as to justify any assumption that the outstanding differences could not be adjusted by the normal means of compromise and accommodation." Kennan later noted what now seems obvious: "changes now sweeping over Central and Eastern Europe are momentous and irreversible."[1] There and elsewhere in the late 1980s, authoritarian and totalitarian states began or accelerated a process of democratization. As a result, the post–World War II structure of international political relations quickly crumbled.

The end of the cold war has forced individual countries to adjust to new strategic, political, and economic conditions. In the East, the most conspicuous landmark of cold war divisions, the Berlin Wall, was demolished and the reunification of Germany ended the very concept of "the East." At the same time, Soviet internal and foreign policy reforms affected all other Eastern European political and economic systems and led within a few years to the dismemberment of the Soviet superpower into its constituent republics. In the West, major steps toward full integration of the European Economic Community were taken in 1992, while novel forms of integration of Asian economies and polities were creating new regional centers of economic and political dynamism in the area dominated by the

Japanese yen. And in the Western Hemisphere—the focus of this volume—the global changes are encouraging corresponding transformations of the paradigms that undergird both U.S. and Latin American hemispheric policies.

This chapter analyzes the rise of a new U.S. approach to regional politics, examining first the principal effects of global changes on the hemisphere. The discussion then turns to the tensions between the coercive and the hegemonic paradigms of hemispheric control in U.S. policy toward Latin America. Finally, the chapter outlines the emergence of a new paradigm of hemispheric security cooperation and suggests the contour of U.S.–Latin American security issues in the remaining years of the twentieth century.

Changes in Latin America's Role in International Relations

In the last two decades the dominant U.S. role in world affairs has changed and U.S.–Latin American relations have undergone a corresponding modification. The diversification of Latin America's foreign relations has resulted from the fragmentation and the multipolarization of world power.[2] The gradual development of a world economy, coupled with more flexible superpower relations and the demilitarization of regional politics, is transforming Latin America's relationship with the United States, Japan, the European Economic Community, and the states of the former Soviet Union.[3]

After World War II, as U.S. hemispheric policy focused on containing and preventing a Soviet presence in the region, Latin American foreign policies became highly sensitive to changes in U.S.–USSR relations. By the late 1980s the major effects of the emerging superpower accommodation were observed throughout the region. This accommodation relieved Latin American governments from the pressure to align their nations in the East-West conflict, thereby opening the way to nonideological approaches in regional and international politics. For example, the peaceful resolution of the Central American conflict via Central American initiatives was easier with the relaxation of tensions between the superpowers. This context contrasted dramatically with the early period of the Reagan administration, which was characterized by an exceptionally tough U.S. approach to the Soviet Union. The political and even military support of Latin American countries for the international coalition that operated in the 1991 Persian Gulf War was an expression of the new atmosphere of cooperation in the political realm. On the other hand, the United States's continuing hostility toward Cuba and its military intervention in Panama raised anew the question of the extent to which the United States is prepared to make fundamental changes in its hemispheric policies.

Worldwide transformations have also had the effect of changing the very concept of Latin America. The gradual integration of Canada, Mexico, and, in the future, some Caribbean economies into the wider North American geo-economic space has contributed to the erosion of the old idea of a single Latin American region. The concept of a coherent region organized as a single actor around regional institutions is being replaced by the recognition of deep diversities and the corresponding need to seek common ground in multilateral forums on how to tackle shared problems. In the process, the notion of a single Latin American region with common interests and a common destiny, always weaker in fact than in belief, has all but disappeared. "Post–Latin America" will be characterized by several subregional systems with different economic, political, and strategic weights.[4] In addition to the region of North American hegemony, which includes Canada, Mexico, the Caribbean, and Central America, it is possible to identify a depressed Andean subregion, an embryonic Brazilian-Argentine axis, and individual countries such as Chile looking for the best way to integrate into world economic, political, and strategic affairs. In this new subregional configuration, Latin American countries will play a role in keeping with their significant new linkages with the developed world; in this sense, Brazil and Mexico are most likely to be major players.

For post–Latin America, traditional foreign policies that were once useful for hemispheric configurations are now obsolete. Accordingly, regional actors are transforming their views and approaches—their paradigms—to address different regional and international issues and to accommodate these new realities. Instead of pursuing old images of regional uniqueness and of institutions that express and organize around presumed commonalities, Latin American countries are now recognizing their deep differences, abandoning the rigid institutions of the past, and refocusing their attention on the development of flexible policies. Consequently, they are seeking and often finding new methods of political cooperation outside of the formal regional institutional framework.

Hegemonic and Coercive Control

In light of these changed conditions, new regional regimes must be developed. The region is clearly moving away from the historic paradigm, which often merely endorsed U.S. policies toward Latin America. During the past decade, Latin American scholars and U.S. Latin Americanists have typically analyzed hemispheric issues from the theoretical perspectives of U.S. hegemony and U.S. hegemonic crisis.[5] The very definition of the issues usually kept the discussion in bipolar terms such as center-periphery, empire-colony, and hegemon-subordinated.

It is possible to analyze this topic from a different point of view—from the standpoint of the need for the United States, particularly in the late nineteenth century, to create a *hemispheric order*: a stable, predictable set of hemispheric relationships—a hemispheric political regime.[6] As a regional hegemon, the United States has often feared the absence of order. Historically, it has tackled hemispheric "anarchy" through different policies designed around two competing paradigms: *hegemonic control* and *coercive control*.

These paradigms emerged in the earliest stages of U.S. foreign policy. From the Jeffersonian utopia of a single hemisphere ruled by one law and speaking one language,[7] to the Wilsonian cooperative approach among the Americas, to the Good Neighbor policy and the Alliance for Progress initiative, a consistent U.S. approach to hemispheric issues has stressed the need for a hemispheric order, supervised by a hegemonic power (the United States), and structured around cooperative policies and multilateral institutions. This approach has been contested by a different view, one that justifies and legitimates the use of coercion to create and maintain an order presumed to be unsustainable without U.S. intervention. From the Monroe Doctrine, to Manifest Destiny, to constant U.S. interventions during Republican and Democratic administrations, this view on hemispheric issues has engendered new instabilities and regional disorder.[8]

Why at different times have U.S. policymakers emphasized one approach or the other? Why is the United States today more inclined to cooperate with Latin American countries in hemispheric affairs? Why has hemispheric cooperation appeared precisely at a moment when there seems to be a crisis of economic cooperation among developed countries?[9] In my view, the decision to exercise hegemonic or coercive control has been contingent on changes in the international strength of the United States and on the nature and diversity of the instruments at its disposal for use in the hemisphere.

During the 1950s and 1960s, when it was economically dominant worldwide, the United States was able to provide incentives for international cooperation by supplying common goods and by prescribing the terms around which this order should be organized.[10] This period, when the country was able to distribute common security goods through multilateral agreements and institutions, thereby exhibiting both global and regional leadership, illustrated the paradigm of **hegemonic control**. The prevailing U.S. approach at this time was to organize a hemispheric order through *institutions* and cooperative policies, but the United States did not forego coercion, as was seen in Guatemala (1954), Cuba (1961), and the Dominican Republic (1965). Nevertheless, it attempted to achieve hegemony through a paradigm that stressed dominance through regional institutional bodies, thus permitting it to organize cooperation around international regimes.[11]

This hegemonic cooperation was achieved through multilateral and multipurpose institutions, which structured the interaction among formally equal countries

Table I. Paradigms of Hemispheric Order

Hegemonic	Coercive
1. *Institutions and Decision-Making Process*	
Multilaterality	Bilaterality
Institutionalized collective interests	No institutionalized collective interests
Multidimensional institutions	Single-issue institutions
2. *Regulations*	
Limits to hegemon behavior	Free hand
Centralized allocation of common goods	Competitive and free market allocation
3. *Sovereignty*	
Formal state equality	State inequality
Collective defense	National security
Regional security through professionalized military	Military politicization and intervention
Organic approach to regional strategic issues	Strategic autism
4. *Participation*	
Stratified	Concentrated and centralized decision-making processes
Leadership	Unstable accommodations
5. *Bloc Formation*	
Interbloc competition	Intrabloc coercion
Use of economic incentives	Use of threats

associated in multilateral organizations. Security became a collective interest and task. Even though participation in these institutions was stratified under U.S. leadership, subordinated Latin American and Caribbean states had a role in the decision-making process. The United States allocated military resources to different Latin American countries, thereby maintaining an intraregional balance of forces. Strategically, the relationship between blocs was one of competition, which strengthened intrabloc relations. Although this situation was rewarding for the hegemon, it imposed limits on its behavior through the creation of a sort of hemispheric "democratic corporatism."[12] (See Table 1.)

After a period of relative decline, the coercive framework for policy-making reemerged in the 1970s and 1980s.[13] Because of economic constraints, the United States lost much of the dominance in world affairs that it had enjoyed in the 1960s and 1970s and so became increasingly unable to manage the hemispheric order. Such a development encourages the use of force.[14] Although the period of Jimmy

Carter's presidency (1977–81) was an exception in this regard, due to unusual international and regional conditions, the orientation of the Carter administration did not pervade all government agencies nor all aspects of U.S.–Latin American relations. Consequently, the detachment from previous policies was not complete.[15]

The paradigm of **coercive control** has been characterized by the preference to generate a regional order without common institutions, regulations, and interests, all of which imply the sharing of values among hemispheric states, but rather on the threat (or actual use) of force to protect U.S. interests. Coercive control was observed most clearly during the Reagan administration, particularly during the enactment of the "rollback policy" in Grenada, Nicaragua, and Panama. U.S. detachment from multilateral organizations in the 1980s to avoid restrictions on its room for maneuver was also indicative of this tendency. Nevertheless, such a form of maintaining hemispheric order is suboptimal, because stability cannot be achieved unless shared interests are developed. As the experience of Central American instability in the 1980s demonstrates, without the cooperation of Latin America, U.S. interests in the region cannot be protected effectively.[16]

As of 1992, U.S. hemispheric policies were in transition once again, this time moving away from the coercive control paradigm toward one somewhat analogous to yet different from the traditional paradigm of hegemonic control. The Bush administration was trying to create a regional order based on hemispheric cooperation around a new kind of international regime, illustrated by the Enterprise of the Americas Initiative launched by President George Bush on June 27, 1990. This new paradigm, which can be labeled *cooperation through partnership*, is different from the hegemonic one because the United States is no longer in a dominant position, nor does it have the resources to provide common goods to the hemisphere. This new regime is cooperative; that is, new norms for free trade enforced through policy coordination and decision-making procedures will be determined bilaterally.

A hemispheric approach characterized by U.S. self-restraint coupled with free trade is not new, having been employed during the Wilson, Roosevelt, and Kennedy administrations.[17] The Bush administration's approach is similar in that it seeks to develop wider commercial spaces as a response to the restrictions appearing in other global markets. It is different because Latin American countries have changed in an extremely important way: economic restructuring in almost all Latin American countries (albeit in different degrees) is reintroducing these economies to the world market. Because national economies are now more liberalized (more open to international trade and more market-oriented), Latin American countries are deeply interested in liberalizing world trade, as demonstrated by the Latin American position in the Uruguay Round of the General Agreement on

Tariffs and Trade. Within this new framework, market mechanisms are more suitable than multilateral institutions to direct U.S.–Latin American relations.

Partnership: A New Paradigm in Hemispheric Relations?

The recent U.S. emphasis on cooperation in the Americas has also been the result of important changes in the international position of the United States as well as internal bureaucratic changes. The former stem from the development of a world economy and include the international diffusion of advanced technology, the surge of international capital markets, and the rapid transformation of industrial organizations and trade patterns.[18] Many of these changes have strongly encouraged the strategic disengagement of the superpowers. As a consequence, the United States is now promoting cooperation through open trade and cooperative approaches to international problems like weapons proliferation, terrorism and international violence, and environmental deterioration. It is also advocating the development of new standards of equity and the enactment of statutes reflecting common principles of law and human rights.[19] Given the current limitations to U.S. global hegemony, the nature of world changes, and the suboptimal character of policies based on coercive paradigms, the new emphasis on partnership emerged in the late 1980s almost automatically.

These structural changes in the international position of the United States have accompanied bureaucratic changes that occurred before and during the presidency of Ronald Reagan.[20] From January 1983 to the end of the decade, the invigorated activity of members of the Democratic party dominated congressional debates on human rights issues. Contributing to the bureaucratic shift inside the Reagan administration were the support of professional diplomats for nonmilitary responses to Latin American crises (as shown in the political defeat of Senator Jesse Helms in February 1986), the isolation—within the Reagan camp—of ideological conservatives from September 1986 on, the dampening effect of the Iran-Contra affair on coercion-oriented conservatives, and the success of silent diplomacy in the Philippines in 1985, in Haiti in 1986, and in Chile and Paraguay in the same period. These forces in the United States were supplemented by events in Latin America, especially the unexpected democratization process in the region and the elections in El Salvador in 1982 and 1984, revealing a civilian preference for a democratic and peaceful resolution of conflicts, and the reinforcement of this movement by the Arias Peace Plan for Central America. Together, these changes persuaded U.S. decision makers that a new cooperative consensus would be more effective in achieving U.S. policy goals than coercion.[21]

The changes in U.S. policy toward Latin America introduced by the Bush

Table 2. Paradigm of Cooperation through Partnership

1. *Institutions and Decision-Making Process*
   Multilateral selectivity
   Institutionalized subregional interests
   Multilateral focused institutions

2. *Regulations*
   Self-restraint
   Negotiated allocation of common goods

3. *Sovereignty*
   Stratified equality
   Segmented collective defense
   Regional security through autonomous professionalized military
   Regional powers in relatively autonomous geo-strategic subregions

4. *Participation*
   Limited and stratified
   Changing coalitions

5. *Bloc Formation*
   Global interdependency
   Free-market principles

administration suggest the emergence of a new paradigm of cooperation in the Western Hemisphere based on a commitment to **partnership**. This new paradigm was visible on several occasions prior to the unveiling of President Bush's Enterprise of the Americas Initiative. Particularly noticeable were those changes in the area of multilateral relations.[22] (See Table 2.)

By the late 1980s the United States could no longer sustain its global political and military projections. Economic constraints and the scarcity of adequate foreign policy instruments at home were supplemented by the trend toward increasing globalization of the economy, which required greater interdependence and reliance on international and hemispheric cooperation. As Richard S. Williamson has indicated, the complexity of contemporary issues on the scientific, economic, and political levels were "outstripping the traditional means by which governments dealt with them. [As a result,] awareness of national interdependency, the importance of regional country and functional groupings has been heightened."[23] To be more effective, the United States increasingly accepted joint efforts and the creation of cooperative regimes in different issue areas. This approach was first seen near the end of Reagan's second term but appeared more clearly during the first years of the Bush administration.

President Bush's emphasis on multilateral cooperation and new forms of partnership is different from the "strategic globalism" of President Reagan, or from the "One Americas" concept of collective security. The Bush approach highlights free trade in the hemisphere as the cornerstone of a new inter-American era of cooperation.[24]

Given the declining importance of state-centered instruments to improve the economic performance of Latin American countries, as well as the current dominance of market-oriented principles in the region, it was easier for a Republican administration to recover the inspiration for a hemispheric order without endangering central values of U.S. conservatives. If coercive tendencies can be overcome, this novel hemispheric situation could create the conditions for a bipartisan consensus on hemispheric matters.

The new multilateral approach has an agenda that goes beyond the Enterprise of the Americas Initiative. According to Secretary of State James A. Baker III, the following items for cooperation need to be defined collectively: "democracy; development; drugs; debt; trade; migration; the environment; nuclear proliferation . . . are neither North American nor Latin American responsibilities. They are the common challenges that we are going to have to confront together to shape successfully our shared destiny. . . . The United States enjoys political stability, peaceful succession of power, *unquestioned civilian authority*, and the steady expansion of human rights. . . . We are committed to helping Latin America wage that successful democratic struggle as well."[25] This agenda closely coincides with the priorities on which Latin American countries have focused in their relations with the United States. A detailed analysis of U.S. linkages with Argentina, Brazil, Chile, Colombia, Cuba, Mexico, and Peru demonstrates that from the Latin American perspective, all the main issues coincide with those mentioned by Secretary Baker: human rights, representative democracy, the Central American conflict, drugs, debt, commercial linkages, nuclear proliferation, the South Atlantic conflict, and military cooperation.[26] This new multilateral approach—or at least a common policy agenda—is a clear departure from the coercive measures previously pursued by the United States.

A second change in U.S. policy is seen in the country's approach to political issues in the hemisphere. In mid-1989 President Bush stated that because the United States and Latin America "share common interests [,] we must work toward a common aim. Our battlefield is the broad middle ground of democracy and popular government, our fight is against the enemies of freedom on the extreme right and on the extreme left." This statement suggests a deviation from the totalitarian-authoritarian approach that informed U.S. policy in the recent past.[27] For the first time in a decade, all sources of political instability are condemned.

In the United States, this policy of strengthening democracy is the product of a previous bipartisan accord and has been carried out through several institutional mechanisms, including the National Endowment for Democracy and special programs of federal agencies—for example, the Democratic Initiatives program of the U.S. Agency for International Development.[28] As an all-embracing concept, this new idea of democracy is also producing a new orientation in U.S. foreign policy, one that is different from the traditional tutelary view of democracy as a condition closely linked to narrowly defined local elites and subservient to U.S. security and economic interests.

A third important change is found in U.S.–Latin American military relations. Since the second Reagan term, which placed a new emphasis on democratization in inter-American relations, one central priority has been to strengthen democratic institutions by supporting civilian over military control. This priority has as a corollary the implication that U.S. economic support will be conditioned on the observance of democratic behavior. The Latin American armed forces were notified that they could not count on the support of the U.S. government for coup attempts.[29] Beyond this basic refusal to support militarism, a permanent U.S. commitment to civilian democratic governments is emerging as crucial to the political future of the region. This is because transitions to democracy do not strengthen civilian governance automatically; Latin American military establishments often maintain high political leverage and use their influence to protect corporate prerogatives. This obviously impedes the transition to complete civilian democratic governance, thereby creating the possibility of permanent political instability.[30]

A fourth change in U.S. policy lies in the area of hemispheric security matters, with the United States now promoting a reduction in the levels of military force. The Bush administration is aware of the need to decrease the economic drain caused by the arms race in the Third World in general and in Latin America in particular. Although the trend toward declining expenditures for weapons has been encouraged in recent years due to regional economic problems, high levels of military expenditures still exist in most Latin American countries. In the last seven years, new weapon technologies have been introduced in the principal countries in the region. In the 1980s substantial amounts of artillery, armored vehicles, tanks, landing craft, frigates and medium-sized ships, helicopters, training aircraft, fighters, missiles, and missile launchers were purchased. The main importer has been Argentina (after the South Atlantic conflict), followed by Colombia, Venezuela, Bolivia, Ecuador, and Uruguay.

Effective curbs on arms transfers are exceptionally difficult to administer. As President Bush noted in 1989:

The security challenges we face today do not come from the East alone. The emergence of regional powers is rapidly changing the strategic landscape . . . in our own hemisphere, a growing number of nations are acquiring advanced and highly destructive capabilities—in some cases, weapons of mass destruction and the means to deliver them. . . . Our task is clear: we must curb the proliferation of advanced weaponry; we must check the aggressive ambitions of renegade regimes; and we must enhance the ability of our friends to defend themselves. We have not yet mastered the complex challenge. We and our allies must construct a common strategy for stability in the developing world.[31]

Traditionally, the United States has sought to enhance its influence over allies in security matters through modern technology transfers. This approach is also economically rewarding for the United States.[32] But since defense expenditures represent a heavy burden on Latin American governments as they seek to overcome economic recession, a new equilibrium between security and economic cooperation must now be found. To increase substantially U.S. military and economic aid unilaterally would be an impossible task. Accordingly, the United States must now seek to identify new ways to establish a credible defense for Latin American countries. A less-burdensome policy would be to support an effective regime for peaceful conflict resolution—that is, one that is respected and endorsed by both the United States and Latin America. A second, complementary policy would be to coordinate arms sales with other developed countries, regulating the flow of arms and weapons technology and thus creating a de facto military balance on the suppliers' and recipients' sides.

The Persian Gulf War complicated the military situation in Latin America. On the one hand, the Bush administration stepped up the process of multilateral control of weapon exports, pressing the Coordinating Committee on Multilateral Export Controls (COCOM) for stricter guidelines. The Australian Group, which shares intelligence information on chemical weapon developments, the twelve-nation Missile Control Regime, and the fourteen-nation Nuclear Supplier Group have been examples of highly diversified networks of multilateral initiatives that are being used as effective mechanisms of arms control. On the other hand, in 1991 the White House asked Congress for the first time since the 1970s to authorize the U.S. Export-Import Bank to support the commercial sales of military products to the members of NATO, Japan, Israel, Australia, "and for 'any other country' which would include the third world."[33] The history of cooperation among the military suppliers of developed countries does not permit much optimism that an effective arms control policy will be accepted or implemented.

Coercive Continuities

Although the Bush administration introduced changes in its foreign policy to adjust to new-world realities, these changes did not spread to all areas of U.S. policy-making.[34] Tensions remained between the general policies noted above and the specific policies of the Bush presidency that continued to be inspired by coercive approaches. The best example of this tension, of course, was the U.S. invasion of Panama in late 1989.

The tendency to define unilaterally an agenda for action and to operate outside of multilateral organizational settings can still be observed in U.S. policy. This is due to two related factors. First, the dominant historical tendency of U.S. policy-makers is to intervene unilaterally in hemispheric affairs, particularly in crisis situations. Even in normal times, multilateralism in security matters has not been common.[35] This tendency to "go it alone" has impeded the development of a workable regional collective security mechanism.

The coercive control approach toward hemispheric issues has also been observed in other areas of U.S. policy. Some members of the Bush administration underlined the utility of being able to use force in foreign policy—as, for example, General Colin Powell, assistant to the president for national security affairs and later chairman of the Joint Chiefs of Staff. His focus was on the Middle East, but the emphasis on "reserving the right to use force" was seen in hemispheric affairs when, for instance, the assistant secretary of state for inter-American affairs, Bernard Aronson, insisted that the United States "has pledged to push democracy in the hemisphere without ruling out the use of force to protect U.S. national interests."[36]

Thus, counterproductive traditional policies have not yet been rejected by U.S. policymakers. One of them, covert action, could conspire against the strengthening of civilian democratic governance in the hemisphere. This danger appeared when William H. Webster, director of the Central Intelligence Agency (CIA), worried about "increasing unrest of 'coup plotting' in Latin American countries (and) declared that a bipartisan policy must be developed to support covert action in the region. . . . Some of the democracies in the region are so fragile . . . that their survival depends on the attitude of their military and the capacity of their military to maintain law and order."[37] This tendency to resort to coercive control over domestic political processes does not encourage genuine progress toward democratic governance and civilian control of the military. Moreover, conspiring covertly to exclude participants from the political process is unlikely to promote stability in the region.

Other continuities with a coercive past can be observed with regard to military assistance issues. The U.S. military assistance policy is an integral aspect of the

U.S. policy not to commit military forces abroad. Hence, in 1989, when the secretary of defense asked the U.S. military establishment to accelerate training and other assistance to military and police forces in Latin America, he carefully observed that "no U.S. troops will accompany Latin American forces on military operations. U.S. troops will be restricted to training and technical aid, such as improving communications."[38]

As an instrument of U.S. foreign policy, security assistance has to be tailored to the shape of civil-military relations. Military assistance can be an important part of bilateral relations between the United States and Latin American governments, but in the process it can encourage direct military-to-military dealings that erode civilian governance and control. This problem has not been clearly understood in Washington. According to a recent analysis:

> Military assistance (FMS: foreign military sales) financing, IMET (international military education and training), and MAP (military assistance program) general costs, and economic support funds (ESF) promote U.S. interests by pursuing a number of mutually reinforcing goals. These include: enhancing the ability of U.S. security partners to deter and defend against aggression and instability; maintaining the cohesion and strength of our alliances; developing sound military-to-military relations that support our diplomatic strategy and enhance U.S. influence and prestige; promoting regional stability; contributing to our access to military bases and facilities abroad, thereby maintaining the strategic mobility of U.S. forces; strengthening the economies of key countries that are attempting to adjust to heavy debt, depressed commodity export prices, and startling changes in the global economic environment; and providing support for emerging democracies while defending existing democratic institutions and values in other countries.[39]

Unfortunately, these goals are often contradictory. In the experience of Latin America, democratic institutions are simply not strengthened by direct military-to-military relations. Without involving democratically elected civilian officials in defense matters, and without really subordinating the military to the executive power, it will be impossible to stabilize domestic polities in Latin America. Consequently, if the United States wishes to strengthen democracy when it gives military assistance to Latin American countries, it must do so only through those civilian officials.

Drug trafficking is another important "security problem" for which the United States has adopted a military solution.[40] In 1989 Secretary of Defense Dick Cheney ordered the Pentagon to develop plans to strengthen the U.S. military presence in the Caribbean Sea and along the U.S. southern border to curb cocaine smuggling.

Initially, some military officers were reluctant to take on the antidrug mission; nonetheless, for the past several years the U.S. military has been expanding its role in the drug war. For some Latin American countries, U.S. military assistance to combat drug producers has been linked to increased funding for military purchases; for example, in Colombia the U.S. Export-Import Bank helped the Virgilio Barco government to finance the purchase of arms needed to cope with drug traffickers. This policy of providing arms to interdict drug trafficking could change regional military balances, impeding reductions in the level of military forces.

Partnership and Security in Latin America

To date, the confusion between U.S. political goals and Latin American security concerns has made it impossible to develop a hemispheric security regime that is capable of sustaining democracy and peace in the hemisphere. Also contributing to this deficiency are the diversity of security paradigms, the crisis of the cold war–era hemispheric security system, and the increasing differences among Latin American countries' positioning in the military arena.

New principles, norms, regulations, and decision-making procedures must now be combined to create specific security regimes informed by the new paradigm of cooperation through partnership. The diversity of conflicts in the hemisphere can only be tackled by creating specific regimes. However, these issue-specific security regimes are difficult to develop because the security interests of the United States have received much more attention than those of Latin America. Cooperative security regimes with a common incentive system for all the parties are not easy to develop and sustain. Regardless of the difficulty involved in their creation, new security regimes will be required if regions are to develop a common approach to enhancing their security in a new global environment.[41] In Latin America, the U.S. presence should not be ignored. Washington's participation in hemispheric security regimes, if genuinely responsive to shared interests, could be an additional reinforcement of global security.

Hemispheric security regimes—whether global or issue-oriented—have commonly embraced all security dimensions, including all aspects of the national defense of individual countries. That links too many issues together. Greater success might be achieved if specific security regimes based on particular dimensions of security—naval, aerial, and territorial—were first established. For example, one hemispheric strategic regime could be developed in the naval area. The incentives for cooperation lie in the fact that all participants are interested in free naval transit in surrounding areas, that is, the Caribbean, Atlantic, and Pacific oceans. Nevertheless, this free transit through sea lines of communication should have some restrictions in order to be supported by all Latin American states. Even though restrictions might be difficult for individual states to accept, agreements may be obtainable. Dumping nuclear waste in the area of Sea Lines of Communications (SLCs) could be forbidden, for instance. In addition, naval bases in neighboring areas could be prohibited. This naval hemispheric regime would require an appropriate enforcement mechanism, and therefore consultation and verification mechanisms and institutions would have to be developed. Joint naval commands for verification and control at the hemispheric level could be highly useful.

A second specific security regime could be established in the aerial field. In addition to supporting naval control and verification procedures, this regime could create a joint agency for the peaceful use of space, using all the facilities provided by President Reagan's National Space Strategy and the U.S. Congress's space policy legislation.[42] Such a security regime should prohibit the installation of strategic landing sites in Latin America's continental and insular territories, as well as ban the use of terrestrial facilities for military space applications. Such an accord could also be used to perform control and verification functions in extensive continental areas claimed by Latin American states. The same role of control and verification could be fulfilled by an aerial security regime protecting Latin America's two-hundred-nautical-mile economic zone.

Finally, a third specific security regime might be a territorial one. The incentive for all parties to participate would be the creation of a conflict control regime to protect the continent from military confrontations and to prevent the internationalization of these conflicts. To achieve these goals, a new Latin American commission for the peaceful management of disputes—established in the context of the Organization of American States—should be supported. In addition to this diplomatic initiative, complementary military policies might be developed. For example, the territorial security regime could emphasize the defensive deterrence potential of local military power. Accordingly, a new U.S. policy toward the Latin American militaries could emphasize a professionalization process that would concentrate training and arms transfers around defensive doctrines and weapons.

At present, the United States seems to perceive drug trafficking and terrorism as the most important issues in the territorial field. From a Latin American perspective, these issues can be handled by police institutions instead of by military ones. To avoid repeating the errors of previous decades—to have a policy toward the Latin American armed forces not focused on defense concerns—it should be emphasized that these problems are not military in nature. Whereas naval, aerial, or territorial security conflicts are derived from the projection of state power, drug trafficking and terrorism are produced by local social and economic conditions, as well as by the absence of domestic political commitments. To deal with domestic policy issues from a military perspective only exacerbates the problems instead of providing effective solutions.

The same could be said regarding the recent U.S. approach to low-intensity conflicts. This kind of hemispheric military activity destroys the possibility of any regional security system because it blends minor political aims with military interests, thereby converting the latter into a second-class linkage. Similarly, U.S. military forces and U.S. covert action should not be used because they permit the development of shared military-security interests. A regional security system can be developed only if all the parties involved renounce the use of military force against each other in seeking to solve political problems. This democratic conviction, so widely disseminated in the domestic politics of the United States, should also be applied to U.S. military policy in Latin America in order to make inter-American military relations more democratic as well.

The development of a completely new paradigm for hemispheric issues around the idea of cooperation through partnership will require the gradual end of coercion and, at the same time, the establishment of cooperative regimes for several issue areas. The reward for all would be the opening of a new era of hemispheric cooperation in security matters.

Notes

1. Kennan, "Future of U.S.-Soviet Relations" and "An Irreversibly Changed Europe."

2. See Whitehead, "Debt, Diversification, and Dependency." A relative, but not absolute decline of the United States in world politics helps to explain Latin America's new room for maneuver. On the nature of changes in U.S. international positioning, see Nye, "Understanding U.S. Strength."

3. This process of change has been incorrectly perceived as a detachment of Latin America from the United States; it has generated either "pessimistic" or "optimistic" views. For a pessimistic scenario that could promote U.S. detachment from Latin America, see Ronfeldt, "A New Dark Age." A different approach is found in Hayes, "The U.S. and Latin America."

4. The idea of a continental uniqueness can be found in the precolonial Inca notion of the *Incarry*, the Spanish America of colonial times, the *América Bolivariana* of the nineteenth century, and integration efforts from the Andean Pact to the Latin American Free Trade Association. On the heterogeneity of Latin American countries, see Fajnzylber, "Democratization," and chapter 1—by Alberto van Klaveren—in this volume.

5. On the Latin American side, see Maira, *¿Una nueva era*. On the U.S. side, see Kennedy, "Can the U.S. Remain Number One?." See also Rico, "Crisis ¿y recomposición?."

6. On U.S. views of Latin American stability and instability, see Schoultz, *National Security*.

7. Jefferson's letter to Monroe in 1801, quoted by Waciuma, *United States–Latin American Relations*, p. 19.

8. Gantenbein, *Evolution of Our Latin American Policy*; Leopold, *Growth of American Foreign Policy*.

9. For an analysis of cooperation among developed countries, see Grieco, *Cooperation among Nations*.

10. Intergovernmental cooperation occurs "when the policies actually followed by one government are regarded by its partners as facilitating realization of their own objectives, as the result of a process of policy coordination." Keohane, *After Hegemony*, pp. 51–52.

11. On cooperation, see Oye, *Cooperation under Anarchy*.

12. See Krasner, *Structural Conflict*, p. 45.

13. A similar argument is found in Craig and George, *Force and Statecraft*, pp. 189–93.

14. The cases of Grenada, Nicaragua, and Panama illustrate this point. Another example is the use of U.S. naval forces for an antidrug patrol in international waters off Colombia.

15. See Schoultz, *Human Rights*, pp. 372–79. Similar arguments can be found in Molineu, *U.S. Policy toward Latin America*, pp. 136–44.

16. See Bull, *Anarchical Society*, chap. 3, and Bodenheimer and Gould, "U.S. Military Doctrines." A clear position on "coercive diplomacy" is Baker, "U.S. Lacks Cohesive Third World Conflict Policy." A critique of this approach is Pastor, *Condemned to Repetition*. For a critique of U.S. "coercive politics" in a more general context, see Nye, "Understanding U.S. Strength." In this context, no stable "set of implicit or explicit principles, norms, rules and decision-making procedures around which actor's expectations converge" could be established.

17. See President Woodrow Wilson's address at Mobile, Ala., October 27, 1913, and the inaugural address of President Franklin D. Roosevelt, March 4, 1933, both in Gantenbein, *Evolution of Our Latin American Policy*.

18. On this concept, see Braudel, *Perspective of the World*, p. 21.

19. Steinbruner, "The Prospect of Cooperative Security."

20. On this subject, see Palmer, "La actual formulación."

21. "The channels linking the United States to the global economy have grown deep and wide. . . . The challenge is therefore to join in partnership with our allies to build a liberal international system supportive of our mutual interests. While American power may have diminished, the American interest in U.S. leadership has rarely been greater . . . its position might be described as 'first among equals.'" Bosworth and Lawrence, "America's Global Role," p. 45.

22. According to U.S. officials, the planning of the new paradigm began two years before it was launched. For an analysis of changes in the U.S. policy toward Latin America from 1984, see Hirst, *Continuidad y cambio*.

23. Williamson, "Toward the Twenty-first Century." He added: "Over the past several decades, the United States has come to an increased recognition that, in many areas, we can be more effective in advancing U.S. objectives if we pursue these objectives in a multilateral context, which allows us to assert values that transcend narrow political interests."

24. Ronfeldt, *U.S. Involvement in Central America*; Bush, "Enterprise for the Americas Initiative." In May 1990, Bush stated that "our task is clear: to make the most of the new opportunities open to us, we must improve our working partnerships in this hemisphere— between countries north and south; between government, business, and labor; and, in the United States, between the different branches of the federal government." Bush, "Commitment to Democracy and Economic Progress," p. 1. For an analysis of the main differences between the approaches of the Bush and Reagan administrations, see Insulza, "Estados Unidos y la nueva realidad internacional."

25. Baker, "Latin America and the U.S.," p. 6. Emphasis added.

26. Van Klaveren, "Las relaciones de los países latinoamericanos."

27. Bush, "Commitment to Democracy." This change was the natural outcome of traumatic experiences in Central America, particularly El Salvador. For a critical analysis of this experience, see Fagen, *Forging Peace*; Pastor, *Condemned to Repetition*; and Shafer, *Deadly Paradigms*.

28. McNeil, "La cara cambiante de la hegemonía." See also Connolly, "Foreign Aid for the 1990s."

29. Cohen, "Shift in U.S. Policy." At the Inter-American Defense College in July 1985, Elliot Abrams, the former assistant secretary of state for inter-American affairs, stated that U.S. economic support would be contingent on democratic practices. In February 1988 he noted that "the option of military rule to 'correct' the alleged errors of the electorate is not acceptable for those who seek the respect or the support of the United States." Abrams, "Obstacles Hindering Latin American Democracy," USIS, Santiago, February 29, 1988.

30. On this topic, see chapter 8--by J. Samuel Fitch—in this volume; Stepan, *Rethinking Military Politics*; Varas, *Democracy under Siege*; and National Democratic Institute for International Affairs, *Civil-Military Relations*.

31. Bush, "Security Strategy for the 1990s."

32. Holmes, "FY 1990 Security Assistance Program."

33. *New York Times*, March 18, 1991, p. C1.

34. Important divergent approaches also were raised. See Fauriol, *The Third Century*.

35. For an analysis of the general trends in U.S. security policy in Latin America, see Varas, *Hemispheric Security*.

36. Powell, "U.S. Foreign Policy"; "Aronson Pledges to Push Democracy." General Powell stated: "Even in these times of fiscal stringency, we must not forget the lesson we learned eight years ago that there is no substitute for defensive strength. America's bipartisan effort to restore the military balance did wonders for our allies'—and the world's—sense of security. When America is weak, the world is a more dangerous place. Our strength has contributed to world stability, and to the possibilities for constructive—and balanced— negotiations with our adversaries on arms control and arms reduction" (p. 31).

37. Nelson, "CIA Chief Warns of 'Coup Plotting.'"

38. "Pentagon Is Ordered to Set Plans."

39. Holmes, "FY 1990 Security Assistance Program."

40. According to President Bush, "our common partnership must confront a common enemy: international drug traffickers. Drugs threaten citizens and civil society throughout our hemisphere. Joining forces in the war on drugs is crucial. There is nothing to be gained by trying to lay blame and make recriminations. Drug abuse is a problem of both supply and demand—and attacking both is the only way we can face and defeat the drug menace." Bush, "Commitment to Democracy and Economic Progress," p. 2.

41. See United Nations, "Report of the Independent Commission on Disarmament and Security," known as the "Palme Report."

42. See Marcia S. Smith, "Space Policy and Funding."

· *Abraham F. Lowenthal*

Chapter Three · CHANGING U.S.

. INTERESTS AND POLICIES

. IN A NEW WORLD

D ramatic global shifts, striking developments across Latin America, and major
changes within the United States are
combining to reshape inter-American
relations. U.S. interests and priorities are being transformed. So are the processes
for making U.S. policies toward the countries of the Western Hemisphere, as well
as the identity and influence of the main actors affecting policy.

With so much in flux, it is impossible to be certain how ties between the United
States and Latin America will evolve in the 1990s, but they will surely be quite
different from those of the 1980s. During the past decade, U.S. policy toward Latin
America—or at least Central America—was fiercely disputed, even if it was
usually only of tertiary significance for fundamental U.S. interests. In the coming
years, Latin America may well become more important to the United States and
yet, paradoxically, be less conspicuous in the U.S. foreign policy debate. Ideological and security concerns were at the heart of inter-American relations during the
1980s; more mundane economic issues are shaping the agenda of the 1990s.

The Impact of Global Changes

Five broad international shifts have transformed the context of inter-American
relations: the collapse of the Soviet Union, the ending of the cold war and the
affirmation of the United States as a world power, the widespread validation of

This essay also appears in Robert Art and Seyom Brown, eds., *U.S. Foreign Policy: The
Search for a New Role* (New York: Macmillan, 1992).

political democracy and free markets, the diffusion of economic power to Europe and Asia, and the underlying restructuring of the world economy.[1]

It is too early to know all the consequences of the former Soviet Union's internal upheavals. In almost any imaginable scenario, however, Moscow will be a considerably smaller factor in Western Hemisphere affairs during this decade than it was in the last two.[2] During the 1970s and 1980s, Soviet ambitions and activities in Latin America were less than U.S. policymakers perceived or claimed, but Moscow did probe opportunistically to expand its influence in the Americas. With the onset of perestroika, the unleashing of centrifugal forces within the Soviet Union, and the end of the cold war, such efforts have virtually disappeared, and they are unlikely to be resumed any time soon, whether the reforms initiated by Mikhail Gorbachev ultimately succeed or fail. Russian involvement in Nicaragua and El Salvador has ended, and Moscow's engagement with Fidel Castro's Cuba has diminished sharply.

The specter that haunted Washington for more than twenty-five years—a "Second Cuba" in the Americas—is now obviously remote. The first Cuba, indeed, has lost much of its interest and credibility, both for erstwhile sympathizers and longtime detractors. Much of U.S.–Latin American relations for the past generation—especially in the Caribbean Basin—was organized around countering and containing Castro's influence. That will be much less the case in the 1990s, when a post-Castro transition is likely finally to occur.

The waning of the cold war is affecting U.S.–Latin American relations in several other ways, some of them potentially contradictory. Regional conflicts are no longer being fueled or exacerbated by superpower competition, but the potentially restraining influence of the great powers is also reduced.[3] The decreased Russian role in Latin America removes a main asserted reason for most recent U.S. intervention in the Americas. But it also diminishes a possible constraint, as the United States no longer faces the prospect of a Soviet reaction elsewhere in the world to a U.S. action in this hemisphere.

The 1989 U.S. invasion of Panama, the deployment in Latin America of U.S. military advisers in the antinarcotics campaign, the extraterritorial enforcement of U.S. drug laws, and the recurrent neo-Wilsonian urge to export democracy all suggest that the unilateral activist impulse of the United States has thus far survived the cold war's demise, and it may well be reinforced, at least for a time, by the military victory against Iraq. But U.S. tolerance for diverse approaches in the Western Hemisphere may also be increasing. Washington would probably have accepted the election as president of Luís Inácio da Silva ("Lula"), the Brazilian labor leader who gained almost 48 percent of the votes in 1989, far more readily than would have been the case any time in the past. The U.S. government absorbed the election of a radical priest to the presidency of Haiti in 1990 with an equanimity that could not have been imagined just five years before, and in 1991

Washington even made strong efforts to help restore President Jean-Bertrand Aristide to office after a military coup removed him. The United States, in short, may find itself in the 1990s freer to intervene in Latin America but less motivated to do so than in recent decades.

The affirmation of political democracy and free market economics is a third trend, related to but distinct from the collapse of the Soviet Union and the waning of the cold war. The command economy has abjectly failed, and the very notion of dictatorship—of whatever stripe—has become illegitimate. No longer can Latin American radicals expect significant extrahemispheric support, ideological or material, for the revolutionary socialist path, or indeed for any approach to development relying on authoritarian rule or statist economics.[4]

A fourth feature of the contemporary international landscape is the rise to prominence of Western Europe and East Asia, with their extraordinarily dynamic economies. By many measures—level of technology, per capita income, currency reserves, and foreign aid disbursements, among others—Japan and the European Economic Community have been catching up to or overtaking the United States. Japan has become the world's major creditor and the greatest donor of official development assistance, and the enhanced integration of the European Community is creating the world's largest market and center of production. Japan and several countries of Western Europe, not Russia, are the real competitors of the United States for influence and markets in Latin America.[5]

Perhaps the greatest international change affecting U.S.–Latin American relations has been the steady transformation of the world economy from a series of loosely connected national markets to an increasingly interdependent global one. The driving force has been technology, which has revolutionized communications, transportation, management, and marketing, and led to the transnational integration of capital and labor. Latin America's role as an exporter of raw materials and a source of unskilled labor has made it extremely vulnerable in a world of synthetics, automation, and global sourcing. But a number of Latin American countries have found profitable places in international production networks.[6] A central challenge for all Latin American nations in the 1990s is to find their niche in the dynamic world economy. U.S.–Latin American relations in the 1990s will be profoundly affected by the strategies Latin America countries adopt to achieve that goal, and by their varying degrees of success in doing so.

Latin America in the 1990s

For Latin America, the 1980s were years of political gain and economic disaster. The advance from authoritarian rule toward democratic politics was as encouraging in its way as the collapse of the communist regimes in Eastern and Central Europe.[7] In country after country, military regimes or personalist dictatorships gave way to democratic civilian governments. In the final months of the decade, Brazil held its first direct presidential balloting since 1960 and Chile its first since 1970—thus bringing elected governments to every country of South America for the first time in a generation. With Nicaragua's internationally observed balloting in February 1990, the most competitive and honest vote in that country's history, elected authorities also hold office in every Central American nation, for the first time ever.

The practice of democracy remains very uneven and precarious across Latin America and the Caribbean, but democratic ideals now unquestionably prevail among elites throughout most of the region.[8] No longer is it commonly asserted that Latin America is somehow predisposed toward authoritarian rule, or that its culture is inherently antidemocratic.[9]

But although Latin America opened up participatory politics during the 1980s, most countries also faced painful economic contraction.[10] From the onset of the regionwide debt crisis in 1982 until the end of 1989, Latin America suffered a 10 percent regional decline in per capita income, with a far more severe drop in some countries and subregions. Unemployment and underemployment rose to record levels, inflation plagued many nations and hyperinflation ravaged a few, and socioeconomic inequalities worsened almost everywhere. Latin America's terms of trade deteriorated markedly, as the real value of most of its traditional exports declined. Its share of world commerce fell during the 1980s, from about 6 to about 3.5 percent, even while the volume of its exports climbed by nearly 50 percent.[11] The region's massive external debt, more than $420 billion in the aggregate by the middle of the decade, created a huge drain of capital that continues into the 1990s. Investment in production and infrastructure has dropped; Latin Americans have had to mortgage their future to service the debt.

Translated into human terms, the statistics on Latin America's plight mean hunger, infant death, boat people and feet people, stunted education, epidemics, street crime and delinquency, and mounting unrest. The political residue of economic failure, in turn, has been the repudiation of incumbent parties in almost every election, increased political polarization in many nations, incipient questioning of the democratic framework in several, and growing insurgencies in a few.

Most Latin American nations have by now adopted programs of economic stabilization and liberalization in order to revive their troubled economies.[12] Throughout the region, governments have been cutting budget deficits, reducing state involvement in the production of goods and services and in the regulation of economic activity, turning to market competition and private enterprise, and moving away from inward-oriented and protectionist policies in order to achieve export competitiveness. Even erstwhile populist politicians, once identified with public enterprises and distributive policies, are now pledged to neoliberal economic reforms. A few Latin American nations—Chile and Mexico, in particular— are already showing positive economic results from the new policies, and there is reserved hope for economic growth in much of the region.

In the early 1990s, however, much of Latin America is also experiencing a growing tension between political and economic liberalization—between opening politics and opening markets. Mounting public disaffection with incumbent regimes in Brazil, Venezuela, and other countries, plus the impressive strength in recent elections of populist candidates and parties—Cuauhtémoc Cárdenas in Mexico, Lula in Brazil, the leftist Frente Amplio and Nuevo Espacio in Uruguay, the socialist MAS and Causa R in Venezuela, and the erstwhile M-19 guerrillas in Colombia—could well lead in the 1990s yet again to new economic policies, revising if not reversing the approach of economic liberalization. The possible emergence of such challenges, in turn, might well produce moves by vested interests and economic elites to restrict democratic competition. How these tensions play out will be central to Latin America's political economy, and thus to inter-American relations, in the 1990s.

Other changes within Latin America will also condition Western Hemisphere relations. The region's fertility rates are slowly declining but the persistent high rates of urbanization in most countries, together with unemployment and underemployment, will continue to produce strong pressures for emigration from many nations.[13] Expanded diplomatic collaboration among Latin American countries and the glimmer of enhanced economic cooperation in several subregions may take on added importance in the 1990s.[14] And U.S.–Latin American relations will surely be affected by the increased differentiation among the nations of Latin America and the Caribbean.

The divergence among the region's countries has always been higher than most U.S. policymakers have assumed, but the differences today are more pronounced than ever. Mexico and many of the Caribbean islands are integrating with the United States in economic and demographic terms, through legal and illegal trade as well as the massive flow of people into the United States.[15] Peru and (to a lesser extent) Colombia are showing signs of *dis*integration. Whole regions of each country are under the control of insurgent movements, counterinsurgent paramilitary groups, or drug traffickers; in Peru, there is a virtual breakdown of the links between formal state authority and social and economic activity more broadly. Brazil remains locked in battles with inflation and economic decline. Chile, in contrast, after the turmoil of the early 1970s and the prolonged Pinochet dictatorship, is now enjoying the fruits of restored democratic politics and a newly modernized economy. Central America wavers uncertainly, facing the promise of peace through exhaustion, but with the possibility of several further years of low-level but deadly conflict. And Cuba, once a vanguard of change, now seems caught in a time warp, reflecting the conditions and concerns of the 1960s while the hemisphere and the wider world have left it behind.

The United States in a Time of Change

The United States has also been changing in ways that bear directly on inter-American relations. Although some of the organizing premises of U.S. policy toward Latin America during the past generation were first fashioned at the turn of the century, they took specific shape in the years immediately following World War II, when the institutions and assumptions of the "inter-American system" were firmly established. The United States was then at the height of its international stature. It accounted for one-third of the world's production, one-third of defense expenditures, and approximately one-third of international trade. Global trade and monetary regimes were established under U.S. leadership, and U.S. largesse fueled the recovery of Western Europe. The dollar replaced gold as the main form of international reserves. Numerous military alliances radiated outward from Washington, and the United States took the initiative on virtually every major international issue.

The worldwide preeminence of the United States in the 1950s was particularly evident in the Western Hemisphere, where U.S. influence rose to unprecedented levels. With a population about equivalent to all of Latin America and the Caribbean, the United States in 1950 produced nine times as much as all the Latin American and Caribbean nations combined, and the U.S. economy overwhelmingly dominated theirs.[16] Almost half of Latin America's trade was with the United States and 37 percent of all U.S. imports in 1950 came from Latin America.[17] U.S. investment in the region quintupled in the twenty years after World War II, as U.S. investors crowded out European competitors and sought opportunities in manufacturing and services to complement earlier involvements in natural resource extraction and public utilities.

It was in this context that Washington's "hegemonic presumption" was extended from the Caribbean Basin to the rest of Latin America.[18] And it was also in this atmosphere that the Organization of American States, the Inter-American Treaty of Reciprocal Assistance (the Rio Treaty), and a host of other mechanisms were devised to facilitate regional political and ideological leadership by the United States, to ensure that Western Hemisphere military security could be protected against extrahemispheric challenges, and to promote the economic interests of the United States, especially of its investors and importers.

During the past four decades, and most sharply in the last two, the fundamental assumptions underlying this U.S. approach to Western Hemisphere relations have eroded. In recent years, the United States has switched from being the world's largest creditor nation to being a very big debtor. The dependence of the United States on imported sources of energy is evident. Large, stubborn, and indeed mounting trade and fiscal deficits reflect an underlying slowing in U.S. rates of productivity and investment, and a decline in the overall competitiveness of the U.S. economy. The dollar is no longer "as good as gold," the United States is not the world's largest supplier of development assistance, U.S. firms are far from the world's most dynamic and aggressive, and U.S. banks have weakened considerably. All of these problems have been underscored by a recession that is increasing unemployment, cutting profits, feeding pressures for protectionism, and creating a high premium on expanding exports.

To be sure, research, higher education, management, and technology have all done well in the United States in recent years, by and large. The competitive advantage of the U.S. economy has accordingly shifted to high-technology industries drawing on skilled workers, as well as to technology-based services and large-scale agriculture. Lower-technology sectors of the U.S. economy, including light manufacturing and many labor-intensive service sectors, have meanwhile come to depend increasingly on migrant labor, largely from Mexico, the Caribbean, and Central America.

The composition of the U.S. population has been changing remarkably. More than one-quarter of the country's population growth since 1980 has been accounted for by immigrants, mainly from Latin America and the Caribbean.[19] Improved health and declining birth rates have combined to produce an aging population, one that may face labor shortages within a decade. The power structure of the United States has also been shifting. Population, wealth, and political clout have been moving west and south, to regions where relations with Latin America are more salient. The close grip on foreign policy formulation of the Boston-New York-Washington WASP establishment has ended, and Hispanic Americans are among the groups vying for increased influence.

With the reduction of East-West tensions, attention in the United States has begun to shift toward domestic problems: a failing primary and secondary educational system, faltering basic industries and infrastructure, decaying cities, environmental degradation, homelessness and worsening public health, the AIDS epidemic, drugs and crime, racial tensions, sharpening disparities of income, a deteriorating work ethic, and declining levels of civic engagement and political participation. Perhaps the most important question facing the United States in the 1990s is whether a national consensus will emerge to address these internal problems, within perceived resource constraints. How that question is answered is bound to affect U.S.–Latin America relations, for Latin America is highly relevant to many of these domestic issues.

The Shifting Agenda of U.S.–Latin American Relations

From the turn of the century, Latin America's significance to the United States has traditionally been discussed in terms of military security, political solidarity, and economic advantage. Latin America, particularly the Caribbean Basin region, was for many years central to the forward defense strategy of the United States. The Panama Canal and the network of military and naval facilities in the circum-Caribbean region were considered vital U.S. security assets. Strategic materials imported from Latin America were also important, during both World War II and the Korean conflict. Pan-American unity, regional solidarity in support of U.S. diplomatic leadership, was a cornerstone of U.S. foreign policy. A virtual Latin American bloc, almost always acting in support of U.S. positions, was key, for instance, during the first few years of the United Nations, when Latin American states by themselves comprised one-third of the membership of the General Assembly. And Latin America was for many years economically important for the United States, mainly as a prime arena for U.S. private investment and as a major source of raw materials needed for the growing U.S. economy. During the first third of the twentieth century, more than half of all U.S. private investment abroad was concentrated in Latin America; in 1950, 40 percent of all U.S. foreign direct investment was still in Latin America and the Caribbean.[20]

For all these reasons, U.S. policymakers have long considered it essential to exclude competing and especially hostile extrahemispheric influences from Latin America and the Caribbean. From World War II through the 1980s, a major goal of successive U.S. administrations was to assure continued U.S. dominance in the Western Hemisphere, particularly in the Caribbean Basin.[21] This was the central aim of John F. Kennedy's Alliance for Progress, of Richard Nixon's Mature Partnership, of Henry Kissinger's New Dialogue, and of both Ronald Reagan's Caribbean Basin Initiative and his undeclared contra war on Nicaragua.

Over the past thirty years, however, Latin America's significance to the United States on these traditional dimensions of concern has been declining. Changes in technology and the waning of the cold war have transformed military defense calculations, and Latin America has become less relevant to U.S. strategic concerns. There is no credible scenario by which the military security of the United States is directly threatened in this hemisphere. The network of military and naval facilities has consequently lost its priority; not even the Panama Canal is as "vital" as it used to be. Latin America's presumed diplomatic solidarity with the United

States has diminished as Latin American nations have increasingly come to act independently and in their own interests, often perceived more in international economic than in regional terms. And Latin America's relative salience to the United States in traditional economic ways has also ebbed. The Latin American share of U.S. foreign private investment has sharply declined—to about 13 percent in the late 1980s—as a result of nationalizations, divestment from Latin America, and massive investment by U.S. firms in other regions.[22] Although some renewed U.S. investment in Latin America is now occurring, not one of the Fortune 500 corporations has as much as 10 percent of its foreign investment in Latin America.[23] With the diversification of global sources and the use of synthetics, the share of U.S. imports coming from Latin American has also dropped (to about 13 percent as well).[24]

It was precisely because Latin America's traditional importance to the United States was steadily dropping that the Reagan administration's intense focus on restoring unchallenged U.S. political, ideological, and security control of the Caribbean Basin seemed so anachronistic and obsessive. This was particularly so in the latter years of the Reagan period, when relations between Washington and Moscow were beginning to thaw but the hostile U.S. campaign against Nicaragua nevertheless continued unabated. The Reagan administration resorted to hyperbolic rhetoric to rationalize a Central American policy that was mainly based on unexamined axioms and ideological fervor. It could not consistently persuade the U.S. public or the Congress that U.S. interests justified military action, covert warfare, or violations of international law because it could not articulate a convincing reason why the United States should be preoccupied with the presence of a hostile regime in a small Caribbean Basin nation.

Coming to office in a radically changing international environment, and after a decade of fruitless partisan wrangling on Central American policy, the administration of George Bush quickly perceived that a different approach to Latin America was advisable. Within its first weeks, the administration distanced itself from the contra war, accepted the framework of a Central American peace plan that had been designed by Costa Rican president Oscar Arias (and rejected by the Reagan government), and began to phase down U.S. involvement in the Nicaraguan conflict.[25] The victory of opposition leader Violeta Barrios de Chamorro in Nicaragua's 1990 election gave the Bush team the satisfaction of seeing the Sandinista regime removed from office, but the basic switch in U.S. signals had already occurred before the Nicaraguan elections and was independent of its outcome. The Bush administration was far less concerned about who governed in Managua than about the deleterious effects on congressional-executive relations of renewed rancor on Nicaragua.

The Bush administration successfully ended the Central America fixation of the

Reagan policy and eliminated its reckless hyperbole. The new administration understood that Latin America should no longer be conceived as a prime target in a supposed Soviet game plan to challenge U.S. power. It recognized that the cold war was waning, that the Soviet Union's earlier-perceived threat to U.S. interests in the Western Hemisphere was evaporating, and that Moscow's influence might actually be mobilized to serve U.S. objectives in the Western Hemisphere.

But the Bush administration did not substitute any clear alternative notion of Latin America's contemporary importance to the United States.[26] For a time, it seemed to aim more to remove Western Hemisphere news from the U.S. press than to develop a long-term strategy for coping with the region's impact on the United States. As the 1990s began, it was an open question whether Latin America would "fall off the map" of U.S. concerns, or whether the region would become more important to the United States in the 1990s.

Those who argued that Latin America would be of diminished interest to the United States asserted, with varying emphases, that as the Soviet Union became less involved in Latin America, the United States would reduce its attention as well. The logic of disengagement was reinforced, in this view, by U.S. budget pressures, doubts that the U.S. private sector would expand its presence in Latin America, negative public attitudes in the United States about the region, and skepticism in Washington about Latin American economic prospects. It was contended that Latin America would be ever more marginal in world affairs, that it would suffer Africa's fate of benign neglect. This perspective on the future of inter-American relations was frequently articulated by those U.S. specialists who had most strenuously emphasized the importance of Latin and Central America to U.S. security in the 1980s, but it was echoed by many Latin Americans and Latin Americanists who feared that the region would be abandoned.[27]

The contrary thesis is that trends in Latin America are increasingly and significantly affecting the United States, and that Washington may therefore be forced to pay attention to the Western Hemisphere—indeed, greater attention than in the past. Latin America is important for the United States, in this view, because of its economic impact and potential, the effects of migration, the region's role in affecting shared problems such as the narcotics trade and environmental deterioration, and its relevance for the core values of U.S. society, particularly respect for human rights.[28]

Latin America's main economic importance to the United States today derives not mainly from U.S. imports and investment but from exports, energy, and finance. Even after nearly a decade of economic downturn and sluggish imports, Latin America still accounts annually for nearly $60 billion of U.S. exports, greater than those to Japan or Germany. If Latin America can fully emerge from the depression of the 1980s, as some countries have already done, it could once again become a growing market for U.S. exports, as it was in the 1970s, and now at a time when an increasing share of the U.S. economy depends on trade and when regaining export competitiveness is a primary challenge facing the United States. A strong expansion of U.S. exports to Latin America could be especially significant in the 1990s, as some U.S. firms may become disadvantaged in a prospectively more integrated European Community. U.S. exports to Eastern and Central Europe in recent years have been less than 2 percent of U.S. exports to Latin America, and even a major expansion of exports to the former Warsaw Pact nations would mean much less to the U.S. economy than simply regaining half the rate of growth of exports to Latin America that was experienced during the 1970s.

Another economic importance of Latin America to the United States—all the more obvious after the Persian Gulf crisis—is as a source of energy; 27 percent of the imported petroleum entering the United States in 1990 came from Latin American and Caribbean nations.[29] Latin America could likewise be salient in the 1990s for U.S. commercial banking operations, not at the artificially high levels that were produced by petrodollar recycling in the 1970s, but at a level substantial enough to make a major difference to the performance of the few money-center banks that have stayed the course in Latin America.

The second major impact of Latin America and the Caribbean on the United States comes from massive and sustained migration to this country from Mexico, the Caribbean islands, and Central America.[30] Nearly 23 million persons of Hispanic American descent now live in the United States, and Latinos are among this country's fastest growing groups. The influx from the Caribbean has also been relentless, amounting to more than 10 percent of that region's population since World War II.[31] These massive migrations are reshaping the United States in many ways—affecting education, employment, public health, business, politics, culture, and mores. They create new links between the United States and the sending countries and a greater U.S. stake in the nature of conditions in these nations.

Latin America's third impact on the United States derives from major problems facing this country that cannot be resolved without sustained cooperation from Western Hemisphere nations. The most dramatic example is narcotics, for Latin American nations produce and transship almost all the cocaine and most of the marijuana entering the United States.[32] Even if the drug curse cannot be removed except by curbing the demand for narcotics within the United States, an effective antinarcotics effort will require detailed and enduring cooperation by Latin American producing and trafficking nations. And Latin America is also potentially important for other issues that will be high on the U.S. agenda in the 1990s: protecting the environment, countering terrorism, combating AIDS and other diseases, and curbing the spread of nuclear weapons and other arms.

A fourth way Latin America matters to the United States has to do with values at the core of U.S. society, especially respect for individual human rights, particularly those of free expression and political organization. As a nation founded on a commitment to the integrity of the individual, the United States cannot condone repression in a region so historically and culturally tied to our own society without risking erosion of its own legitimacy. Whenever Latin American governments have engaged in substantial violations of human rights, the domestic political process of the United States has pushed the region higher on Washington's foreign policy agenda. The growing Latin American and Caribbean diaspora in the United States will reinforce this historic tendency in the 1990s.

These four aspects of Latin America's importance for the United States have implications for U.S. policies in the hemisphere in the coming years. They suggest not only why the United States may well rediscover Latin America, but also that it may concern itself more than heretofore with the region's internal economic, social, and political conditions.

In an earlier era, when what mattered most to Washington was obtaining military bases, preserving access to raw materials, protecting investments in extractive industries, and gaining diplomatic support from client states, the U.S. government could perhaps afford to turn a blind eye to internal conditions within Latin America, overlook poverty and inequity, and make its peace with unattractive dictators. But if what will concern the United States about Latin America in the 1990s is the capacity for the region to buy U.S. products and continue servicing debt obligations to U.S. banks, assured access to secure energy sources, the rate and volume of migration and its relation to U.S. labor requirements, the prospects for effective cooperation on tough shared problems like drugs or the environment, as well as the protection of human rights—then Washington should come to recognize an important stake in the region's fundamental well-being.

Far from becoming irrelevant, Latin America's problems and opportunities may be understood as virtually "domestic" concerns of the United States. More precisely, many of the issues at the heart of U.S.–Latin American relations in the 1990s will be "intermestic"—based on the international spillover of domestic trends and involving both international aspects and actors.[33] The line between domestic policy and Latin American policy will be hard to define.

The Policy-making Process: New Issues, New Actors

As the main issues in U.S.–Latin American relations have been changing, the processes for policy-making have likewise been transformed. Trade, investment, finance, immigration, narcotics control, resource development, environmental protection, and public health are not primarily questions for the diplomatic or military establishments that have usually dominated the formulation of Latin American policy. These issues engage the participation, instead, of many different executive departments and agencies, and also of Congress and many of its committees. Congress is inevitably involved in all matters where legislation or budgetary resources are required, and most of the questions on the inter-American agenda in the 1990s will require either or both. State and local authorities, corporations and trade unions, and many other nongovernmental organizations are also substantially engaged.

The process of making "Latin American" policy has become much more complex in recent years. The State Department, the Pentagon, the Central Intelligence Agency, and the U.S. Information Agency have become less influential in the formulation and implementation of Western Hemisphere policies, while larger roles are being played by Treasury, Commerce, Agriculture, the Office of the Special Trade Representative, the Export-Import Bank, the Overseas Private Investment Corporation, the Drug Enforcement Administration, the Environmental Protection Agency, and the Immigration and Naturalization Service. This trend is likely not only to continue but also to accelerate in the 1990s.

The tendency in the past twenty years for nonstate actors to be ever more involved in making Washington's Latin American policy will also likely persist. Large multinational corporations with investments in Latin America and commercial banks with loans there may have a diminished stake in the region, but small businesses are more engaged, exporting products to Latin America or producing components in the region. Trade unions are also more involved, and they will have reason for intensive participation as the trend toward greater economic integration with Mexico and the Caribbean Basin countries continues, as is likely now that a proposed North American Free Trade Agreement has been negotiated and that the Caribbean Basin Initiative has been extended. Latino groups are seeking a larger role in shaping U.S. attitudes and policies toward Latin America, and their influence will be enhanced in the 1990s by the strategic concentration of Hispanic voters in California, Texas, and Florida, crucial states in national electoral terms.[34]

The process of shaping U.S. policies toward Latin America in the 1990s will probably be much less a matter of partisan debate between Democrats and Republicans, liberals and conservatives, than it was in the 1980s, when the Reagan administration's highly ideological approach heightened domestic political controversy. Immigration, trade, and narcotics issues elude familiar "liberal" and "conservative" divisions, for those who favor restrictive policies on some of these matters may support otherwise "liberal" social programs, whereas those who favor letting market forces reign freely may well be "conservative" on other questions. Cross-cutting conflicts among interest groups will likely multiply in the next years.

As strategic and security issues diminish and economic and social questions take their place, policy will be increasingly made by the pull and haul of advocacy, negotiation, and compromise. Growers, manufacturers, commercial firms, workers, consumers, environmentalists, law enforcement officers, human rights groups, civil libertarians, Hispanic Americans of various origins and perspectives, scholars, foundations, the media—these and other groups will compete to shape policies in a highly fragmented and easily permeable policy-making environment.[35] Some Latin American governments, Mexico foremost among them, are beginning to recognize that there will be expanded scope for influencing the U.S. policy-making process; the 1990s may well see much better organized and more visible Latin American lobbying efforts.

Indeed, the politics of the United States and of Latin America are becoming much more intertwined as a result of mass migration and its feedback effects as well as the explosive improvements in communications. Mexican, Caribbean, and Central American politicians now raise campaign funds and compete for influence in the United States. U.S. politicians appeal to Latinos, the fastest-growing group of voters, in part by reference to Latin America–related issues. Interest and affinity groups—labor unions, chambers of commerce, religious and human rights groups, professional associations, scholars, journalists, and others—build transnational networks that promote their causes on both sides of porous frontiers.[36] The alliances and coalitions that are formed vary from issue to issue and country to country, defying simple categories of analysis.

The United States and Latin America in the 1990s: Some Tentative Predictions

Yogi Berra is supposed to have observed that "it is always difficult to make predictions, especially about the future." This sage observation is more relevant than ever today, in a world that is changing with such breathtaking speed. No one in 1988 foresaw the Soviet Union's swift turn toward market economics, the breakup of the Soviet bloc and then of the union itself, Germany's rush to unification, China's crackdown at Tienanmen Square, South Africa's steps toward ending apartheid, or Iraq's invasion of Kuwait and the collective international response. Nor was it then imaginable that the return to democracy in Chile would be so smooth; that the Peronist party would take power in Argentina and quickly abandon so many of its historic policies; that the United States would deploy 24,000 troops to topple the government of Panama and that this action would be greeted with apparent enthusiasm both in Panama and the United States and with quiet acceptance elsewhere in the hemisphere; that a Marxist labor leader would come close to being elected president of Brazil, or that the son of a Japanese immigrant would actually be elected in Peru; that the Sandinistas would hold free elections in Nicaragua and accept defeat; or that the Mexican government would initiate negotiations with the United States and Canada on a Free Trade Agreement. Surprise has been virtually the only constant recently, and it would be foolhardy to predict the detailed shape of inter-American relations in the 1990s.

With more than the usual diffidence, therefore, I offer four general propositions about U.S.–Latin American relations in the 1990s:

1. Until and unless a new framework for U.S. foreign policy takes hold, U.S. policy toward Latin America will change only slowly, in uncertain and perhaps contradictory ways.

The habits of thought and patterns of action that long dominated U.S. foreign policy generally, and policy toward Latin America in particular, will not change overnight, even after widespread recognition that the cold war era has ended. The foreign policy elite and the broader American public still lack an agreed new vision of this country's place in the world, and of the nature and priority of various threats to U.S. interests. Policy will consequently often be shaped by inertial tendencies—unexamined axioms, bureaucratic and personal rivalries, institutions and budgets in search of new missions, and the competitive claims of different constituencies. Until new concepts and criteria for ordering U.S. priorities are widely accepted, established policies will have the advantages of familiarity and of well-placed and experienced advocates, and they will often prevail long after their initial rationales have been eroded.

More specifically, it is likely that the United States will continue to be drawn toward countering revolutionary nationalist movements in the Caribbean Basin border region, even though the reasons for U.S. involvement in such civil strife have become ever more tenuous. It is likewise probable that U.S. policy toward Cuba will not alter much until and unless major changes occur on the island, even though it is obvious by now that the strategic assumptions underlying the old policy are no longer valid; the constituency for reshaping policy toward Cuba may be too weak to prevail against entrenched interests and familiar arguments in a context of general uncertainty. And although Washington is increasingly concerned with economic issues, U.S. policy will probably continue to be shaped by the specific interests of particular interest groups, rather than by a national economic strategy for the hemisphere.

2. It will make even less sense than before to think about a general Latin American policy of the United States, for the countries of the Americas are changing their relations with the United States in diverse and contradictory ways.

To some extent, the pattern of the interwar years has been reasserting itself. As in the 1920s and 1930s, the United States is becoming far more closely engaged with Mexico and the Caribbean Basin than with South America, and other world powers are competing with the United States for influence on the South American continent.

Mexico is embarked on a course that, if sustained, will make that country increasingly a North American nation, ever more different in structure, approach, and international outlook from the countries of South America. More than 70 percent of Mexico's trade is already with the United States, compared with 18 percent of Argentina's, 28 percent of Brazil's, and 18 percent of Chile's. More than half of all U.S. exports to Latin America and the Caribbean in 1989 went to Mexico (compared with 39 percent in 1980), even before Mexico further reduced its tariffs and committed itself to free trade negotiations with the United States. More than 6 percent of Mexico's work force is now employed in the United States, and its workers remit at least $2–3 billion annually back to Mexico. Mexico and the United States are linked in myriad ways, and the trend toward specially designed bilateral policies and instruments is accelerating.[37]

The Caribbean Basin Initiative and especially the much more important underlying human initiative of sustained mass migration have linked the United States, particularly southern Florida and the eastern seaboard, with the Caribbean islands. It is instructive that U.S. airlines and telephone companies regard the Caribbean as "domestic," not foreign; it is ever more difficult to define the border between the mainland and the Caribbean in economic, social, demographic, and political terms. Again, special regional policies are gaining ground, reinforcing the de facto integration of the Caribbean islands into the U.S. community.[38]

It is much less clear how the Central American nations and Panama will relate to the United States in the 1990s.[39] It may be that the intense U.S. involvement of the 1980s (and the 1920s before them) will continue, albeit in modulated tones. But it is equally likely that the United States will eventually disengage, finding cosmetic devices to cover a substantial reduction of U.S. military and economic programs, as was the case during the late 1920s, the 1930s, and the 1970s. The rapidity with which Washington has in practice diminished its announced commitments to economic reconstruction in Nicaragua and Panama is instructive. Ambivalence and contradiction, not a clear-cut policy, are probable in the U.S. relationship with Central America.

The Andean countries—especially Colombia and Peru—will be more salient for the United States as a problem region, with particular reference to drug trafficking and guerrilla insurgencies. The U.S. military, narcotics control, and law enforcement establishments will be major shapers of the U.S. approach, which will also be greatly determined, in turn, by the success or failure of local efforts to regain control of the national territory. Tensions are likely to increase over U.S. efforts to pressure local authorities to accept U.S. priorities and tactics for dealing with the drug issue.[40]

The Southern Cone nations—Argentina, Chile, and Uruguay—have been reverting to the kind of diverse international ties they had before World War II, with the United States receding to a secondary role corresponding with its lack of large specific interests. Chile may defy this trend, at least for a time, because of its ability and willingness to act as a model interlocutor for U.S.-preferred regional economic policies and to take considerable advantage of the U.S. market, but Washington is unlikely to give sustained attention to distant Chile.[41] Argentina's strenuous efforts to adjust its historic foreign policy in order to align itself with Washington are equally unlikely to produce a lasting reciprocal interest by the United States.[42]

A big question mark in U.S.–Latin American relations is the future of Brazil, a megacountry of some 155 million inhabitants, the tenth largest economy in the world, with vast resources and a modern industrial infrastructure. It is difficult in the early 1990s to foresee whether Brazil will by the end of the century have regained the dynamism of the 1970s or else sunk deeper into economic and social difficulties. Nor is it yet clear how Brazil will organize its economy and politics to confront its major challenges. No approach yet adopted has succeeded in fully mobilizing Brazil's resources so that the country can achieve its long-touted potential. Competing visions are still being tried out; whatever general tack Brazil eventually chooses will shape its relationship with the United States.

3. U.S.–Latin American relations in the 1990s will be broadly influenced by how Latin American nations respond to the changing world economy, and by their relative success in mobilizing domestic resources and attracting external capital.

It is not yet clear in the early 1990s whether the overall net impact of major global and regional shifts will be to spur Latin American nations to further diversify their markets and sources of capital and technology, to spawn renewed and more effective efforts at intraregional integration, to push Latin America and the United States toward enhanced hemispheric partnerships, or to leave some or many Latin American countries without partners, marginal in a world of blocs built fundamentally around the dynamic northern economies. Each of these possibilities is real, and much will depend on Latin American decisions and strategies. Different countries may well move in contrary directions.

At present, most Latin American countries are embarked on programs of economic stabilization and liberalization, attempting to integrate themselves more effectively into the world economy. But the domestic political base for these neoliberal and internationalist approaches is precarious in many cases, and the current policies may not be long sustained. If neoliberal recipes are not soon perceived as successful, it is uncertain what will follow. Inward-oriented national populist movements may regain strength in some countries, with or without support within the armed forces. But there will also be efforts to develop new approaches—to strengthen the state's role in building infrastructure, providing education and services, promoting equity and justice, and guiding economic development while perhaps restricting its role in production, employment, and regulation.[43] Some Latin American countries doubtless will seek new paths during the 1990s, but it is not yet obvious what those will be or where they will lead.

4. By the same token, the single biggest factor shaping U.S.–Latin American relations in the 1990s is likely to be whether and how the United States confronts its own economic, social, and political agenda.

President George Bush's Enterprise for the Americas Initiative of 1990—promising a reduction of Latin America's official debt owed to U.S. government agencies, offering some aid to facilitate investment in Latin America's economic recovery, and holding out the prospect of hemispherewide or subregional free trade agreements—offers a positive vision of how inter-American relations could evolve in the 1990s.[44] Although the initiative was notably short on specifics and has been very slow in implementation, it reflects the Bush administration's inchoate recognition that revitalized Western Hemisphere partnerships could be immensely helpful to the United States in a period when cold war blocs are breaking up, economic power and military prowess are diffusing, new international economic and political rivalries are intensifying, and the global challenges to health, the environment, and governance are taking center stage.

But a viable Western Hemisphere policy for the United States will depend most of all on a program for this country's economic reconversion and recovery. No proposals for relieving Latin America's debt burden or for opening U.S. markets to Latin American exports will be implemented and sustained unless they are part of an overall strategy for restoring dynamism to the U.S. economy. No significant special policy of trade preferences for Latin America can be put into effect if broad domestic U.S. interests—including small business and organized labor—will be badly hurt. Nor would any such program affect Latin America's development prospects as much as expanded growth that would bring higher prices and enlarged markets for Latin American exports. Probably no U.S. measure to support Latin America's development directly would be as effective in helping the region as reducing the fiscal deficit of the United States and thereby relieving pressure on world interest rates—provided that this can be done without curbing Latin American exports to the United States.

The United States will not be able to adopt and sustain policies that facilitate Latin American progress and build strong Western Hemisphere cooperation unless it undertakes effective programs to ease the transition from marginal sectors in its own economy, integrate immigrants more humanely, reduce the domestic demand for narcotics, and curtail environmentally damaging practices. But the United States has not been able or willing in recent years to adopt and implement such policies consistently. While preaching discipline abroad, it has run up unprecedented domestic budget deficits. While pressing for global free trade, it has put into effect ever more protectionist policies, sector by sector, and pressures have mounted to adopt more restrictive immigration policies as well. Washington has often succumbed to the temptation of blaming Latin American nations for drug trafficking and environmental deterioration rather than enlist international cooperation on the basis of domestic efforts and achievements.

More than forty years ago, as the cold war was just beginning to take shape, George Kennan (in his classic "X" article in *Foreign Affairs*) argued that the main way the United States could influence the Soviet Union was by its own domestic actions—by creating "among the peoples of the world generally the impression of a country which knows what it wants, which is coping successfully with the problems of its internal life." Kennan closed his eloquent statement of the containment doctrine by asserting that "the issue of Soviet-American relations [was] in essence a test of the overall worth of the United States as a nation among nations."[45]

U.S. relations with Latin America in the 1990s and beyond will also test this country's mettle, but in a new way. The challenge of the next generation will be in some ways even more difficult than in the last, for it will involve mobilizing the national will and resources to combat a number of different but linked problems, some of them undramatic and subtle, rather than to face one clear adversary against which it was relatively easy to keep score.[46]

The future of relations with Latin America and the Caribbean will depend, more than anything, on what this country does to rejuvenate its economy and deal with such issues as drugs, education, and the environment. If the United States continues to muddle through in coping with these issues incrementally, relations with Latin America will remain more or less as they have in recent years. If the United States turns to these issues with a shortsighted and rearguard approach—becoming more protectionist, restrictionist, punitive, and interventionist—inter-American relations could instead enter a much more conflict-ridden phase, with far greater hostility than we have seen.

But if the United States finally turns forcefully to its domestic agenda, Washington will have strong reasons to forge important Western Hemisphere partnerships. The best futures for Latin America and the United States are one and the same—a vigorous U.S. commitment to confront its own accumulated problems. Nearly five hundred years after the visit of Christopher Columbus, the countries of the New World find their destinies intertwined.

Notes

I am grateful to Robert Art, Bruce Bagley, Peter D. Bell, Sergio Bitar, Richard Bloomfield, Michael Desch, Richard Feinberg, Albert Fishlow, Samuel Fitch, Peter Hakim, Jonathan Hartlyn, Terry Karl, William Leogrande, Ricardo Luna, Heraldo Muñoz, John Odell, Guillermo O'Donnell, Robert Pastor, John Sheahan, Gregory Treverton, Viron P. Vaky, Raymond Vernon, and my graduate students at the University of Southern California—all of whom commented helpfully on a previous draft, and to Daniel Broxterman, Tina Gallop, Kathy Matthes, Leslie Mohr, and Susan Smolko for their valuable research and logistic assistance. I also appreciate the comments made on presentations of these ideas at seminars organized by the Foro Latinoamericano in Santiago, Chile; by the Consejo Argentino de Relaciones Internacionales in Buenos Aires; and by the Center of International Studies at the University of Southern California.

1. For a fuller discussion of these five trends and their implications for U.S.–Latin American relations, see Inter-American Dialogue, *The Americas in a New World*, chap. 1. See also chapter 1—by Alberto van Klaveren—in this book and Andrew Hurrell, "Latin America and the New World Order."

2. On the changing Soviet role in Latin America, see Mujal-León, *The USSR and Latin America*; Mikoyan, "Soviet Foreign Policy"; Stanchenko, "The Soviet Union and Central America"; Miller, *Soviet Relations with Latin America*; Valkenier, "*Glasnost* and *Perestroika*"; and Blasier, "Moscow's Retreat from Cuba."

3. Karl, "Central America."

4. Castañeda, "Latin America."

5. For a succinct appraisal of the Japanese and Western European roles in Latin America, see Inter-American Dialogue, *The Americas in a New World*, pp. 8–11. For more extensive comments on Japan, see Stallings, "Reluctant Giant"; Peter H. Smith, "Japan, Latin America"; and Watanabe, "Latin America in Japan's Foreign Policy." On Europe's role, see van Klaveren, "Latin America and Europe," and the various extremely useful reports published by IRELA in Madrid.

6. See Landau, Feo, and Hosono, *Latin America at a Crossroads*. See also Gereffi, "New Patterns of Industrial Integration."

7. Latin America's turn toward democracy has spawned an extensive literature. See, for example, O'Donnell, Schmitter, and Whitehead, *Transitions from Authoritarian Rule*; Diamond, Linz, and Lipset, *Democracy in Developing Countries*; and Mainwaring, O'Donnell, and Valenzuela, *New Democracies*. For recent overviews, see Hakim and Lowenthal, "Latin America's Fragile Democracies," and Remmer, "Democracy and Economic Crisis."

8. See Pastor, *Democracy in the Americas*, Torres Rivas, *Centroamerica*; R. Barros, "The Left and Democracy"; and chapter 8—by J. Samuel Fitch—in this volume.

9. Such statements were common only a few years ago and may still be encountered in some texts. See, for example, Harrison, *Underdevelopment Is a State of Mind*.

10. For a useful overview of Latin America's economic crisis of the 1980s, see Kuczynski, *Latin American Debt*. See also Jeffry Frieden, *Debt, Development and Democracy*.

11. See United Nations Economic Commission on Latin America and the Caribbean, *Preliminary Overview of the Economy*.

12. See Williamson, *Progress of Policy Reform* and *Latin American Adjustment*.

13. For a useful discussion of the causes and consequences of Latin America and Caribbean migration to the United States, see Commission for the Study of International Migration and Cooperative Economic Development, "Report." See also the excellent series

of research studies prepared for the commission and published in a five-volume series edited by Sidney Weintraub.

14. See Frohmann, *Puentes sobre la turbulencia*, and Tomassini, *Nuevas formas de concertación regional*. See also Hirst, "Reflexiones para un analisis politico."

15. On Mexico's "silent integration" with the United States, by now increasingly vocal, see Reynolds, "Mexican-U.S. Interdependence." See also Lowenthal and Burgess, *The California-Mexico Connection*.

16. The U.S. gross national product in 1950 was over $355 billion and Latin America's was less than $40 billion. See U.S. Bureau of the Census, *Historical Statistics*, and United Nations Economic Commission for Latin America, *Economic Bulletin*.

17. See U.S. Bureau of the Census, *Historical Statistics*.

18. I coined the *hegemonic presumption* phrase, signifying an unquestioned belief that Latin America is a rightful sphere of U.S. influence, in my contribution to the bicentennial series in *Foreign Affairs*. See Lowenthal, "Ending the Hegemonic Presumption."

19. U.S. Bureau of the Census, *Statistical Abstract*.

20. See U.S. Bureau of the Census, *Historical Statistics*.

21. See Lowenthal, *Partners in Conflict*, chap. 2.

22. See U.S. Bureau of the Census, *Statistical Abstract*.

23. See Wiarda, *Democratic Revolution*.

24. See U.S. Department of Commerce, *U.S. Foreign Trade Highlights, 1988*.

25. See Pastor, "George Bush and Latin America," and Perry, "In Search of a Latin American Policy." Cf. Heine, "De la negligencia benigna."

26. See Fauriol, "The Shadow of Latin American Affairs."

27. For U.S. versions of this thesis, see Falcoff, "A Look at Latin America"; Ronfeldt, "A New Dark Age"; and Wiarda, "United States Strategic Policy." Cf. Abrams, "Looking South."

28. The following paragraphs draw from my earlier writings. Cf. esp. "Rediscovering Latin America" and *Partners in Conflict*, chap. 3.

29. U.S. Department of Energy, *Petroleum Supply Monthly*.

30. Commission for the Study of International Migration and Cooperative Economic Development, "Report."

31. See Pastor, *Migration and Development*, and Domínguez and Domínguez, "The Caribbean."

32. For fuller discussions of U.S.–Latin American narcotics linkages, see Bagley and Tokatlian, *Economía y política del narcotráfico*; Mabry, *Latin American Narcotics Trade*; MacDonald, *Mountain High*; and U.S. Congress, Senate, Committee on Governmental Affairs, *Cocaine Production*.

33. The term *intermestic* was introduced by Bayless Manning in his article, "The Congress, the Executive, and Intermestic Affairs."

34. Ayón and Anzaldua Montoya, "Latinos and U.S. Policy."

35. For an early statement of the ways in which much of U.S. policy toward Latin America is shaped by an extraordinarily fragmented and permeable policy-making process, see Lowenthal and Treverton, "The Making of U.S. Policies toward Latin America." This paper was published in Spanish in *Foro Internacional* (Mexico), 1978.

36. Schoultz, *Human Rights*. Cf. Thorup, "Politics of Free Trade," and Dresser, "Exporting Conflict."

37. For a good overview, see Weintraub, *Marriage of Convenience*. Cf. Bilateral Commission on the Future of United States–Mexican Relations, *Challenge of Interdependence*, and Pastor and Castañeda, *Limits to Friendship*.

38. See Pastor and Fletcher, "The Caribbean in the Twenty-first Century." Cf. Quick, "The International Economy and the Caribbean."

39. For a constructive set of proposals on how the United States should relate to Central America, see International Commission for Central American Recovery and Development, *Report*. Cf. Karl, "Central America," and Robinson, *Intervention or Neglect*.

40. See Marcella and Woerner, "Strategic Vision"; McClintock, "War on Drugs"; and Bagley, *Myths of Militarization*.

41. For the history and context of U.S.-Chile relations, which suggest that a reduction of U.S. involvement is likely, see Sater, *Chile and the United States*, and Muñoz and Portales, *Elusive Friendship*.

42. On Argentina's changing policies, see Escudé, "La politica exterior de Menem"; Russell, "El idealismo periferico"; and Borón, "Relaciones internacionales de Argentina."

43. See United Nations Economic Commission for Latin America and the Caribbean, *Changing Production Patterns*; Fishlow, "The Latin American State"; and Wise, "In Search of Markets."

44. For a fuller discussion, see Lowenthal, "Rediscovering Latin America." See also Feinberg, "Bush's Enterprising Initiative," and Schott and Hufbauer, "Free Trade Areas."

45. X, "Sources of Soviet Conduct," *Foreign Affairs* (July 1947): 566–82.

46. On the broad U.S. agenda for the 1990s, among many other references see Nye, *Bound to Lead*; Nau, *Myth of America's Decline*; Chancellor, *Peril and Promise*; Halberstam, *The Next Century*; and Gergen, "How Is America Changing?." I have expanded on my own views about the U.S. agenda in "The United States in a Fast-Changing World."

Rosario Espinal

Chapter Four THE RIGHT AND THE NEW RIGHT IN LATIN AMERICA

hat do Fernando Collor de Mello, Alfredo Cristiani, León Febres Cordero, Augusto Pinochet, Anastasio Somoza, Mario Vargas Llosa, and José Videla have in common? At first one is tempted to say that they share little, if anything, in common. Yet one is hard pressed not to lump their names together when one thinks of the Right in Latin America. What, then, is the reason for this paradox? The ambiguity derives from the fact that, in the twentieth century, Latin American countries have witnessed a variety of political regimes, all of which could be labeled right-wing depending on the criterion employed to define right-wing politics. Should repression, so widespread in the Latin American political experience, be the key indicator in identifying right-wing regimes?[1] Should one instead focus on the anticommunist stance of the regime, which was so central to the Right during the cold war? Or should one instead define the Right in terms of an economic ideology, be it a promarket stance?

The discomfort that most analysts of Latin American politics would experience in answering these questions points at the ambiguities surrounding the definition of the Right. This is particularly the case in Latin America due to the limited correspondence between the three indicators listed above. For instance, military regimes in Latin America, which have been the most repressive, have been frequently statist, not market-oriented. On the other hand, to associate the Latin American Right exclusively with military regimes would be ill-advised, for some military regimes have pursued reformist policies even while exhibiting repressiveness (the case of General Juan Velasco Alvarado in Peru is a case in point). Finally, it would be unwise to associate the Latin American Right exclusively with neoliberal projects that only gained popularity in the 1980s and have been endorsed by military and civilian governments of the most diverse nature.

Notwithstanding the problems associated with any attempt to define the Latin American Right as a political movement or form of government—whether one emphasizes actors, policies, or ideologies—three characteristics seem useful in understanding the evolution of the Right in Latin America from the 1930s to the present: (1) a systematic use of violence against selected groups of citizens in an attempt to exclude them from the political process, (2) an anticommunist bias of the regime, particularly during the cold war, and (3) a market-oriented ideology. If these factors would positively correlate with one another, then the most rightist regime would be highly repressive, anticommunist, and market-oriented. But this is not a reflection of what is found in Latin America, nor is this indicative of what has occurred in advanced capitalist societies in the post–World War II period, when the Right has not been associated with dictatorships at all. Consequently, the three characteristics, more than providing a means for classifying right-wing regimes, help us to examine the metamorphosis undergone by the Right in post–1920s Latin America.

This chapter develops three main arguments about the Right in Latin America. The first is that it is inappropriate to associate the Latin American Right exclusively with repressive military regimes, for two reasons: (1) some military regimes have been reformist in spite of their repressiveness, and (2) since the 1980s, political organizations of the Right, like the Democratic Front (FREDEMO) in Peru, have gained ascendancy, while civilian right-wing governments, such as that of Collor de Mello in Brazil, have been democratically elected to office. The second argument is that a distinctive characteristic of the Right in contemporary Latin America is its neoliberal economic orientation—namely, its promarket and anti–big-government stance. This movement, which I call the *New Right*, has sought to compete electorally in various Latin American countries, beginning in the early 1980s with the electoral inroads made by the National Action party (PAN) of Mexico. The third argument is that notwithstanding sweeping neoliberal economic reforms throughout the region and some electoral gains made by right-wing parties in the 1980s,[2] a main problem of the New Right in Latin America is the lack of well-organized political parties capable of competing electorally in the newly installed democratic regimes. This weakness is the result of several factors: the previous predominance of the military within the Latin American Right, a well-entrenched populist orientation of both right- and left-wing governments, the consistent failure of the market in Latin America to provide the means for social mobility to large segments of society, and, more recently, the adoption of a neoliberal platform by historically powerful populist parties like the Institutional

Revolutionary party (PRI) in Mexico, the Peronists in Argentina, and Democratic Action in Venezuela.

The Right and the Military

To assess the relationship between the Right and the military in Latin America is not an easy task. Although both traditional and modern authoritarian regimes (the old caudillo-led dictatorship and bureaucratic-authoritarianism) were right-wing in that they were highly repressive and anticommunist or antisubversive, they differed profoundly in their conception about the nature of the relationship between the state and private capital. Highly personalistic, military-led dictatorships (those of Somoza in Nicaragua and Rafael Trujillo in the Dominican Republic) wished to develop significant state autonomy vis-à-vis private capital. A liberal ideology was alien to these regimes, for they sought to reproduce economically what they had set out to do politically: the exclusion of competition. Here assaults on foreign and local capital by the dictator were common, while "nationalizations" of foreign companies, instead of having a redistributive purpose as they had elsewhere in Latin America, were designed to favor the dictator's own market power as an individual capitalist. This was typical of highly dependent societies in Central America and the Caribbean, where the penetration of foreign capital had severely undermined the opportunities for local investors, and dictators came to fill the political vacuum created by the failure to carry out liberal reforms at the turn of the century.

In contrast to personalistic dictatorships, the new authoritarianism of the Southern Cone in the 1960s and 1970s (the bureaucratic-authoritarian regimes) had as a priority the opening of the economy to private investors, with international capital playing a major role.[3] This was the case in situations as dissimilar as that of Brazil, where the state was a major partner in economic ventures; or that of Chile, where the state sought to provide favorable conditions for private business. These authoritarian regimes were certainly right-wing in that they were repressive, politically exclusionary, and anticommunist. Yet they differed—owing to when they assumed power and the prevailing socioeconomic and political conditions in each country—in their conception about the nature of the relationship between the state and private capital.

In Brazil, the military government installed in 1964 found a society of great disparities (regionally and class-based), a fairly secure elite, and a country with significant natural resources and the geographic extension that allowed for a dream of grandiose capitalist development. A major infusion of foreign capital, coupled with the technocratization of the state apparatus, led to the formation of a vital business class with much at stake in the survival of the Brazilian state as a partner in economic ventures, though it sometimes feared the state as an economic competitor.[4]

Unlike the Brazilian generals, the Argentine military in 1976 found a politically divided society, but one more homogeneous in social standing. The notion of "law and order" as understood by the military became more prominent here. Repression, political exclusion, and anticommunism (more precisely defined as antisubversion) all ran high. In the area of economic policy, however, the regime was ambivalent. By the late 1970s, it was clear that the Argentine economic model of autarkic industrialization with significant social concessions to the working class was in trouble. Torn between a growing fiscal crisis and entrenched corporatist prerogatives, the military government fluctuated between orthodox policy-making and state expansionist policies.[5] The end result was the persistence of a sluggish economy, a distrustful entrepreneurial class, and mobilized labor unions.

The Chilean experience under Pinochet was similar to that of Argentina and Brazil with respect to the extensive use of repression, the anticommunist bias, and the national security discourse of the regime, yet it was quite different in the area of economic restructuring. Unlike in Argentina, where social interests remained entrenched in the state despite widespread political repression, in Chile Pinochet presided over a major dismantling of the state in its dual function as producer of goods and services and as distributor of social benefits. Pinochet used state power to launch a major restructuring of the Chilean economy in line with neoliberal principles.[6] The emphasis on agro-exports was vital as Chile repositioned itself early in the new international division of labor. As a result, business benefited considerably at the expense of other constituencies. In his endeavor, Pinochet, unlike the Argentine generals, found a weaker opposition, for not only had the Chilean working class never achieved the corporatist power of Peronist unions, but the attack on socialism as it was practiced under Salvador Allende and the degree of polarization leading to the 1973 coup d'état gave Pinochet greater power in promoting an antileftist program. That is, Pinochet's government assumed a mandate to dismantle socialism and crush leftism as no other military regime had done in the region.

Thus, generally speaking, right-wing, military-led regimes in post–1920 Latin America were of four types: (1) the military-caudillo variety, where the state was instrumental in limiting the growth of the private sector, as market mechanisms were undermined by the dictatorial state (the Trujillo and Somoza dictatorships); (2) the developmentalist military regime of Brazil, which relied on a partnership between business and government; (3) the unstable Argentine juntas, which failed to promote economic growth, whether government- or market-led; and (4) the neoliberal dictatorship of Chile, which favored an export-led market economy.

These regimes were similar in their repressiveness, exclusionary policies, and anticommunist or antisubversive stance; yet they had diverse agendas concerning the role of the state and the market in the economy.

Neoliberalism and the New Right

Right-wing politics defined in terms of the supremacy of the market over the state as the regulatory principle of social relations originated in Latin America only in the 1980s. This is illustrated by a set of very diverse experiments in the region, including the Chilean neoconservative experience under Pinochet, the neoliberal shifts within the PRI under the de la Madrid and Salinas de Gortari administrations in Mexico, and the strong, if not decisive, electoral performance of FREDEMO in the 1990 Peruvian elections. I refer explicitly to these three cases because they illustrate a problem examined in this chapter—namely, the weakness of promarket right-wing parties in Latin America. This explains why neoliberal projects have been fostered by the most diverse political regimes and organizations, including the military in Chile, a traditionally populist party like the PRI in Mexico, and a newly formed political organization like FREDEMO in Peru.

Unlike in England and the United States, where in the 1970s and 1980s the Conservative and Republican parties campaigned on neoliberal ideas, in Latin America neoliberalism initially entered politics through the policy-making arena. Experiences here vary depending on the type of political regime considered, but the objective was the same everywhere: the implementation of neoliberal economic reforms designed by technocrats. In Chile, the military government imposed neoliberal economic policies, including sweeping privatization, at a time when most sectors of society were systematically excluded from the political process. In Mexico, a traditionally populist-corporatist party like the PRI underwent in the 1980s major internal reordering in an attempt to adapt to the new international conditions imposed in part by the debt crisis. Beginning with the de la Madrid administration, the PRI under the leadership of highly trained technocrats implemented painful neoliberal reforms and, in so doing, confronted well-entrenched interests such as those of organized labor. It was only in Peru, where none of the elected governing parties were strong supporters of neoliberalism (Fernando Belaúnde showed lukewarm support for it, while Alán García sought to reject it altogether), that a political movement in the opposition led by the Freedom Movement rallied in favor of neoliberal ideas in the 1990 elections. These cases also illustrate that neoliberal policy-making in contemporary Latin America transcends right-wing governments and parties, for center-left parties like the PRI implemented important neoliberal reforms as part of the restructuring plan. Nor is it possible to assume that neoliberal policies—unpopular at times—were more likely to appear under military regimes, for they were implemented as well by civilian governments. This is the case because neoliberal reforms (fiscal austerity, privatization, lower tariffs) in Latin America were not simply the expression of an ideological choice but were linked to the structural reorganization of state-society relations, owing to the debt crisis and the limitations of dependent industrialization.[7]

Beginning in the 1970s, the Latin American corporatist state—authoritarian for the most part—found itself torn between societal demands for incorporation (by marginal business groups, workers, peasants, and the unemployed) and demands to meet external debt payments. Hesitant to turn its back on these demands, but hard pressed to implement austerity programs, Latin American governments faced great instability and serious legitimation problems in the 1980s. Within this context, the assault on the state by neoliberal ideologues and technocrats was evident, yet neoliberalism as a broadly defined political movement remained at first alien to most citizens, who depended on government patronage or state assistance at best. Trying to muddle through the economic crisis, Latin American countries witnessed the demise of military regimes in the 1980s, along with the return to civilian politics.

One important attempt to damage the legitimacy of the patronage state and to promote a neoliberal agenda beyond the sphere of policy-making was the publication of Hernando de Soto's *The Other Path* in 1987. Here one finds an eloquent presentation of an antistatist, neoliberal vision with a potential populist appeal based on the specific conditions of a Latin American society. De Soto's antistatism was rooted in a critique of the inefficient Peruvian state—inefficient for rich and poor alike. Unlike the unpopular neoliberal policies that swept Latin America in the 1980s, de Soto's manifesto was a comprehensive statement rooted in the life experience of the average Latin American citizen. *The Other Path* was a discursive strategy aimed at reconstructing political identities with a neoliberal foundation among the large and growing segments of society making up the so-called informal sector.

In brief, economic liberalization favored by neoliberal policy-makers (initially representatives of international agencies) changed the content of public policy in Latin America.[8] On the other hand, neoliberal manifestos such as that of de Soto helped transform the content of political discourse, shifting it to the Right as it emphasized antigovernment ideas. Constrained by the debt crisis and a changing international economy, governing parties like the populist PRI in Mexico implemented neoliberal policies alien to the party's own traditions. But more important, the return to democracy in Latin America, and the neoconservative revolution in advanced capitalist countries, favored the growth of political organizations, like

FREDEMO, that openly endorsed neoliberal ideas. As a result, the market became a major referent in discussions about economic policy in Latin America in the 1980s.

Neoliberal Policy-making as Right-Wing Politics

In the mid-1970s, during the early stages of the prolonged economic crisis that still affects Latin America, specific countries found themselves in different positions to deal with the emergency and accept the neoliberal prescription initially provided by international creditors. The differences were related, in particular, to the nature of the relationship between business and the state and the level of incorporation and mobilization of popular sectors.

Some countries, like Brazil, Mexico, and Venezuela, had a diversified business class as a result of the expansion of import substitution and export industrialization in the 1960s and early 1970s. Here there was collaboration between business and government, and popular sectors did not pose a major threat either because they were incorporated through corporatist structures as in Mexico and Venezuela, or because they were disorganized or suppressed by a repressive state as in Brazil. Notwithstanding important differences among these countries in terms of social structure and the nature of the political regime, they had in common business classes that benefited tremendously from state patronage during the economic expansion of the 1960s and 1970s.

Other countries, like Argentina, Chile, Peru, Uruguay, and to a lesser extent Ecuador, experienced economic decline in the early and mid-1970s due to the exhaustion of import-substitution industrialization. Here business was distrustful of both government and popular sectors. In the Southern Cone, the decline of import-substitution industrialization, coupled with expanded social services and new demands for incorporation by popular sectors, limited capitalist expansion (the victory of Allende in the 1970 Chilean elections and the return of Juan Perón to the presidency of Argentina in 1973 represented traumatic experiences for business in these countries). In the Andean countries, the situation was one of persistent oligarchic power and unfulfilled expectations for reform fueled, in part, by military-led populism.

Here two questions are relevant in an attempt to understand differences and similarities between these countries. How successful was neoliberal policy-making in these various contexts after the economic crisis deepened in the late 1970s and early 1980s? And what was the likelihood of a neoliberal surge once competitive politics was reintroduced in the 1980s? The first question concerns the ability of governments to proceed with neoliberal reforms, initially imposed by foreign creditors. The second refers to neoliberalism as a political project. Although public policies and political projects intermix, they are distinguished here for analytic purposes because neoliberalism as a set of policies initially entered Latin America from the state down, imposed to cure economic ills with little regard for popular needs or ideological affinities. On the other hand, neoliberalism as a political project is a comprehensive system of ideas politically contested that seeks to modify state-society relations by emphasizing the central role of the market in the production and allocation of resources in society.

In Mexico, where the PRI not only enjoyed an unchallenged hegemony but also served as the institutional backbone of the corporatist system, policymakers were in a more advantageous position to introduce adjustment policies, even when the program was alien to the party's own traditions. Policymakers could more easily isolate themselves from short-term social pressures because they had great control over the state and party apparatuses. Notwithstanding the costs in terms of political hegemony, the PRI proceeded under the de la Madrid administration to implement orthodox economic policies (lower trade barriers, cuts in public spending, devaluations, diversification of exports, and debt payments) and to undo the corporatist system that the PRI had fostered for forty years.[9] All of this came about after Mexico's latest statist and populist manifestation, with President José López Portillo's announcement in September 1982 of a temporary debt moratorium and the nationalization of private banks.

Like Mexico, Venezuela profited from oil revenues throughout the 1970s. Yet, with a more modest industrialization project, the debt crisis took longer to explode in Venezuela and electoral turnovers helped to keep hope for change alive. This ended when social democrat Carlos Andrés Pérez, who previously had presided over the oil boom, proceeded shortly after taking office in early 1989 to implement stabilization measures (increases in the price of gasoline and transportation, liberalization of the exchange market, and budget cuts, among others). The need for fresh credit after Jaime Lusinchi's announcement of a moratorium forced Pérez to put aside any other priority he may have had upon assuming office. The government announced the stabilization package in the midst of great political uncertainty: FEDECAMARAS, the business federation, and the Confederation of Venezuelan Workers (CTV) disagreed on new pay raises, while the government in a major anticorporatist move sought to disassociate itself from the negotiation process. The immediate outcome was rioting in the streets and repressive actions by the government to control the unrest.[10]

In Argentina and Brazil, the process of economic decline in the 1980s was more dramatic than in either Mexico or Venezuela. Hyperinflation became an endemic problem. By the end of the military regime in Argentina, there was little consensus about how to revitalize the economy. After taking office in December 1983, Raúl

Alfonsín promised *concertación* but was unable to deliver much of it: the organized labor movement was uninterested in making further sacrifices, while business had little incentive to invest in a volatile economy and polity.[11] In an attempt to reverse the course of action, the Alfonsín government announced in mid-1985 a "heterodox shock" (the Austrial Plan), but the program was soon in trouble: prices rose again and workers frequently went on strike. Meanwhile, the government relied once more on public spending to reactivate the economy.[12] Ironically, it was left to newly elected Peronist president Carlos Saúl Menem to promote neoliberal economic reforms by 1990.

In Brazil, the economic crisis represented a major blow to the country's hope of becoming a major world contender. In the early 1980s, the military government was torn between sustaining benefits to business and technocrats and adjusting to new international demands (for debt payments, lower tariffs, more competitive exchange rates, and so forth). The inability to deal effectively with both led to business disillusion with the military, but the civilian government installed in 1985 did little to solve the economic problems. At first, a business class highly dependent on the state was not inclined to accept prescriptions of the International Monetary Fund (IMF).[13] Following the Argentine experiment, the Sarney government tried a heterodox shock (the Cruzado Plan) in early 1986 to tackle hyperinflation, but the plan was also soon in trouble: inflation was back, business became more dissatisfied with the government's economic policy, and popular protests intensified. The 1989 elections delayed resolution of the problems, but the victory of the right-wing candidate, Fernando Collor de Mello, ensured the enactment of neoliberal economic reforms in 1990.

It is in Chile, however, that we find the most consistent implementation of neoliberal economic policies. In comparative terms, Pinochet's regime was in a better position to reorganize the economy than any of his military counterparts in the region. Reacting to the Allende experience, Pinochet assumed a mandate in the mid-1970s to dismantle socialism, foster market relations, and reorient economic priorities in favor of the export sector. With most social sectors excluded from the political process, he had great autonomy to pursue his reforms, including extensive privatization of the economy.

In the Andean countries, variations in neoliberal projects were also the outcome of structural developments and political conjunctures.[14] In Peru, and to some extent in Ecuador, the emphasis on the market and neoliberal policies followed the collapse of populist military regimes. Antistatism and a promarket view were emphasized as an alternative to state-led development, yet there was little agreement among business factions and politicians on how to pursue a neoliberal program. Ultimately, Fernando Belaúnde in Peru and León Febres Cordero in Ecuador, who portrayed themselves as promoters of neoliberalism, proved to be more interested in public spending than expected. Subsequently, major neoliberal economic reforms were delayed by their successors, Alán García and Rodrigo Borja, respectively. A different case was Bolivia, where neoliberal reforms were successfully implemented in 1991.

Overall, the Latin American experience with neoliberal policy-making shows that, although forced to implement neoliberal policies, most governments tried to resist or soften adjustment measures whenever possible. The reasons seem obvious: given the debt crisis and the depressed prices of major export products, the political cost of economic adjustment was high. In fact, the most controversial issue was not whether one believed the market or the state to be the engine of progress, but who was to pay the price of adjustment.

Unlike in advanced capitalist countries, where a neoliberal ideology was fostered in the context of an economy soon to recover, in Latin America the socioeconomic consequences of adjustment were troublesome, while the possibilities for economic recovery seemed even more remote. Moreover, the neoliberal measures prescribed for Latin America (such as budget cuts, devaluations, lower tariffs, and wage competitiveness) were largely the opposite of what neoliberals actually did, for instance, in the United States—namely, to allow large public deficits, increase protectionism, and favor an overvalued currency. Thus, despite the efforts of highly educated technocrats from Latin America and abroad to portray the market as the source of economic prosperity, even business was reluctant to fully support sweeping neoliberal reforms in Latin America.

Party Politics and the New Right

Due in part to a worldwide crisis of socialism and in part to its own internal problems, the Latin American Left was unable to provide an alternative vision for the society to be built at the end of the twentieth century. The hope that a critical stance on "real existing socialism" would ease the way into a truly "democratic socialism" had vanished by the mid-1980s. Instead of socialism, Latin America witnessed the installation of democratically elected governments, whose primary task was to manage the region's most severe economic crisis in this century. Governing parties ranged from center-left to center-right, but regardless of their ideological coloration they all shared the failure to solve the acute economic and social problems oppressing their nations.

As the 1980s closed with a deepening of the economic crisis and its disastrous social consequences (hunger, high rates of unemployment, and increased crime, among others), party politics acquired new twists in a newly democratized Latin America. Old populist parties like the PRI pursued the newly adopted neoliberal strategies. Meanwhile, a truly neoliberal Right, as represented by the National Action party (PAN) in Mexico and the Freedom Movement in Peru, made some electoral inroads. In examining changes in party politics and the role and prospects of the New Right in a democratic Latin America, it is useful to consider three issues: the strength of the party system, the nature of the populist experience, and how the Right might organize politically.

In countries with fairly stable party systems and a significant populist experience of social incorporation,[15] whether through political parties as in Mexico and Venezuela, or through personalized leadership with Peronism as in Argentina, center-left parties (the PRI, Democratic Action, and the Peronists) faced in the 1980s and 1990s the painful process of undoing their own political legacy. With inauguration of the de la Madrid administration in 1982, the PRI turned to neoliberal policy-making; so did Democratic Action in Venezuela and the Peronists under Carlos Menem in Argentina at the end of the 1980s. What is striking about these countries is not only the metamorphosis experienced by their center-left parties, which suddenly began advocating neoliberal restructuring, but also the fact that those changes constrained the growth of neoliberal right-wing parties. In Mexico, the PAN, having made inroads in the local elections of 1983 and 1985, failed in the 1988 elections to break the PRI hegemony. More important, it lost support with respect to the newly formed National Democratic Front (FDN) led by Cuauhtémoc Cárdenas, which positioned itself to the left of the PRI.[16] In Argentina, the Union of the Democratic Center (UCD) was unable to garner massive support in 1989—despite much expectation to the contrary. Moreover, after the elections, some of the UCD's top leaders joined the Peronist administration of Carlos Menem in an attempt to push through neoliberal reforms by then endorsed by Menem.[17] Finally, Venezuela lacked a neoliberal party with the capacity to mobilize the electorate.

What will ultimately happen to populist parties, like the PRI and the Peronists, that have endorsed neoliberal reforms to solve the economic crisis remains unknown. A guess is that both Democratic Action in Venezuela and the PRI in Mexico may be in a better position than the Peronists in Argentina to implement the changes and survive politically, for at least two reasons: (1) the more advantageous position of Mexico and Venezuela in the international economy as oil producers, and (2) the greater stability of the Mexican and Venezuelan political systems. Yet, paradoxically, the absence of military regimes in the recent history of these countries may encourage military action if civilians fail to respond effectively to social demands and aspirations, as illustrated by the attempted coup in Venezuela of February 1992.

In the 1980s, other Latin American countries witnessed significant attempts of the Right to organize politically. These are countries that in the past experienced oligarchic electoralism, followed by military-led populism. The most dramatic example is Peru, but Ecuador somewhat fits the description. In Ecuador, the Right rallied in the early 1980s behind Febres Cordero and his Front of National Reconstruction (FRN). Febres Cordero was equipped with competent neoliberal technocrats to pursue neoliberal reforms, but a slim margin of victory coupled with congressional opposition from the center-left were major obstacles to his restructuring plans. Thus, promises for sweeping neoliberal reforms soon vanished, and the poor performance of the Febres Cordero administration was a major blow to the New Right in Ecuador.[18]

In Peru, the traumatic military populism of Velasco Alvarado, the dubious commitment of Belaúnde (1980–85) to neoliberalism, the populist style of Alán García (1985–90), the electoral gains made by the United Leftist Front at the municipal level in the early 1980s, and the radicalization of the Shining Path all contributed to the growth of the New Right with FREDEMO, led by prominent Peruvian novelist Mario Vargas Llosa. Notwithstanding the electoral victory of Alberto Fujimori in the runoff elections in 1990, FREDEMO obtained a formidable 39 percent of the votes cast. Whether this percentage reflects a stable constituency of the New Right or a temporary allegiance to FREDEMO remains to be seen. A more pressing question is, What will happen to the Freedom Movement, the organization that provided the neoliberal content to the coalition that produced FREDEMO?

What was unique about the Peruvian experience with FREDEMO was the support the movement received from various social groups, including business, middle-income groups, and prestigious intellectuals like Mario Vargas Llosa. The vote for FREDEMO was, for instance, consistently higher in upper- and middle-class neighborhoods.[19] Communicating the neoliberal message to large segments of the lower classes remains, however, the great challenge for the Latin American New Right. Here de Soto's contribution was significant in that it represented a comprehensive attempt to foster among lower-income groups (the informals) a sense of their position in the marketplace and the advantages they could derive from it. Nonetheless, voting results in the 1989–90 Peruvian elections did not reveal widespread support for neoliberalism among the poor.[20]

Finally, the inevitability of economic reforms with neoliberal overtones in Latin America can be illustrated by two very different cases of recent democratization. One is the program of economic reforms introduced by Brazilian President Collor de Mello in early 1990. The other is the endorsement of Pinochet's neoliberal reforms by the Christian Democratic–led ruling coalition that won the 1989 elections in Chile. In both of these countries, however, the New Right faces major challenges and opportunities. In the case of Brazil, where right-wing presidential candidate Collor de Mello defeated the leftist candidate Ignacio Lula Da Silva of the

Workers' party (PT) in 1989, it remains to be seen whether or not the Right will foster a strong right-wing party during the Collor de Mello presidency. This will depend in part on the success of the government's economic reforms, although it will depend even more on the willingness of Brazilian right-wing politicians to rely less on personalistic politics and more on party structures. The latter is particularly problematic given the history of elitism and personalistic clientelism that has characterized that country's politics.

In Chile, if it was true that the majority of the electorate said no to an additional eight-year term for Pinochet in the 1988 plebiscite, the results of the December 1989 elections seemed hopeful to the New Right. Notwithstanding the solid victory of the center-left coalition led by the Christian Democrats, the showing of presidential candidate Hernán Büchi,[21] a former cabinet member in charge of the country's finances under Pinochet, demonstrates the possibilities that are open to the civilian New Right in a democratic Chile. Advantageous to the Right is that Pinochet left the Chilean economy performing better than any other in the region, with a lower rate of inflation and a booming agro-export sector. Yet the future electoral performance of the Chilean Right is somewhat difficult to predict. Much will depend on the strength and performance of the Christian Democratic–led ruling coalition (which includes a variety of left-wing parties) and the ability of right-wing politicians to foster modern political organizations in the 1990s.

Conclusion

The Right in Latin America has changed significantly over time, and no single indicator is sufficient to illustrate the changes. In examining the evolution of the Right in Latin America since 1920, this essay has relied on three factors: (1) the systematic use of violence against selected segments of the citizenry in order to exclude them from the political process, (2) the anticommunist bias of the regimes, and (3) the prevailing market-oriented or neoliberal ideology. Even though the military has been a major actor in right-wing regimes, right-wing politics has an important civilian component in contemporary Latin America. Indeed, since the 1980s right-wing politics came to be identified not with militarism, but with neoliberalism. Yet neoliberalism in Latin America more than being a societal-based political project was largely imposed by technocrats through policy-making under both military and civilian governments. Moreover, center-left parties such as the PRI and the Peronists came to endorse neoliberal programs that were alien to their own traditions in an attempt to deal with the debt crisis in the 1980s.

With the return to democracy in the 1980s, right-wing political organizations holding neoliberal ideas gained ascendancy in several Latin American countries.

The PAN in Mexico, UCD in Argentina, and FREDEMO in Peru are outstanding examples. Yet parties of the New Right still remain weak throughout the region. For one thing, some are relatively new or reflect more a political movement than a party per se, as in the case of FREDEMO in Peru. Second, they espouse promarket ideas that are not only alien to most Latin Americans but also are associated with policies implemented under the auspices of the International Monetary Fund, which various constituencies have explicitly rejected by rioting, striking, or denouncing as unfair.

Despite the strong push toward market liberalization by international agencies and the United States, the success of the New Right in a democratic Latin America ultimately lies in the capacity of its leaders to foster political organizations and transform the political identities of the citizenry, replacing statist myths with individualistic ideologies. This is not an easy task in highly impoverished societies where the market has historically failed to provide opportunities for many. Yet, short of these ideological transformations and economic reforms, neoliberalism will remain a set of policy recommendations designed in Washington at best, or policy prescriptions imposed from outside and above and rejected by a majority of the Latin American citizenry. If it is the latter, then conditions in the 1990s could be favorable for the resurgence of militarism in Latin America. Yet civilian regimes currently in place in Latin America retain considerable capacity to muddle through the economic crisis, if for no other reason than the fact that in the post–cold war era, with communism no longer a viable alternative, the options available to the military for claiming legitimacy in government are more limited.

Notes

I wish to thank Alex Dupuy and Howard Winant for helpful comments on an earlier draft of this paper. I appreciate the support of Jonathan Hartlyn, who provided more than just editorial help. I also thank Alejandra Bizzanelli for her research assistance.

1. Here I refer only to capitalist societies. A discussion of repression in communist countries is beyond the scope of this chapter.

2. These reforms include the privatization of state-owned enterprises, lower tariffs, competitive exchange rates, and low or no fiscal deficits.

3. See O'Donnell, *Modernization*.

4. For a discussion of the social and political implications of these class alliances, see Cardoso, "Associated-Dependent Development."

5. Robert Kaufman argues that Argentina was harder pressed than Brazil to implement orthodox economic policies (monetary and fiscal contractions, wage controls, and devaluations) because it had to cross higher "confidence thresholds" among external and domestic investors due to its international isolation and domestic polarization. See Kaufman, *Politics of Debt*, pp. 11–14.

6. For a discussion of Chile's experiment with neoliberal economics, see Foxley, *Latin American Experiments*.

7. A comparative discussion of the economic crisis and its consequences is found in Ghai and Hewitt de Alcántara, "Crisis of the 1980s."

8. Canak, "Debt, Austerity, and Latin America."

9. For a more detailed analysis of these changes, see Kaufman, "Economic Orthodoxy."

10. For a detailed analysis of these events, see Miriam Kornblith, "Deuda y democracia en Venezuela."

11. In 1986 private investment shrank by 10 percent. Maxfield, "National Business," p. 83.

12. In 1987 Argentina witnessed a 37 percent expansion in public investment. Ibid.

13. For a discussion of the role of business in the Brazilian transition, see Cardoso, "Entrepreneurs and the Transition Process." Sylvia Maxfield discusses business positions toward IMF demands in "National Business."

14. Conaghan, Malloy, and Abugattas, "Business and the 'Boys.'"

15. By "fairly stable party systems," I mean the longevity of parties.

16. Fox, "Towards Democracy in Mexico?."

17. Edward Gibson, "Democracy and the New Electoral Right."

18. For a discussion of the Febres Cordero administration, see Conaghan, "Dreams of Orthodoxy."

19. See Durand, "La nueva derecha peruana."

20. Ibid.

21. Hernán Büchi received 29 percent of the votes cast.

· *Marcelo Cavarozzi*
·
·
Chapter Five · THE LEFT IN LATIN AMERICA:
·
·
. THE DECLINE OF SOCIALISM
·
·
· AND THE RISE OF POLITICAL
·
·
· DEMOCRACY
·
·

eginning in the mid-1930s the Latin American Left has evolved from a situation of relative homogeneity to one of extreme diversity. This tendency has been related to two distinct sets of factors. The first has to do with the dominant *organizational models* within the Left. These have developed from the pattern associated with the quasi-monopolistic position that the Soviet-linked Communist parties enjoyed during the 1930–55 period to a mode of diversity and competition among different organizational formats. Organizational models can be correlated with specific political strategies. However, the political goals of any organization or group—whether a political party, a guerrilla group, a confederation of neighborhood associations, or a church-related community organization—vary over time. And even more important, different models of organizations tend to generate distinct patterns of political action. These patterns, as much as their formal ideologies, influence the performance of organizations and the behavior of their members.

The second factor contributing to the heterogeneity of the contemporary Left is related to its *programmatic aspects*, that is, the substantive goals that define a political or social organization as part of the Left. For half a century, the substantive core of the Latin American Left evolved around three principles:

1. A positivistic belief in social progress. This belief was associated with the premise that progress was, by and large, the consequence of goal-oriented political action, rather than the result of the mere interplay of social forces.

2. The idea that private property had either to be abolished or, at best, to be made to play a secondary role in the organization of the economy. Thus, either socialism or state capitalism would replace private capitalism as the dominant "mode of production."

3. The identification of imperialism as one of the main obstacles to achieving progressive change in Latin America. Anti-imperialism (the condemnation of the interests and strategies of the United States and, to a lesser extent, other capitalist countries) became one of the engines of left-wing political action.[1]

During the 1980s, two of these principles—the belief in social progress and the abolition of private property—were radically weakened. As a consequence, the consensus around what is and what is not leftist has been broken. In part because of the breakdown of this consensus, the boundaries of the contemporary landscape of the Left have been blurred and are in constant flux. Political democracy has become a much more central issue of the ideological and intellectual controversies surrounding the definition of the core elements of the Left. Although these controversies are by no means settled, it is apparent that political democracy has become a strategic issue for significant segments of the Left. Some have interpreted this as the rapprochement of socialism and democracy; this is probably correct, provided that we do not forget that the definition of socialism itself is undergoing a profound reconsideration.

Thus, as we come closer to the present, we should think in terms of Latin America's "Lefts," rather than of a single, or even a predominant, Left. The principal goal of this chapter is to analyze the historical and contemporary reasons for the growing diversity of the Left in the Western Hemisphere. In addition, because both the identity and the strategies of social and political actors are the result of interactive processes, this essay will also consider the interests and actions of "the other"—the Left's opponents—and try to ascertain how those actions have helped shape what the actor is and what it does. Although this is true of any social actor, in the case of Latin America's Left it is most directly relevant to an understanding of how the Left and U.S. interventions in Latin America have been related since the late 1940s. The perceptions and actions of the United States vis-à-vis the Latin American Left became a decisive element in the construction of the latter's identity; similarly, as the essays by Alberto van Klaveren (chapter 1) and Abraham Lowenthal (chapter 3) indicate, the real and imaginary threats that the Left posed to "political stability" became a key consideration in the design and implementation of U.S. foreign policies within the region in the era of cold war anticommunism.

The Communist Parties and the Popular Front Strategy

In 1935 the Communist International, led by the Soviet Stalinists, abandoned the ultra-leftist course followed since the early 1930s and embraced a Popular Front strategy. The rationale behind this shift was that the antifascist struggle made advisable the joining of forces with the parties representing the national bourgeoisies in defense of the democratic institutions and of the social gains (*las conquistas sociales*) of the popular classes. Allegedly, both democratization and the advancement of social justice were being threatened by the authoritarian blitzkrieg led by the Latin American imitators of Benito Mussolini and Adolf Hitler.

The outcomes of this new strategy were quite uneven in Latin America. In some cases, it made it easier for the Communist parties to be accepted, however reluctantly, into the political arena. The best example of this trend was in Chile, where the Communist and Socialist parties joined the National Workers' Confederation in allying with the Radical party to create the Popular Front (Frente Popular). In 1938 the Frente's presidential candidate, the Radical senator Pedro Aguirre Cerda, defeated his conservative opponent. Although the Frente was formally dissolved less than two years later, mainly as a result of the feuding between the socialists and the communists, the latter would again be part of Radical-led winning presidential coalitions in 1942 and 1946.[2] Costa Rica, in 1942, provided another successful example of the Popular Front strategy: although a so-called Frente Popular was not officially created and the communists prudently changed their name to that of Popular Vanguard (Vanguardia Popular), they joined with President Rafael Calderón's oligarchic faction and the Catholic church in forging a governmental coalition that remained in power until 1948.[3]

Cuba in 1940 and Guatemala in 1946 were two cases where the communists made an abrupt transition from illegality to power sharing. In Guatemala, the communists supported Juan José Arévalo's reform-oriented government; in Cuba, in a more surprising twist, the Communist party joined Fulgencio Batista's 1940 cabinet. At that point, the former sergeant retained some of the traits that had made him appealing to the anti-Machado rebels of the mid-1930s and had yet to turn into the communist hunter of the 1950s.

During the 1930s and 1940s, the fortunes of the Communist parties were much less propitious in the continent's three largest countries: Argentina, Brazil, and Mexico. In the first case, the result was largely determined by the communists' lack of political skill: they implemented their antifascist doctrine against the party of the dispossessed. They branded Peronism as a creole version of fascism and did nothing to prevent Juan Perón's successful electoral blending of the workers of metropolitan Argentina and the poor of the country's backward north—although, in the latter case, the Peronist alliance also included traditionalist provincial oligarchies. The Argentine communists never recovered from their 1946 blunder; they turned from the continent's most powerful left-wing party—measured in terms of its organizational capabilities and the size of its membership—toward political futility.[4] Their Mexican and Brazilian counterparts followed quite different political trajectories; however, the outcomes were hardly more satisfactory. The Mexican communists, after dissipating some of their energies in devising successive plots to assassinate Leon Trotsky, were completely overshadowed by Vicente Lombardo Toledano, his contradictory partnership with the PRI, and his blend of progressivism and nationalism. This was acknowledged even by Joseph Stalin, who considered Lombardo his main interlocutor in Mexico.[5]

In Brazil, after the emergence of Getúlio Vargas, the Communist party was somewhat more successful in retaining the support of segments of the urban working class. The repression following Luis C. Prestes's unsuccessful 1935 putsch (and the long march of the 1930s), and the implementation of the corporatist regulations of the Estado Novo, did not wipe out the Communist party, but it drastically limited the range of political activities that it could effectively undertake. After a brief renaissance in the mid-1940s, the party was banned in 1947 and remained in the shadows of the state unions, while it was incapable of gaining a foothold in the countryside.[6]

The parallel failures of the Argentine, Brazilian, and Mexican communists, despite their different styles of action, might be attributed to the political contexts in which the three had to operate: contexts characterized by the combination of state-controlled unions and inchoate and fragile party systems. Neither the Brazilian state officials, nor the Mexican labor bureaucrats, nor Perón tolerated any effective competition in their rather successful seduction and cajoling of the labor force. And except for a brief period in the mid-1940s in Brazil, the communist activists could not thrive by promoting political mobilization associated with electoral politics.

One must go beyond the largely accurate argument that national-popular regimes and populist movements proved to be more difficult political rivals than established party systems for the activities of communists and other left-wing groups. The communists, as well as other more significant political actors, constructed a political rhetoric that misinterpreted the events of the 1930s and early 1940s in Latin America. This was a period when in several Latin American countries labor repression was intensified. This phenomenon often coincided with both the articulation of fascist ideologies, which had become fashionable in Europe beginning in the previous decade, and the formation of fascist and quasi-fascist parties and even of armed groups eager to emulate Hitler's storm troopers.[7]

The spatial and temporal overlapping of the two phenomena—that is, on the one hand, more intense political repression and, on the other, the emergence of a vibrant fascist imagery—did not necessarily mean that fascist regimes were being established in Latin America, however. During the Great Depression, several Latin American states began undergoing a process of substantive change; moreover, new class and sectoral alliances were formed. But neither the new Latin American state nor the emerging, and more complex, class alliances were those typical of fascism.

During the interwar years, in five or perhaps six Latin American countries— Mexico, Brazil, two or three Southern Cone countries, and, to a limited extent, Colombia—import-substitution industrialization began to unfold. The urban working classes grew in size and diversity. Besides, in several other countries, and especially in the areas around the Caribbean Basin, the mobilization of plantation workers, and less often of peasant or rural laborers, became more intense. In some countries, and not excluding occasions of violent repression, the most common response was to tolerate, or even to encourage worker participation—either in unions or through state-supervised collective bargaining or both—and, at the same time, to attempt to control it. In others, from El Salvador and Nicaragua to Colombia's Atlantic lowlands, the most common response was the intensification and expansion of state repression.

In both cases, however, the incorporation of the labor force (workers and peasant laborers) into what could be described as the arenas of social citizenship became a political issue. Whether the incorporation aborted, as in the cases of the oligarchic regimes and sultanistic dictatorships surrounding the Caribbean Basin, or whether it succeeded, as in the Southern Cone and Mexico, the communists tried hard not to lose a perceived opportunity. In order to become the organizers and representatives of the workers, the communists resorted to the most varied, and sometimes contradictory, tactics. In certain cases, like the parties in Chile and Argentina, they allied with the Radical party and other groups that seemed to fit the pure ideal type of the reform-oriented bourgeois party pictured by Georgi Dimitrov in his textbook on popular fronts. Yet in these and other countries, the communists also found less reputable partners within the ranks of oligarchic factions—even among opportunistic military leaders like Batista. They were often against the Catholic church, as in Argentina and Guatemala, but sometimes they allied with *los curas*, as they did in Costa Rica.

All of this suggests that the antifascism of Latin America's communists was more an ideological patina than a concrete guide for political action. In fact, the communists pragmatically sought their partners in every corner of the political spectrum. But the concrete practices of Latin American Communist parties departed in a more radical way from the official creed. Socialism, defined as the goal of abolishing private property and doing away with the bourgeoisie, was replaced by a different developmental model or politico-economic matrix: that of state-centered capitalist modernization.

This matrix was supported by three pillars that were cemented by the roles the state played: (1) political regulation of the economy, (2) state tutelage of class relationships, and (3) development of the autarkic closed-economy model associated with import substitution and protectionism. Although the state-centered matrix underwent different historical stages and its construction was promoted by the most diverse types of political regimes, the specific demands advanced by the Communist parties—and even less often by other segments of the Left as well— seldom went beyond the limits defined by the matrix. Nor were the specific policies advocated by the Communist parties—whenever they were in a position to influence governmental outputs—a daring attempt to build socialist economies. From the mid-1930s to the mid-1950s, the mainstream of the Left (that is, the Communist parties) became the progressive pole of the broad continuum of developmentalist statism. Thus, Latin American communists abandoned the idea of promoting an alternative model of social and economic development. Their goal was more modest: they sought to encourage the expansion of political democracy and to promote social justice.

Why did the communists support state-centered modernization? One of the most important aspects of the new development matrix was its emphasis on autarkic industrialization and import substitution. The state was instrumental in erecting protective barriers through tariffs and the manipulation of the exchange rates, and in providing incentives through credits with negative interest rates and by subsidizing foreign imports of intermediate and capital goods. All of this favored the growth of the domestic manufacturing sector. In addition to the belief that this process would provide the material basis for the rise of the national bourgeoisie, the communist Left perceived industrialization to be directly linked to the expansion of the organized industrial work force—namely, the carriers of socialism according to most of the interpretations of Marxist thought that coexisted within the Left.

The state-centered matrix was also defined by a trend of incorporation of the popular sectors into the market and the national polity. This trend was largely a result of the actions of state institutions, which played an equally strategic role in the design and implementation of the welfare state. In the areas of health, housing, education, social security, and transportation subsidies, the services rendered by public or state-financed institutions had a progressive impact on income distribution.

Conversely, the rhetoric and beliefs of the noncommunist Left, and most notably the Trotskyist sects, vis-à-vis the Latin American welfare state, were more heterogeneous and ambiguous than those of the Communist parties.[8] Whereas the latter and certain segments of the emerging populist Left—most notably Lombardo Toledano in post–Cárdenas Mexico—evaluated the welfare state rather positively, the Trotskyists tended to condemn it as part of the attempts of capitalist classes and "their" states to seduce the masses. A general pattern emerged: whenever the Left was linked, directly or indirectly, to policy-making, it tended to favor the expansion of the welfare state. The reason was obvious: parties seeking the support of the masses had to prove their political effectiveness to their actual and potential followers, even before the advent of socialism.

Carlos Díaz Alejandro has demonstrated convincingly that a third element was part of the state-centered matrix in the Southern Cone and Brazil: the implicit regulation of inter- and intrasectoral conflicts through "moderate" levels of inflation.[9] Although the Left never advocated inflation explicitly, the context of monetary instability legitimated the actions of labor unions, inasmuch as wage negotiation often led to continuous bargaining sessions and frequent work stoppages.

In summary, from the 1930s to the mid-1950s the dominant slogans of Latin American communists were progressivism and reform rather than socialism. In turn, the basis of their political strategy was to strengthen their positions within the labor movement while trying to penetrate the institutions of the "bourgeois" state, operating according to its rules. Their aim was not to abolish this state.

Latin America's postwar political landscape underwent a dramatic change with the advent of the cold war, however. During the Roosevelt presidency, the United States moved away from the policies of direct intervention and the big stick, which had prevailed since the turn of the century. The new approach inaugurated by Franklin D. Roosevelt combined neglect, restraint (as, for example, in the controversy with Mexico over the nationalization of oil companies decreed by Lázaro Cárdenas), and, in some cases, off-shore supervision and domestically generated military repression. The latter method was used especially in the small states of Central America and the Caribbean, where sultanistic authoritarian regimes were buttressed and newly created National Guards replaced U.S. marines in maintaining "law and order" and protecting imperial interests.

Furthermore, after 1941, when the Soviet Union joined the Allies in the war against Germany, the concerns about the spread of communism in Latin America became a much lower priority in the United States's Latin American agenda. In fact, the State Department was more preoccupied with the pro-Nazi inclinations of Argentine army officers than with the appointment of communist ministers in Cuba, Costa Rica, or Chile.[10]

This picture changed dramatically with the beginning of the cold war. During the dozen years following 1947, anticommunism became a decisive factor in U.S. foreign policy toward Latin America. This shift helped turn the tide of the previous decade. The second half of the 1930s and the war years had been a period of continuous expansion of the Communist parties and movements in the continent. After 1947, the decline of their influence was a trend that knew few exceptions in

Latin America. This was largely a result of the combination of targeted repressive and preemptive policies. Distinct policy packages and repressive methods were used in each country, however, depending on the type of political regime.

Democratic Chile, the relatively less democratic Brazil, and Costa Rica outlawed the Communist parties and, more broadly, made life much more difficult for Communist-dominated or Communist-associated labor unions. Reliable opposition hunters such as Rafael Trujillo, Anastasio Somoza, and the Salvadoran military refocused their guns, and leftists became their preferred targets. When Fulgencio Batista returned to power in Cuba in 1952 as a result of a military coup, he would not dream of appointing communists to his cabinet; rather, he began chasing them in the streets and the universities. In Guatemala, the Central Intelligence Agency and the U.S. secretary of state, John Foster Dulles, decided that Arévalo's successor, Jacobo Arbenz, was too soft on communism. Because Arbenz had also committed the sin of trying to deal with the United Fruit Company assuming that he was the head of a sovereign state, he was ousted from power by a band of mercenaries led by a dissident officer, Carlos Castillo Armas. Not surprisingly, after 1954 life became more difficult for Guatemalan leftists and other political dissidents.[11]

In addition, the cold war arsenal developed a new and more sophisticated weapon: the anticommunist reformist politician. José ("Don Pepe") Figueres from Costa Rica was the first and most effective example of a breed that developed primarily in the Caribbean Basin. Rómulo Betancourt, also an extremely resourceful political leader, had to wait almost a decade to implement his version of the formula after the military put an end to Venezuela's democratic *trienio* in 1948.[12] The political formula of the new brand of reformists combined the liquidation of the Left, whether conducted through political means or direct military repression, with the preemption of the social and economic reforms advocated by the communists. The reformists relied on an anti-oligarchic political discourse, while promoting state-led industrialization and the expansion of the welfare functions of the state.

The reforms introduced by Figueres, especially after he returned to power through the electoral road in 1952, were not substantively innovative. Most of them had been long implemented in the Southern Cone countries and in Mexico, and even by his predecessor Calderón. The difference was that they were designed to win the support of the masses away from the Left. In a sense, Figueres anticipated the programs of the Alliance for Progress.[13]

Other potential reformist leaders were thwarted by the armed forces in their efforts to gain power. The military in Peru, and to some extent in the Dominican Republic, were as opposed to reform-oriented politicians as they were to communists. Victor Raúl Haya de la Torre and Juan Bosch, who were longtime foes of the

Peruvian armed forces and of Trujillo respectively, were prevented from reaching the presidency—because elections in their countries were either rigged or annulled if the "wrong" candidate emerged victorious—or were overthrown shortly after assuming office.

Figueres and several other influential anticommunist reformists from Latin America and the United States made a crucial mistake beginning in late 1956, however. When Fidel Castro and the other survivors of the Granma expedition reached the Sierra Maestra and began fighting against Batista's troops, the reformists thought they had found the figure who embodied all their virtues and could carry their banners into dictatorial Cuba and democratize it. They supported Fidel and his companions and helped the Cuban Revolution to succeed. In doing so, they unintentionally contributed both to a radical change in the continent's political history and to a dramatic shift in the course of the Latin American Left into a new riverbed.

The Cuban Revolution and Its Impact on the Left: From "El hombre nuevo" to Militarism

From the perspective of his country's history, Fidel Castro was the quintessential figure of the Cuban Revolution. With his persona and his pre-1959 political career, he represented all the myths and social processes that would explain how a score of survivors fighting in the isolated hill country of Oriente province—whose population and economic structure were far from being representative of Cuba's sugar-producing lowlands—were able to defeat a relatively well-trained and well-paid professional army. The son of a Galician immigrant, a former student leader, a lawyer, and a brilliant orator, Fidel possessed all the attributes of a successful Cuban politician. After staging an unsuccessful attack on the Moncada barracks in 1953 and defying the dictator with his "History Will Absolve Me" defense, he went first to Batista's jails and then into exile, only to return to the island in a boat in 1957 after recruiting his army abroad. He was able to present his struggle credibly as the continuation, and logical conclusion, of the heroic but unfinished nationalistic crusades of José Martí and the anti-Machado rebels of the early 1930s.

Despite all of this, it was not Fidel, but Ernesto ("Che") Guevara, the Argentine-born revolutionary who, until his death in October 1967, came to symbolize most vividly the features of the Cuban Revolution that made it so appealing to the Left in Latin America and elsewhere. Guevara's image was more cosmopolitan than Fidel's, which partially explains why it was more easily appropriated by the new movements and ideological currents of the 1960s, as well as by the intellectuals of

Paris's Left Bank and Berkeley's Telegraph Avenue. But the principal reasons for Che's appeal were less mundane. During the 1960s, he represented more explicitly and more dramatically than Fidel the two decisive departures that the Cuban revolutionaries made with the Left's political past.

The first disjuncture was related to Guevara's absolute rejection of capitalism in its different variants and shapes. Until Che's sudden and surprising immersion in the field of economic policy-making, it was not entirely clear what was the specific mix of state socialism and industrial and rural cooperativism that he and the other ideologues of the new Cuban economy were advocating. However, Guevara left no doubt about the fact that the new model intended to abolish capitalism altogether, as well as replace the ideal of the profit-maximizer bourgeois with that of the socialist "hombre nuevo."[14] This implied a radical departure from the practices of the Communist parties during the previous quarter century, a shift from trying to make capitalism more progressive to founding socialism.

The second break with the past was no less decisive. The gradualist strategy of attempting to penetrate the institutions of the "bourgeois state" in order to reform them from within was abandoned. It was replaced by the more radical quest for the hegemony of the socialist forces and their ideology. To do away with capitalism, whether in its oligarchic or modern industrial variants, the new revolutionaries concluded that it was necessary to destroy the bourgeois state and to abolish its core institutions.

The destruction of the old state was largely conceived as a military task. The revolutionary Left correctly calculated that the Latin American armed forces would not graciously accept their withering away; hence, they concluded that the creation of alternative, nonbourgeois state institutions had to be invariably associated with successful armed insurrections. Within this vision, in fact, political power could emanate only from the barrel of the gun.[15]

In turn, the New Left regarded political parties and democratic rules as a mere facade of bourgeois domination, and the mechanisms and rules of bourgeois political democracy were perceived as a threat to the Left. Bourgeois democracy was not seen as simply formal; it was allegedly opposed to more genuine types of democracy. Within these visions, real or substantive democracy was equated, on the one hand, with greater social and economic egalitarianism and, on the other, with citizen political participation at the grass-roots level.

During the early and mid-1960s, the successes of Guevarism were ideological rather than political. Che's manuals became standard textbooks in university classrooms from Mexico City to Concepción, Chile. But the promised transformation of the Andes into South America's "Sierra Maestra" (the Cuban mountain range from where the revolution emerged triumphant) never materialized. Instead, there was a succession of disasters. These ranged from the defeat of the armed groups led by Yon Sosa and Turcios in Guatemala to the military's successful neutralization of Hugo Blanco's attempt to mobilize the peasants in the southern Peruvian Sierra, to the ill-fated guerrilla movements of Colombia and Venezuela.

But the most disappointing aspect of the guerrilla strategy inspired by Guevara was not its military failure, but its utter political irrelevance. Even in those cases in which it had an impact on significant numbers of the population in the countryside, rural guerrilla warfare failed to produce major alterations in the region's national political landscape. There was only one case where rural insurrectionary tactics contributed to the installation of a progressively inspired regime: after defeating the guerrillas in the mid-1960s, the Peruvian military decided to preempt any future threats by deposing the conservative government of Fernando Belaúnde Terry and founding an inclusionary regime that implemented programs of social and economic change and sought to encourage the controlled mobilization of the Peruvian poor.

The death of Che Guevara in Bolivia in October 1967 highlighted the shortcomings of rural *guerrillerismo* in Latin America and especially of its versions for export. Guevara and the score of Cubans, Argentines, and Bolivians who accompanied him in the Bolivian incursion were unable to develop any recognizable support; on the contrary, they were betrayed by the few peasants who joined their group and were easily gunned down by the "special forces" trained by the U.S. military.

Che's death became a watershed in the history of the Left in Latin America. Although the basic premises of the insurrectionary strategy associated with the Cuban Revolution were not abandoned, there was a significant shift in the methods. This shift, which was both ideological and practical, began with the rejection of the basic principles of Guevarism: the purity of the socialist pedigree of Latin American progressive forces and the vanguard role of the rural guerrillas in the revolutionary struggle.

The emergence of the post-Guevarist dogma was legitimized by the founding of the Organization for Latin American Solidarity (OLAS) in Havana in 1967. From that date forward, the advocates of armed struggle sought to link their actions with the demands and platforms of those noncommunist progressive and/or nationalistic forces that did not call themselves socialist. The new potential partners included political parties, unions, and class organizations. Although the tactics of armed struggle were not abandoned, they became progressively subordinated to the goal of influencing, or even infiltrating, preexisting political groups that did not adhere to the guerrillas' tenets. Even when the countryside remained the main theater of operations, the impact on urban politics emerged as the main concern. The creation of a force resembling Mao Tse-Tung's peasant army continued to be the goal of only a few zealots.

In the late 1960s and early 1970s, the image, if not the reality, of armed struggle became contiguous to the broader national political scenes, and especially to developments in the so-called *frentes de masas* (mass popular organizations). The impact of this shift was felt almost everywhere, but it was particularly significant in several countries where the appeal of armed struggle had been weak during the 1950s and early 1960s, especially in the Southern Cone.

During the postwar period, the fortunes of the Left had differed widely in the three Southern Cone countries; however, the 1970s witnessed an unexpected convergence of their trajectories. The Left experienced an unparalleled rise in popularity, involving the reinvigoration of some of the old players of the parliamentary game and the emergence of new movements that supported armed struggle and developed close ties with university students and intellectuals.

Chile became the foremost example of the rise of a traditional left-wing parliamentary alliance, a phenomenon that overlapped with the emergence of new militant warriors. In September 1970, the Popular Unity (Unidad Popular) coalition scored a narrow victory in that year's elections, and Salvador Allende became the first elected socialist president on the continent. In fact, the Communist and Socialist parties had been important players of Chilean politics since the 1930s. Nevertheless, only after the formation in 1957 of the Revolutionary Front of Popular Action (FRAP—Frente Revolucionario de Acción Popular), the predecessor of Unidad Popular, and the sealing of the traditional and bitter rift between the two left-wing parties, did the Left become a serious contender for political power.[16] The rise to power of the left-wing coalition coincided with the emergence in the late 1960s of a new organization advocating armed struggle, the Movement of the Revolutionary Left (MIR—Movimiento de Izquierda Revolucionaria). Led by a group of radicalized students from the University of Concepción in southern Chile, the MIR later gained support among the larger student audiences of Santiago's universities. After resorting to bank robberies and political assassinations during the presidency of Eduardo Frei (1964–70), the *miristas* offered their "conditional support" to the Unidad Popular government. The MIR's support was greeted much more warmly by some of the more militant members of Allende's own Socialist party than by their usually more cautious Communist partners, or by Allende himself.[17]

In Uruguay, the Left had been electorally much weaker than in Chile. But the Communist party had nevertheless enjoyed a significant influence within the labor movement. In 1970 that party led a cluster of small groupings, from the Socialists to the Christian Democrats, in founding the Broad Front (Frente Amplio). In addition, a newly created Marxist guerrilla group, the Tupamaros, gained considerable appeal among the urban population—especially among the young—by resorting to Robin Hood tactics, while the government of conservative Colorado president Jorge Pacheco Areco curtailed democratic freedoms and the power of the congress. In 1971 the Frente Amplio successfully challenged the traditional electoral oligopoly of Colorados and Blancos and captured almost 20 percent of the national vote, while narrowly missing victory in the country's capital, Montevideo.[18]

In Argentina, the fortunes of the Left did not improve until 1969. The Argentine Communist party did not benefit from the post-1955 proscription of its arch-enemy, Peronism, and it remained an irrelevant force. Its futility was matched by the other small groupings of the Left, including splinter groups from the old Socialist trunk that turned into ill-fated guerrillas in the mid-1960s. The rise of antiauthoritarian social protest, beginning with the 1969 Cordobazo, changed Argentina's political landscape, however. General Juan Carlos Onganía's dream of founding a new millennium of social peace and administrative politics led, on the contrary, to the growth of new militant unions, the emergence of various guerrilla groups, and the return of Peronism to power in 1973. This return coincided with an altogether new phenomenon; for the first time in the history of this populist movement, a self-proclaimed left-wing group, the Montonero guerrillas, gained considerable influence within it. The Montoneros became the largest force in the repoliticized Argentine universities, and they inspired the creation of initially successful organizations among the urban marginal population and within the mostly conservative Catholic church. Largely as a result of Perón's affectionate tutelage over *mis muchachos* (my boys), the Montoneros enjoyed the upper hand both during the 1972–73 electoral campaign of the FREJULI (the electoral front engineered by Perón) and the short-lived presidency of Héctor Cámpora.[19]

The rising electoral and political fortunes of the Left in the Southern Cone were not merely a result of the shifting strategies of those supporting armed struggle. In fact, other factors were more important, such as the diminished appeal of the nonleftist parties in Uruguay and Chile, the mobilizational climate that swept Argentina in the wake of the collapse of Onganía's military dictatorship, and the mood of student revolt coming from Europe that made a first stop in Mexico City and then spread throughout most of Latin America in the late 1960s. In both Chile and Uruguay, the respective guerrilla movements—the MIR and the Tupamaros—were outweighed in popular support and electoral significance by the traditional parties of the Left. While the Montoneros had for a short while the approval of the old leader, they were resisted by the other members of the Peronist coalition, including the powerful unions, and the protofascist clique that surrounded Perón and controlled his wife and successor, María Estela "Isabelita" Martínez.[20]

The point, however, was that the imagery of the armed Left—popular insurrection, terrorist tactics, and the condemnation of "bourgeois democracy"—enjoyed a temporary supremacy that prompted more moderate politicians from the Left and the nationalist ranks, ranging from the Chilean communists and Salvador Allende to Perón, to adopt, or at least not to challenge, the antiparliamentary and confrontationist rhetoric of the insurrectionary groups.

The rise of the Left in the Southern Cone in the early 1970s proved to be a short-lived phenomenon. In 1973 in Uruguay and Chile, the military launched successful coups that put an end to the continent's two oldest traditions of constitutional democracy. Similarly, the 1974 turn to the right of the Peronist government both presaged and, at the same time, failed to prevent the 1976 Argentine coup. The Southern Cone's "new" authoritarian regimes specifically targeted the Left for extermination, and although all oppositions, whether leftist or not, suffered the unparalleled levels of repression that the military applied, the Left—especially the rank-and-file members of unions, student groups, and the civilian organizations linked to armed groups—experienced the most severe and lethal repression.

The novelty of the Southern Cone military dictatorships of the 1970s was not limited to the development of sophisticated and effective methods of repression, however. Their leaders concluded that the definitive elimination of subversive threats went beyond the mere extermination of the militants; a radical alteration of the "distorted" organizational patterns of Latin American societies was also required. Hence, the military regimes pursued the refoundation of their societies. The long-term project of the military combined, on the one hand, the proposed eradication of state interventionism and the imposition of an unrestricted market economy and, on the other, the drastic narrowing of the political realm—the contraction of the range of social conflicts and controversies to be settled through political means. The world view of the military did not exclude a gradual return to a limited political democracy; but in this version of democracy, representative institutions would be subject to the permanent tutelage of the armed forces and would be largely devoid of political content.

The installation of the Southern Cone military regimes became a historical watershed, transcending the lifespan of the regimes themselves and having an impact on most of the continent's countries. The 1973 coups in Chile and Uruguay were the starting points of two distinct trends. On the one hand, they signaled the beginning of an authoritarian surge that swept most of the continent. This surge led, among other significant effects, to the political defeat of the left wing, primarily by direct military repression. On the other hand, the coups of the 1970s unleashed an even more profound transformation of Latin American societies that would irreversibly change their economic and social structures and the dominant ideological paradigms. The period opening with the Southern Cone coups witnessed the collapse of the state-centered matrix; as a consequence, the linkage between "developmentalist statism" and economic growth was broken. This process reverberated on the left: the transformations of the 1970s, culminating with

Latin America's 1982 debt crisis, had a significant impact on the social and political mobilization of the working classes and other popular sectors. Thus, one of the most decisive parameters in determining patterns of action and the potentialities of the Left was altered. Initially so promising for the Left, the 1970s swiftly turned into a decade of serious historical defeats.

Are the Thousand Flowers Blossoming or Wilting?

In addition to the emergence of a new, more aggressive military regime—the "foundational" dictatorships of the Southern Cone—other types of authoritarian regimes were partially relegitimated by the prevailing antidemocratic mood. The category of political authoritarianism includes different types of regimes. The Southern Cone military dictatorships of the 1970s belonged to the newest variant of authoritarianism in Latin America, one combining the repressive demobilization of highly mobilized societies with the implementation of economic policies focused on anti-inflationary and trade-liberalization goals.

There were at least three other types of authoritarian regimes in the continent's capitalist societies. One of them was the surviving developmentalist regime of the 1960s, the Brazilian dictatorship that came to power in 1964. The 1970s were highlighted by President Ernesto Geisel's attempt to use the 1968–73 economic boom as a launching pad for a controlled political opening that envisioned a gradual return to civilian rule. The second type was that of the traditional military dictatorships still prevailing in Paraguay and several Central American and Caribbean countries—from Somoza's Nicaragua to Duvalier's Haiti—which fit to a greater or lesser degree the sultanistic pattern. The military-dominated regimes of Honduras, El Salvador, and Guatemala should also be included in this category. Finally, the third type was best exemplified by the Peruvian military regime, which tried to implement a program blending social reform and controlled political mobilization. Ecuador's military regime and Torrijos's Panama were watered-down and hybrid versions of the latter type.

One factor contributing to the relegitimation of authoritarianism in Latin America was the change that U.S. foreign policy underwent in the post-Kennedy years. The Alliance for Progress had as one of its major goals the containment of communism in Latin America. Alliance ideologues thought that a program of social reform carried out by civilian politicians would be the most effective recipe for achieving that goal, although as the Bay of Pigs invasion demonstrated, this strategy did not exclude the possibility of resorting to more direct military means when the communist threat was deemed to be serious and imminent.

Beginning in the Johnson administration, the belief in the effectiveness of political democracy in Latin America gradually eroded. The makers of U.S. foreign policy returned to the more traditional approach associated with the practices that prevailed during the Eisenhower administration. These practices stemmed from the belief that the military, whether in power or behind the power, was the most reliable shield against communism and the most likely institution to keep political order. In both the Johnson and Nixon administrations, there were several examples of this revaluation of the political role of Latin America's military: the open support of the 1964 Brazilian military takeover, the 1965 invasion of the Dominican Republic, and the 1970–73 attempts to destabilize the Unidad Popular government in Chile.

Although they continued to pay lip service to democracy and condemned some military takeovers, U.S. foreign policymakers, in fact, supported Latin America military authoritarianism during the two decades following 1964. There was a significant exception to this trend, however. Between 1976 and 1980 under Jimmy Carter, U.S. foreign policy temporarily shifted course and most U.S. government agencies distanced themselves from the military regimes. The main practical effects of this detour were the condemnation of the human rights violations committed by the armed forces and the more neutral stand taken by the United States vis-à-vis some of its former authoritarian allies, including Anastasio Somoza in Nicaragua and Joaquín Balaguer and the post-Trujillo military in the Dominican Republic.[21]

Most of the consequences of the Carter policies were intended, or at least they were not unwelcomed. These included the concessions that some of the military governments were forced to make in the area of human rights, especially in Uruguay and Argentina, and the implementation of the first largely fraud-free election in the Dominican Republic in over a decade, which resulted in the victory of the main opposition party in the 1978 presidential contest. But in Nicaragua the results were disappointing: contrary to the intentions of the U.S. government, Somoza's fall from power led to the establishment of a coalition government within which the Marxist Sandinistas clearly enjoyed the upper hand.

Many Latin American leftists interpreted the victory of the Nicaraguan rebels as part of a worldwide trend of socialist resurgence and concomitant U.S. defeat that had supposedly started in Vietnam. They were wrong. The Sandinistas became the only winners within a political camp that had experienced all types of political and military calamities during the 1970s. The Left's victory in the Nicaraguan revolution and the beginning of its protracted, and largely successful, struggle against the U.S.-sponsored contras overlapped with the inroads that another guerrilla army, the Frente Farabundo Martí de Liberación Nacional (FMLN), made against the Salvadoran military.[22]

The turn of events in Central America contributed to an optimistic reading of the 1970s on the part of certain sectors of the Left. The proponents of this perspective acknowledged the setbacks suffered during the previous decade. However, they maintained that except for the effective antiguerrilla campaigns of the governments of Venezuela, Colombia, and Mexico, most of those defeats had been inflicted by authoritarian governments run by the armed forces. Therefore, they argued, although one could not deny that the defeats had been costly, they also largely represented the "naked expression of capitalist domination," uncovering the veils of formal democracy and reiterating the futility of parliamentary practices. Besides, the more interventionist stand adopted by Ronald Reagan in "fighting communism" in Nicaragua, El Salvador, and the whole Caribbean Basin provided a blunt demonstration that "imperialist aggression" was ready to step in when the domestic repressors faltered.

Militarism thus remained one of the predominant strains of thought and action within the Left during the early and mid-1980s. But more segments of the Left— old and new alike—began to question terrorism and, more generally, the use of violence in political action. Significant guerrilla groups continued to operate in El Salvador, Guatemala, and Colombia; the Shining Path (Sendero Luminoso) became a relevant actor in Peruvian politics, and the newly created Patriotic Front "Manuel Rodríguez" began engineering terrorist operations against General Pinochet's regime. On the rest of the continent, however, left-wing advocates of violence either vanished or were exterminated, and even in Chile and Peru the stronger segments of the Left supported nonviolent strategies. Still, some of the crucial debates within the Left continued to unfold around the question of what would be the most efficient method for defeating the "bourgeois" regimes, whether democratic or authoritarian, and gaining political power.

In concentrating on the traditional themes of the conquest of the state, the Left failed to realize that the Latin American societies it had known for more than half a century were rapidly fading away. Although claiming that theirs was the discourse of the future, leftists began to be isolated in the past. As a consequence, during the 1980s the Left lost the ideological momentum it had enjoyed in Latin America during the previous five decades. Even under conditions of extremely harsh repression or successful developmentalist drives, the Left had been able to infuse its struggles with a progressive aura that had sustained the enthusiasm of its supporters and evoked the fears of its opponents. This trend was dramatically reversed during the 1980s. For the first time in the post-1930 period, the Left was relegated to a defensive position.

This ideological debacle was closely related to the collapse of the state-centered matrix. The breakdown of the Latin American states went beyond the crisis of their fiscal and monetary mechanisms. It also severely weakened public authority; in certain cases, this process involved the almost-total unraveling of the (state-centered) rules regulating daily interaction among people. More specifically, the collective actors of the past decades—business associations, labor unions and other organizations of the popular sectors, and the cadres of state managers and public technocrats—partially evaporated. These sectoral organizations and collective informal groups oriented toward political action saw their capacity to engage their individual members shrink dramatically. The allegiance of individuals to organizations and to collective projects diminished substantially. At the same time, the patterns of interaction among different collective actors became more disorganized as the formal and informal rules governing those interactions lost their effectiveness.

This dramatic shift in the region's political culture especially affected the popular sectors. But, among all political actors in Latin America, it was the Left, supposedly the closest to the domain of the popular sectors, that proved to be the most inept in adapting to change. In fact, several of the "old" left-wing parties, and some of the more recently created organizations, renovated their discourse and veered in the direction of unambiguously supporting political democracy. Uruguay's Broad Front, the Renovada faction of the Chilean Socialists, the Workers' party (PT) in Brazil, Mexico's Party of the Democratic Revolution (PRD—Partido de la Revolución Democrática), and the M-19 in Colombia were some of the most prominent examples of this trend, whereby political democracy came to be accepted by the Left as a legitimate and valuable end in itself.

But the democratic *aggiornamento* did not prevent the Left's parties and organizations from playing a marginal role during the wave of democratization that swept South America during the 1980s. This was the most significant indication of the ideological demise of the Left. During the 1980s, all of South America's military regimes either transferred power to constitutionally elected civilian regimes or initiated transition processes leading in that direction. The last year of the decade symbolically synthesized the period. It was inaugurated by the surprising ouster of Paraguay's dictator, Alfredo Stroessner, by his less surprisingly disloyal relative and fellow general, Andrés Rodríguez. Stroessner had been in power for thirty-five years, and his replacement opened the path toward a real transition to democracy in his country. The year ended with the confirmation of the results of the 1988 Chilean plebiscite and the presidential election in Brazil. In December, Patricio Aylwin won election as the candidate of the joint opposition's front in Chile, and Fernando Collor de Mello defeated the Workers' party candidate, Luís Inácio da Silva ("Lula"), to become Brazil's first freely elected president since 1961.

In every case the transition to a democratic regime was not the result of an opposition's frontal assault characteristic of popular movements, much less of actions associated with left-wing organizations. In some instances the replacement of military dictatorships was largely caused by the operation of factors internal to the regime, whether an implosive rupture (Argentina) or a military-led end of a sultanistic autocracy (Paraguay). In other cases, the route was that of a negotiated transition, with or without a decisive electoral defeat of the authoritarian government. Examples of the first variant were the plebiscites in Uruguay and Chile, and of the second, the exit from power of the Brazilian and Peruvian military.

It is especially noteworthy that in the two cases in which intense mobilizations of civil society were directed against the authoritarian regimes—Chile and Brazil—the Left failed to bring about the desired democratic reforms. In Chile, massive urban protests began in 1983, when a severe financial crisis signaled the failure of the military's first monetarist experience, and the mass movements and the opposition parties demanded the immediate end of the dictatorship. Their motto was, "Pinochet should resign now"; however, after three years of confrontation and a limited opening, the regime was able to neutralize the protests and to enforce the path designed by the 1980 authoritarian constitution. In Brazil, the rebirth of civil society during the 1970s, and the mass rallies for *diretas-já* (direct presidential elections now) contributed to the loss of the strategic initiative by the military regime around 1982. The military was still capable of maintaining the indirect nature of the 1985 presidential election, however, and only the split of the government party and the indecisiveness of the last military president, General Figueiredo, paved the way for the victory of the opposition's candidate, Tancredo Neves.

The ideological crisis of Latin America's Left was certainly intensified by the collapse of the communist regimes of Eastern Europe and the Soviet Union. The socialist economies of the East had already become an uninspiring (if still apparently viable) model, and their disintegration did little to improve the appeal of the Left among Latin Americans. The events that unfolded between 1989 and the banning of the Communist party in the Soviet Union were even more harmful for the self-image of the leaders and activists of the Left. Not only the supporters of the minority orthodox Communist parties, but also the members of most of the other political groupings and organizations that defined themselves as left-wing, found themselves in a political terrain devoid of any credible reference to the utopias that had inspired their actions for more than half a century.

From the perspective of the Latin American Left, the crumbling of the communist regimes of Eastern Europe only accelerated a process that was largely determined by domestic factors in Latin America. During the late 1980s, the Latin American Left was already involved in a losing battle, demanding a return to the era of state developmentalism and the reconstitution of the heroic social actors of the past. These actors—the working class, the peasantry, and the urban poor—were to be the builders of socialism. In fact, the patterns of collective action of workers, peasants, and the poor were also disintegrating, largely because they had been centered on the state—and the Left could hardly make sense of the novel types of behavior of the underprivileged.

The economic and politico-cultural mutations of the 1980s have affected all sectors of the Left throughout Latin America. However, four main segments have reacted in very different ways to them. These segments are the *izquierda basista* (the grass-roots Left), the proponents of millenaristic violence, guerrilla movements, and the political Left.

The Izquierda Basista

Organizations and groups belonging to the grass-roots Left have emerged in almost every country in Latin America since the 1970s. Some were connected to processes of popular mobilization against the authoritarian state or the organizations it controlled. The most significant examples were the "new unions" in Brazil and Mexico. Typically, *basismo* also appeared in association with neighborhood associations often sponsored by progressive sectors of the Catholic church, the Ecclesiastical Base Communities (CEBs). The basistas distrust all mechanisms of political representation, and they believe that participatory democracy is the only *real* democracy. In this vision, the state, whether authoritarian or democratic, is regarded as inherently evil, while civil society is good. Basistas have often resorted to the creation of political parties such as Brazil's PT. Once transitions to democracy occur, however, these parties become ambivalent organizations. Although they operate in the arenas of representative democracy and occasionally hold elected governmental positions, basistas have not ceased to claim that the extension of participatory mechanisms implanted in civil society is the only way truly to democratize Latin American societies. In practice, the basista parties have confronted a difficult dilemma. On the one hand, when acting in the political arena, they are faced with the same opportunities and constraints that other parties encounter. To increase their chances of success, they have had to resort to the same practices of negotiation and compromise that they criticize. Obviously, compromise often requires the postponement of grass-root demands (sometimes sine die).

On the other hand, the disorganization of the Latin American state has gone hand in hand with the weakening of civil society and its organizations. The result has often been dwindling participation. Instead of the vibrant grass-root mobilizations envisioned by the basistas, the reality of contemporary Latin America has been the mockery of direct democracy (*asambleísmo*) by left-wing militants. The most dramatic example of this trend has been the PT. The Trotskyist sects that coexist within it have been able to infuse the party's program and rhetoric with a language alien to the majority of the party's voters and sympathizers. The latter have often become alienated and have withdrawn.

Proponents of Millenaristic Violence

Peru's Shining Path (Sendero Luminoso) is the foremost example of this virulent and novel form of armed warfare. As Carlos Iván Degregori has argued, Sendero is neither an Andean nor a premodern movement; rather, it articulates an ideology and a praxis that both negate reality and try to solve ambiguities and bottlenecks by asserting that its leader is the "fourth sword of Marxism" (after Marx, Lenin, and Mao).[23] The Colombian Army of National Liberation (ELN—Ejército de Liberación Nacional) has resorted to some of Sendero's tactics, although they have been much more limited in scope. Actions of extreme cruelty, often directed against the masses these movements claim to represent (in the case of Sendero, the Indian peasants of Peru's southern Sierra), are often combined with the most irrational variants of terrorism (in the case of the ELN, for example, the bombing of oil pipelines that produced major ecological disasters).

Millenaristic violence thrives when there is a high degree of state decomposition and societal segmentation. It offers no credible image of the future, but rather a redemptive retreat into some form of primitive, and extremely authoritarian, collectivist utopia.

Guerrilla Movements

Only a score of guerrilla groups survived the onslaught of the 1970s. From the Southern Cone to the sierra of Guerrero, Mexico, where Lucio Cabañas was killed in 1974, the guerrillas were effectively wiped out by military forces that resorted to every method available, whether legal or illegal, in the "war without battles," as one of Héctor Aguilar Camín's characters described it. Furthermore, the guerrillas failed to overcome an even more serious obstacle: the indifference of the masses. In the early 1970s, however, there was a precursor of what would become the only way to avoid doom. Teodoro Petkoff, a leader of the Venezuelan guerrillas, negotiated an amnesty whereby his forces laid down their weapons in exchange for the possibility of running for elective office. The Movimiento al Socialismo (MAS) was thus born. It became Venezuela's third, albeit minority, party in a game that nevertheless continued to be dominated by the country's two major parties, Acción Democrática and COPEI.

The most significant recent example of a process of negotiated reinsertion of the guerrillas into parliamentary life has developed in Colombia since the late 1980s. During that decade a resurgence of political violence led the country into a situation of virtual statelessness. Politically related violence had never been completely eliminated after the years of La Violencia (1948–58) and the beginning of the National Front governments of 1958–74. In fact, the oldest and strongest of the country's guerrilla groups, the Revolutionary Armed Forces of Colombia (FARC—

Fuerzas Armadas Revolucionarias de Colombia), was a legacy of that early period. During the 1970s and 1980s, other guerrilla groups either were created or expanded their operations. Chief among them was the Movement of the 19th of April (M-19), which took its name from the date of the 1970 election that apparently fraudulently denied the presidential victory of the daughter of the former populist dictator, Gustavo Rojas Pinilla. Other groups included the EPL and the ELN, both formed in the 1960s, and Quintín Lame, founded in the 1980s, which emerged from radicalized elements of groups of Colombia's southwestern departments.[24]

But the explosion of violence was not only related to expanded guerrilla activity. In fact, the most cruel and spectacular episodes of terrorist violence and assassinations were engineered by the drug cartels (especially by the Medellín group) and the paramilitary groups they helped spawn, which successfully hunted left-wing leaders and activists. The failure of the pacification effort of President Belisario Betancur (1982–86) and the all-out war declared by his successor, Virgilio Barco, against the drug cartels (bringing about a sequel of lethal retaliations) seemed to indicate entry into a new era of complete lawlessness and the breakdown of political order. However, during the last year of Barco's government and the first year of President César Gaviria's, negotiations led to the reintegration into parliamentary politics of three of the country's guerrilla groups: the M-19, the EPL, and Quintín Lame. More important, the M-19's president, Antonio Navarro Wolff, first joined Gaviria's cabinet as minister of health, then headed the M-19 list of candidates who scored an impressive plurality victory in the elections for the constituent assembly. The M-19 became one of the three major actors in the drafting of Colombia's new constitution, enacted in July 1991, alongside Gaviria's faction of the Liberal party and a faction of the Conservative party. The success of the M-19's reintegration, and the realization on the part of the Coordinadora Guerrillera Simón Bolívar (formed by the FARC, the ELN, and a dissident faction of the EPL) that it faced a no-win situation, prompted the rest of the guerrillas to enter into negotiations with Gaviria's government in 1991.

The relevance of the Colombian case resides in the fact that the reintegration of the guerrillas into parliamentary politics has been part of a process of completing the democratization of a still-oligarchic political society. Colombia's political map is being redrafted; in addition to the emergence of a third political force associated with the Left, the governing Liberal party itself is undergoing a process of political modernization that has undermined, but not entirely erased, the power of the party's clientelistic barons.

The Political Left

During the early 1990s, three distinct elements coexisted within that sector of the Left that has unequivocally chosen parliamentary life and therefore carries on its activities through political parties. The first is exemplified by broad left-wing coalitions that, on acquiring political power, have failed to advance policy options significantly different from those implemented by the conservative parties that preceded them in power. Jaime Paz Zamora's coalition in Bolivia and Rodrigo Borja's government in Ecuador are the two foremost examples of this first subtype. The absence of reformist proposals by these two coalitions indicates their failure to address the dominant theme of the late 1980s and early 1990s—economic adjustment. Passive political adjustment to the policies initially designed by their conservative predecessors, Paz Estenssoro and Febres Cordero, also indicates that access to governmental spoils has become the overriding objective of the erstwhile reformists of the two Andean countries.

The second type of political Left includes those parties that are still pursuing the full democratization of the political systems of which they are a part. Although Mexico's PRD and Paraguay's *independientes* have yet to be a force in their country's transition to democratic consolidation, securing political democracy is unarguably the top priority of the two forces. This partially justifies their inability to deal with the issues of economic adjustment and restructuring.

The two main parties of the Chilean New Left, the *socialistas renovados* (Socialist party) and the Partido por la Democracia (PPD), constitute the most successful examples of renovation within the Left. First, the Socialist party and the PPD have realized that a prerequisite for the achievement of power in the postauthoritarian era is the building and consolidation of a party system embracing various political and ideological options. In Chile, as well as in other countries such as Argentina and Nicaragua, this means that the right-wing forces would unquestionably choose to act through parliamentary parties, thus renouncing an authoritarian option. From this perspective, the building of a party system comes to be conceived as the extension of a political "safety net." This net would perform two crucial functions in the process of democratic consolidation: prevent authoritarian regressions and effectively weave key social and economic actors into a system defined by its pluralism and the predominance of compromise over violent confrontation. In the arena of political institutions, democratic consolidation would require the party system to provide both conservative social and economic forces and their opponents with credible alternatives, and to help to build majoritarian coalitions within presidential systems.

The other challenge confronting the Chilean New Left is the need to devise a progressive alternative to the cul-de-sac resulting from the end of the long cycle of growth associated with import-substitution industrialization and state interventionism. This involves building alternative policy-related and societal mechanisms for regenerating economic dynamism, and for reincorporating the excluded sectors of the population into labor and consumer markets. The Chilean Left is beginning to realize that this is one of the keys to the consolidation of democracy.

One of the principal challenges of the new democracies in Latin America is to overcome the failure of governments to interweave the networks of public and private mechanisms that could provide a forum for the negotiation and settlement of divergent positions and interests concerning key economic issues. This task is largely the responsibility of the Left.

The Chilean New Left and, more ambiguously, its Uruguayan counterparts (which still face the difficult task of bringing together the Frente Amplio and the Nuevo Espacio) seem to be advancing on this path. Conservative parties are increasingly preaching reliance on the automatic mechanisms of the market, within which sheer economic power is obviously the dominant currency. At the extreme, this means that some key decision-making channels would become fully privatized. The result could be the "voiding" of democracy rather than its breakdown. This voiding would imply that the settlement of who governs, and how, would have little impact on the substance of governance. In other words, the democratic selection of officials, and the full observation of the constitution and the laws, might not have a significant impact on the creation of public arenas for the definition and settlement of collectively important issues.

A Final Caveat

The crumbling of the socialist regimes of Eastern Europe and the Soviet Union only accelerated the decay of the Latin American Left. The impact of the international events of recent years is being felt in a more indirect, albeit important, way by the Left, however. U.S. foreign policy vis-à-vis Latin America is being radically redefined with the end of cold war anticommunism. First, issues such as drug production and trafficking, migration to the United States, and degradation of the environment are becoming more important than fighting the remnants of the guerrilla movements of the last quarter century. Second, purely economic issues are determining more directly the behavior of the different agencies of the U.S. government; one consequence is that the secretaries of Commerce and the Treasury and the head of the Federal Reserve Board have become more important to Latin America than the secretary of state or the Pentagon. Third, Latin America as a whole, with the exception of Mexico, has become an even more marginal area in the making of U.S. foreign policy.

Manuel Noriega in the Central American isthmus and Saddam Hussein in the Persian Gulf provide powerful clues about how U.S. military interventions will be decided in the future. The combination of a crucial issue such as drugs or oil and "bad behavior" as defined by U.S. officials, rather than ideology, will be the determining factor. It is not yet apparent how the Left will react to this crucial transition.

Notes

1. See, for example, the speech of Che Guevara before the United Nations General Assembly, December 11, 1964 (reprinted in Mallin, *"Che" Guevara on Revolution*, pp. 112–26), and Debray, *Strategy for Revolution*.

2. Gil, *Political System of Chile*, pp. 67–73.

3. Bell, *Crisis in Costa Rica*, contains the most comprehensive coverage in English of events leading up to the revolution of 1948.

4. Rock, *Argentina*; Peter H. Smith, *Argentina*.

5. Hamilton, *Limits of State Autonomy*; Ashby, *Organized Labor*.

6. Levine, *The Vargas Regime*; Skidmore, *Politics in Brazil*.

7. Many disparate political groupings and personalities used the fascist rhetoric, including the Guatemalan dictator Jorge Ubico; the founders of Mexico's PAN; General José Felix Uriburu and his associates, and the early 1940s Perón in Argentina; the "nacista" Jorge González von Marees and his opponent, the Radical Arturo Olavarria and his ACHA group, in Chile; Uruguay's Herrerismo; the Brazilian *integralistas* and their successful repressor, President Getúlio Vargas; and several factions of Colombia's Conservative party.

8. The 1930s witnessed the definitive eclipse of the anarcho-syndicalist Left. During the previous half century, the anarchists had thrived on the outright refusal of the capitalist classes to let the "social question" (*cuestión social*) become an item of the political agenda. The anarchists' absolute rejection of the capitalist state was symmetrical with the repressive strategies of the oligarchic states of the pre-1930 era. The confrontation between two totally incompatible societal visions could be settled only through the obliteration or withering away of one of them.

Another sector of the Left that lost ground after the Great Depression was that of the parliamentary Socialist parties associated with the traditions of European social democracies. The reasons for their decline were almost exactly the opposite of those operating in the case of anarchism. The Socialist parties had been especially significant in the River Plate region, where their influence was associated with the liberalization of the restrictive parliamentary institutions of the oligarchic state. The liberalization process, which involved the democratization of congressional practices, the expansion of the party system, and the implementation of fraud-free electoral regulations, was interrupted in the late 1920s. The Socialists never recovered.

A caveat is needed here: Chile's Socialist party was founded much later than its Southern Cone counterparts, and it bore little ideological resemblance to them. It was born in the aftermath of the twelve-day Socialist Republic in 1933 and its positions vis-à-vis parliamentary democracy were always ambiguous. In fact, some of its factions were influenced by Trotskyism and supported the abolition of the institutions of the capitalist state—even through a workers' insurrection.

9. Díaz Alejandro, *Essays*. Díaz Alejandro also argued that in other Latin American countries where "early" or "late" state-centered development was also predominant, unions and other popular organizations were not strong enough to prevent wages and salaries from being disciplined by orthodox economic policies pursuing stabilization. Mexico was the example he used for "early" state-centered development, whereas Colombia and Peru were "late" cases. Beginning in the 1940s and throughout the 1950s, "inflationary" countries experienced annual inflation rates ranging from 20 to 50 percent. From a long-term perspective, this was a "moderate" rate of inflation.

10. Wood, *Dismantling of the Good Neighbor Policy*.

11. Gleijeses, *Shattered Hope*; Immerman, *The CIA in Guatemala*.

12. It should be noted, however, that Betancourt's position vis-à-vis the communists was more ambiguous in the 1940s than in the 1950s. Much of Figueres's earlier and more militant anticommunism had to do with the fact that the left-wing party was part of the governmental coalition of President Calderón that was defeated by Figueres's army in the brief civil war of 1948.

13. Ameringer, *Don Pepe*.

14. The major attributes of the "new man" were his predisposition to sacrifice everything, including his own life, for the sake of the revolution, and the emphasis on moral incentives. Solidarity, rather than profit seeking, was the engine motivating the new socialist man. During the 1960s, the subordination of women was certainly not a major preoccupation of either Cuban revolutionaries or the Latin American Left in general; the issue of the "mujer nueva" would be raised by the feminist Left a decade later.

15. The replacement of communist "popular-frontism" by revolutionary armed struggle as the most effective road to socialism implied a return to a Leninist conception of hegemony. Lenin and Antonio Gramsci inspired two alternative definitions of hegemony. As the latter accurately pointed out, Lenin's conception was inextricably linked to the political experience of the founder of the Soviet state, which was nurtured by the "gelatinous" context of Russian society. That experience could be alluded to by the metaphor of the "war of maneuvers"—that is, the successful stormings of the winter palaces of capitalist states and the defeat of their armies, signaling the triumph of socialist revolutions. Conversely, Gramsci argued that the conquest of power in "Western" nations, with their more complex and stronger civil societies, required more subtle and broad-based methods. Thus, in the West politico-military victory was dependent on the prior or parallel achievement of cultural supremacy over the bourgeoisie.

16. Allende missed achieving the presidency by a slim margin in 1958, when the right-wing independent Jorge Alessandri was elected in a four-candidate race in which the Christian Democrats and the Radicals also received significant support.

17. Constable and Valenzuela, *Nation of Enemies*.

18. Collier and Collier, *Shaping the Political Arena*, esp. pp. 647–52.

19. Cámpora became Peronism's presidential candidate when the outgoing military president, General Alejandro Lanusse, vetoed the candidacy of Juan Perón. Cámpora was elected in March 1973 and assumed the presidency on May 25. For an overview that relates this era to the broader panorama of the Argentine political economy, see William C. Smith, *Authoritarianism*.

20. It was Perón himself who prompted the demise of the Montoneros. In disagreement with the unexpected radical course that Cámpora followed during his first weeks in office, Perón engineered a palace coup that brought about the resignation of the new president and his vice-president, as well as the displacement of the Montoneros and their political allies. Later in 1973, after he had been elected president, Perón explicitly condemned the tactics and ideology of the Montoneros and the Marxist Revolutionary Army of the People (ERP—Ejército Revolucionario del Pueblo). When Perón died in mid-1974, his wife, as vice-president, assumed the presidency.

21. Schoultz, *Human Rights*.

22. The FMLN was never able to duplicate the success of its Sandinista neighbors: its military foes were much more effective than Somoza and his National Guard, and the Salvadoran oligarchy was more powerful as a social actor and more closely allied to the

military than the inchoate Nicaraguan propertied classes. In addition, the advent to power—in 1982—of José Napoleón Duarte's Christian Democrats, who tried to implement a reformist program and whose presence assured continuing U.S. military and economic aid, further hurt the FMLN.

23. Degregori, "Origins and Logic of Shining Path," p. 37.

24. Hartlyn, *Politics of Coalition Rule*, esp. pp. 216–24.

Part Two · ISSUES

· Riordan Roett

Chapter Six · THE DEBT CRISIS AND

. ECONOMIC DEVELOPMENT

. IN LATIN AMERICA

A s the "lost decade" of the 1980s closed, the Latin American debt crisis assumed a Janus-like quality. For the international financial community, "the debt crisis is seen to be almost a thing of the past."[1] As one ranking World Bank official commented at the annual meeting of the Inter-American Development Bank in Nagoya, Japan, in April 1991, "what we have left is just the rump of the debt problem."[2] Writing from a different perspective about the same issue in its second *Human Development Report* (1991), the United Nations Development Programme (UNDP) stated that "the economic problems of the 1980s have hit [Latin America] hard. The debt crisis, high interest rates, barriers raised against Latin American exports, and low commodity prices—all wrought havoc with some of the region's past achievements in human development."[3]

Depending on whether you are an international banker or an ordinary citizen in Latin America, both views have validity. Latin America, in the early 1990s, has returned to the international financial markets with something of a vengeance; the poor and marginal in Latin America continue to be malnutritioned, poorly educated and housed, and without jobs. Both situations, somewhat ironically, are due to the courageous and successful process of economic restructuring undertaken at the end of the last decade by a new generation of political leaders in the region. That program of reform has led to a renegotiation of the private commercial bank debt on terms only marginally favorable to the Latin American states; but the reforms and the renegotiation have restored the creditworthiness of the region for the first time in more than a decade. What it has not done is address the social and human legacy of the lost decade for the majority of Latin Americans: "Average inflation rates soared about 100% during the 1980s in Argentina, Bolivia, Brazil and Peru—eroding real wages and discouraging investment. Open unemployment remained relatively constant between 1980 and 1989, but employment shifted towards less productive activities. Production per head fell, along with living standards, and malnutrition and infant mortality started to rise in many countries."[4]

The origins of the Janus-like profile of Latin America in the 1990s—a profile that, on the one hand, suggests that the debt is not a problem and, on the other, highlights the social malaise the debt crisis created—are found in the difficult, but correct, decision of the region to undertake a program of economic liberalization. The economic and social development models of the postwar period were found wanting by political leaders elected in the late 1980s and early 1990s. The new realities of the interdependent, global economic system have forced a reconsideration of the hemisphere's role in world affairs. Competitiveness and productivity are the sine qua non for success in today's complex world. Opportunities for regional cooperation are better than at any time in the region's history; protected, closed economies make little sense in a period of integration and cross-border economic collaboration.

The market orientation that has been adopted appears to offer the best opportunity to address the pending agenda of development issues that have gone unanswered for decades. Finally, the new economic model may provide an opportunity to come to grips with the burden of debt accumulated during the last few decades. Interest payments require sizable stocks of foreign exchange that can be earned primarily through increased exports and new capital investments. By the end of 1991 it was clear that the Brady Plan, announced by the U.S. Treasury secretary in March 1989, was the only feasible policy response for dealing with the outstanding stock of debt. Latin America has decided to be realistic and work within the new parameters. Threats of unilateral moratoria have disappeared. The International Monetary Fund (IMF) is again welcome in the capitals of the region. The international bond markets have reopened and new capital flows have begun to return to Latin America.

There are a number of explanations for this turn of events. The first was the inauguration of George Bush in January 1989. He proceeded to redefine the debate about U.S. policy in Latin America. A deal was cut with congressional Democrats to end U.S. support for the contras in Nicaragua and seek democratic elections and to work toward a negotiated settlement of the civil war in El Salvador. Both issues had polarized relations between the Congress and the White House throughout the 1980s. Bush also undertook a series of economic initiatives to benefit the hemisphere. The first was the Brady Plan in March 1989 to prod the private commercial banks toward a greater degree of debt reduction, and the second was the June 1990 Enterprise for the Americas Initiative. The 1990 initiative stressed the interdependence of debt reduction, trade, and investment.

This essay will (1) provide a summary of the evolution of the debt crisis in the 1980s and (2) consider the state of play in the early 1990s, that is, the status of the Brady Plan, the momentum of economic liberalization in the region, and the implications of the Janus-like dichotomy of Latin America—a region now internationally creditworthy yet possessed of the overpowering social agenda inherited from the lost decade.

The Debt Crisis in Perspective

As Pedro-Pablo Kuczynski has cogently summarized:

> There is . . . no great mystery about the origins of the debt crisis in Latin America: first, and most important, an extremely high level of external debt, most of it at floating interest rates; second, the impact of a very large rise in international interest rates, mostly denominated in dollars at a time of a rising U.S. dollar, upon the service of this debt; third, an eventual, but not immediate, decline in export earnings due to a deep international recession; and, finally, as in most debt crises, a loss of confidence on the part of the lenders, who initially started to lend at shorter terms and eventually stopped altogether, precipitating the suspension of debt service.[5]

During the 1950s and 1960s, the economies of Latin America and the Caribbean expanded. The growth was uneven but the quality of life for millions of citizens improved. Income distribution remained badly skewed against the poor but in many countries an expanding middle class offered new opportunities for mobility and inclusion in the modern sectors of the economy. The pattern slowed in the 1970s due to the heavy burden of oil import bills after the first petroleum crisis in 1973. It was also caused by the slower growth in the industrial countries during the decade, which reduced the demand for commodities exported by the developing nations.

Confronted with a decision to continue growing or introduce substantial cutbacks in spending, the region's governments opted for continued growth. To do so meant to borrow—hence, the massive public sector deficits that burden the region today. While the private sector borrowed, it was overshadowed by governments and the state agencies that garnered the bulk of the new lending flows. Flush with petrodollars, the world's commercial bankers were willing and anxious to find new customers. Latin America and the Caribbean were a godsend for them. The assumption of the borrowers was that world economic conditions, though not good, would not further deteriorate, allowing them to service the new debt. Careless about details, the region's financial and political leaders did not understand the implications of borrowing from commercial banks at floating interest rates and relatively short maturities.[6] As Barbara Stallings has commented:

In the 1970s there was a peculiar combination of cooperation and competition among the banks. Cooperation arose because the large loans were syndicated. A lead manager brought together a group of banks, which could number in the hundreds, and each took a piece of the loan and shared the risk. Competition entered as the largest banks vied for the "mandate" to organize syndicates and obtain the front-end fees that were more lucrative than interest payments. Thus the lone investment banker traveling to a Latin American city in the 1920s in hopes of selling a $50 million loan was replaced by "pin-striped salesmen" (who) crowded each other in Intercontinental hotel lobbies and the reception rooms of finance ministers in order to offer $500 million. Also unlike the 1920s, U.S. banks were joined in the competitive fray by European and Japanese institutions as the 1970s moved on.[7]

The shift to private commercial bank loans paralleled a drop in loans from industrial countries and from the international financial institutions. These loans were generally at fixed interest rates and relatively long maturities. The 1970s also saw a drop in direct foreign investment in Latin America. And the savings level dipped in the region, public deficits grew, and erratic exchange rate and interest rate policies impacted growth levels.

In the 1990s—a decade that will see almost all of Latin America and the Caribbean governed by civilian, democratic regimes—it is crucial to remember that there were few such governments in the 1970s. On the continent, only Colombia and Venezuela were democratic in the 1970s. Military authoritarian regimes were still in their heyday. They eagerly turned to the international commercial banks to maintain the only credibility they possessed—the capacity to generate high levels of growth. The policy decision to borrow was made by a small group; without functioning parliaments, interest groups, and the free press to challenge their authority, it was easy to justify the new credits as necessary for growth and development.

The situation was even worse if one considers whether or not the borrowed funds were invested or saved; the evidence strongly suggests that they were not. They were spent on "pharonic mega-projects" with limited utility for social development, were dispensed as payoffs, evaporated amid old-fashioned corruption, or left the country as flight capital, never to be seen again.[8]

The ship began to founder in the late 1970s. International oil prices tripled in 1979. The inauguration of Ronald Reagan in 1981, and the policies of his administration, heightened the international economic crisis of 1980–82, which produced unprecedented interest rate levels.[9] Interest payments exploded for the Latin American countries. In the short run, they borrowed more to service the debt. But export earnings were dropping precipitously as demand dropped sharply in the developed world. The banks reacted poorly to the Malvinas-Falklands war in mid-1982; confidence was weakening that Latin America was sufficiently stable to continue to service its debt; and a state of war, unthinkable just months before, raised new fears of disruption in the region.

The Crisis Erupts

In response to the turbulence in the world economy, high interest rates, and diminished export earnings for the Third World, the commercial banks stopped lending in mid-1982. In August of that year, Mexico informed U.S. officials that it was almost out of foreign exchange reserve and could no longer service its debt. During the "Mexican weekend" of August 13–15, the patchwork response that continues today was cobbled together by the U.S. government and international financial institutions.[10]

Some observers believed that Mexico was an isolated case and that a package of international loans would be sufficient to tide it over. This belief was strengthened by the political nature of the debt announcement in Mexico; the Mexican leadership heralded the nationalization of the banking system and the reimposition of exchange controls by President José López Portillo on September 1. The international community was quickly disabused of this false impression in Toronto in September 1982. At the joint annual meeting of the International Monetary Fund and the World Bank, it was suddenly clear that Brazil was the emperor without clothes. Within eight weeks of the Toronto meeting, where Brazil failed to negotiate significant new loans, it too sought a moratorium on the repayment of principal to its commercial bank creditors. Within weeks, the rest of Latin America, with the exception of Colombia, moved to reschedule its outstanding debt.

From the position of the industrial country governments, it was critical to avoid a breakdown of the international financial system. Key to any policy response was a continuation of interest payments by the debtors; otherwise, the private commercial banking system would be in serious danger of collapse. Of particular concern to the U.S. Federal Reserve System and to the White House was the poor health of many of the major banking institutions in the United States. U.S. banks were saddled with bad loans in the housing, agricultural, and energy sectors. To be hit with a moratorium by Third World debtors would prove disastrous.[11] Everything had to be done to maintain interest payments.

Paul Volcker, the head of the U.S. Central Bank, led the charge for the industrial countries. He organized a series of restructuring committees of international commercial banks whose task was to "advise" each of the debtors. The actual purpose of the committees was to coordinate the politics of the renegotiations among the commercial banks and to "police" the Latin American and Caribbean debtors to be sure they were tempted neither by a declaration of unilateral default nor the urge to organize a debtors "cartel."[12]

Stabilization and Adjustment

An immediate consequence of the 1982–83 debt crisis was the necessity of programs of economic stabilization and adjustment. The IMF played the critical role in this process. As Howard Handelman and Werner Baer have written:

> All stabilization and adjustment programs require considerable economic sacrifice from much of the population. Such programs usually try to contain the forces that have produced inflation and to correct distortions that have grown out of the inflationary process. Orthodox programs, favored by the International Monetary Fund . . . and by monetarist policymakers, involve some combination of currency devaluation, reduction of import controls, credit restrictions, reduction of government subsidies on basic consumer goods (including fuel and basic foods), higher prices for public utilities, freeing of prices, wage repression, reduction of public employment, and reduction of the fiscal deficit. These policies usually produce a slowdown of economic growth, or even a period of decline. Thus, stabilization confronts policymakers with the problem of how to allocate economic sacrifices. Should they be evenly shared by all socioeconomic groups, or should they be borne more heavily by specific sectors?[13]

The answer, of course, is clear. The heaviest burden has been carried by the poorest segments of Latin America. Government after government undertook IMF-monitored programs of adjustment and stabilization. The quickest way to achieve IMF goals, necessary for multilateral and private commercial bank credits, was by cutting the "social" budget. This was feasible in some countries because military governments could do so without fear of rebuke. Fledgling democracies did it with trepidation—or postponed the inevitable for a year or two until forced to take the steps required to maintain their creditworthiness.[14] From the perspective of the industrial world, the issue was whether or not the Latin American governments would bite the bullet and do as they were told—or react collectively.

Latin America Reacts

The latter concern was a real one, from the position of the commercial banks and the industrial countries. As the frightening dimensions of the combined international economic crisis and the adjustment measures that were being demanded by the combined creditors became apparent to Latin American leaders, they reacted. On February 11, 1983, President Osvaldo Hurtado of Ecuador wrote to the executive secretaries of the Economic Commission for Latin America and the Caribbean (ECLAC) and the Latin American Economic System (SELA). The Ecuadorean chief executive requested the two entities to "prepare as soon as possible a set of proposals designed to develop the response capacity of Latin America and to consolidate its systems of co-operation."[15]

The two organizations drafted a document entitled "The Bases for a Latin American Response to the International Economic Crisis" in May 1983. The document was discussed at a meeting in Quito that month and again in August, when a decision was taken to convene a heads-of-government conference in January 1984 in Quito. In the interim, the Inter-American Economic and Social Council (CIES) of the Organization of American States (OAS) organized a "Specialized Conference on External Financing in Latin America and the Caribbean" in Caracas in September 1983. The ECLAC-SELA basic document served as a "reference" for the Caracas conference. Regrettably, the moribund meeting in Venezuela would prove to be the only spark of interest on the part of the OAS to join the debate about the resolution of the debt crisis.

In January 1984, at the heads-of-government meeting, a "Declaration of Quito" and a "Plan of Action" were approved. The declaration called for an immediate response from the creditor countries to ameliorate the dramatic fall in living standards and the economic and financial crisis that afflicted the region. It was widely noted that a democratic trend had begun in Latin America. Newly elected civilian regimes were desperate to find a solution both to the impossible situation they had inherited from their predecessors and the further worsening of the economic situation in the mid-1980s.[16]

In May 1984, the presidents of Brazil, Colombia, Mexico, and Argentina issued a joint letter that dramatically called for help from the industrial countries. It was ignored. In June 1984, seven Latin American heads of state addressed an urgent letter to the Group of Seven, about to convene for its annual economic summit in London. The letter called for a "constructive dialogue among creditor and borrowing countries." The Latin Americans stated that it was impossible to imagine that their financial problems could be resolved only by "contacting banks or through the isolated participation of international financial organizations." Deflecting the Latin American's entreaty, the final communiqué of the London Summit brusquely rejected the call for negotiations and offered "help" only if the Latin governments reduced their spending and worked to put their houses in order.

The growing frustration of the Latin American political leaders led to the organization of the Cartagena Consensus group in June 1984. Speaking at the opening of the meeting, President Belisario Betancur of Colombia stated: "Latin America's foreign debt service has become so burdensome that it threatens the very stability of the international monetary system and the survival of the democratic process in various countries."[17] The Cartagena conference strongly endorsed the Quito declaration and called for a response from the industrial countries. The Cartagena group's finance ministers and foreign ministers met subsequently in 1984 and in 1985 but without any meaningful outcome. Another letter was addressed to the economic summit, meeting in June 1985 in Bonn; it too was unsuccessful.

It was clear that the strategy of the industrial countries was one of buying time—of the "containment" of the crisis by dealing with one country at a time and avoiding any "contamination" of the rest while the worst case was dealt with. Thus, a series of emergency packages, bridge loans, and credits were forthcoming from 1982 through 1985. A drastic cutback in the living standards in the debtor countries was the other side of the coin, of course. The region severely cut imports and generated large trade surpluses to pay the interest on the outstanding debt. Latin America, by 1983, had become a capital exporter, an anomaly in the theoretical development literature. Latin American governments, desperate to retain access to the international financial community, particularly for critical revolving trade credits needed to support the export surplus program, accepted the creditors' scheme.

Why did Latin America's efforts to act collectively fail? There is no easy answer to the question. A number of reasons account for the politically ineffective strategy of the Latin American states. Many were new democracies and their leaders were uncertain of how far they could go in pressing their case with the industrial countries. Any effective strategy would require the participation of both Mexico and Brazil—and one or the other was usually following its own strategy during the 1980s. The tactics of "divide and conquer" by the industrial countries were brilliant—from their perspective. The United States was given the "lead" in responding to Latin America and it was able to apply Paul Volcker's "quarantine" scheme with great success. Latin America found that it had few allies in the industrial world, and the Third World was a sympathetic but ineffective ally in the debt struggle. As Richard Feinberg has written: "The Latin American nations—individually or collectively—never really had their own debt strategy. . . . Whereas the creditors—public and private—overtly organized to coordinate strategies for managing old debts as well as for providing new loans under certain conditions, the debtors remained independent from each other. Individual debtors, too, failed to devise or articulate very clear strategies beyond seeking to remain current on interest payments, regain credit worthiness, and minimize the costs of refinancing."[18]

Democracy also provided a surprising "escape valve" for the tensions in the Latin American countries. Contrary to many fears that the debt crisis would destroy fledgling democracies, they have survived the lost decade and have been able to convince their people of the need to work with, not against, the international financial community.[19] There are other reasons, of course, but these would appear to be the major lines of thought as to why collective action produced little, if any, progress in the 1980s.

The Baker Plan

By 1985 the industrial governments sensed a sharp increase in "debt fatigue." At his inauguration in July 1985, President Alán García declared that Peru would allocate no more than 10 percent of its annual export earnings to service the debt. A "Declaration of Lima," signed by the Latin American leaders attending the Peruvian ceremony, called on the industrial countries to accept coresponsibility for the debt crisis and to recognize the linkage between interest payments and export earnings. At the same meeting, the Support Group was created to assist the Central American Contadora process in Central America. Fidel Castro convened a widely reported, but ineffective, series of debt meetings in Havana in the summer of 1985. And at the United Nations General Assembly meeting in September 1985, Presidents José Sarney of Brazil and Alán García of Peru, among others, were sharply critical of the lack of response to the plight of the debtor countries.

In the ensuing years, significant political changes had taken place in Washington, D.C. The most important change was the transfer from the White House to the Treasury of James A. Baker III. As Treasury secretary, Baker was now the Reagan administration's coordinator for a response to the debt crisis. The second Reagan term, while virulently ideological in its Central American policy, was more benign on broader hemispheric issues. At the joint meeting of the IMF and the World Bank in Seoul in October 1985, the Baker Plan was announced. It had three components: the first called for continued adjustment among the debtor countries, and the second stipulated that the private commercial banks would lend an additional $20 billion over a three-year period; based on the third, the World Bank and the Inter-American Development Bank would provide new loans totaling $9 billion over three years.

The Baker Plan made good headlines but it did little to address the debt burden.

The economic summit in Tokyo in June 1986 laconically endorsed the Baker Plan but did not indicate any change of policy on the part of the industrial countries. At the Venice economic summit, in June 1987, Baker announced an "enhancement" of the Baker Plan that he termed a "Menu of Options." The menu was a wish list of possible financial mechanisms for reducing Latin America's debt ranging from debt-equity conversion schemes, to exit bonds, to project lending, and on-lending. But the menu failed to reduce the debt. Many governments were wary of debt-equity schemes because they increased foreign ownership of vital resources and proved to be inflationary; capital markets were—and are—underdeveloped in most countries and the widespread use of equity swaps as a debt solution was not feasible. In addition, the secondary markets for debt-backed equities and securities are relatively thin in the region and such instruments often fluctuate sharply in response to political statements or short-term economic developments in the debtor countries.

The announcement of the Menu of Options had been preceded by a dramatic decision at Citicorp, the lead bank in the restructuring process and one of the major creditors of all of the Latin American states, that it would allocate $3 billion to its loan-loss reserve fund precisely to protect itself from bad Third World loans. The U.S. Treasury and the Federal Reserve supported the decision; other commercial banks in the United States did not, as a comparable move by them would be highly costly in terms of earnings and investor returns.

The year 1987 saw a series of initiatives that indicated no one had any new answers to the debt crisis. In September, the conservative *Financial Times* of London questioned whether or not a "bits and pieces" approach was sufficient:

> The question is whether muddling through is still the best strategy or whether the governments of the developed countries should themselves provide resources to solve the problem.
>
> Muddling through is always easy, but is it enough? It is difficult to believe that the running sore of developing country debt will be healed without a willingness of major developed countries to contribute to the treatment.[20]

That theme was echoed by the newly organized Group of Eight Latin American states, which met in Acapulco, Mexico, for its first summit meeting in 1987. In the final document, the group declared: "The economic crisis undermines democracy in the region because it neutralises the legitimate efforts of our peoples to improve their living standards. It is contradictory that the same people who call for democracy also impose, in world economic relations, conditionality and adjustment schemes that compromise that very democracy, and which they themselves do not apply in correcting their own imbalances."[21]

Latin America Adjusts

Quietly, the democratic governments of Latin America had begun to realize in the middle of the lost decade that the old development models of the early post–world war years were now inadequate. Some countries came to that realization sooner than others. Many viewed the dramatic reversal of Chile's economic fortunes in the mid-1980s with quiet admiration but often with the fear that it required an authoritarian regime to implement such drastic structural adjustment measures. The fact that the administration of Mexican President Miguel de la Madrid was beginning to do the same strengthened the apprehension. It was widely believed that the changes under way in Mexico were due to the pervasive influence of the Institutional Revolutionary party (PRI) and its massive bureaucratic strength throughout the country.

The failure of the Cruzado Plan in Brazil in 1986 and the slow collapse of President Raúl Alfonsín's Austral Plan in Argentina further cautioned Latin America's leadership from embracing the siren call of deep adjustment.[22] But by the late 1980s, a number of countries had adopted far-reaching goals of internal change. The economies of the region were being opened to new investment, privatization schemes were under way to transfer to the private sector inefficient and bloated state companies, and it became widely recognized that the internal debt was in most countries as serious, if not more so, than the external debt. Exchange rate policies had to be adjusted; exports needed to be diversified and interest rates stabilized.

Latin America's leaders understood that they remained highly vulnerable to exogenous developments and trends. But by the last years of the decade, muddling through was all that was available. The international financial system had reached a "steady state." Restructuring of the region's debt was an ongoing process, but always on a case-by-case basis. Volatile interest rates had steadied and dropped. Thanks to the absorptive capacity of the U.S. market, the region's export push succeeded in generating high trade surpluses for many countries.[23]

Did Latin America receive many benefits from its adjustment in the mid-1980s? It obtained very few. Indeed, the situation tightened in 1987–88 as regional banks in the United States began to write off Latin American debt. The Bank of Boston, for example, announced in December 1987 that it would write off $200 million. It was widely understood that the bank had given up hope of repayment of that portion of its loan portfolio to the debtor countries. Other regional banks followed throughout 1988. The decision of the "regionals" to opt out polarized the U.S. banking community. The so-called money center banks, primarily in New York and California, had comparatively thin reserves against their loans to the Third World but were under pressure within the Baker Plan to make new loans. The regional banks, with relatively small exposure, were healthier than the money center banks and able to reserve quickly against possible losses—and to opt out of any forced new lending.

By 1988–89 the decade's crisis had abated. The industrial countries were occupied with East-West questions. There was the general impression, with the exception of Chile, Bolivia, and Mexico, and a few of the smaller Central American and Caribbean states, that Latin American governments were irresolute, disorganized, well-meaning perhaps, but unwilling to understand the major trends in the globalization of the world economy. If they were unable to understand the need to restructure in order to compete, there was little that the industrial countries could or would do to help them. Democracy had survived. Elites had not brought back the billions of dollars of flight capital that would provide a comfortable cushion for efforts at renewed growth in the region. And efforts such as those of the Group of Eight, and other regional groups, were ineffective and incapable of backing up their desperation with any action that would be seen as threatening to the industrial countries.

That perception changed sharply in the United States at the end of the Reagan administration. The new government of Mexican President Carlos Salinas de Gortari, which took office in December 1988, made it clear in 1989 that continued restructuring without debt relief was unacceptable. The Salinas government's willingness to challenge the conventional wisdom of the 1980s regarding the debt strategy was matched in the United States by a growing concern with the bilateral relationship. A period of "Mexico-bashing" in the mid-1980s had yielded to a realization that American foreign policy and security interests were deeply impacted by events in Mexico. If debt was a higher priority for Mexico, it would need to be for the United States as well.[24]

The Brady Plan

The year 1988 was a "slide year" in debt discussions. With the upcoming presidential election in the United States, it was clear that the Reagan administration would take no new action. Besides, Treasury Secretary Baker was deeply involved in running the campaign of then Vice-President Bush. With the victory of the Bush-Quayle ticket in November 1989, the debt issue moved quickly. The president-elect met with Mexican President Salinas in Texas. It was "leaked" during the transition that the new American government would move beyond the Baker Plan and the Menu of Options soon after the inauguration in January 1989.

Secretary of the Treasury Nicholas Brady announced what has been termed the "Brady Plan" in March 1989. It stressed voluntary debt reduction by the banks—

writing off loans in negotiation with the developing countries—as well as new lending to help them pay off old loans and develop the means to produce more foreign exchange and put their debt burden behind them. The plan relies heavily on the IMF and the World Bank to lend money to those countries undertaking structural reform to help them to cut back on their outstanding obligations. A total of $28.5 billion was originally put forward in support of the new program, $24 billion from the IMF and the bank and $4.5 billion from the government of Japan. The goal was to reduce interest outflows by $7 billion a year for three years—but it was quickly pointed out that the U.S. target would require $40 to $50 billion of new funds.

At first, the private commercial banking community, highly vulnerable to reduction of its Third World debt exposure, resisted. Throughout 1989 it signaled its fatigue with Third World debt. In September 1989, Manufacturers Hanover announced that it would add $950 million of a Japanese infusion of $1.4 billion of fresh capital to its loan-loss reserve fund. Chase Manhattan followed with a decision to increase its loan-loss reserve by $1.9 billion. And J. P. Morgan stated that it would add $2 billion to its reserve, a step that left it with 100 percent of its medium-and long-term exposure to Third World debt fully covered. The Morgan message was loud and clear. It indicated that it was turning its back on the new lending component of the Brady Plan. Now that it was fully covered, it had the flexibility to do with its loan portfolio what it wanted, without the pressure to grant new loans so that the old ones could continue to be serviced.

A second obstacle was the inability of the United States to provide more public funding for debt reduction. The debate between the U.S. private commercial banks and the Bush administration was clear—and bitter. The banks urged the Bush team to make more resources available in order to encourage them to undertake greater debt reduction and to provide guarantees for new loans. When he announced the bank's loan-loss reserve decision, the chairman of Morgan stated: "We are very concerned about debtor countries' rising expectations of the magnitude of debt reduction possible under the Brady initiative, when sufficient resources to encourage sizable voluntary debt reduction programs have not been provided by industrial countries."[25]

By the end of 1989, a brief power struggle erupted. The players were the banks, the Third World countries, and the governments of the industrial countries. The central question was, Would the U.S. government and the other industrial countries provide sufficient "enhancements" for the private commercial banks to proceed with debt reduction? The banks were challenging a deficit-ridden U.S. administration to make a massive financial contribution to allow debt reduction to move ahead. To the degree that Latin America and the Caribbean are viewed by the industrial world as an area of special responsibility for the United States, they look to Washington to resolve the issue, with minor contributions from the Japanese, who are seeking ways to buy friends with their trade surplus.

The issue was clear: ". . . fundamental is the question about whether sufficient official funds will be available to provide significant debt relief for qualifying countries."[26] By 1990 few observers were willing to bet that the official funds would be made available. An alternative, of course, was for the industrial governments to apply more coercion against commercial banks to forgive debts, "a step that so far they have felt unable to take. Given a quasi-voluntary format, it is far less clear that there is enough."[27]

If a turning point—which broke the logjam in 1990–91—can be identified, it was the Brady Plan negotiation between the banks and Mexico. The government of President Salinas, inaugurated in December 1988, had inherited a difficult economic and political situation. Although the initial reforms undertaken by his predecessor, Miguel de la Madrid, appeared promising, they had not yet restored confidence in the country's economy. The social fallout from the debt crisis in the 1980s had generated a strong, populist reaction to the Salinas candidacy. Only the indefatigable efforts of the ruling Institutional Revolutionary party, which has never lost a presidential election, guaranteed Salinas's hairline victory.

Salinas entered office with an excellent economic team; most of its members had worked with him in the 1980s in the de la Madrid government. Salinas was determined to continue the "deepening" of the reform process and to press immediately for international financial concessions to restore the creditworthiness of Mexico. That was essential, he reasoned, to begin to put the 1980s behind him and to begin to attract new direct foreign investment and capital flows. Ironically, what was viewed by Mexico as an important breakthrough when it was completed in February 1990 was interpreted otherwise internationally. One commentator stated that "the jury is now in on the 1989 debt restructuring agreement between Mexico and the international financial community. Unfortunately, the deal is a bad one for Mexico. The agreement, signed on Feb. 4, falls far short of the country's needs, has not and will not produce the desired effects, and leaves the nation in a woefully weak position for future negotiations."[28] Even the *Financial Times* (London), more laconically, stated that "one hates to spoil a good party. But it is now clear that if Mexico eventually puts its debt problem behind it, the contribution from the new debt accord will have been modest indeed."[29]

Throughout 1990, additional voices were raised to express misgivings about the Brady Plan. The Institute of International Finance (IIF) in Washington, D.C., a think tank that speaks on behalf of the commercial banks, stated in May that the plan had encouraged an "alarming increase in country arrears to commercial bank creditors." The IIF report blamed the Brady initiative for engendering "a loss of discipline in the [international financial] system and the build-up of payments arrears to commercial banks and official agencies."[30] The IIF concern reflects a related issue of growing concern in financial circles: the health of the private commercial banks. Third World debt is a critical element in the poor state of health of the commercial banks but it is only one element. Bad loans in the real estate and energy sectors, the impact of the Savings and Loan fiasco, and a general sluggishness in the American economy have raised questions about the future of the private banking system as we now know it. The Latin American debt remains a problem for the private banks as much as it does the governments of the region. It was in mid- or late 1990 that the terms of reference about the Latin American debt changed. The stark reality confronting Latin America in the 1990s was summarized by the Economic Commission for Latin America and the Caribbean in late 1989: "The economic crisis that has affected Latin America and the Caribbean during most of the 1980s persisted during the last year of the decade, as the average per capita product fell for the second year running, this time by 1%, while inflation averaged the unprecedented 1,000%. . . . The region's expanding trade surplus continued to be insufficient to cover the huge burden of debt service and only five Latin American and Caribbean countries managed to meet those commitments fully and timely in 1989."[31]

ECLAC continues to report that the net resource transfer abroad in 1989 reached nearly $25 billion—the equivalent of almost 18 percent of the value of the region's export of goods and services and of approximately 3 percent of its gross domestic product. If Mexico is excluded from these figures, the net resource transfer abroad in fact increased to nearly $23 billion, from less than $18 billion in 1988. The 1989 performance suggests that "most of the countries of the region seem now to be reaching the limits of their capacity for adjusting to external constraints, on the basis of their present structures of production."[32] But just as ECLAC was issuing its pessimistic assessment, the international financial markets rediscovered Latin America. That rediscovery has changed the nature of the debate regarding regional debt in the 1990s.

The Enterprise for the Americas Initiative

An additional factor in the debt debate emerged in June 1990 with the announcement at the White House of the Enterprise for the Americas Initiative. Heralded as a "new partnership for trade, investment, and growth" in the Americas, it called for free and fair trade within the hemisphere; domestic and foreign investment, new capital flows, a reduction in debt burdens, and an improvement of the environment; and additional support for debt and debt-service reduction.

As reported one year later, the initiative was "a triumph of timing which promised rewards for the sort of reforms the Latin Americans had already be-gun."[33] But the movement on specifics has been slow. In mid-1992, negotiations were nearly completed on the North American Free Trade Agreement (NAFTA) with Mexico, Canada, and the United States seeking a new concept of North American trade. "Framework" agreements for freer trade have been signed with sixteen countries, as well as the southern common market of Argentina, Brazil, Paraguay, and Uruguay. Chile received the first Enterprise debt reduction and investment package in 1991. Progress has been made in raising $1.5 billion from the United States and other industrial countries for the creation of an investment fund proposed by President Bush. The fund is intended partly to support privati-zation efforts.

The problem has been the U.S. Congress, which has vocally endorsed the program but has been slow to pass legislation necessary for further action. Of all the trade, food, and foreign aid credits the president wants to make available for debt reduction, only forgiveness on some of the food debt has been authorized. Bills granting reduction on the rest were moving slowly through both houses in 1992.

The most dramatic result of the initiative has been the enthusiasm of the Latin American governments. When President Bush visited South America in December 1990, he received an enthusiastic endorsement of the initiative. All of the Latin heads of states, during their visits to Washington, have supported the program. Combined with the economic restructuring that continues throughout the hemi-sphere, it has changed the tone and the nature of the debate about U.S.–Latin American ties for the first time in decades.

What remains to be done is substantial. But the probably successful conclusion of the NAFTA will provide an important impetus for further trade action. Invest-ment is returning to Latin America. But it is the stock of debt that remains the principal uncertainty to sustained, renewed growth in the hemisphere.

The New Realities of the 1990s

The successful conclusion of the Brady Plan for Mexico was followed with agree-ments for Venezuela (March 1990), Costa Rica (May 1990), and Uruguay (January 1991) (the formalities and legalities often took many additional months of discus-sion, but the fundamental agreement was the essential element in the negotiation). Chile and Colombia continued their effective policy of not seeking to renegotiate their foreign debt by prudent macro-economic management and, in the case of Chile, an early commitment to liberalization, privatization, and opening of its economy to foreign investment on very favorable and competitive terms.

By 1991 the generalized commitment to reform in Latin America was recognized worldwide. Salinas in Mexico, Aylwin in Chile, Menem in Argentina, Pérez in Venezuela, and others were publicly and politically supportive of a rapid shift from the post-1945 economic development models. Only Brazil's President Fernando Collor de Mello, who was personally in favor of such reform, found himself blocked by a recalcitrant congress, regional interests, and a new constitution— approved in 1988—that tied the government's hands from moving rapidly to join the other countries in the hemisphere.

That commitment, and the successful completion of the Brady Plan negotiations, rekindled investor interest in the region—suddenly and dramatically. In January 1991 the *Economist* commented on Secretary Brady's plan, recognizing that while vague at its initiation, "nonetheless, in an admittedly modest way, his idea is beginning to work."[34]

At about the same time, the Inter-American Development Bank (IDB) released the findings of a study indicating that continued reform measures—trade liberalization, the return of flight capital, foreign investment, and internal structural reforms—would yield important benefits: "Under these conditions GDP growth rates of between 3.9 and 5.2 percent are financially sustainable for Argentina, Brazil, Colombia, Chile, Mexico, and Venezuela, provided that some additional net borrowing is channeled to the region. For the seven major Latin American countries, the stock of debt, at $365 billion in 1989, would stabilize at under $380 billion at the end of the century, even without additional debt reduction. The ratio of debt to export earnings would improve from 313 percent in 1989 to 128 percent in the year 2000."[35]

It was also in 1991 that the Janus-like nature of the situation in Latin America and the Caribbean became apparent. Although the IDB study cited above appears sanguine, the annual report of the bank, issued in April 1991, stated that economic reform programs in Latin America had worsened poverty in the region.[36] According to the report, "drastic fiscal adjustment, inflation and stabilization programs have unquestionably exacerbated the problems of poverty existing at the beginning of 1990."[37]

As 1991 progressed, the lines of the debate were clear. Financial markets were moving quickly to capitalize on the strenuous reform efforts of the democratic regimes in Latin America. They had paid little attention to the results—or the implications—of the adjustment process in the late 1980s. The international organizations concerned with social development were attempting to emphasize the cost of the adjustment. But financial markets—and, at times, governments— appeared less than interested.

One important indication of the growing financial interest in Latin America was the pattern of growth in the region's stock markets. In the early 1980s, stock markets were viewed with suspicion. By the early 1990s, the International Finance Corporation (IFC) reported, "the debt crisis of the 1980s forced developing countries to rely more heavily on equity finance. The embracing of free market principles made rapid development of financial infrastructure a priority. But the IFC also stresses the emergence of competitive 'world class' companies, with a growing appetite for equity finance."[38] As the appetite for new capital grew in 1991, it was reported that Latin America's private and state-owned companies sold over $5 billion of bonds to investors outside their borders in the last two years."[39] The first customers for the new line of debt and equity were wealthy Latin Americans. They had billions of dollars in flight capital outside their countries; it had begun to return. One estimation is that Mexicans brought home $10.7 billion in 1989 and 1990, partly by buying Mexico's internationally traded bonds. Venezuelans repatriated nearly $2 billion and Chileans $1.4 billion.

Quickly, high yields and the improved credit ratings of the issuers in the region attracted North American and European institutions. American insurance companies turned to Latin debt to replace the battered junk bonds in their portfolios. Japanese investors became interested. In 1991 a dozen new funds were investing in Latin stock markets as well as internationally traded shares and bonds.[40]

Even Brazil, by the middle of 1991, had begun to drop its pariahlike reputation of the 1980s. It came to agreement on settling outstanding interest arrears with the private commercial banks and offered a new plan for settling the stock of debt. Salomon Brothers reported that, as a result of the ongoing efforts to normalize the region's international financial relations, capital flows into Latin America grew from $5 billion in 1989 to over $13 billion for 1990.[41] The expectation that all of the major debtor countries in Latin America would return to the international capital markets was proven correct with both Brazil and Argentina able to do so in the last quarter of 1991.

Also by mid-1991 it was widely accepted that Latin America had escaped "the Jaws of Debt."[42] The combination of prudent financial management, macroeconomic reforms, and the attractiveness of Latin America companies that were set up to be privatized had galvanized the international financial markets. But given world economic conditions and the fragile social and political coalitions that have been forged in the countries of the region to achieve the drastic reforms, the critical issue is whether this trend will continue.

Conclusion

As the Latin American debt crisis enters its second decade, it is no longer a crisis for many. The international financial community now views the region—at least, its major countries—positively. The commitment to economic restructuring in the late 1980s by the democratic political leaders has succeeded in attracting the return of flight capital and new capital inflows. The successful Brady Plan negotiations were an essential prerequisite for new investment. Continued reform and liberalization, particularly the privatization of state corporations, has proven to be attractive to investors in search of new and profitable opportunities.

There are clearly dangers. The lack of an agreement in the Uruguay Round of the General Agreement on Tariffs and Trade (GATT) can impact negatively on Latin America's agricultural exports. The emergence of world trading blocs will have implications for the countries of the region. The continued sluggishness of the U.S. economy is of concern to the governments in the hemisphere. And the allure of Eastern Europe as an alternative to Latin America continues to concern the region.

But the rapid negotiations on the North America Free Trade Agreement among Mexico, the United States, and Canada; the South American Common Market (MERCOSUR) of Argentina, Brazil, Paraguay, and Uruguay; a possible common market among the countries of Central America and Mexico; and the bilateral free trade agreements being discussed—Chile and Mexico, Chile and the United States—offer new and important trade and investment opportunities in the hemisphere for the first time in its history.

The critical variable that is infrequently discussed is the cost of adjustment and the decrease of living standards during the 1980s. The challenge of the 1990s is to link the new flows of investment capital to social investment. Latin America's social agenda needs to be given a high priority between now and the end of the century. New capital investment should lead to higher levels of productivity. But that will require skilled, healthy workers who are in short supply in the region given the lack of social investment in recent years. Continued political stability and social peace, at some point, will necessitate a shift in investment priorities on a sustained basis.

The task is not impossible. New resources are now available. The challenge to the successor governments—to follow those who undertook the hard decisions about economic liberalization and privatization—is to maintain the outward-looking economic model of recent years and address the human development challenge that confronts all of the states in the region. As the UNDP study asserts, "the lack of political commitment, not of financial resources, is often the real cause of human neglect."[43] The citizens of the region now await a repetition of the successful financial and economic engineering of recent years in improving the quality of life and addressing the human development imperative of Latin America and the Caribbean.

Notes

1. See "Last Rites in Sight for Debt Crisis," *Financial Times*, April 10, 1991.
2. Ibid.
3. United Nations Development Programme, *Human Development Report*, p. 34.
4. Ibid.

5. Kuczynski, *Latin American Debt*, p. 73.

6. For a comparative analysis of Latin America's phases of indebtedness, see Stallings, *Banker to the Third World*.

7. Ibid., pp. 97–98.

8. Capital flight is discussed in Lessard and Williamson, *Capital Flight*.

9. As I have written elsewhere, "by 1981 the warning signals were apparent to those who wanted to see them. While the ratio of debt service to export earnings in countries such as Indonesia, Korea, and Malaysia remained below the 'safe' level of 15 percent, the debt service ratios in Brazil and Chile rose above 30 percent and reached 35 percent in Mexico and Argentina. World Bank estimates indicate that a single percentage point change in short-term dollar interest rates has an impact each year of more than $1.2 billion on the combined net debt service of Mexico, Brazil, and Argentina, Latin America's three largest borrowers. From 1979 to 1981 the debt servicing of these three key countries rose by $10 billion, or 170 percent." Roett, "The Debt Crisis," pp. 242–43.

10. For background on the Mexican debt crisis, see Ayala and Durán, "Development and Crisis in Mexico," pp. 243–64.

11. The position of the private commercial banks is summarized in Canavan, "The Threat to the International Banking System," pp. 53–59.

12. On the strategy of the industrial countries, see Roett, "How the 'Haves' Manage."

13. Handelman and Baer, "Economic and Political Costs," pp. 2–3.

14. See Wiesner, "State of the Debt Crisis," pp. 25–31.

15. For a discussion of the 1983–84 response of Latin America, see Roett, "Latin America's Debt."

16. For one of the earliest analyses of the relationship between debt and democracy, see Roett, "Democracy and Debt in South America."

17. See Roett, "Latin America's Response," pp. 153–61.

18. Feinberg, "Latin American Debt," p. 60.

19. For a discussion of the survival of democratic regimes in spite of the debt overhang during the 1980s, see Drake, "Debt and Democracy," pp. 39–58.

20. "Strategy for LDC Debt," *Financial Times*, September 30, 1987, p. 26.

21. "Acapulco Sparks a Sense of Unity," *Financial Times*, December 1, 1987, p. 6.

22. For a discussion of the Austral and Cruzado plans, see Kaufman, *Politics of Debt*.

23. David Mulford, a key architect of the Reagan administration's responses to the debt crisis and a major player in the Bush administration, summarizes his viewpoint in "View of the Reagan Administration," pp. 81–86.

24. For background on the Mexican debt, see Trebat, "Mexican Foreign Debt."

25. Sarah Bartlett, "Third World Debt Woes," *New York Times*, September 23, 1989, p. A1.

26. Stephen Fidler, "One Step Closer to a Lighter Burden," *Financial Times*, January 23, 1990, p. 16.

27. Ibid.

28. Jorge C. Castañeda, "Mexico's Dismal Debt Deal," *New York Times*, February 25, 1990.

29. "A Modest Deal for Mexico," *Financial Times*, January 17, 1990, p. 18.

30. Stephen Fidler, "Brady Debt Plan 'Encourages Arrears,'" *Financial Times*, May 4, 1990, p. 3.

31. *CEPAL News*, December 1989, p. 1.

32. Ibid., p. 3.

33. "Bush Initiative Translates Slowly into Action," *Financial Times*, July 18, 1991, p. 7.

34. See "Money in the Well," *Economist*, January 5, 1991, p. 62.

35. Inter-American Development Bank, *The IDB*, p. 5.

36. "Latin American Poverty 'Deepened' by Reforms," *Financial Times*, April 8, 1991.

37. Ibid., p. 7.

38. "A Decade of Change in Emerging Markets," *Financial Times*, May 31, 1991, p. 6.

39. "The Latin Market Comes to Life," *Economist*, June 8, 1991, p. 77.

40. Ibid.

41. "Latin American Borrowers Set to Re-enter the Market," *Financial Times*, August 27, 1991, p. 17.

42. "Latin America Escapes the Jaws of Debt," *Wall Street Journal*, August 29, 1991.

43. United Nations Development Programme, *Human Development Report*, p. 1.

· *Roberto Bouzas*

Chapter Seven · U.S.–LATIN AMERICAN

. TRADE RELATIONS:

. ISSUES IN THE 1980S AND

· PROSPECTS FOR THE 1990S

Following the 1982 external debt crisis in Latin America, financial issues became a leading concern in hemispheric economic debates and trade matters were relegated to a secondary role. This order of priorities is likely to be reversed in the 1990s, as foreign trade and investment return to the forefront under the influence of far-reaching policy transformation and an evolving international trading system.

In the 1980s the importance of the United States as a trading partner for Latin America increased substantially, whereas the role of the region as a supplier to the United States diminished markedly. This change aggravated the typically imbalanced nature of U.S.–Latin American trade relations. However, it did not affect all countries in the region to the same extent or with similar intensity. Rather, the trend further strengthened the by-now historical process of economic differentiation within Latin America.

The trade policies of the 1980s also departed from their dominant postwar status. On the one hand, U.S. policies became more assertive, fostering U.S. objectives by a combination of discriminatory practices, procedural protectionism, and aggressive unilateralism; consequently, the scope of trade frictions expanded significantly. On the other hand, particularly in the late 1980s, Latin American trade regimes generally moved away from the protectionist stance typical of import-substitution industrialization (ISI). This shift was the result of such factors as the perceived failure of inward-oriented development models, the export imperative arising from the need to finance large interest payments, and policy conditionality (the provision of financial assistance subject to policy commitments) enforced by international financial institutions (IFIs).

It is an interesting contrast—and one that suggests a potential for conflict in the future—that precisely when Latin American trade regimes have become more outward-oriented, U.S. trade policies have shifted toward a more assertive and, to a certain extent, protectionist stance. However, the turn of the decade has given rise to enhanced expectations regarding the potential for hemispheric trade cooperation. The launching of negotiations to create a North American Free Trade Agreement (NAFTA) and the Bush administration's proposal to gradually move toward a Western Hemisphere Free Trade Agreement (WHFTA) undoubtedly contributed to this new sentiment.

Although U.S.–Latin American trade and investment relations are likely to expand substantially in the 1990s—especially when compared to the dismal record of the previous decade—a number of fundamental questions still remain. How is the prospect for enhanced hemispheric trade cooperation to be made compatible with mounting U.S. domestic pressures in favor of protection and a more aggressive U.S. stance on international trade issues? Will recent changes in Latin American trade regimes and gradual accommodation by countries in the region to U.S. demands reduce hemispheric trade conflicts? More fundamentally, is the near prospect of NAFTA and the trade component of the Bush initiative likely to lead to regionalization in the hemisphere or, rather, to further differentiation within Latin America? This chapter explores major developments in hemispheric trade relations in the 1980s and, by addressing some of these questions, it provides a number of insights for the 1990s.

U.S.–Latin American Trade Relations in the 1980s

During the 1980s, two major trends in hemispheric trade relations could be observed. First, throughout the decade there was a dramatic decline in the importance of the region as a trading partner for the United States. This shift was influenced, on the one hand, by the external debt crisis, which sharply reduced Latin American import capacity, and, on the other, by the relatively high share of primary commodities (particularly oil) in Latin American exports to the United States.

Second, Latin America as a whole reversed the tendency toward regional diversification of its foreign trade pattern, which had characterized most of the postwar period. Actually, throughout the 1980s the region became more dependent on the United States both as a source of imports as well as an outlet for regional exports. This reinforced a long-standing feature of hemispheric trade relations: the disparate relative importance of the partners.

Table 3. Latin American Share of U.S. Foreign Trade, 1980–82 to 1987–89

	1980–82	1987–89
Latin American Share of U.S.		
Total Foreign Trade[a]	17.0%	12.5%
Share of U.S. Total Exports		
Latin America	16.9	13.4
Mexico	6.6	6.4
South America	7.4	4.4
Caribbean	2.9	2.6
Share of U.S. Exports to Latin America		
Mexico	39.1	47.3
South America	43.8	33.2
Caribbean	17.1	19.5
Share of U.S. Total Imports		
Latin America	15.3	11.7
Mexico	5.4	5.3
South America	6.1	4.9
Caribbean	3.8	1.5
Share of U.S. Imports from Latin America		
Mexico	35.3	45.4
South America	39.9	41.8
Caribbean	24.8	12.8

Source: Author's calculations based on data from U.S. Department of Commerce, *U.S. Foreign Trade Highlights, 1989* (Washington, D.C.: GPO, 1990), p. x.
a. Imports and exports.

Latin America as a Market and a Supplier

In the last decade, aggregate U.S.–Latin American trade flows (exports plus imports) as a share of total U.S. trade fell by about a quarter, from an average of 17 percent in 1980–82 to just over 12 percent in 1987–89 (Table 3). The diminishing importance of the region as a trading partner for the United States affected its role both as a supplier of U.S. imports and as an outlet for U.S. exports. Whereas the latter might have been expected as a result of the fall in imports brought about by the external debt crisis, the former was particularly disturbing, especially because it took place in a period of rapid U.S. import growth.

U.S. Exports

The external debt crisis and the forced adjustment that followed the rationing of international credit in the early 1980s sharply curtailed Latin America's import capacity. Given the role of the United States as a leading supplier to the region, this turnaround in demand severely hit U.S. exporters. Only in 1988 did the value of U.S. exports to Latin America exceed the peak recorded in 1981; by 1989 they were just 17 percent above the values recorded at the beginning of the decade. But this was not the case for all subregions: whereas by the end of the decade U.S. exports to Mexico and the Caribbean had grown vigorously, those to South America were still 18.1 percent below the peak achieved before the external debt crisis.[1]

As a result of falling import capacity, the Latin American share of total U.S. exports fell from 16.9 percent in 1980–82 to 13.4 percent in 1987–89 (Table 3). Again, although the importance of all subregions as outlets for U.S. exports diminished, the intensity of the contraction varied widely. South America experienced the largest fall, contributing to most of the overall reduction, while the decrease in Mexican and Caribbean shares was more moderate. Indeed, following rapid import growth in the late 1980s, by 1989 Mexico turned out to be a more important market for U.S. exports than at the beginning of the decade.

These divergent trends produced a major change in the trade flows between the United States and the various Latin American subregions. Whereas Mexico and the Caribbean increased their shares (the former markedly), South America experienced a sharp reduction (Table 3).

U.S. Imports

Throughout the 1980s, the value of U.S. imports from Latin America grew—albeit with some fluctuations—by almost 50 percent. Again, this expansion was unequal among the various subregions: while imports from Mexico and South America expanded vigorously, those from the Caribbean fell by more than a third.

Notwithstanding U.S. import growth from Latin America, the region's market share fell from 15.3 percent of total U.S. imports in 1980–82 to 11.7 in 1987–89 (Table 3). Although this contraction affected all Latin American subregions, it was most intense for the Caribbean (its share almost halved) and, to a lesser extent, South America.

The relatively disappointing performance of Latin American exports to the United States is partly explained by the region's considerable dependence on primary commodities, particularly oil. As Table 4 shows, in the early 1980s primary commodities (including oil) accounted for more than three-quarters of U.S. imports from the region, a much higher share than total U.S. imports (42 percent). Although the composition of U.S. imports worldwide changed throughout the decade (the share of primary commodities fell), imports from Latin America remained heavily concentrated in primary products (45.3 percent in 1987–89). Given the performance of primary commodity (especially oil) prices throughout the period, it comes as no surprise that U.S. imports from countries

Table 4. Commodity Composition of U.S. Imports, 1980–82 to 1987–89 (Percentage of total imports)

	World	Latin America	Mexico	South America	Caribbean
1980–82					
Primary commodities[a]	12.0%	24.9%	12.3%	32.9%	30.2%
Mineral fuels	30.0	51.3	52.5	43.3	57.4
Manufactured goods[b]	55.3	22.5	32.0	20.9	9.7
Not classified	2.7	1.3	3.2	2.9	2.7
1987–89					
Primary commodities[a]	8.9	20.9	12.4	26.0	35.4
Mineral fuels	10.4	24.4	16.2	35.0	18.3
Manufactured goods[b]	77.7	51.3	67.0	36.9	42.5
Not classified	3.0	3.4	4.4	2.1	3.8

Source: Author's calculations based on data from U.S. Department of Commerce, *U.S. Foreign Trade Highlights, 1989* (Washington, D.C.: GPO, 1990), p. x.
a. Excluding mineral fuels.
b. Standard International Trade Classification (SITC) 5+6+7+8.

and subregions with higher-than-average shares of primary commodities in total exports experienced, as a general rule, a relative contraction. In the case of Mexico, the high rate of growth of manufacturing exports to the United States helped to counteract the impact of falling oil prices on aggregate export values.[2]

The United States as a Market and a Supplier

Traditionally, the United States has been an important Latin American trading partner, although this has varied widely by subregion and country. As a general rule, as one moves southward in the hemisphere, the U.S. share of foreign trade falls markedly.[3] Throughout the 1980s, in contrast to previous years, the importance of the United States both as a supplier and as an outlet for regional exports has increased, with the share of two-way trade rising from below a third of total Latin American external trade in 1980–82 to 37 percent in 1987–89 (Table 5).

The rising concentration of Latin American exports in the U.S. market is mostly explained by the performance of Mexico and South America. In fact, the United States absorbed 61.4 percent of Mexican exports by the end of the decade, as compared to 56.6 percent in 1980–82. The U.S. share of South American exports also expanded, from 21.5 percent in 1980–82 to 28.6 percent in 1987–89. For the Caribbean, exports to the United States as a share of total exports remained stable at around 48 percent.

Table 5. U.S. Share of Latin American Foreign Trade, 1980–82 to 1987–89

	1980–82	1987–89
U.S. Share of Total Latin American Foreign Trade[a]	32.3%	37.0%
U.S. Share of Total Exports		
Latin America	32.7	37.2
Mexico	56.6	61.4
Caribbean	48.2	48.8
South America	21.5	28.6
U.S. Share of Total Imports		
Latin America	31.9	36.7
Mexico	62.0	67.2
South America	27.1	30.3
Caribbean	22.6	37.4

Source: Author's calculations based on data from International Monetary Fund, *Direction of Trade Statistics Yearbook* (Washington, D.C.: IMF, 1990), p. x.
a. Exports and imports.

U.S. exports to Latin America increased even more sharply, with the U.S. share rising from 31.9 percent in 1980–82 to 36.7 percent by the end of the decade (Table 5). However, this shift was more broadly based and affected all subregions. Import concentration rose most rapidly in the Caribbean, pushed by a diminishing share of crude petroleum in total imports.

These trends enhanced the role of the United States in Latin American external trade. Thus, not only a larger share of regional exports was rendered more vulnerable to fluctuations in U.S. aggregate demand, but also U.S. trade policies became more relevant in determining Latin American access to external markets.

U.S.–Latin American Trade Balances

Aggravated by the external debt crisis, U.S. trade deficits with Latin America increased almost fivefold between 1980–82 and 1987–89 (Table 6). By the end of the period, however, they were still relatively minor compared to total U.S. disequilibria, accounting for just over 7 percent of aggregate U.S. trade deficits.

Again, these figures mask sharply divergent paths between U.S. trade balances with Mexico and South America, on the one hand, and the Caribbean, on the other. Whereas in the former cases the United States went from a slight surplus in 1980–82 to a deficit in the late 1980s, in the case of the Caribbean U.S. trade balances shifted from a sizable deficit in the early 1980s (about 10 percent of total

Table 6. U.S. and Latin American Trade Balances, 1980–82 to 1987–89

	1980–82	1987–89
U.S. Trade Balance[a]		
World	−$38.179M	−$126.681M
Latin America	−1.850	−9.141
Mexico	701	−3.500
South America	994	−7.549
Caribbean	−3.567	1.953
Latin American Share of U.S.		
Overall Trade Deficit	4.8%	7.2%
Latin American Trade Balance[a]		
World	−$6.853M	$ 11.984M
United States	−3.103	4.723
U.S. Share of Latin American Trade Balance	45.3%	39.4%

Sources: Author's calculations based on data from U.S. Department of Commerce, *U.S. Foreign Trade Highlights, 1989* (Washington, D.C.: GPO, 1990), p. x, and International Monetary Fund, *Direction of Trade Statistics Yearbook* (Washington, D.C.: IMF, 1990), p. x.
a. Totals may not add up due to minor discrepancies in coverage.

U.S. disequilibria) to a surplus in 1987–89. Overall, and notwithstanding the Caribbean Basin Economic Recovery Act of 1984, by the late 1980s the Caribbean was the only subregion where the United States was still recording trade surpluses.

The picture from the Latin American standpoint looks somewhat different. Mirroring the importance of the United States as a trading partner, bilateral trade balances closely followed the pattern of overall Latin American balances, moving from a deficit position in the early 1980s to a surplus position by the end of the decade. In both periods the United States accounted for a large share of Latin America's overall trade balance: whereas in 1980–82 deficits with the United States amounted to about 45 percent of total Latin American trade disequilibria, in the late 1980s bilateral surpluses contributed to almost 40 percent of the region's excess of exports over imports.

U.S.–Latin American Trade Policy Issues

J. Michael Finger has characterized U.S. trade policies in the postwar period as a combination of liberalization and selective protection. Indeed, the fact that the major objective of U.S. trade policy in the first three decades of the postwar period has been the creation of an open world trading system has been no obstacle to episodes of discrimination and/or selective protection.[4] For most of that period, however, the United States fostered an open world trade environment by means of a benevolent approach based on the principles of multilateralism and nondiscrimination.

Since its inception in 1947 and until the late 1970s, the General Agreement on Tariffs and Trade (GATT) was the main vehicle for promoting U.S. trade objectives. Yet for Latin America, it generally ranked second to bilateral negotiations or other multilateral forums, such as the United Nations Conference on Trade and Development (UNCTAD).

Within this broader context, market access issues have provided most of the flesh for hemispheric trade disputes in the postwar period. Outstanding controversies have included the discriminatory nature of the structure of U.S. protection (tariff escalation, tariff peaks, and nontariff barriers), the issue of preferential treatment for less developed countries (LDCs), and high protection in Latin America.

The Structure of U.S. Protection

One major Latin American complaint about the structure of U.S. protection has been the relatively high nominal tariffs levied against products that are of export interest to the region. Although there is widespread agreement that GATT has succeeded in reducing developed countries' nominal tariffs,[5] these reductions have been mostly restricted to products actively traded among industrialized countries. In fact, successive GATT negotiating rounds have failed to reverse the bias of industrial countries' tariff schedules against industrial products of export interest to less-developed countries. In particular, although average U.S. tariff rates for manufactures fell from 59 percent in 1932 to about 7 percent in the 1970s and to just over 3 percent after full implementation of the reductions agreed to in the Tokyo Round, tariff rates have remained comparatively high for some consumer goods and textiles, products for which LDCs have developed comparative advantages.[6]

GATT also failed to deal appropriately with the issue of tariff escalation (low or zero tariff rates on raw materials and increasingly higher rates as the scale of processing advances). This has resulted in high protection for processed raw materials and semimanufactures and has provided a disincentive to the development of downstream, value-added industries processing raw materials in LDCs. For example, although post–Kennedy Round U.S. nominal tariff rates for a sample of twenty-one major nonoil commodities at different stages along the processing chain cannot be regarded as exorbitant, tariff escalation resulted in protection rates that were two or almost three times higher than nominal rates.[7]

Table 7. Coverage Coefficient of U.S. Nontariff Barriers for Latin American Exports, Classified by Major Product Groups, 1986

All foods	26.3%
Agricultural raw materials	33.8
Fuels	—
Ores and metals	24.3
Manufactures (excluding chemicals)	11.8
Chemicals	21.8
Total Latin American Exports Affected by U.S. NTBs	9.7
Total Latin American Exports to U.S. (excluding fuels)	18.9

Source: Adapted from R. Goncalves and J. A. de Castro, "El proteccionismo de los países industrializados y las exportaciones de la América Latina," *El Trimestre Económico* 56, no. 222 (April–June 1989): 443–69.

Similarly, although the prohibition of nontariff barriers (NTBs) has been one of the basic pillars of GATT, these barriers have remained extensive in various sectors and industries of export interest to Latin American countries (outstanding examples include agriculture, textiles, and apparel). Furthermore, since the early 1970s developed countries' NTBs proliferated, giving rise to complaints that they were severely limiting access to developed countries' domestic markets. Between 1966 and 1986 the NTB index for major product groups rose by 37 percent for all industrial countries and by 30 percent for the United States.[8] One study estimated that by the mid-1980s about 18 percent of Latin American exports to the United States (excluding fuels) faced some type of NTB, with a much higher incidence for certain countries (Table 7).[9]

Thus, tariff and nontariff barriers in combination have served to discriminate against products of export interest to Latin America (and, more broadly, to LDCs). Edward J. Ray found evidence that "NTBs have been used in the U.S. and abroad to substitute for lost tariff protection by industries that experienced tariff cuts in the Kennedy Round and . . . to complement tariff protection in industries that already had relatively high tariff protection."[10] Another study has argued that the post–Kennedy Round structure of tariffs and NTBs in the United States systematically discriminated against imports of consumer durables, processed agricultural products, and textiles—all products for which the Latin American countries displayed comparative advantages.[11]

Preferential Treatment

Historically, Latin American nations (and LDCs generally) have demanded preferential access to developed country markets on the grounds that "apparent symmetry of non-discriminatory and reciprocal trade policies [do] not correspond with the actual asymmetry of the world economy."[12] In the 1960s, this demand was reinforced by the evidence that the post–Kennedy Round pattern of protection across major industrial countries continued or even increased barriers against imports of consumer goods, textiles, and manufactured foodstuffs—products of special interest to LDCs. Eventually, preferential treatment also became an issue when a number of specific codes were concluded in the Tokyo Round.[13] However, preferential treatment was at odds with the most-favored nation (MFN) principle of GATT and, as such, it was opposed by the United States throughout most of the postwar period.

The preferential arrangements of the countries of the European Economic Community (EEC) with former colonies as well as activism by LDCs induced a change in the traditional U.S. stance. As a result, in 1968 UNCTAD II approved a resolution calling for the institution of a Generalized System of Preferences (GSP) to grant the exports of less-developed countries nonreciprocal, duty-free access to developed country markets. The door for effective implementation of GSPs was finally opened three years later, when GATT authorized a ten-year waiver to the nondiscriminatory intent of the MFN clause, requiring only that the preferences be extended to all LDCs.[14]

Then, in 1974 the U.S. Congress passed legislation authorizing the president to execute a GSP for a maximum of ten years. Implementing legislation explicitly excluded a list of "import-sensitive" products, authorized the president to designate as import-sensitive any product previously declared eligible, and made provisions to "graduate" (remove GSP benefits from) countries on the basis of their export success. Many Latin American countries viewed these limitations as excessively restrictive.

Thus, the U.S. Generalized System of Preferences has failed to provide LDCs with preferential access to the U.S. market precisely in those areas in which they have comparative advantages.[15] The reason is straightforward: in those areas the pressure of special interests in developed countries has been most powerful. As a consequence, economic sectors capable of maintaining relatively high tariff barriers and of benefiting most from nontariff barriers were also generally in a position to prevent the extension of preferential treatment to selected LDC exports.

GSP renewal in late 1984 provided an opportunity to assess how U.S. trade policy objectives had evolved. The new program intensified its restrictive character: labor conditions and rights, protection of U.S. patents and intellectual property rights, promotion of freer trade in services, and so-called unfair trade practices were introduced as new elements to be considered in determining a country's eligibility. Furthermore, the renewed GSP abandoned the nonreciprocal feature of the original program and thus became an instrument for extracting trade concessions from LDCs. In fact, after 1984 "reciprocity" became a guiding principle for the United States in granting concessions to individual countries, giving rise to new controversies with LDCs in general and with the Latin American countries in particular.[16]

U.S. imports under the Generalized System of Preferences have never represented a high share of total U.S. imports.[17] But the arrangement has benefited a significant portion of LDCs' manufactured exports. In the mid-1980s, for instance, about 25 percent of Argentine and Brazilian manufactured exports and about 13 percent of Mexican exports to the United States were duty free under the GSP.[18]

Import-Substitution Industrialization and Latin American Trade Regimes

One major source of friction in U.S.–Latin American trade relations in the postwar period has been the high protection associated with the strategy of import-substitution industrialization followed by most Latin American countries. The original rationale for ISI was that, due to their role as primary commodity exporters, Latin American countries were subject to a long-run terms of trade deterioration that limited their ability to benefit from technical progress achieved in the industrialized world.[19] It was argued that to get around that "structural" limitation, each Latin American country should develop a domestic manufacturing base. This, in turn, would demand protectionist trade regimes characterized by high nominal tariffs, widespread quantitative restrictions on imports, and heavily regulated foreign exchange markets. In practice, the analytic rationale in favor of ISI was rapidly reinforced—and to a large extent distorted—by domestic vested interests.

Indigenous incentives favoring high protection were compounded by GATT's failure to stimulate LDCs' participation in the process of multilateral trade liberalization. There is a consensus that until the mid-1970s GATT had been unable to bring about significant reductions in LDCs' nominal tariffs, partly because of the limited incentives for LDCs to engage in reciprocal tariff concessions, which had been the cornerstone of successive negotiating rounds. This situation did not change substantially in the subsequent Tokyo or Uruguay rounds of GATT trade talks. Furthermore, for most of the postwar period, GATT provided Latin American countries (and LDCs generally) the means to maintain high nontariff barriers.[20]

The 1980s, however, witnessed some major changes. As ISI became increasingly discredited as a development strategy and international financial institutions enhanced their role in domestic policy-making as a result of the external debt crisis, Latin American trade regimes generally moved toward liberalization.

Whether motivated primarily by domestic reasons or by conditionality imposed by IFIs, this process of Latin American trade liberalization was largely unilateral. In most cases, residual high-protection practices have been more the result of balance-of-payments constraints than of autonomous trade policy decisions. Relatively rapid trade liberalization in Latin America removed one major controversial issue in hemispheric trade relations. Nevertheless, the shift in U.S. trade policy toward aggressive unilateralism and procedural protectionism created new sources of conflict, most of which are likely to remain throughout the 1990s.

U.S. Trade Policy in the 1980s and Its Impact on Latin America

Generally speaking, the last two decades have been a period of rapid change in U.S. trade policies. The erosion of the overwhelming U.S. economic dominance of the early postwar years, a perception of "unfair treatment" on the part of the country's trading partners, and the apparent decreasing effectiveness of GATT to foster its trade objectives all led to a shift in the United States's approach to international trade issues. This transition accelerated markedly in the 1980s.

Hemispheric trade relations were heavily influenced by these new U.S. trade policy directions, the most outstanding being (1) discrimination based on economic grounds, (2) increasingly restrictive use of trade-remedy laws, (3) mounting recourse to aggressive unilateralism, and (4) inclusion of a whole set of "new issues" as part of U.S. trade policy objectives.

Discrimination
Although U.S. trade discrimination was not completely new, most previous episodes had been driven by security and/or strategic considerations. This was true of the 1983 Caribbean Basin Initiative, the 1985 free trade agreement (FTA) with Israel, and the 1990 Andean Initiative. In the late 1980s, however, a new brand of U.S. trade discriminatory policies emerged with the conclusion of the Canada–U.S. Free Trade Agreement (CUSFTA) in 1988 and the launching of negotiations with Mexico and Canada to create a North American Free Trade Agreement in 1990.

Although strategic and security considerations were important in CUSFTA and NAFTA negotiations, trade policy objectives seem to have played a much larger role than in the past. There is a consensus that CUSFTA was a by-product of mounting U.S. (particularly congressional) uneasiness about GATT's ability to advance U.S. interests.[21] Similarly, trilateral negotiations to create NAFTA can be regarded as partly motivated by the impasse of the Uruguay Round of multilateral trade negotiations, by the perception of a continuing deterioration in the U.S. stance on trade, and by sustained progress toward European unification.[22]

It is still an open question whether economic incentives favoring discrimination in U.S. trade policies will evolve into a "regionalist" stance or instead will be part of a building-block approach to multilateral liberalization. To some, discriminatory policies of the United States in the late 1980s were used to promote its trade objectives among "like-minded" trading partners. To others, however, they suggested that bilateralism and regionalism were likely to become increasingly influential. Most share the view that such approaches, if unrestrained, may run counter to an open multilateral trade environment.[23]

Some Latin American observers regard the long-term proposal to create a Western Hemisphere Free Trade Area in the Enterprise for the Americas Initiative as a clear indication of the United States leaning toward discrimination and, eventually, regionalism. Even if this perception proves to be exaggerated, the creation of NAFTA will have long-lasting effects on hemispheric trade relations.

Procedural Protectionism
Procedural (or contingent) protectionism has expanded markedly since the early 1970s, partly as a result of mounting U.S. preoccupation with "unfair" trade practices and a deteriorating trade position.[24] Three major provisions of U.S. trade-remedy laws are involved: (1) Section 201 ("escape clause"), (2) Section 701 (subsidized imports), and (3) Section 731 (dumping).

For the most part, every important piece of U.S. trade legislation passed since the mid-1970s has made these provisions more restrictive.[25] Significant changes in conditions relating to antidumping (ADD) and countervailing duties (CVD) include a transfer of authority for ADD and CVD actions from the Department of the Treasury to the Department of Commerce (Trade Agreements Act of 1979); expanding the definition of unfair trade practices to facilitate acceptance of petitions, to ease the requirements for positive determination, and to expedite retroactive imposition of penalties (Trade and Tariff Act of 1984); and expanding CVD and ADD statutes specifically to cover products that use subsidized inputs and to impose new rules to guide the practice of "cumulation" in injury investigations (Omnibus Trade and Competitiveness Act of 1988). Increasing restrictiveness of CVD and ADD statutes have resulted in a notable rise in the number of annual filings (requests) and actions (investigations effectively carried forward).[26]

As of early 1988, Latin American and Caribbean countries accounted for a disproportionately large share of CVD orders issued and imposed. In fact, about 47 percent of CVD orders in place (a proportion much larger than the 11.6 percent Latin American share of U.S. imports) were aimed at imports from the region.[27] These orders applied mostly to semi-industrialized countries (Argentina, Brazil, and Mexico) and basically affected products such as textiles, apparel, and footwear. Furthermore, about 90 percent of orders in place by mid-1988 had been issued following enactment of the Trade Agreements Act of 1979 and almost a third following approval of the Trade and Tariffs Act of 1984, indicating the extent to which both facilitated petition procedures (Table 8).

Conversely, ADD orders against imports from Latin America were proportional to the region's share of total U.S. imports (according to 1988 figures, 10 percent and 11.6 percent, respectively). By 1988 most duties in place affected imports from semi-industrialized Latin American countries (Table 9). Once again, most actions (about three-quarters) were imposed following approval of the 1984 Trade and Tariffs Act.

In the 1980s "escape clause" provisions were used less often than ADD and CVD filings and actions. The escape clause (Section 201 of the Trade Act of 1974 as amended by subsequent legislation) is the U.S. legal counterpart of GATT Article XIX, which allows signatory countries to temporarily elude some of their obligations when imports cause (or threaten to cause) injury to domestic industries. The relatively small number of escape clause cases filed in the 1980s has been the result of more flexible requirements for obtaining contingent protection under Section 301 (presidential retaliatory authority), Section 701 (subsidized imports), and Section 731 (dumping), as approved by the 1979 Trade Agreements Act.[28] It is interesting to note that notwithstanding the decline in the absolute number of escape clause cases filed between 1975–80 and 1981–87, the proportion of them resulting in protective actions increased by nearly a quarter.

Broadly speaking, at least 50 percent of investigations carried forward under Section 201 since 1975 concerned products of interest to Latin America—for example, steel, tobacco, footwear, sugar, honey, flowers, copper, and zinc. In the 1980s, the most remarkable case was the petition filed against carbon and alloy-steel imports, which led to a series of voluntary export-restraint agreements (VRAs) with such countries as Brazil, Mexico, Trinidad and Tobago, and Venezuela.[29] The frequent resort to "gray area" measures—like VRAs or Orderly Marketing Agreements (OMAs)—as a result of escape clause petitions generated extensive criticism not only in Latin America but among other U.S. trading partners as well.

Aggressive Unilateralism
In contrast to ADD, CVD, and escape clause statutes, Section 301 of the Trade Act of 1974 is a coercive mechanism that grants retaliatory powers to the president of the United States. It originated as an authorization to carry forward actions against "unjustifiable or unreasonable" import restrictions on U.S. goods and services (such as dumping, subsidies, or other "unfair" trade practices) and on U.S. access to supplies. The Trade Agreements Act of 1979 and the Trade and Tariff Act of 1984 expanded the scope for retaliatory activity, setting time limits for the U.S.

Table 8. Countervailing Duty Orders on Latin American Exports (Orders in place as of August 15, 1988)

Country	Product	Year Imposed
Argentina	Woolen garments	1978
	Nonrubber footwear	1979
	Wool	1983
	Leather wearing apparel	1983
	Cold rolled steel sheet	1984
	Oil country tubular goods	1984
	Textiles and apparel	1985
Brazil	Castor oil	1976
	Cotton yarn	1977
	Scissors and shears[a]	1977
	Pig iron	1980
	Agricultural tillage tools	1985
	Castings	1986
	Brass sheet and strip	1987
Chile	Standard carnations	1987
Ecuador	Fresh cut flowers	1987
Mexico	Leather wearing apparel	1981
	Toy balloons	1982
	Litharge	1982
	Ceramic tile	1982
	Carbon black	1983
	Castings	1983
	Cement	1983
	Bars, rebars, and shapes[a]	1984
	Lime	1984
	Bricks	1984
	Auto glass	1985
	Textile mill products	1985
	Porcelain cooking ware	1986
Peru	Cotton sheeting and sateen	1983
	Cotton yarn	1983
	Rebars	1985
	Textiles and apparel	1985
	Pompom chrysanthemums	1987
Uruguay	Leather wearing apparel	1982
Venezuela	Electrical conductor aluminum rods	1988

Source: "The Omnibus Trade and Competitiveness Act of 1988: Its Impact on Latin America and the Caribbean," SP/DCC.I.T., no. 3 (Caracas: SELA, 1988), p. 164.
a. Revoked with outstanding entries.

Table 9. Antidumping Duties on Latin American Exports (Orders in place as of August 15, 1988)

Country	Product	Year Imposed
Argentina	Barbed wire	1983
	Carbon steel wire rods	1984
Brazil	Pipe fittings	1986
	Butt-weld pipe fittings	1986
	Construction castings	1986
	Disc wheels	1987
	Orange juice	1987
	Brass sheet and strip	1987
Chile	Sodium nitrate	1983
	Standard carnations	1987
Colombia	Fresh cut flowers	1987
Dominican Republic	Portland cement	1983
Ecuador	Fresh cut flowers	1987
Mexico	Elemental sulphur	1973
	Cooking ware	1986
	Fresh cut flowers	1987
Venezuela	Electrical conductor aluminum rods	1988

Source: SELA, "The Omnibus Trade and Competitiveness Act of 1988: Its Impact on Latin America and the Caribbean," SP/DCC.I.T., no. 3 (Caracas: SELA, 1988), p. 181.

trade representative (USTR) to issue recommendations for action and extending presidential authority to cover practices on which no internationally agreed-upon set of rules yet existed (such as trade in services, high-technology products, and trade-related investment issues).

The 1988 Omnibus Trade and Competitiveness Act (OTCA) also amended Section 301, expanding its scope to include as policy targets restrictions to U.S. investments, infringement of U.S. intellectual property rights, inadequate protection of labor rights, and state procurement and export targeting policies. OTCA also requested the USTR to explicitly identify unfair trade practices in "priority" countries and eventually initiate investigations. These investigations were subject to the same requirements as those carried forward under Section 301. These enhanced retaliatory powers became known as Section Super 301. OTCA also enacted Section "Special 301," requiring the USTR to identify foreign countries that deny adequate protection to U.S. intellectual property rights and to select a group of priority countries to initiate investigations.

More than 70 percent of Section 301 cases involving Latin American countries were initiated in the 1980s and an overwhelming majority involved either Argentina or Brazil (Table 10). The only Super 301 case against a Latin American country involved Brazilian import license practices. The case was finally concluded in 1990 following a major overhaul of the Brazilian trade regime.

Section Special 301 has also affected a number of countries in the region. In mid-1989 the USTR included Brazil and Mexico in a list of seventeen countries under "priority observation" because of their practices regarding intellectual property rights protection.[30] Four other Latin American countries (Argentina, Chile, Colombia, and Venezuela) were "under monitoring." However, no action was taken.

It is interesting to note that the implementation of Sections 301, Super 301, and Special 301 has served to promote U.S. trade objectives as if they were U.S. "rights." The fact that these criteria have been defined unilaterally has greatly enhanced the potential for trade frictions.

New Issues

In the 1980s trade debates widened to include so-called new issues dealing with matters like trade in services, protection of intellectual property rights (TRIPs), trade-related investment measures (TRIMs), trade in high-technology products, and, more recently, labor rights and environmental standards. These issues, which traditionally have not been part of the trade agenda, have jumped to the forefront as a result of rapid technical progress, changing production and business structures, and falling protection "on the border."

Large sections of both the 1984 Trade and Tariffs Act and the 1988 Omnibus Trade and Competitiveness Act have been devoted to defining U.S. policy with regard to these new areas. They became guiding principles for U.S. trade policy both at the bilateral and multilateral levels. In particular, the United States pushed them forcefully into the agenda of the Uruguay Round.

Currently, there is no internationally agreed-upon set of rules to govern the new issues. As a result, U.S. objectives have been defined and pursued unilaterally. In particular, bilateral arrangements like the Canada–U.S. Free Trade Agreement and the U.S.–Israel Free Trade Agreement have been used to implement U.S. goals, establishing international precedents before an international consensus has emerged. Most Latin American countries have also felt U.S. pressure to yield on the new issues. Outstanding examples have been the use of Section Super 301 and Special 301 measures or the inclusion of new issues as priority items in bilateral framework agreements signed with various Latin American countries after 1987.[31]

In the 1980s these new issues became a major source of conflict in U.S.–Latin American trade. Bilateral controversies were frequently aggravated by the fact that many of them intertwined with domestic policies whose objectives were other

Table 10. Section 301, Super 301, and Special 301 Cases against Latin American Countries (as of January 1, 1991)

Year Initiated	Country	Against	Issue
Section 301:			
1975	Guatemala	Cargo-preference laws alleged to discriminate against U.S. shipping interests.	Petition withdrawn following bilateral consultations.
1977	Brazil South Korea China Japan	Japanese agreements with Brazil, Korea, and China on thrown silk alleged to restrict access of U.S. silk exporters to Japanese market.	Japan adjusted restrictions in 1977; case terminated in 1978.
1979	Argentina	Requirement that marine insurance on trade with Argentina be placed with Argentine insurance firms.	Case suspended in 1980; renewed talks possible.
1981	Argentina	Alleged break of agreement with the U.S. by imposing restrictions on export of hides.	U.S. increased tariff on leather in 1982; case terminated.
1982	Brazil Japan South Korea Taiwan	Restrictions on imports of nonrubber footwear alleged to deny market access for U.S. exporters.	Brazil offered to liberalize in 1985; case pending.
1983	Brazil Spain Portugal	Export subsidies and quantitative restrictions in soybean market alleged to restrict U.S. exports.	U.S. has requested additional talks; case pending.
1983	Argentina	Argentine postal system's monopoly on air courier operations alleged to be unreasonable barrier to services.	Argentina lifted restrictions in 1985.
1985	Brazil	Computer policy alleged to restrict investment and imports, subsidize production, and violate intellectual property rights; self-initiated by USTR.	Sanctions suspended in 1988. Case terminated in 1989 after Brazil adjusted its restrictions.

Table 10. *Continued*

Year Initiated	Country	Against	Issue
1986	Argentina	Differential export tax on soybeans alleged to subsidize export of soybean products.	Argentina plans to remove export taxes; case suspended.
1987	Brazil	Pharmaceutical patent laws alleged to provide inadequate protection for U.S. intellectual property owners.	U.S. applies sanctions in 1988. Sanctions suspended in 1990 following Brazilian commitment to improve patent protection.
1988	Argentina	Pharmaceutical patent laws alleged to provide inadequate protection for U.S. intellectual property owners.	U.S. has declared against Argentine policies and threatened sanctions. Argentine commitment to improve patent protection.
Section Super 301:			
1989	Brazil	Brazil designated as "priority country" due to its regime of import restrictions alleged to deny market access to U.S. exporters.	Brazil removed from the "priority country" list following major overhaul of the trade regime in 1990.
Section Special 301:			
1989	Brazil Mexico	Designated as countries on the "priority watch list" due to alleged inadequate protection of U.S. intellectual property rights.	Mexico was removed from the "priority watch list" in 1990 following a commitment to change its patent protection legislation.
1989	Argentina Chile Colombia Venezuela	Designated as countries on the "watch list" due to alleged inadequate protection of U.S. intellectual property rights.	No action taken.

Sources: Adapted from SELA, "The Omnibus Trade and Competitiveness Act of 1988: Its Impact on Latin America and the Caribbean," *SP/DCC.I.T.,* no. 3 (Caracas: SELA, 1988), and U.S. International Trade Commission, *Operation of the Trade Agreements Program: 42nd Report, 1990* (Washington, D.C.: USITC Publication 2403, July 1991).

than regulating international trade flows. Generally speaking, foreign investment, patent protection, and service-sector policies were regarded by most Latin American governments as part of their—rapidly shrinking—arsenal of development policies. Patent protection policies, for instance, were typically associated with the broader issue of technology transfer. Similarly, regulatory policies for the service sector (such as banking, telecommunications, and transportation) were regarded as closely connected with developmental priorities. The well-known controversies between the United States and several Latin American countries regarding patent protection for pharmaceutical products and between the United States and Brazil concerning the computer industry illustrate the tensions that have arisen.

By the early 1990s, most Latin American countries had changed their positions on the new issues. Under the weight of aggressive unilateralism, conditionality imposed by international financial institutions, and the modest results of previous policies, most countries in the region shifted to views more compatible with U.S. policy guidelines. But divergent national interests are likely to remain influential in policy formulation, particularly in sensitive areas such as trade in services. Furthermore, as the trade agenda expands to include previously uncovered issues, the potential for conflict will certainly increase.[32] But this problem is not unique to trade relations in the hemisphere. On the contrary, it is precisely the increasingly controversial nature of the issues included in the Uruguay Round that has made it so difficult to reach an agreement by the originally scheduled date.[33]

U.S.–Latin American Trade Relations in the 1990s

As the 1990s unfold, three forces will continue to shape U.S. trade policy: (1) the multilateral orthodoxy dominant for the first three postwar decades, (2) the post-1970s protectionist stance, and (3) the bilateral and/or regional approach reinvigorated in the 1980s. Which one will eventually prevail is still an open question and, as M. Hart argues, "a superpower like the United States (could) ride off in several directions at once for a considerable period of time."[34]

It is unlikely that the impasse of the Uruguay Round of multilateral trade negotiations will lead either to a breakdown of the multilateral trading system or to major and rapid breakthroughs in the most critical trade disputes. On the one hand, the former seems difficult to conceive when globalization and interdependence have advanced so far.[35] On the other hand, because the current agenda includes highly controversial issues and some of the main partners (particularly the EEC) seem interested in completing their internal economic unification before tackling some of the most daunting multilateral issues, a path-breaking agreement appears unlikely in the near future. The most probable scenario seems to be an eventual completion based on a relatively more modest compromise. Similarly, there are few reasons to anticipate that U.S. domestic forces in favor of protection will recede in the 1990s. On the contrary, the eroding position of the United States in the world economy will probably ensure that trade tensions will persist, reducing the prospects of a benevolent multilateralist revival. Thus, the most likely scenario for U.S. trade policy in the present decade is one of continued eclecticism. In this context, aggressive unilateralism and discrimination will remain major tools of U.S. trade policy.

Discrimination may provide the United States with a means of making domestic pressures compatible with prevailing international constraints, notwithstanding its potentially deleterious effect on the multilateral trading system. Discrimination may also prove highly instrumental in gradually advancing U.S. views regarding the controversial new issues on the international trade agenda. If such a scenario prevails, it is likely that at least some Latin American countries will be among the prime targets of U.S. trade policy.

Just a decade ago, the idea of a free trade area in the Western Hemisphere may have appeared to be completely out of the question for various reasons. Multi-lateralism was still the guiding principle of U.S. trade policy, notwithstanding selective episodes of discrimination. In addition, prevailing trade policies and development ideologies throughout Latin America were unyielding on the issue of trade liberalization. However, times have changed. On the one hand, as trade conflicts with other industrial countries have deepened and as GATT has become less suited to foster U.S. trade objectives, discriminatory bilateral and/or regional approaches have gained respectability in the United States. On the other hand, trade policy reform has advanced substantially throughout Latin America as a result of both changing development paradigms and the conditionality of interna-tional financial institutions. In particular, growing dissatisfaction with inward-oriented economic policies and with what is regarded as an especially adverse international economic environment have contributed to a warm Latin American reaction to the prospect of FTA negotiations with the United States.

What is the likelihood of a Western Hemisphere Free Trade Agreement? Is NAFTA indicative of an overall trend, or is it a special case that will not be replicated elsewhere in the hemisphere, much less on a hemispheric scale? Be-cause U.S. desires to push for a WHFTA will largely depend on the future evolution of the international trading system—and particularly on the changing relationship between major trading partners—a definitive answer cannot be pro-vided. However, existing incentives to move in that direction can still be identified. Furthermore, even if the process of FTA creation does not go beyond NAFTA, the very existence of NAFTA will have far-reaching implications for hemispheric trade relations in the 1990s.

Regionalization or Further Differentiation in Latin America?

The incentives to enter into a free trade agreement (or, generally speaking, pursue further economic integration) are not just economic; they are also political and strategic. Nevertheless, even if economic factors do not dominate the negotiations between two countries, any successful agreement will have to be based on solid economic grounds if it is to be sustained in the long run.

The potential implications of prevailing asymmetries should be one of the leading issues in the debate on the creation of FTAs between the United States and the Latin American countries. What is at stake is not so much a question of relative size but, more fundamentally, of levels of development and other differences in key economic parameters (wage and productivity levels, income distribution, and relative prices). Among other things, such disparities will influence the likelihood and extension of "polarization effects" as well as the distribution of net economic gains and adjustment costs across member countries. It is surprising that the issue of asymmetries and how to deal with their potential effects in the case of NAFTA—the first free trade agreement among partners with such divergent levels of economic development—has attracted so little attention thus far.[36]

Generally speaking, the economic incentives for FTAs may be classified into three broad categories. First, net static welfare gains (or losses) stem from the reallocation of resources following reciprocal trade liberalization. Second, dynamic gains (or losses)—for example, scale economies, external economies, polarization effects, effects on investment flows, and enhanced economic efficiency—result from an enlarged market and can, in fact, have more important implications than static effects. And third, "defensive" reasons—such as the maintenance of market access, improvement of bilateral relations, or avoidance of discrimination—can also provide an economic rationale for a free trade agreement.[37]

U.S. net static gains from the creation of FTAs with Latin American countries and/or subregions will be limited by prevailing differences in economic size. Even Brazil and Mexico (the two largest economies in Latin America) are relatively small when compared to the United States.[38] Moreover, trade with Mexico (the third largest trading partner of the United States) represents just 6 percent of total U.S. foreign trade, although it contributes about 50 percent to aggregate U.S.–Latin American trade flows. These facts imply not only that U.S. net welfare gains will be small, but also that a handful of Latin American trading partners—especially Mexico—will be responsible for the vast majority of them.

This view is shared by a U.S. government report, which states that the benefits accruing to the United States as a result of a free trade agreement with Mexico "would be small in relation to the size of the U.S. economy at least in the near to medium term," as the Mexican economy is small compared to that of the United States and a large portion of bilateral trade already encounters low tariff and nontariff barriers.[39] In fact, rapid trade liberalization throughout Latin America since the late 1980s has limited the potential for trade expansion. However, after a decade of widespread economic stagnation, present trade values may be a misleading indicator of the region's trade potential. As historically closed economies, the Latin American countries may have vast room for increased tradeability. Notwithstanding these qualifications, most Latin American countries—and the region as a whole—are likely to remain a minor U.S. trading partner for the next decade, particularly if import growth continues to be restrained by a balance-of-payments constraint that is seriously aggravated by the limited availability of financing.

Although difficult to quantify, U.S. dynamic gains would also be small as a result of the disparity in relative sizes. This overall conclusion would not change substantially if a WHFTA—rather than a more restricted agreement—is considered. In fact, at least as far as scale economies and investment diversion are concerned, NAFTA would be sufficiently large to allow for most of the expected effects to operate without going beyond it. If this were correct, from the standpoint of dynamic gains a hemispheric arrangement would be largely redundant.[40]

This leads to so-called defensive reasons, mostly arising as a reaction to events taking place in other parts of the world. The process of European unification may improve the terms of trade of participating countries vis-à-vis the rest of the international community, including the United States.[41] Similarly, the dynamics of a wider trade area may divert investment to the unified market, affecting nonparticipating countries. There is already some evidence that European economic unification and mounting difficulties in GATT have provided a favorable environment for CUSFTA and NAFTA to progress. However, it is worth emphasizing that U.S. "defensive motivations" to create preferential trade arrangements would not involve all Latin American countries to the same extent and may not be limited to the region. In fact, the United States may also find likely—and faster-growing—partners in other regions of the world, such as the Pacific Basin.

Limited U.S. incentives to enter into free trade agreements with the Latin American countries may be counterbalanced by the fact that aggregate adjustment costs would also be small, therefore reducing the domestic opposition that such initiatives may generate.[42] In any case, although aggregate costs may be small, they are likely to be concentrated in a number of regions and sectors, hence strengthening domestic resistance. As a result, domestic opposition in the United States will be more intensive the larger the envisaged FTA.

In conclusion, from the viewpoint of the United States and under foreseeable international economic conditions, an overwhelming economic rationale for a hemispheric FTA does not seem to exist. Instead, it is likely that the United States will find it both more attractive and more politically viable to follow a selective approach to FTAs in the hemisphere, emphasizing closer association with a limited number of partners. If strategic and foreign policy considerations also play a role—as they will certainly do—the case for a selective approach might actually be strengthened.

From the standpoint of Latin American countries, incentives to enter into FTAs with the United States are also highly heterogeneous. In fact, enthusiasm about the possibility of such negotiations is more the result of a perceived lack of alternatives and an increasingly marginalized position in the world economy than of any rigorous economic assessment.

At one extreme, countries with a relatively high concentration of foreign trade with the United States, low levels of protection, and exports subject to relatively high U.S. tariffs might find an FTA attractive from a static point of view. Mexico is typical of such a country. Indeed, by the late 1980s about two-thirds of Mexico's foreign trade and an even higher proportion of its trade in manufactures were concentrated in the United States. Similarly, although tariff rates for most U.S.– Mexican trade are low, some Mexican products are subject to high nominal tariffs and, therefore, might benefit from export expansion under an FTA. Similarly, Mexican exports face the familiar problems of tariff escalation and extensive nontariff barriers.[43] Furthermore, rapid trade liberalization since the mid-1980s has sharply reduced the room for trade diversion and associated welfare costs.

At the other extreme, Southern Cone countries (including Brazil) may find that an FTA with the United States could have large potential costs related to trade diversion.[44] These countries have a well-diversified trade pattern regionally (the United States is just one of various important trading partners) and, at least in the case of Brazil, comparatively high—though falling—protection. As W. Fritsch argues, a free trade agreement with the United States would be tantamount to unilateral liberalization with the additional welfare cost of trade diversion. This would seriously question the rationale for such an approach.[45] Furthermore, because nontariff barriers are useful in restricting access to the U.S. market, how these would be treated in a potential FTA would heavily influence the potential impact of an agreement.

Dynamic effects would also differ markedly among the Latin American countries. In the case of Mexico, the potential effect of an FTA with the United States on direct investment—and, more generally, on capital flow—could be sizable. Extensive intraindustry and intrafirm trade between the United States and Mexico already demonstrates the intimate relationship between foreign investment and the flow of trade. The Mexican economy could also take full advantage of economies of scale and external economies by securing access to domestic and foreign firms in an enlarged market. An agreement could also improve the general business climate as a result of diminished uncertainty regarding the future evolution of domestic economic policy and stable access to Mexico's overwhelmingly largest export market. For Mexico, a NAFTA could act as an anchor for economic reforms, further promote the interpenetration of the North American economies, and provide an environment more conducive to obtaining appropriate financing for large current account deficits.

For other countries in the region, however, these incentives may be less relevant. On the one hand, economies of scale and external economies might be unimportant for many commodity-based economies, like those of the Caribbean, Central America, and some Andean countries.[46] On the other hand, the potential effect on portfolio and direct investment flows of an FTA might be more restricted for countries other than Mexico, as they would not enjoy the locational advantages of the latter or—because many of the benefits from capital flow diversion are likely to be largely dependent on exclusiveness—they would suffer the disadvantage of being "latecomers."[47]

For the Caribbean and Andean countries, the incentives to enter into FTAs with the United States will have to be assessed against the fact that they currently enjoy or are likely to enjoy more generous-than-GSP duty-free access to the U.S. market. However, because the Caribbean Basin Economic Recovery Act (CBERA) and the Andean Trade Preferences bill (still under congressional consideration in mid-1992) exclude many products of export interest to the beneficiary countries (like textiles, apparel, footwear, leather, sugar, and tuna), there may be an incentive to yield on nonreciprocity in exchange for more extensive product coverage. Furthermore, for the Andean countries the cost-benefit analysis would have to consider the fact that preferences would be granted for a limited period.[48]

It seems likely, therefore, that the greatest incentives for Latin American countries to enter into FTAs with the United States would be defensive in nature—that is, maintaining market access, improving bilateral relations, and avoiding discrimination. These motives would be enhanced by the proliferation of subregional agreements throughout the hemisphere or by the progressive constitution of a hemispheric FTA. Although the trade diversion effects of NAFTA may be limited when compared to the size of the U.S. economy,[49] their significance for third-country exports could be considerable, especially for products that face comparatively high nominal tariffs or NTBs on entering the U.S. market. Equally important, discrimination against Latin American exports in regional markets may become an additional source of concern. Although Mexico's foreign trade with other Latin American countries is small, other countries engage in substantial intraregional trade. Thus, FTA agreements between the United States and other Latin American countries may place third countries in the region at a disadvantage vis-à-vis members of the FTA, creating additional incentives to join.

Conclusion

In the 1980s, the enormous impact of the external debt crisis on the U.S.–Latin American economic agenda turned attention away from trade and investment issues. In the shadow of the debt, however, important transformations took place in the realm of trade. Many of their far-reaching effects will be felt in the present decade.

The fact that by the late 1980s Latin American trade regimes had moved toward liberalization has not removed the potential for trade conflicts with the United States. This is partly the result of a parallel U.S. trade policy shift toward discrimination, procedural protectionism, and aggressive unilateralism, enlarging the scope of trade frictions. Furthermore, as the trade agenda has expanded to incorporate the so-called new issues, it is likely that differences between U.S. principles and Latin American perceived interests will continue into the 1990s.

More recently, the launching of negotiations to create a NAFTA and the announcement of the Bush administration's long-run objective to create a hemispheric FTA have introduced a new major issue in hemispheric trade relations. In particular, divergent U.S. incentives to enter into FTA negotiations with individual Latin American countries and/or subregions and contrasting interests on the part of the latter regarding the value of making such agreements with the United States are likely to help consolidate the process of economic differentiation within Latin America, instead of pushing toward "regionalization" on a hemispheric scale.

Under foreseeable international economic conditions, Latin American countries (and their patterns of integration into the world economy) are likely to grow more distinct in the future, as they have in the recent past. However, progressive differentiation within the region will not preclude more intense economic interactions throughout the hemisphere. Dealing imaginatively with closer—but more diversified—economic interactions between the United States and the Latin American countries will be one of the main challenges of a constructive trade agenda for the 1990s.

Notes

1. For the purpose of this section, three subregions are distinguished: Mexico, the Caribbean (the Caribbean islands, Central America, Suriname, and Guyana), and South America.

2. When compared with the Caribbean average, this is also true of Costa Rica and the Dominican Republic.

3. In 1987–89 the range varied between 77 percent for the Dominican Republic and 61.4 percent for Mexico to 4 and 12 percent for Paraguay and Uruguay, respectively.

4. See Finger, "Ideas Count, Words Inform." Outstanding episodes of U.S. discrimination were the exclusion of communist countries from the MFN clause, the support for the creation of the European Community for Steel and Coal, the U.S.-Canadian automotive agreement, the Generalized System of Preferences, and the support to limit codes negotiated in the Tokyo Round to signatory countries. Among others, selective protectionism was extensive in agriculture, textiles, apparel, and steel.

5. For a comprehensive analysis of the evolution of the world trading system and its institutions in the postwar period, see Jackson, *World Trading System.*

6. See Ray, *U.S. Protectionism.*

7. See Fritsch, "Latin America's Export-Growth Imperative."

8. For an exhaustive inventory of nontariff barriers, see Laird and Yeats, "Trends in Nontariff Barriers."

9. See Goncalves and de Castro, "El proteccionismo de los países industrializados." When fuels are included, the rate falls to slightly below 10 percent.

10. Ray, *U.S. Protectionism,* p. 25.

11. Ray and Marvel, "Pattern of Protection."

12. Hamilton and Whalley, "A View from the Developed World," p. 33.

13. Nau, "The NICs in a New Trade Round."

14. Jackson, *World Trading System.*

15. See Ray, *U.S. Protectionism.*

16. SELA, "América Latina y el proteccionismo norteamericano."

17. By the mid-1980s, U.S. duty-free imports under GSP were equivalent to about 4 percent of total imports (see Ray, *U.S. Protectionism*) and to about 20 percent of MFN dutiable imports from beneficiary countries (see Laird and Sapir, "Preferencias arancelarias").

18. Ray, *U.S. Protectionism.*

19. The classic argument is provided by Prebisch, *Economic Development of Latin America.*

20. Dam, *The GATT.* GATT Article XVIII(b) and (c) allow LDCs to impose quantitative restrictions due to balance-of-payment difficulties or for infant-industry purposes.

21. Factors frequently mentioned as enhancing the attractiveness of CUSFTA to the United States include (1) modest accomplishments by the Tokyo Round of multilateral trade negotiations, (2) failure of the 1982 GATT ministerial meeting to agree on a new round of trade negotiations, (3) uncertain prospects for the Uruguay Round finally launched in 1986, and (4) approval of the European Unification Act.

22. The bilateral focus of the United States regarding Mexico was apparent even previous to NAFTA negotiations. In 1985, before Mexico had become a member of GATT, both governments concluded an agreement on subsidies that entitled Mexican exports to the injury test. In 1987 they signed a framework agreement that became the primary mechanism for consultation and exchange on trade and investment issues. Finally, two years later the framework agreement was expanded by the Understanding Regarding Trade and Investment Facilitation Talks.

23. See Schott, "More Free Trade Areas?"; Baghwati, *World Trading System at Risk*; and Krueger, "The Case for Free Trade."

24. *Procedural protectionism* is the design and enforcement of trade-remedy laws in a protectionist manner (Grinols, "Procedural Protectionism").

25. Since the mid-1970s, the U.S. Congress has passed four major pieces of trade

legislation: the Trade Act of 1974, the Trade Agreements Act of 1979, the Trade and Tariffs Act of 1984, and the Omnibus Trade and Competitiveness Act of 1988.

26. Grinols, "Procedural Protectionism."

27. SELA, "Omnibus Trade and Competitiveness Act."

28. Grinols, "Procedural Protectionism."

29. SELA, "Omnibus Trade and Competitiveness Act."

30. In 1990 Mexico was removed from the "priority country list" after its government pledged to enact new patent protection legislation.

31. By late 1991 the United States had signed framework agreements with Bolivia, Chile, Colombia, Costa Rica, Ecuador, Honduras, Mexico, and MERCOSUR (Argentina, Brazil, Paraguay, and Uruguay).

32. The environment is emerging as an interesting issue. Its increasing relevance for international trade was revealed during congressional debate on extending "fast-track authorization" to negotiate NAFTA.

33. Tussie, "Developing Countries."

34. Hart, *North American Free Trade Agreement*, p. 54. See also Lawrence and Schultze, *American Trade Strategy*.

35. Although such a scenario is unlikely at present, increasing trade conflicts and mounting protectionism among major trading partners could produce more conflictive "economic blocks." This would have significant implications for a potential WHFTA.

36. Castañeda, "Mexican Perspective," mentions potentially sizable costs as a result of "polarization effects."

37. Net static welfare gains for countries entering into a FTA will be larger (1) the more they are "natural" trading partners, (2) the lower are their trade barriers to the rest of the world, and (3) the higher are the preexisting obstacles to bilateral trade. For dynamic effects, see El-Agraa, *Theory and Measurement*. On defensive reasons, see Schott, "More Free Trade Areas?."

38. Brazil and Mexico's GDP are, respectively, about 5 and 3 percent of the United States's GDP.

39. See U.S. International Trade Commission, "The Likely Impact . . . of a Free Trade Agreement with Mexico."

40. It is certain that increasingly difficult access to world markets as a result of mounting protectionism among major trading partners would enhance the attractiveness of a regional preferential arrangement on dynamic grounds.

41. Dornbusch, "Policy Options for Freer Trade."

42. This may support FTAs with countries like Chile or Costa Rica. In fact, an agreement could provide a clear signal at a minimal adjustment cost to the rest of the hemisphere regarding U.S. policy preferences.

43. It should be emphasized that the impact on market access of an FTA with the United States will be heavily dependent—at least for countries exporting manufactures and certain agricultural products—on the treatment given nontariff barriers (including contingent protection).

44. Bouzas, "A US-MERCOSUR Free-Trade Area."

45. Fritsch, "O plano Bush e o interesse nacional."

46. Fritsch, "New Minilateralism."

47. Countries already taking part in the agreement will develop an interest in maintaining discrimination and benefiting from exclusiveness.

48. The Andean Trade Preferences bill grants duty-free access to imports from Bolivia, Colombia, Ecuador, and Peru for ten years. In 1990 Congress amended the CBERA to extend indefinitely the benefits originally expected to be phased out in 1996.

49. See U.S. International Trade Commission, "The Likely Impact . . . of a Free Trade Agreement with Mexico."

· J. Samuel Fitch

Chapter Eight · DEMOCRACY, HUMAN RIGHTS,

. AND THE ARMED FORCES

· IN LATIN AMERICA

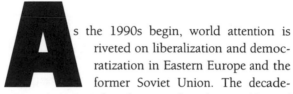s the 1990s begin, world attention is riveted on liberalization and democratization in Eastern Europe and the former Soviet Union. The decade-long democratic transition in Latin America is less dramatic than the crumbling of the Berlin Wall, but the end of military rule has transformed the political life of the region's four hundred million inhabitants. The North American stereotype of Latin America as a region dominated by military dictatorships and state terror has become more and more out of date. A more appropriate image might be long lines of ordinary citizens—mostly poor, men and women, young and old—casting their vote, often with surprising results.

Today, elected civilian administrations govern all but three of the twenty Latin American republics.[1] Only Cuba seems—thus far—unaffected by the democratic tide. The Duvalier dynasty in Haiti and the thirty-six-year dictatorship of General Alfredo Stroessner in Paraguay have fallen.[2] The U.S. invasion overthrew Panamanian strongman Manuel Noriega in 1989 and installed in his place the opposition candidates whose election victory Noriega had refused to recognize. In a hotly contested and closely monitored election, Nicaragua's Sandinistas lost overwhelmingly to the U.S.-backed opposition. Brazil and Chile now have their first democratically elected governments in decades. Among the democratic regimes established in the 1980s, Argentina, Brazil, El Salvador, Guatemala, and Uruguay have completed peaceful presidential transitions; Bolivia, Honduras, and Peru are now in their third successive term of constitutional government; Ecuador is beginning its fourth. All have had one or more electoral transfers of power to the opposition.

Still, it would be a serious mistake to assume that democratization is irreversible or to confuse formal democratic structures with fully consolidated democratic regimes. Civil-military conflicts are still present, at times erupting in confrontations that threaten the stability of civilian governments. In Haiti and Panama, military coups have derailed the transition process. Despite some progress in negotiations with insurgent groups, civilian governments in Colombia, Guatemala, and Peru face continuing internal wars that have resulted in widespread human rights violations and substantial militarization of nominally civilian regimes. Political rights have been restored to almost all of the region's population, but basic social and economic rights have suffered from the worst economic crisis since the 1930s. In 1992, President Alberto Fujimori seized dictatorial powers in Peru with the backing of the military. The 1992 coup attempt in Venezuela—after more than thirty years of democratic rule—is a dramatic reminder that very few of Latin America's democracies have consolidated—much less institutionalized—effective civilian control of the armed forces.

The issue for the coming decade is whether the democratic gains of the 1980s can be sustained. Will the 1990s witness another cycle of coups and military regimes, like those that ended earlier eras of constitutional rule? Will civil wars and economic crises lead to creeping military takeovers and new forms of garrison states within formally democratic shells? Or will effective democratic regimes be consolidated and deepened? Protecting human rights, avoiding the militarization of democratic governments, and extending democratic reforms will present difficult challenges for Latin American leaders. After a decade of preoccupation with Central America, U.S. policymakers also face new policy questions. In an era of limited U.S. resources and competing demands for support of democratization elsewhere, what is the U.S. role in supporting democracy and human rights in Latin America? How can U.S. policy accommodate the diverse circumstances of Latin American democracies without losing its coherence? What is the role of U.S.–Latin American military relations and the inter-American military system in a democratic Latin America?

Civil-Military Conflict in the New Democracies

A central fact for both policymakers and analysts dealing with Latin America today is the substantial diversity in patterns of civil-military relations and levels of conflict between civilian governments and the armed forces.[3] Since the return to democratic rule in 1983, **Argentina** has experienced repeated confrontations between civilian and military authority.[4] In the early years of his administration, President Raúl Alfonsín made a concerted effort to subordinate the armed forces to civilian control. The military's defeat in the war with Great Britain and civilian repudiation of the military government's human rights violations divided the armed forces and isolated the military from their traditional civilian allies. Alfonsín's decision to place military officers on trial for "disappearances" and torture provoked an intense military reaction but received near-unanimous support from the civilian public. Alfonsín strengthened the civilian Ministry of Defense, replaced the traditionally autonomous service commanders with a new Joint Chiefs of Staff, and fired a number of generals for speaking publicly on political questions. The military budget was slashed from 5 percent of gross domestic product to less than 2.5 percent.[5] Military salaries declined dramatically, with increasing numbers of officers taking second jobs outside the military. Budget restrictions reduced military conscription and curtailed training programs and exercises.

The last three years of the Alfonsín government were marked by a broad-scale retreat in the face of repeated rebellions of junior officers, led by hard-line special forces veterans of the Malvinas-Falklands war. The first revolt in April 1987 was countered by a massive mobilization of civilian groups in defense of the democratic regime. Nevertheless, confronted with military refusal to carry out orders to suppress the rebellions, the government twice acceded to rebel demands for the resignation of the army chief of staff and eventually conceded a de facto amnesty for human rights violations committed during the military government. Faced with a growing economic crisis, Alfonsín was forced to speed up the transfer of power to Carlos Menem after the Peronist victory in the 1989 elections.

In contrast to Alfonsín, Menem sought to lower the level of civil-military tension in order to concentrate on the country's economic problems. The December 1990 revolt by *carapintada* leader Mohamed Seineldín was quickly suppressed and harshly punished, in part because for the first time noncommissioned officers played a major role in the uprising.[6] Later that month, Menem pardoned the imprisoned leaders of the military government, despite sharp civilian criticism. Although the release of the juntas and the purge of the carapintadas has lessened the danger of future revolts, over time military subordination to civilian rule has weakened; increasingly, the armed forces bargain with civilian authorities as autonomous forces.[7]

In **Brazil**, civil-military confrontations have been avoided by conceding to the armed forces a high level of institutional prerogatives and a voice in the new government.[8] The economic and political problems of the Sarney administration (1985–90) strengthened the military's role as a major political actor in the new regime. A proposal to create a civilian ministry of defense was abandoned in the face of strong military opposition. High-ranking officers played a major role in José Sarney's victory over opposition efforts to institute a parliamentary system and to limit his presidential term. When the Constituent Assembly abolished the National Security Council, Sarney transferred its staff to the new National Defense

Council. Brazil's first directly elected civilian president, Fernando Collor de Mello, has attempted to restrict the military's tutelary power, downgrading the military-dominated National Intelligence Service and terminating programs to develop a nuclear weapons capability. Collor's efforts have, however, been hampered by his weak political base and declining popularity in the face of persistently high rates of inflation and unemployment. At the same time, cuts in military budgets and falling military salaries have further eroded military confidence in the civilian regime.[9]

The military's allegiance to democratic rule is highly conditional. Given the international climate, a constitutional regime is seen as desirable, but the armed forces have insisted on a de facto veto power to ensure that civilian governments do not jeopardize Brazil's pursuit of its "permanent national objectives." In part because of the Brazilian military regime's greater economic success and its gradual, controlled transition, the armed forces retain substantial support from economic elites and the political Right, which share the military's concerns over Brazil's weak parties and civilian inability to manage the economy.

In **Uruguay**,[10] civilian and military leaders have fashioned a negotiated return to the status quo ante, with the aid of strong traditional parties and a history of military subordination to constitutional authority.[11] Except on the delicate question of officers accused of human rights violations, during the administration of President Julio María Sanguinetti (1985–90) military leaders generally refrained from intervening in policy disputes. Civilian leaders, in turn, displayed little interest in military policy, conceding substantial autonomy to the armed forces in matters such as military education and doctrine. Congressional cuts in military budgets and declining salaries generated some military complaints, but military allegiance to the constitutional regime seems secure as long as that regime remains dominated by the traditional Colorado and Blanco parties. Nevertheless, the flare-up in civil-military tensions over the appointment of a civilian minister of defense and naming of service commanders by President Luis Alberto Lacalle suggests that, even in Uruguay, conflict still exists over the extent of civilian authority over the armed forces.

In the new Andean democracies, civil-military relations have been less overtly conflictual than in Argentina but less stable than in Uruguay. In **Peru**,[12] the first civilian government, under President Fernando Belaúnde, was marked by Belaúnde's single-minded dedication to completing his term of office, despite a deteriorating economy and a growing internal war with the Sendero Luminoso and Tupac Amaru guerrillas. His successor, APRA's Alán García, initially profited—economically and politically—from his decision to unilaterally limit Peru's repayment of its foreign debt. Three years later, the economy was in shambles, with negative growth rates (−10 percent in 1989), skyrocketing inflation, and free-falling currency markets. The guerrilla war quickly spread to Lima and its surrounding shantytowns, with a steadily rising death toll of combatants and bystanders. Despite widespread military opposition, particularly in the air force, García created a new Ministry of Defense in place of the separate ministers for each military service. Nevertheless, the initial ministers have been retired officers who appear to function as intermediaries between the government and the military, rather than as agents of civilian authority. In early 1989, rumors of a coup against García were rife, with the press speculating about possible dates. But largely because of strong international opposition and the fear that a coup would lead sectors of the Left to join the armed opposition, military leaders decided to tough out García's last year in office. Alberto Fujimori, a political unknown, was the surprise victor over Mario Vargas Llosa in the 1990 elections. However, the president's limited base of organized support led to fears of increased military influence in the new government.[13] After less than two years in office, Fujimori closed the opposition-controlled congress and assumed the power to rule by decree. Leaders of the armed forces endorsed the new "emergency regime" and pledged their support for the government.

In **Ecuador**,[14] the first civilian government under Jaime Roldós and, after his death, Osvaldo Hurtado was characterized by a policy of mutual accommodation, with the military adhering to its constitutional role and the new government taking care not to offend the armed forces. In contrast, Hurtado's conservative successor, León Febres Cordero, became embroiled in a personal dispute with the air force commander, which led to two revolts by air force personnel, including a short-lived kidnapping of the president. Reliable sources suggest that the army was prepared to intervene if the 1989 elections had been won by populist Abdalá Bucaram,[15] but the second round went to center-left candidate Rodrigo Borja. Among civilians and military officers, support for a military role as political arbiter is strengthened by the country's fragmented party structure and weak civilian commitment to constitutional rule.

Despite several coup attempts and repeated rumors of military conspiracies, **Bolivia** has maintained its fragile constitutional system through three successive governments.[16] President Hernán Siles Suazo (1982–85) was, however, forced to call elections a year early because of deteriorating economic conditions. His successor, Víctor Paz Estenssoro, imposed a draconian anti-inflationary "shock treatment," which eventually stabilized the economy at the expense of widespread unemployment and the dismantling of the state mining company. Popular opposition to the austerity program, particularly from the powerful mine workers' union, was crushed by the use of army troops to control protest strikes and demonstrations. Potential deadlocks in the 1985 and 1989 elections were avoided by pacts between the eventual victors and the Alianza Democrática Nacionalista (ADN) headed by former military ruler Hugo Banzer, who has emerged as a key figure in the new regime. The stability of the democratic regime has been bolstered by U.S.

and Latin American support in moments of crisis and by the internal divisions of a weak military, discredited at home and abroad by its reputation for corruption and drug trafficking.

For the first time in recent memory, all of the Central American countries have elected civilian governments. Yet military relations with civilian leaders are complicated by the long tradition of military domination of Central American politics.[17] By South American standards, the Central American militaries have historically been weakly professionalized. Until recently, most operated more like police or national guard forces than armies, often with direct ties to civilian elites and military-dominated parties. Despite recent increases in technical and organizational development, most officers still view the armed forces as the ultimate arbiters of political power.

In **El Salvador**,[18] the threat of a cutoff in U.S. economic and military aid forced the armed forces into an uneasy partnership with the Christian Democratic government of José Napoleón Duarte. Civil-military relations were marked by sharp but largely covert conflicts over government policies and the conduct of the war against the FMLN guerrillas. Despite widespread human rights violations, even after curbing the gross excesses of the early 1980s, only a handful of lower-ranking military personnel were sanctioned. The 1989 election of conservative ARENA President Alfredo Cristiani brought closer government relations with the military but more tensions with the United States. The brutal murder of six Jesuit priests and two women following the November 1989 FMLN urban offensive resulted in indictments of four officers; two were subsequently convicted—but only after intense U.S. pressure and international condemnation. The change of government in Nicaragua and declining American support for continuation of President Ronald Reagan's cold war Central American policies put pressure on both the FMLN and the Cristiani government to reach a negotiated settlement to the civil war that has claimed over 70,000 lives. Despite the historic agreement, the provisions for cuts in the armed forces and creation of a new national police force presage serious tensions over the future role and powers of the military. As in Colombia, paramilitary groups are likely to continue the war by other means.

Guatemala has made a concerted effort to forge a new pattern of civil-military relations to replace the military-elite alliance that had ruled the country since the CIA-sponsored overthrow of the Arbenz government in 1954.[19] Under the leadership of Defense Minister General Héctor Gramajo, the "professionalist" faction of the army supported the Christian Democratic government of President Vinicio Cerezo (1985–90) against intense opposition from business groups and two major coup attempts. Yet, as critics have pointed out, the new regime institutionalizes a high degree of military autonomy and preserves military control over wide areas of national policy deemed vital for national security.

In **Honduras**, the absence of a serious guerrilla threat and a less interventionist military tradition have facilitated military acceptance of civilian rule. During the 1980s, the region's second largest U.S. military aid program provided an additional incentive for the military to refrain from overt military intervention. As in Ecuador, the chief threat to the stability of the post-1982 constitutional regime has come not from the armed forces, but from civilian failure to agree on democratic norms and attempts to enlist the military as allies in partisan conflicts. Still, the military retains a high level of autonomy from the government and dominates national security policy.[20]

The Risk of Renewed Military Intervention

As the country-by-country analysis suggests, many of the structural conditions that led to earlier periods of military intervention are still present, although with some important modifications. In particular, the current democratic regimes began with significantly higher legitimacy in the eyes of virtually all segments of the public. Especially in those countries that experienced extensive human rights violations under military rule, political democracy was revalued as a goal in and of itself.[21] Having suffered the worst of the repression, the political Left gained a new appreciation of the rule of law and democratic protection against state violence. Members of the political Right (and the United States) learned that the military was often an unreliable ally. Military rule did not necessarily guarantee political access or promotion of their economic interests, even in conservative military regimes. In countries with radical/reformist military leaders, economic elites were among the first to clamor for a return to democracy. In Brazil, Ecuador, and Peru, the legitimacy of democratic regimes has been enhanced by constitutional changes that eliminated the disenfranchisement of illiterates. With universal suffrage and high levels of participation in presidential elections, it has become much harder for ideological minorities to claim to represent the true "will of the people" against democratically elected governments.

On the negative side, partly as a result of previous periods of military rule, civilian institutions are still relatively weak and fragmented. In countries with strong traditional parties, those parties have tended to dominate posttransition elections, maintaining centrist governments and decreasing military objections to civilian policies. But even the traditional parties have been riven by internal factions and personalism that diminish their capacity to govern effectively. Countries with weak party systems have emerged from military rule even more fragmented. In Ecuador, for example, a dozen different parties are represented in the congress, making it difficult to construct legislative majorities or to encourage responsible opposition. The 1988 presidential elections were contested by ten different presidential tickets. In Brazil, in one sense there are no "major" parties.[22] Despite the introduction of the French system of two-stage presidential elections, which produces formal majorities in the second round, first-round results in both countries indicate that the eventual winners had less than 30 percent support; second-place finishers typically had less than 20 percent in the first round. Brazilian President Collor's National Renovation party—which did not exist a year before his election—won only 20 seats in the 559-person legislature.[23] Fragmented, weakly institutionalized party systems produce personalist or minority governments with narrow, unstable bases of public support. Representative institutions, such as legislatures and provincial/local governments, remain underdeveloped and underfunded, leaving the stability of these countries dangerously dependent on the personal popularity of the president. As witnessed in the dramatic loss of popular support suffered by Collor, Alfonsín, and García,[24] personal leadership is vulnerable to rapid public disillusionment.

Weak political institutions are particularly dangerous in countries where the armed forces have achieved a high degree of organizational and technical development. The principal examples of stable civilian regimes in Latin America are countries, such as Colombia, Mexico, and Venezuela, that developed strong civilian institutions *prior* to the development of strong, sophisticated militaries. Without the strengthening of the institutions of democracy—parties, legislatures, judiciaries, and other mechanisms of representation and conflict resolution—the organizational imbalances between civilian and military institutions reinforce the political self-confidence of the armed forces and undermine respect for civilian authority.

The effort to strengthen political institutions and legitimize constitutional democracy has been systematically undermined by the foreign debt crisis. During the 1980s, Latin America transferred roughly $25 billion a year in net capital flow to the developed countries. Civilian governments experimented with orthodox and heterodox policies to pay the debt, combat inflation, and promote economic growth, but with little effect. At the end of the decade, per capita income for the region was substantially below what it was in 1980. Argentina's per capita income has fallen below the 1970 level. In the month of January 1990, real wages fell by 20 percent; purchasing power for lower-income Argentine workers was 33 percent less than the 1989 average and 50 percent below the average for the 1980s. In other countries, the decline has been less dramatic, but economic stagnation and decreased employment opportunities have resulted in falling real wages and growing underemployment. The working class has borne the brunt of the economic crisis, but the middle class—particularly public employees—has also suffered serious losses as a result of hyperinflation and IMF-imposed austerity programs. In 1989 inflation exceeded 4000 percent in Argentina, 3500 percent in Nicaragua, 3000 percent in Peru, and 1500 percent in Brazil, averaging 1000 percent for the region as a whole.[25] The inability of democratic governments to restore economic growth or control inflation has produced a significant loss of public confidence. In past decades, this kind of economic failure would have quickly resulted in military coups.[26]

The survival of constitutional democracy in the midst of this prolonged economic crisis is itself a significant achievement.[27] To date, the major political effect of the debt crisis has been severe public punishment of incumbent parties at the next presidential election. Thus far, no governing party in the new democracies has won reelection since the debt crisis began in 1982. The discrediting of the political establishment is reflected in the electoral success of outsiders—Collor and Lula in Brazil, Fujimori in Peru, and, to a lesser extent, Menem in Argentina. Less visible but perhaps more important has been the increase in public support for revolutionary or military alternatives to democratic regimes. Although these are still minority viewpoints, the overwhelming public support for democracy in the early 1980s has visibly eroded.[28]

Military Role Beliefs and Coup Decisions

Military officers' conceptions of the legitimate role of the military in politics play a critical role in mediating military responses to the political environment. The failures of institutional military rule had a positive effect in discrediting the "national security and development" role beliefs that dominated the Latin American militaries in the 1960s and 1970s. Extended military rule resulted in internal factionalization, weakening of professional norms, corruption, and major losses in institutional prestige. In Brazil and Peru, military governments could point to some major achievements, despite their other failures; in the Southern Cone, human rights violations produced an even deeper loss of institutional legitimacy.

Decreased military self-confidence in their capacity to govern has led to a general rejection of the view that the armed forces should establish long-term military governments when necessary to ensure national security. Nevertheless, most military schools continue to teach the national security doctrines of earlier decades. National security is still broadly defined to include a wide range of political, socioeconomic, and international factors. This all-encompassing concept of security transforms domestic and foreign policy issues into "military" issues, encouraging military demands for a voice in nonmilitary policy decisions. Despite increased interest in external defense roles among the navy and air forces of the more professionalized militaries, army officers remain preoccupied with internal security threats.[29] In most countries, the hard-line variant of the national security doctrine—stressing the ideological character of the "subversive threat"—gained ground during the 1980s. Still, most officers are extremely reluctant to return to direct military rule.

In most cases, the result of this combination—lack of military self-confidence in their capacity to govern along with a simultaneous lack of confidence in civilian political leadership—has been formal adherence to the constitutional regime mixed with assertions of the military's traditional role as political guardians.[30] In this view, the armed forces reserve the right to intervene to protect "vital national interests" or ensure "national security" in times of political crisis. This view of the military as a suprapolitical, autonomous institution is institutionalized in existing patterns of military thought and perpetuated by the lack of a positive civilian program for military reform. As long as the military defines its role as the guardian of national interests and/or national security, the stability of the new democracies will remain dependent on a complex military calculus, weighing the costs and benefits of intervention in particular situations using traditional coup decision criteria.

With varying degrees of intensity, **public opinion** has generally opposed potential military coups. None of the military revolts of the last decade had widespread civilian support, even from the military's traditional allies. Formal and informal pacts among members of the political leadership have significantly reduced the number of civilians "knocking at the barracks door." Still, as noted above, civilian support for democracy appears to be weakening.

Given the depth of the economic crisis, **public disorders** have been less common than many observers expected. Food riots in Venezuela in 1989 resulted in several hundred deaths; looting of supermarkets in Argentina led to a presidential decree authorizing military intervention in the event of "internal commotion," which—at least in spirit—contradicts the new National Defense law reserving internal security functions for the police.[31] Still, strikes and labor protests have been surprisingly moderate. Labor militancy has been diminished by the repression of radical leaders under military rule and by the enormous growth of the reserve army of the underemployed. Particularly in the Southern Cone, labor leaders have consciously tried to avoid destabilizing the new democracies.

Except in those countries facing long-standing insurgencies, the **communist threat** has dramatically receded. Except perhaps in Brazil, electoral support for the Left has generally declined, despite economic conditions seemingly favorable to leftist parties and radical populists. The collapse of communist regimes in Eastern Europe and glasnost in the former Soviet Union have undoubtedly contributed to the crisis of the Latin American Left; voter rejection of the Sandinista regime in the Nicaraguan election has deepened the crisis.

External support for democratic regimes has been a significant factor in overcoming potential coup threats. The U.S. threat to cut off military aid is perhaps less important than the potential denial of assistance in debt rescheduling, but it still carries some weight for militaries facing shrinking budgets and increased difficulties financing purchases of replacement parts for aging arms inventories. Moral and diplomatic support for democracy from other Latin American democracies and from Western Europe also contributes to an international environment that is widely perceived as hostile to military regimes.

Many of the current civil-military tensions are rooted in conflicts over the military's **institutional interests**—its budget, status, professional autonomy, and political influence. In countries where the military has traditionally enjoyed a high degree of autonomy and power, civilian attempts to reduce military prerogatives are inherently controversial. Although most officers remain sensitive to the institutional costs of recent military regimes, those memories are fading in time relative to the success or failure of the current civilian governments. In a perverse way, the economic crisis has also become a deterrent to military rule. Given the obvious political costs of economic stabilization and austerity programs, few officers see any institutional advantage in assuming direct responsibility for managing the debt crisis.

On balance, military calculations of the costs and benefit of intervention have come out in favor of continuing military support for civilian governments, at times grudgingly, sometimes by relatively narrow margins. Military revolts have generally centered around corporate or personal grievances, which lack the nonmilitary backing necessary to achieve intramilitary consensus for a coup, especially in the face of domestic and international opposition. The situational factors that have thus far discouraged new military coups (except in Panama and Haiti) are, however, by their nature subject to change. Weak political institutions, seemingly endless economic crises, and the loss of public support for democratic governments are likely to produce temporary interventions in some of the new democracies. Given military reluctance to return to direct military rule, the coups of the 1990s are likely to be limited to installing caretaker governments and calling new elections.

At the same time, there is impressionistic evidence of a cautious military groping toward new models of civil-military relations. Many officers speak of military coups and especially military governments as things of the past. Although this perception seems largely based on international events—and is therefore likely to change in the event of coups in any of the major countries or a change in U.S. policy—there appears to be a general expectation that civilian governments will remain the norm for the foreseeable future. If so, the critical question for the 1990s may not be the stability of the current regimes, but rather, How democratic are the patterns of civil-military relations that have emerged in the 1980s?

Patterns of Civil-Military Relations in the New Democracies

In fully democratic regimes, civil-military relations—the interactions between the armed forces, the state, and society—are marked by two essential characteristics. First, the military is politically subordinate to constitutionally designated civilian authorities. In all of its many variants, democratic theory rejects the idea of a politically autonomous military acting as guardians of national security or "national interests." Second, the armed forces are professionally and institutionally subordinate to democratic control. Civilian authorities are ultimately responsible for **defense policy**. The president and the congress define the threats against which the country must be protected and determine the allocation of resources between defense and other priorities. The armed forces are *professional advisers* to civilian authorities and *institutional instruments* for execution of the government's defense policies. Civilian authorities are also responsible for defining **military policy**, that is, defining the norms and creating institutional mechanisms to establish and operate the system of civil-military relations.[32] Abdication of civilian responsibility for military policy means, in effect, that the armed forces dictate the terms of civil-military relationships.

This ideal model suggests a typology of civil-military relations in the Latin American democracies, based on varying degrees of military subordination to or autonomy from democratic control.[33] Furthest removed from the democratic model are the cases of **military dominance**, in which civilian governments are effectively subordinated to the armed forces, rather than vice versa. The military's policy choices are imposed on civilian presidents, who govern at the sufferance of the military commander(s). The clearest example of this pattern was Panama under Noriega, who twice deposed the presidents he had designated. The Haitian army has likewise twice overthrown elected presidents who challenged military leaders.

A second pattern is characterized by extensive military participation in national policy-making. The armed forces exercise a **tutelary** role with respect to civilian authorities, speaking publicly on national policy issues even when these fall outside of the strictly military sphere. Civilian groups, including the president, seek to influence policy by mobilizing military allies. In Brazil, under Sarney, six of the twenty-six cabinet ministers were active-duty officers, who intervened—along with other military leaders—in policy debates over constitutional revisions, agrarian reform, and labor legislation.[34] In Guatemala, despite their formal constitutional subordination to the president as commander in chief, the armed forces exercise substantial power on all matters related to national security broadly defined.[35] The army plays a key role in the Poles of Development program and interagency committees that coordinate government policy in insurgent-contested zones. The State Security Council, consisting of military and civilian ministers, is headed by the Army Secretariat of Intelligence.

Chile is perhaps the most complex case. The Constitution of 1980 was clearly designed by Augusto Pinochet to provide a tutelary role for the armed forces in subsequent civilian governments. The military controls four of the eight seats on the National Security Council, which can be called into session by any two of its members. The president is *not* the commander in chief of the armed forces and cannot remove any of the current service commanders except with the concurrence of the Security Council. The new Organic Law of the Armed Forces guarantees the military total institutional autonomy from civilian control, including a predetermined floor for the military budget. Under President Patricio Aylwin, the civilian coalition government has rejected the tutelary model but has had only limited success in asserting its control over the armed forces. Pinochet's decision to remain as army commander after stepping down as president increases the likelihood of an eventual confrontation over the role of the military in the new regime.[36]

The third pattern is **conditional military subordination**. In these cases, the armed forces refrain from overt intervention in political matters. However, they reserve their right to intervene to protect national interests and guarantee national security in times of crisis. Both the definition of "national interests" and the determination of what actions are warranted in crisis situations are decisions reserved to the armed forces. Bolivia, Ecuador, Honduras, and Peru appear to fit this pattern. Senior officers rarely make overtly political public statements or pronouncements on national policy matters. Nevertheless, because the military is only conditionally loyal, civilian governments defer to presumed or privately expressed military opinion on issues that might provoke military discontent. The armed forces thus exert an indirect, anticipatory political influence on nonmilitary policies without overtly contravening the norm of an apolitical military. Within this pattern, the armed forces typically exercise a high degree of institutional autonomy and a quasi-monopoly over internal and external defense policy. The minister of defense is normally a military officer; service commanders are selected by the president but only within the narrow limits permitted by institutional regulations. The president and the congress set the military budget, but military doctrine and military education are the exclusive preserve of the armed forces.

In the fourth pattern, **consolidated democratic control**, the armed forces are politically and professionally subordinate to the appropriate civilian authorities, including a civilian minister of defense. Civilian governments can prevail on matters where military officers disagree with civilian policy without threatening the stability of the democratic regime. Among the new democracies, only Uruguay and Argentina during the initial years of the Alfonsín government approximated this pattern. Even in Uruguay, military subordination to democratic control did not include the human rights issue. In both Uruguay and Argentina, the military still retains a substantial degree of de facto institutional autonomy.[37]

In regimes with **institutionalized democratic control**, the armed forces voluntarily accept civilian control because they have internalized democratic professional norms.[38] Conflicts between civilian and military authorities are handled within established institutional channels. In periods of crisis, public attention is focused on constitutional mechanisms of conflict resolution, rather than on rumors of military intervention. In Latin America, Venezuela has made the greatest progress toward institutionalized democratic control. But even in Venezuela, a breakdown of civilian control is still not unthinkable.[39]

Within this typology, important variations also exist in the level of conflict over the distribution of power and autonomy in civil-military relations, which in turn affects the stability of these relationships.[40] These differences reflect major cross-national variations in the extent of military control over the transition process, the degree of repression and ideological hardening of the military during the previous military regime, and the historical model of civil-military relations under earlier civilian governments.[41] Thus, civilian authorities in traditionally democratic Uruguay encountered significantly less *military* resistance than in Argentina, where democratic control implies a major loss of military prerogatives compared to recent decades. Since taking office in 1989, President Menem has chosen to reduce the level of conflict by tacitly ceding the military's right to bargain with the civilian government on institutional issues and in effect restricting, at least temporarily, the scope of effective civilian control.[42] In the tutelary regimes, there are likewise important differences in the degree of *civilian* acceptance of the military's extensive political and professional prerogatives. In Chile, the new civilian leaders have argued for a return to the traditional norms of military subordination and resisted military attempts to preserve a tutelary role in the new regime. In both Chile and Argentina, the strengthening of hard-line military factions under military rule complicates efforts to achieve civilian control. Likewise, in Central America a long history of military domination reinforces military claims to power sharing, which weak civilian presidents have been unable to resist. If, however, the revolutionary Left (or Right, in the case of Nicaragua) can be incorporated into democratic politics via negotiated settlements of the Central American wars, these power-sharing arrangements are likely to be more actively contested.

In the long-term, the tutelary model is likely to be unstable. Given the ideological differences between civil society and the armed forces, allowing the military to function as a pressure or veto group within a civilian regime diminishes the capacity of the regime to be responsive to civilian interests. Accommodating the military's policy preferences may diminish tensions in the short run, but ultimately it undermines regime legitimacy. Sooner or later the lack of autonomy from military pressures will lead to public perception of these regimes as pseudo-democracies. In the past, such limited democracies have proven to be inherently unstable.[43]

Conditional military subordination is likewise not conducive to the long-term survival of the new democracies. In effect, civilian governments are tolerated as long as they respect the institutional interests of the military and avoid serious national crises. Given the structural conditions under which Latin American democracies operate, political and economic crises are inevitable. In crisis situations, the military can either intervene temporarily to replace the government or demand a reversal of the policies perceived to have led to the crisis. The first alternative increases the probability of a subsequent return to more permanent intervention and direct military rule; the second increases the likelihood of a shift toward the tutelary model and a greater military role in the determination of state policy.

Current patterns of civil-military relations are therefore subject to varying degrees of instability. There is clearly no automatic process of movement toward more democratic patterns; reversions to less democratic models are also possible, in some cases probable.

The Military and Human Rights: Dealing with the Legacy of the Past

By far the most difficult and contentious single issue in civil-military relations has been the question of accountability for human rights violations by members of the armed forces. No other issue illustrates so dramatically the limits of civilian rule or the dilemmas facing democratic leaders in dealing with the military. In the Southern Cone, Brazil, and Central America, the military regimes of the 1970s committed extensive violations of the fundamental right to physical integrity, as well as less dramatic violations of political and economic rights. Kidnappings, torture, and "disappearances" of political prisoners became institutionalized mechanisms in the military's war against "subversion." The climate of fear created by clandestine military organizations was an important instrument of political control, even after the elimination of the guerrilla organizations against which they were initially directed. In most cases, prior to turning over power to their civilian replacements, military governments granted blanket amnesties protecting military personnel from prosecution for acts committed "in the line of duty." With the return to civilian governments, human rights groups demanded investigation and prosecution for human rights abuses. Public support for these demands varied, roughly in relation to the number of victims.

In Argentina, with nearly 9,000 documented "disappearances" in the military's antisubversive campaign,[44] Alfonsín's pledge to punish human rights violations was integral to his victory in the 1983 elections. Once in office, Alfonsín sent to the congress legislation that repealed the military's self-amnesty and provided for automatic appeal of all decisions of the Supreme Military Tribunal to civilian courts. A national commission was established to investigate the fate of the disappeared persons. The commission conducted lengthy public hearings, taking testimony from relatives, friends, and victims of the repression. Its report—broadcast in a nationwide television special and published in an instant best-seller—documented the existence of a clandestine military-police network of detention centers where persons suspected of subversive connections or sympathies were systematically tortured and, in most instances, summarily executed. Criminal charges were subsequently filed against the nine army, navy, and air force commanders who constituted the first three military governments. After the Supreme Military Tribunal found no cause for prosecution, the cases passed into the civilian Court of Appeals, which eventually sentenced two members of the first junta to life imprisonment, imposed varying prison terms on three others, and acquitted the rest. Subsequently, similar charges were filed against a growing number of other officers.

Adverse military reaction to the trials was intense and virtually unanimous. Despite Alfonsín's repeated statement that individual officers would be tried, not the military institution, in practice the trials became a collective civilian condemnation of the armed forces. For the military, the trials could not be a judgment against individuals, as the counterrevolutionary campaign involved all three branches and all levels of the military hierarchy. In the military view, the "struggle against subversion" was an internal war, in which more officers died than in the Malvinas. Faced with a terrorist war directed primarily at the police and military officers, the military responded by adopting terrorist methods and organization.[45] Torture was justified as a necessary tool to extract intelligence information to break the tight cell structure of the Montoneros and ERP guerrillas. The "dirty war" continued even after the guerrillas were defeated, because the enemy was not only the armed opposition and its support network, but all those holding ideological positions contrary to "Western Christian civilization" as well. Many officers felt some ambivalence about the trial of the juntas, because these were also the generals responsible for the failures of the military regime and the disaster in the Malvinas. As charges were brought against lower-ranking officers still on active duty, military resistance quickly stiffened. Military reaction to the trials also reflected other discontents—declining salaries, the loss of institutional prerogatives, and constant criticism in the press and mass media—which were widely perceived as attempts to undermine or destroy the armed forces. Defense of the "war against subversion" was thus a moral defense of the institution.[46]

Belatedly recognizing the depth of the military opposition, Alfonsín sent to the congress the "Ley de Punto Final" creating a date after which no new charges could be filed. The new law galvanized the efforts of human rights groups, which quickly

pressed charges against several hundred additional officers, many of whom had been lieutenants and captains in the 1970s. The breaking point occurred in April 1987, when an army major refused to appear in court and declared a barracks revolt against the army chief of staff for failing to defend the institution. Despite a massive civilian mobilization to defend the regime, other military units refused to repress the rebellion. Although President Alfonsín announced that he had negotiated the surrender of the rebels "without concessions," he subsequently sent to the congress the "Law of Due Obedience," which effectively exonerated all junior officers of responsibility for human rights charges on the grounds that they "could not resist" obeying the orders of their superiors. Two subsequent revolts in 1988 extended military demands to include the dropping of charges against rebel officers, the freeing of those already convicted of human rights violations, and public vindication of military actions in the "dirty war." Shortly after coming to power, President Menem announced the termination of all military trials and pardoned most of the officers still in prison.[47] A year later, he pardoned the convicted members of the juntas.

In Uruguay, human rights violations under military rule involved fewer executions but more extensive use of torture against a much smaller population.[48] Following the installation of a civilian government in 1985, individual court cases began to be filed against a growing number of military, police, and prison personnel. A small group of former guerrillas still in prison was pardoned, but proposals to grant amnesty to the military sparked sharp debate. In 1986 top military leaders sparked a crisis by refusing to issue orders compelling officers to appear in court. Under strong pressure from President Sanguinetti, legislators representing the two traditional parties approved a complex legal formula by which the state agreed to forego its right to prosecute crimes committed under military rule. The de facto amnesty was widely opposed by the political Left as well as many supporters of the opposition Blanco party. Human rights groups spearheaded a campaign to gather petition signatures equal to 25 percent of the electorate in order to force a national referendum on repeal of the nonprosecution law. When petitions with more than 630,000 signatures were returned, the Electoral Tribunal delayed its ruling but ultimately failed to disqualify enough signatures to prevent the referendum. Influenced in part by the bitter conflicts in neighboring Argentina, moderate and conservative groups rallied behind warnings from Sanguinetti and Defense Minister General Hugo Medina that repeal would lead to a civil-military confrontation that could destabilize the democratic regime. After a heated and divisive campaign, the repeal initiative failed by a margin of 53 to 41 percent.

In Brazil, the urban guerrilla groups of the early 1970s were a far less serious threat to the military regime. Despite the formation of various antisubversive units within the military, the number of executions and cases of torture was smaller, especially in relation to its population. Faced with a united military refusal to permit trials of active or retired officers, the political leadership has ignored the human rights issue.[49] The only investigation was conducted and later published by human rights activists, aided by the Catholic church, who smuggled out military court documents from the trials of political prisoners.

In Chile, the new Christian Democratic government confronted similar issues. Several thousand supporters of the Allende government and MIR militants were killed in the 1973 military takeover and the ensuing suppression of the Left. Thousands more were held as political prisoners; many were tortured. After 1974, the repression became more selective and centralized under the Directorate of National Intelligence (DINA), which assassinated opponents of the regime in Chile and abroad. In 1978 the military government issued a blanket amnesty to all military personnel. Most of the documented disappearances during the military regime occurred prior to the amnesty, but a number of highly visible cases happened during the 1980s. High-ranking officers made clear their opposition to any repeal of the amnesty law.[50] Pinochet also warned that no civilian court would be permitted to touch anyone who acted under military orders, even for acts that occurred after the amnesty. Nevertheless, the Aylwin government named a high-level panel to investigate human rights cases, arguing that it was necessary to tell the truth about human rights abuses, by the military government or by antiregime groups, even it were not possible to do justice to the victims. The report of the Commission on Truth and Reconciliation detailed over two thousand deaths and disappearances and sparked new demands for modification of the amnesty law to permit officers to be tried (but not sentenced) for crimes committed prior to 1978. But the government's reluctance to risk a confrontation with the military and opposition from the conservative bloc in the senate have thus far prevented the necessary changes.[51]

Accountability for human rights violations committed by previous military governments is a true dilemma for the new democracies. If, as in Brazil, the perpetrators are not held accountable, the armed forces may conclude that future violations can be committed again with impunity.[52] On moral and legal grounds, the case for self-amnesty is untenable under the international conventions to which these countries were signatories. In Uruguay, despite extensive disclosure of the general pattern of repression, justice was denied to individual victims by a vote of the people after a divisive national debate. In Argentina, the CONADEP investigation and the trial of the juntas disclosed the unpleasant truth that many of the military's civilian supporters had chosen to deny. The result was a significant loss in support for the military among its traditional allies and a strengthening of civilian determination to avoid a repetition, captured in the title of the CONADEP report *Never Again*. The cost in Argentina was also high: a bitter civil-military polarization and repeated confrontations, setting in motion a government retreat behind convoluted legalisms with little or no credibility and, ultimately, a forced amnesty, despite public opposition. The cost also includes the diversion of the Alfonsín administration from the task of defining a new role for the armed forces in the democratic regime, and the progressive loss of civilian control over the armed forces. The experience of Argentina and Uruguay is evidence that the rule of law cannot be created simply by writing new constitutions or installing democratic governments. Nor can the law be imposed on the armed forces if they reject the moral basis of that law. In Chile, who will try Pinochet for the crimes committed by DINA, which reported directly to the president? Subordinating the armed forces to the rule of law will, in most cases, be a long and difficult process.

Fighting Internal Wars

Conflicts over human rights violations have also been prominent in El Salvador, Peru, Colombia, and Guatemala. In each of these cases, elected civilian governments face long-term internal wars against guerrilla forces that do not accept the legitimacy of the current regime. In wars where the enemy wears no uniform and relies on its ability to blend with the civilian population, the killing of noncombatants by government forces is a common occurrence.[53] Sometimes these deaths are inadvertent; often they occur in revenge for alleged sheltering or support for guerrilla forces. Guerrilla forces routinely engage in assassinations of local officials, "informers," and individual members of the police and armed forces. Often the military retaliates in kind. Some of the most brutal and cold-blooded violations have occurred at the hands of paramilitary death squads, composed of right-wing terrorists, private security forces, members of the police, and/or military personnel operating outside of their regular units. Such forces have been tacitly condoned and protected by many officers who view them as useful in eliminating or intimidating real or potential guerrilla sympathizers. In El Salvador, Archbishop Romero is the best known among thousands of death squad victims. In Colombia, the death squads have targeted supporters of the Unión Patriótica (UP), which was created as a legal party following peace negotiations between the government and the FARC guerrillas. Since 1985, more than a thousand UP members have been assassinated, including two of the party's presidential candidates.

Civilian governments have been unable to control these violations. In most cases, they have been unwilling to risk losing military support by sanctioning those responsible. Despite President García's pledge to punish the officers involved in the massacre of several hundred Sendero Luminoso prisoners after the 1986 prison uprisings, it took over three years for one colonel and one lieutenant to be sentenced to prison terms by the Supreme Council of Military Justice.[54] In numerous other cases, military courts have simply ruled that no homicide occurred. The case of the six Jesuit priests and two women murdered at the University of Central America in San Salvador is the first instance of indictments or convictions of military officers in the long history of that civil war. In countries with weak, intimidated judiciaries, and shadowy wars of terror and counterterror, the law of war is routinely ignored. Civilian inability to control paramilitary death squads or sanction human rights violations has seriously diminished regime legitimacy by baring the limits of the rule of law and demonstrating the inability of civilian governments to protect their own citizens.[55]

In all four cases, internal war has also resulted in significant militarization of civilian regimes. Militarization takes place on several different levels. Following the historic pattern of military autonomy, most civilian governments assume that the military will run the war and the civilians will run the rest of the government. But civil wars are rarely fought that way. Effective antiguerrilla warfare requires coordinated social and economic policies, "civic action" projects, and psychological warfare campaigns. Civilian failure to implement the kinds of policies the military deems necessary to defeat the guerrillas results in increased civil-military tensions and decreased military respect for civilian rule. Given the inherently political character of counterinsurgency warfare, the eventual result is usually military demands for a greater policy voice on matters directly and indirectly related to the war effort. Internal war thus creates pressures toward the tutelary model of civil-military relations, even in countries like Colombia with a long history of civilian rule.[56]

In addition, military authorities become the de facto territorial government in contested areas of the country. In 1988 ten of Peru's twenty-four departments, with over half of the national population, were officially emergency zones in which local military commanders exercised both military and civil functions.[57] In these conflicts, not only the government, but also political life itself becomes militarized. On both sides, military violence is directed against other citizens. With or without elections, bullets are the ultimate political currency. The expression of political opinions and political participation—for or against the government—exposes the noncombatant public to armed violence from the other side. In such cases, elections do not necessarily constitute democratic regimes.[58] Without the rule of law, effective political representation, and freedom to organize without fear of violence, civilian regimes are at best partially democratic; at worst, they become indistinguishable from their military predecessors.

In a less dramatic fashion, military involvement in antidrug missions presents a similar risk of militarization of democratic regimes.[59] As in counterinsurgency missions, the enemy—for instance, peasant producers of coca leaf or marijuana—

is part of the local population. Like counterinsurgency, drug eradication also involves the military in a wide range of related policy issues—crop substitution, development programs, domestic intelligence operations, and so forth. For nationalist sectors of the public and the armed forces, it also involves the problem of the military acting as agents for the United States, shifting the burden away from the insatiable American demand for drugs onto local economies desperate for any kind of employment.[60] The biggest risk is military corruption, especially in militaries that have only recently achieved intermediate levels of professionalization. In most countries, noncommissioned and junior officers are typically paid $50 to $300 a month. Even generals' salaries are insignificant compared to the bribes the drug cartels can pay for protection or intelligence. If the drug lords with their private armies manage to subvert significant fractions of the military, as they did to a degree in Bolivia in the 1970s, what democratic government will be able to resist this new alliance of economic and military power? Fortunately, like the problem of internal war, the drug problem is specific to a relatively small number of countries.

Latin American Policies for Democratic Consolidation

Redefining existing patterns of civil-military relations and avoiding militarization of civilian regimes will require a long-term effort. There are no magic solutions or easy alternatives to patterns rooted in historical experiences, political structures, and socioeconomic contexts that are quite different from those of Western European or North American democracies. Civilian leaders must therefore develop long-term strategies for promoting more democratic relations with the armed forces. These strategies must take into account the diverse starting points and distinctive balance of political forces in each country. The agenda of issues facing civilian leaders varies substantially, as does their margin for maneuver vis-à-vis military leaders intent on maintaining their traditional power and prerogatives. There will be no single path to consolidation of a democratic model of civil-military relations. Within these diverse national strategies, the common objective must be to reduce the risk of military intervention by changing the conditions that contribute to that risk.

Avoiding a new round of coups or militarization of democratic regimes requires, first, empowering civilian institutions.[61] Democratic consolidation cannot succeed without civilian commitment to constitutional rules for political conflict and increased capabilities for effective government. Strengthening legislative and judicial institutions is essential to reduce the burden of political responsibilities on already-overloaded executives. In some countries, formal pacts among the major political parties to defend the democratic regime will be necessary to survive the economic crisis and growing public disillusionment. Political leaders must take the primary responsibility for defending against a breakdown of democratic politics.

Second, democratic leaders must develop a basic consensus with respect to the missions to be assigned to the armed forces. To the extent that democratic political forces have no clear definition of the role of the armed forces in a democratic society, they invite nondemocratic forces to fill that void with their own defini-tions. Integrating the military in democratic regimes requires a legitimate profes-sional mission.[62] External defense missions are clearly easier to reconcile with democratic control, but for Latin American militaries a reserve, if not an active, role in internal security is probably unavoidable. Use of the military in secondary missions, such as civic action, drug control, or economic development functions involves a risk of military involvement in related policy conflicts. It also implies different force structures, training patterns, and professional norms. At a mini-mum, a strategy for democratic control of the military requires a conscious military policy that defines the kind of military that democratic leaders desire.

Third, civilian leaders must acknowledge that the context of civil-military relations is different in Latin American democracies and that civil-military con-flicts are deeper and more intractable than in other democracies. Integrating the military within democratic regimes will require constitutional innovations and new institutional mechanisms that permit those conflicts to be managed in ways that are consistent with democratic norms. One example might be a national security council composed of civilian ministers and legislative representatives, to whom all general officers have guaranteed access to speak on matters of national security when their professional conscience requires dissent from government policies. Another might be legal standing for officers to appeal to the courts when civilian decisions violate professional norms. Norms of professional behavior must allow for military dissent on national security issues within democratic channels. If such channels do not exist, conflict and opposition will be expressed in ways that undermine democratic regimes.

Finally, civilian leaders must take seriously their responsibility in internal security. This involves clearly delineating the respective roles of the armed forces, the police, and other security forces in defending the democratic state against attempts to impose an alternative regime by force. In countries faced with serious insurgencies, it also involves the coordination of political, social, and economic policies with military operations in an integrated strategy of internal defense. By definition, internal war involves the use of state violence against one's own citizens. The laws and norms governing the rights of combatants and noncombat-ants in domestic conflicts cannot be less demanding than those applied to interna-tional wars. Failure to enforce those norms diminishes regime legitimacy and aggravates the security problem. If, as many analysts argue, the internal security doctrines of past decades undermined democracy and contributed to human rights violations,[63] democratic leaders and analysts must assume the responsibility for developing alternative counterinsurgency doctrines appropriate for democratic regimes. If not, the "Argentine solution" will remain the default alternative.

U.S. Policies for Democratic Consolidation

In the 1980s, the international environment was an important factor supporting Latin American efforts to promote political democracy, in contrast to previous decades when the United States supported military coups against governments hostile to U.S. interests and backed military regimes that promised to suppress the threat of communism. The reversal of these policies under the Carter and Reagan administrations increased the legitimacy of democratic regimes (and the legitimacy of U.S. policy) and encouraged transitions to civilian government in countries still under military rule.[64] Support for democratic governments from the United States, Western Europe, and Latin democracies played an important role in deterring potential coups in Bolivia, Ecuador, El Salvador, Honduras, and Peru. In each case, however, international support for democracy succeeded because it *reinforced* domestic groups and sectors of the military opposed to military intervention. Given the present structural conditions in Latin America, domestic conditions will not always be favorable to democratic survival. In Haiti, U.S. and OAS sanctions have thus far had little effect.

U.S. policies should therefore be directed to the long-term goal of democratic consolidation, acknowledging that there will be reverses and that the crucial policy choices have to be made in Latin American capitals, not in Washington.[65] Given the diverse circumstances of individual Latin American countries, U.S. policy should emphasize consistency in upholding democratic governments and democratic *principles* of civil-military relations,[66] acknowledging the diverse strategies appropriate to encouraging movement toward more democratic relationships with the armed forces. Applying those principles in the 1990s will require more sophisticated and nuanced policies than in the 1970s, when military governments were the chief obstacle to democracy and the principal agents of human rights violations. In the decade ahead, as in the 1980s, major violations of human rights will occur under civilian regimes, not military dictatorships. Military intervention will most likely occur not against, but *within* elected governments. U.S. policy must therefore move beyond simple distinctions between civilian and military governments to focus on the long-term goal of consolidation of stable democracies and democratic civil-military relations.[67]

The most effective U.S. strategy would be to concentrate on the underlying causes of military intervention. Latin American efforts to strengthen civilian institutions could be assisted through the National Endowment for Democracy. Technical assistance to legislatures and judicial institutions would be particularly valuable. However, the most urgent and dramatic need is for economic support from both the United States and other industrial democracies. The legitimacy of civilian regimes in Latin America depends in part on their ability to manage the economic crisis more effectively than their military predecessors.[68] Thus far, international economic conditions and the policies of the creditor nations have forced democratic governments to adopt policies that differ only marginally from those imposed by force under military rule. A significant U.S. initiative on debt relief beyond the Brady Plan is essential to sustain the political viability of democratic regimes in the region. It would be ironic—though not unprecedented—if U.S. economic policies undermined our political objectives in the region or if U.S. efforts to aid nascent democracies in Eastern Europe reduced economic support for struggling democracies in Latin America.

Another complex issue facing the United States is the future of its military assistance programs. In the 1950s and 1960s, these programs provided the country with considerable direct and indirect influence over the Latin American militaries. The United States maintained an extensive network of military advisers throughout the region, held a near-monopoly on foreign military training, and had a dominant position as arms supplier through direct sales and transfers of surplus U.S. equipment. Although the extent of U.S. influence was often exaggerated by supporters and critics of military aid, that influence was nevertheless important, particularly when U.S. policies aimed at "containing communism" coincided with the institutional interests and ideological orientation of Latin American officers.

In subsequent decades, U.S. military influence sharply declined.[69] Human rights restrictions barred much of the region from grant aid and training programs. Despite increased funding for military aid under the Reagan administration, almost all of the increase went to El Salvador and Honduras. Excluding those two countries, grant military aid declined from roughly $110 million a year in 1969 to an average of $35 million in the mid-1980s. Transfers of surplus equipment, which averaged $33 million a year from 1950 to 1968, totaled less than $1 million for 1980–86 combined. The number of Latin American military personnel receiving U.S. training dropped from a high of 9,000 in 1962 to roughly 2,000 a year during the Reagan years. In 1983 U.S. grant military aid constituted an estimated 1 percent of Latin America's military expenditures; excluding El Salvador and Honduras, the figure was roughly 0.1 percent. By the late 1970s, the U.S. share of the Latin American arms market had dropped to less than 10 percent. Moreover, U.S. support for democracy is less compatible with Latin American military interests and ideology than the goal of fighting communism. Antidrug programs will provide a new source of funding for direct and indirect military assistance programs to countries of particular concern—that is, Bolivia, Colombia, and Peru—but their limited geographic scope and the tendentious issues involved make it unlikely that drug aid will become a significant source of U.S. military influence over their Latin counterparts.

A logical argument could be made for phasing out U.S. military aid programs to the region, but that argument is not likely to be persuasive in Washington as long as guerrilla insurgencies and drug exports continue to be a problem in Central and South America.[70] Continuation of current small-scale military aid programs could provide a modest reward for military support for civilian regimes and a symbolic sanction for those guilty of gross violations of human rights or clear departures from democratic civil-military relations. To be effective as an instrument for democratic consolidation, military aid must be denied to governments—including elected democratic governments—that fail to prevent and/or punish systematic violations of fundamental human rights. Denial of military aid to such governments is appropriate, as in virtually every case the armed forces are either directly responsible or the only force capable of controlling paramilitary groups committing such violations.[71] To be credible, U.S. decisions to permit or deny military aid must be based on independent reporting of violations by groups such as Amnesty International, the United Nations, and the Organization of American States, rather than the State Department's human rights reports. However accurate the latter may be, they will always be suspected of prejudice based on other U.S. interests in the government in question.

Distinguishing democratic governments from elected but nondemocratic governments likewise involves difficult judgments for U.S. policymakers. In the past decade, the United States has emphasized the importance of honest, competitive elections as a key measure of political democracy. In the decade ahead, it must place more attention on the conditions under which elections are held, particularly the freedom to organize politically without fear of government or opposition violence. Distinguishing undemocratic patterns of civil-military relations also involves multiple criteria and often limited data. Nevertheless, countries where a civilian president serves at the sufferance of the military commander are arguably as undemocratic as nonelected governments and hence should be denied U.S. military aid. Regimes where the military controls a significant number of cabinet posts or positions in the national security council, or exercises a policy veto, are at best partially democratic and should be treated as such. Military aid should be conditional upon certified progress toward greater democratic control in order to avoid tacit U.S. endorsement of regimes whose legitimacy and stability are suspect.

The United States also needs to reexamine the International Military Education and Training Program (IMET) and other U.S. contacts with Latin American officers to ensure that these programs implement U.S. policies in support of democracy and human rights. In the past, IMET has relied heavily on the assumption that U.S. values and beliefs about civil-military relations would be conveyed automatically through simple exposure to the U.S. model. Particularly in the case of attitudes that run counter to the predispositions of Latin officers, conscious efforts must be made to explain and defend the U.S. position. Despite bureaucratic resistance, some changes have occurred in U.S. training programs. The law of war, with specific applications to internal war, is now an integral part of the curriculum at the School of the Americas. Formally and informally, military subordination to constitutional authority is encouraged. At the same time, the American training experience often reinforces ideological predispositions that encourage resistance to democratic control of the armed forces. Traditionally, senior-level courses have stressed a cold war view of geopolitics and global defense, as well as the military's role in "nation-building." Although these courses appear nonpolitical to U.S. officers, their content is clearly political and controversial from the perspective of civil-military tensions in Latin America. By presenting the U.S. view of regional security as professional and nonpolitical, such courses reinforce the tendency of Latin officers to view their opposition to the foreign and defense policies of civilian governments as apolitical rather than as a violation of civilian control. Shifting the emphasis to more technical courses would provide needed military skills with fewer unintended political side effects. U.S. efforts to involve the Latin American militaries in the war on drugs should likewise be systematically reviewed to eliminate programs that run counter to the goal of more democratic civil-military relations.

One of the most important steps the United States could take would be to expand IMET to provide technical training for *civilian* personnel involved in defense policy and civil-military relations.[72] Latin American democracies face a desperate shortage of civilians with expertise in areas like military budgets, weapons procurement, strategy, and military education, which have traditionally been the exclusive preserve of the armed forces. Congressional staffs, defense ministry officials, and presidential advisers need training and opportunities to study mechanisms for civilian oversight and control of intelligence agencies and the armed forces. Such a program could offset the negative effects of *military* assistance programs on the organizational imbalances between civilian and military institutions in Latin America. Without competent civilian personnel, democratic control of the armed forces will remain a utopian aspiration.

Both the United States and Latin American governments should consider revamping or abandoning the Inter-American Military System (IAMS) created in the late 1940s. Although formally a multilateral instrument for regional security, in practice IAMS has functioned largely as a mechanism for coordinating Latin American participation in U.S. global strategy for the cold war against the Soviet Union and world communism. In dealing with the security crises of the 1980s— the Malvinas-Falklands war, the Central American wars, and the U.S. invasions of Grenada and Panama—the United States and other parties have ignored the Rio Treaty. The Inter-American Defense College and the Inter-American Defense Board, both headquartered in Washington, D.C., provide a small number of senior training courses and diplomatic sinecures, respectively. The periodic conferences of American army commanders (and their naval and air force counterparts) have served mostly for the interchange of like-minded views on the threat of ideological subversion arising from the "international communist movement." The entire system is based on a presumption of common national interests and common security threats to Latin America and the United States. This "hemispheric" vision of regional security is not shared by most democratic governments in Latin America, nor even by most military officers.[73] The disintegration of the Soviet Union and the thaw in U.S.-Russian relations are likely to accelerate these divergences, although changes in threat perceptions and military doctrines will occur slowly, lagging considerably behind actual events.

Except where drugs are a major concern, both Central and South America are likely to be assigned lower priority on the U.S. agenda of security issues. To the extent that political violence and insurgency become decoupled from automatic gains in Soviet or Cuban influence, Latin American officers may find even less U.S. support for their security concerns. To the extent that international economic conditions continue to frustrate Latin American efforts to control inflation and promote economic growth, fewer officers will view U.S. and Latin American interests as compatible. On the right as well as the left, the next generation of Latin American officers is likely to be strongly nationalistic. For better or worse, increased professionalization of the Latin American militaries has resulted not only in local suppliers of training and arms, but also in militaries with greater ideological autonomy from the United States and a greater capacity to produce their own military doctrine. In the long term, the Latin American democracies will have to develop their own mechanisms for military cooperation and regional security.

Ending on a Note of Hope

By design, this analysis has stressed the limitations of Latin American democracies and of current patterns of civil-military relations. A realistic assessment of the prospects for the future offers no cause for complacency. Yet it would be equally wrong to be overly pessimistic. At the beginning of the 1970s, few foresaw the democratic forces that would overturn the military dictatorships seemingly entrenched throughout the region. At the beginning of the 1980s, who would have predicted the breadth of the democratic wave that followed? Who would have believed that these fragile new democracies could survive ten years of economic crisis? At the beginning of the 1990s, we should consider not only the problems, but also the democratic achievements of the last decade. The transition from Alfonsín to Menem was the first transfer of power between two democratically elected presidents in Argentina since 1928. For the first time in eighty years, Peru has had three constitutionally elected presidents in succession.[74]

While the economic prospects are dismal, the international context has perhaps never been so favorable for democratic consolidation. The radical changes in the world balance of power and the end of the cold war will necessarily force a reappraisal of the assumptions underlying military doctrine and civil-military relations at both the regional and national levels, in the United States and in Latin America. Despite the negative weight of the past, the opportunity exists for a civil-military effort to define an alternative model of civil-military relations that is both democratic and Latin American.

Notes

This chapter is part of a larger study of civil-military relations in the new Latin American democracies that began with field work in Argentina in 1985, supported by a travel grant from the American Philosophical Society. Portions of the analysis have been developed in papers for the Inter-American Dialogue. Members of the Dialogue and especially its director, Abraham F. Lowenthal, have been generous with their insights, encouragement, and criticism. I am also indebted to my colleagues Andrés Fontana, Augusto Varas, Juan Rial, Ernesto López, Felipe Aguero, Genaro Arriagada, Lou Goodman, and Alfred Stepan for sharing their scholarship, their support, and their passion for a better understanding of the military's role in democratic consolidation.

1. Haiti is currently under a civilian interim president following its second coup against an elected civilian president. In Paraguay, General Andrés Rodríguez deposed longtime dictator Alfredo Stroessner and then ran for president with the backing of dissident elements of the official party in elections that were at best semicompetitive, due to the lack of time permitted for organization of an opposition campaign. Given the focus of this volume on U.S.–Latin American relations, this chapter defines democracy in political terms—that is, competitively elected governments, extensive political participation, and sufficient legal guarantees and freedom from violent coercion to permit meaningful and autonomous electoral choices.

2. On civil-military relations in Paraguay, see Bouvier, "Decline of the Dictator"; Abente, "The Military in Paraguay"; Lezcano, "El régimen militar de Alfredo Stroessner"; Jose Garcia, "The Crisis in Paraguay"; and Riquelme, *Hacia la transición a la democracia*. On Haiti, see Maingot, "Problems of a Transition to Democracy," and Wilson, "Military Rule."

3. Varas, "Military Autonomy and Democracy"; Aguero, "The Military in Processes of Political Democratization" and "The Military and the Limits to Democratization"; Marcella, "Latin American Military Participation in the Democratic Process."

4. On Argentina, see Fontana, "La política militar"; Varas, "Democratization and Military Reform in Argentina"; Pion-Berlin, "Civil-Military Relations" and "A House Divided"; Norden, "Democratic Consolidation"; Potash, "Alfonsín and the Argentine Military"; Cavarozzi and Grossi, "From Democratic Reinvention to Political Decline"; Gleijeses, "Decay of Democracy in Argentina"; and Borón, "Authoritarian Ideological Traditions."

5. Norden, "Democratic Consolidation," p. 12. If one takes into account the rapid inflation that devalued military appropriations before they could be spent, in the late 1980s the cuts went even deeper. Potash, "Alfonsín and the Argentine Army," p. 5.

6. Fraga, "Permanente inestabilidad," pp. 8–13.

7. If the current relative economic stability gives way to another round of hyperinflation, the stage may be set for a more overt reassertion of military power. In 1990 a key figure in the Semana Santa revolt warned of the danger of a military coup by the generals and called on President Menem to change the policy direction of the government, reviving the alliance of "those political, business, *military*, and social sectors that make up the majority of Argentines" (emphasis added). Major Ernesto Barreiro, "If Menem Falters in Argentina," *New York Times*, March 23, 1990, p. A35. The military partner in this alliance would be the *carapintada* sector of the military responsible for the revolts against Alfonsín. In the classification scheme suggested below, this could represent a shift to a "tutelary" regime.

8. See Stepan, *Rethinking Military Politics*, pp. 69–127; Eul-Soo Pang, "The Darker Side of Brazil's Democracy," p. 22; Mainwaring, "The Transition to Democracy"; Lamounier, "Challenges to Democratic Consolidation"; Zagorski, "The Brazilian Military"; Alexandre Barros, "The Brazilian Military"; and Cavagnari Filho, "Autonomía militar y construcción del poder."

9. "Forças Armadas—para que?" *Noticiario do Exército*, no. 8 078 (October 4, 1990): unpaged.

10. On Uruguay, see Gillespie, "Reconsolidation of Democracy"; Stepan, *Rethinking Military Politics*, pp. 116–18; Perelli, "Legacies of the Transitions to Democracy"; Rial, "Las relaciones cívico-militares"; and Weinstein, *Uruguay*, pp. 104–12, 127–29.

11. Stepan, *Rethinking Military Politics*, pp. 116–18.

12. On Peru, see Mauceri, "The Military, Insurgency"; Woy-Hazleton and Hazleton, "Political Violence"; Wise, "Political Responses to the Debt Crisis"; Rubio Correa, "The Military in Peruvian Politics"; McClintock, "The APRA Government and the Peruvian Military" and "Prospects for Democratic Consolidation"; García-Sayán, *Democracia y violencia en el Perú*; and Pásara and Parodi, *Democracia, sociedad y gobierno*.

13. See Washington Office on Latin America, "The Killing Fields of Peru."

14. On Ecuador, see Conaghan, "Ecuador" and "Politicians against Parties"; Isaacs, "Obstacles to Democratic Consolidation"; Bustamante, "Fuerzas Armadas en Ecuador" and "The Armed Forces of Colombia and Ecuador"; Schodt, *Ecuador*, pp. 135–71; and Martz, *Politics and Petroleum*, pp. 247–395.

15. Author interview with a retired army general, Quito, Ecuador, July 1988.

16. On Bolivia, see Barrios, "The Armed Forces and Democratization." For an optimistic view, see Mayorga, "Tendencias y problemas de la consolidación."

17. Aguilera, "The Armed Forces, Democracy and Transition" and "The Development of Military Autonomy."

18. On El Salvador, see Montgomery, "Pacts and Politics," and Baloyra, "Negotiating War."

19. On Guatemala, see Schirmer, "Rule of Law" and "Oficiales de la Montaña"; Robert García, "Guatemala under Cerezo"; Yurrita, "Transition from Military to Civilian Rule"; Handy, "Resurgent Democracy"; and Jonas, "Contradictions."

20. Adair, "Civil-Military Relations," p. 6 and passim. Adair notes that the military controls a majority of the seats on the National Security Council and that congressional approval of the military budget and the designation of the commander in chief is largely pro forma. See also Morris, Honduras, pp. 83–85, 125–27.

21. O'Donnell, "América Latina."

22. Gillespie, "Praetorianism versus Party Systems"; Conaghan, "Politicians against Parties," pp. 4–16; Isaacs, "Obstacles to Democratic Consolidation," pp. 6–14; Mainwaring, "Institutional Dilemmas."

23. Latin American Weekly Report WR-90-07, February 22, 1990, p. 3. The candidate of the largest party in the congress, the PMDB, received less than 5 percent of the presidential vote.

24. García's popularity rating in public opinion polls dropped from 93 percent in 1985 to 15 percent in 1988 (and to less than 10 percent in 1989). Mauceri, "The Military, Insurgency," p. 39. Alfonsín's personal popularity dropped from 48 percent in 1984 to 9 percent in 1989; approval of his government's performance dropped from 82 percent in 1984 to 36 percent in 1989. Catterberg, "La consolidación," p. 13. After less than two years in office, Collor's government was rated positively by 8 percent of the respondents in one survey and negatively by 63 percent. "Year-end Marks New Low for Collor," Latin American Weekly Report WR-92-01, January 9, 1992, p. 5.

25. Lowenthal, "The United States and South America," p. 3; Latin American Weekly Report WR-90-09, March 8, 1990, p. 7; "Region Sees Low Growth, High Inflation," Latin America Weekly Report WR-90-01, January 11, 1990, pp. 6–7. In 1990 the regional average was even worse, but only four countries were over 1000 percent, compared to twelve with less than 100 percent. Provisional figures for 1991 suggest a regional average of roughly 100 percent, with only three countries in triple-digit figures. "Inflation Update," Latin America Weekly Report WR-92-04, January 30, 1992, p. 11.

26. Cavarozzi and Grossi, "From Democratic Reinvention to Political Decline," p. 19. In the three months prior to the 1964 coup in Brazil, inflation was running at an annual rate of 175 percent. Precoup inflation was roughly 500 percent in the overthrow of Allende in Chile and the coup against Isabel Perón in Argentina.

27. Drake ("Debt and Democracy") argues that democracies are better able to survive adverse economic conditions than their authoritarian counterparts, even though their chances for survival would be greater under less adverse circumstances.

28. Isaacs ("Obstacles to Democratic Consolidation," pp. 16–19) presents survey data showing that a substantial minority of the urban public in Ecuador believe that dictatorship solves problems better and is less corrupt than democracy.

29. Perelli, "The Military's Perception of Threat"; Pion-Berlin, "A House Divided," pp. 15–32.

30. Rial, "The Armed Forces and Democracy," pp. 280, 285–90.

31. "Siempre listos: Los planes del Ejército ante el aumento de la tensión social," Página 12, no. 839, February 22, 1990, pp. 1–4.

32. Fontana, "La política militar," p. 2.

33. Cf. Varas, "Civil-Military Relations."

34. Stepan, *Rethinking Military Politics*, pp. 93–114; Rizzo de Oliveira, "O aparelho militar." President Collor reduced the number of military ministers from six to three in a reorganized cabinet of twelve members, thus preserving the military's presence in relative terms.

35. Schirmer, "Rule of Law," pp. 3–6.

36. See Varas, "The Chilean Military."

37. Gillespie, "Reconsolidation of Democracy," pp. 3–7.

38. Thus, institutionalized democratic control is distinguished from situations like the early Alfonsín years, where the military accepted a substantial degree of civilian control, largely because the internal divisions of the military and intense civilian hostility left the military no other alternative.

39. "After 32 Years of Democracy, Fears of a Coup in Venezuela," *New York Times*, 10 August 1990, p. A3. Enrique Baloyra found that as recently as 1983, more than half of a national sample believed that "coups were sometimes justified" and a third agreed that "the current situation in Venezuela justifies a coup." At the same time, democracy was strongly preferred over military dictatorship ("Public Opinion about Military Coups"). Felipe Agüero notes that many officers are critical of various control mechanisms, which they view as contrary to military efficiency and professionalism ("The Military and Democracy in Venezuela"). Initial explanations of the February 1992 coup attempt stressed a combination of corporate grievances, tensions over government attempts to find a diplomatic resolution of the dispute with Colombia over the Gulf of Venezuela, and the perception that public opinion would be favorable, given the sharp drop in public support for President Carlos Andrés Pérez.

40. The typology parallels Stepan's classification in terms of military prerogatives and military contestation (*Rethinking Military Politics*, pp. 99–100). Distinguishing between the professional/institutional and political dimensions of military subordination/autonomy/dominance would, however, produce a three-dimensional model instead of Stepan's two-dimensional classification. An alternative classification developed by Augusto Varas focuses on differences in military autonomy or civilian control based on differential state capacity to control military institutions and differences in levels of military corporateness (Varas, "Military Autonomy and Democracy," pp. 9–12). See also Rial, "The Armed Forces and the Question of Democracy," pp. 16–17.

41. See Aguero, "The Military and the Limits to Democratization," pp. 18–31, and Perelli, "The Legacies of Transitions to Democracy."

42. Fontana, "La política militar," p. 23; Norden, "Democratic Consolidation," pp. 16–17.

43. Fitch, "Military Professionalism."

44. CONADEP, *Nunca Mas*, p. 293.

45. Garzón Valdés, "The Argentine Military and Democracy," p. 8. On the moral defense of the "war against subversion," see also Graziano, "Messianism and Atrocity."

46. Fontana, "La política militar," p. 12.

47. Wynia, "Peronists Triumph."

48. Based on figures from Amnesty International, Lawrence Weschler estimates that roughly 2 percent of the population was "detained for interrogation"; one-tenth of that number received extended prison sentences (*A Miracle, A Universe*, p. 88). Servicio Paz y Justicia (*Uruguay Nunca Más*, pp. 285, 417–30) puts the total number of short-term detentions at roughly 4,000 and another 5,000 formally charged, of whom nearly 50 percent were imprisoned from three to eight years. A Uruguayan senate investigation

documented 170 disappearances; SERPAJ estimates 78 deaths during imprisonment. On the handling of the nullification law, see Perelli, "Amnistía sí."

49. Stepan, *Rethinking Military Politics*, pp. 69–70; Zirker, "Democracy and the Military in Brazil"; McCann, "Modernizing Authoritarian Rule," p. 46. Dassin, *Torture in Brazil*, pp. 79, 235–38, lists 125 disappeared persons. Out of 7,300 political prisoners tried in military courts, 1,900 testified that they had been tortured. According to military records, another 10,000 persons were interrogated but not brought to trial.

50. Fruhling, "Justicia y violación," p. 8 (figures from the Vicaría de la Solidaridad). The Chilean Commission on Human Rights (ibid., p. 9) estimates over 400 deaths related to human rights violations between 1981 and 1987. General Pinochet threatened that the state of law would end "the day they touch any of my men." *Latin America Weekly Report* WR-89-42, October 26, 1989, p. 3. Air Force General Mathei, generally recognized as the "moderate" member of the Chilean junta, also warned against opposition attempts to modify the amnesty law. Shirley Christian, "Chilean General Warns Opposition on Amnesty," *New York Times*, August 1, 1989, p. 1.

51. "Rettig Report Tallies Pinochet's Dead," *Latin America Weekly Report* WR-91-11, March 21, 1991, p. 2. The Aylwin government also instituted a program of financial compensation to the victims of human rights abuses during the military government. The trial of General Manuel Contreras, the former head of DINA, and General Espinoza Bravo for the car-bomb murder of former ambassador Orlando Letelier in Washington, D.C., may, however, serve as a Chilean surrogate for Argentina's trial of the juntas. "Letelier Two Are Finally Indicted," *Latin America Weekly Report* WR-91-40, October 17, 1991, p. 8. This case is being heard under a provision that permits the Chilean Supreme Court to take over cases involving foreign governments. A new 1991 law also permits some cases to be transferred to civilian jurisdiction from military courts that have thus far stonewalled attempted prosecutions.

52. See Aspen Institute, "State Crimes," pp. 3–4. Note, however, that the presumed causal relationship between lack of accountability and future violations is based on behavioral assumptions rather than on any empirical evidence demonstrating that effect.

53. Peruvian figures on the victims of political violence since 1980 show only slightly fewer "civilian" casualties than "guerrillas"; the latter category undoubtedly includes some bystanders reported as combatants. Woy-Hazleton and Hazleton, "Political Violence," p. 17–18.

54. *Latin America Weekly Report* WR-89-50, December 21, 1989, p. 12.

55. Bourque and Warren, "Democracy without Peace."

56. Chernick, "Negotiations and Armed Conflict," pp. 19–22. Mauceri ("The Military, Insurgency," pp. 22–43) provides an excellent analysis of civil-military tensions in Peru.

57. Woy-Hazleton and Hazleton, "Political Violence," p. 8. See also Rubio Correa, "Perception of the Subversive Threat."

58. See Karl, "Imposing Consent?."

59. Goodman and Mendelson, "Threat of New Missions"; Washington Office on Latin America, *Clear and Present Dangers*. The Reagan administration's emphasis on "narco-terrorism" and alleged links between drug traffickers and guerrillas encouraged U.S. and Latin American officials to frame the drug problem as a security issue, i.e., "the war on drugs" (Muñoz, "Las relaciones entre Estados Unidos y América Latina").

60. Woy-Hazleton and Hazleton, "Political Violence," p. 20; Sharpe, "Drug War."

61. Stepan, *Rethinking Military Politics*, pp. 128–45; Baloyra, "Democracy Despite De-

velopment"; Diamond, Lipset, and Linz, "Building and Sustaining Democratic Government."

62. Fitch, "Military Professionalism," pp. 133–39; Gamba, "Missions and Strategy."

63. Crahan, "National Security Ideology"; López, *Seguridad nacional*. See also Pion-Berlin, "Latin American National Security Doctrines."

64. See Portales, "Democracia y derechos humanos," and Fitch, "United States Human Rights Policy."

65. See Lowenthal, "Learning from History," pp. 262–63.

66. One of the major criticisms of Carter's human rights policies was that those policies were selectively applied to right-wing military dictatorships but not Marxist dictatorships (Kirkpatrick, "Dictatorships"). In Haiti, the lifting of portions of the U.S. economic embargo and the forced repatriation of Haitian refugees reinforced the army's resolve to defy international pressures to reverse the 1991 overthrow of President Aristide (Howard French, "Bravado Replaces Anxiety as Balance Tips for Supporters of Coup in Haiti," *New York Times*, February 7, 1992, p. A3).

67. See "Comeback for the Region's Military?," *Latin America Weekly Report* WR-91-16, May 2, 1991, pp. 6–7. On the conceptual poverty of the distinction between civilian and military regimes, see Remmer, "Exclusionary Democracy," and Ronfeldt, "Patterns of Civil-Military Rule."

68. Peeler, "Deepening Democracy," p. 15. Peeler argues that democratic consolidation will require redistribution of economic resources in favor of the poorest sectors, which is the opposite of the trend under current stabilization policies.

69. A more detailed analysis is contained in Fitch, "Inter-American Military Relations." See also Millett, "Limits of Influence."

70. On the dominance of security interests in U.S. policy toward Latin America, see Schoultz, *National Security*.

71. Thus, depending on the circumstances, it might be appropriate to deny military aid but to continue economic or humanitarian aid. The fungibility of budgetary resources reduces the practical impact of cutting one form of aid but not the other; nevertheless, except in El Salvador and Honduras, the current levels of military aid are not high enough to directly deter actions that the military is otherwise determined to pursue. The primary importance of giving or withholding military aid is symbolic, in legitimating (or denying international approval of) military actions. In situations where the military is split or faced with domestic opposition to intervention, international support or condemnation can affect military behavior.

72. A small-scale "expanded IMET" program is now in operation but directed primarily at civilians involved in weapons procurement.

73. Child, "The Inter-American Military System," p. 3, "Geopolitical Thinking," p. 155, and *Unequal Alliance*; Brigagao, "The Institutional System," p. 151; Fáunde-Ledesma, "The Inter-American System," pp. 183–84; Caffrey, "The Inter-American Military System"; Zagorski, "'South Atlantic Zone of Peace,'" p. 16; Guedes da Costa, "Bases da Postura dos Paises Sudamericanos."

74. Woy-Hazleton and Hazleton, "Political Violence," p. 1.

· Bruce M. Bagley and Juan G. Tokatlian

Chapter Nine · DOPE AND DOGMA:

. EXPLAINING THE FAILURE

· OF U.S.–LATIN AMERICAN

· DRUG POLICIES

he conceptualization of the "drug problem" in the United States and much of
Latin America and the Caribbean underwent a dramatic transformation during
the 1980s. At the outset of the decade, U.S. policymakers viewed drug trafficking
and consumption primarily as criminal and public health issues. For their part,
most Latin American and Caribbean officials either neglected these questions or
saw them as basically American problems that would have to be resolved in the
United States by U.S. authorities. As of 1990, however, there was apparently
widespread consensus among both U.S. and Latin American leaders that drug
production, smuggling, and abuse constituted significant threats to national security and societal well-being throughout the hemisphere. The concatenation of a
complex set of international, regional, and country-specific factors produced this
remarkable—albeit still tentative and uneasy—convergence of national perspectives.

This chapter seeks to explain the underlying factors that generated this convergence and to examine its implications for the "war on drugs" in the United
States, Latin America, and the Caribbean. The central argument of the essay is that
despite the emergence of a conceptual consensus around the definition of the drug
phenomenon as a serious national security threat, U.S. efforts to "impose" an
"antidrug" national security regime during the 1980s proved ineffective in halting
drug cultivation, processing, and trafficking in the hemisphere because from the
perspective of most Latin American and Caribbean leaders, the U.S.-inspired

regime lacked legitimacy, credibility, and symmetry. To construct an operative international drug regime in the 1990s will require that the U.S. government abandon the coercive, punitive, and unilateral policies that have guided its anti-narcotics strategy to date and replace them with a more cooperative, multilateral framework that takes into account the complex and multifaceted nature of both demand and supply within the interdependent political economy of the hemispheric drug trade.

Drugs and National Security: The U.S. Perspective

In the United States, the explosive surge in crack consumption, the accompanying increases in drug-related crimes in many American cities, and the attendant rise in U.S. media coverage of drug issues clearly fanned public awareness of and leadership concern with the country's drug epidemic.[1] Unfolding events in Latin America also focused public attention on these topics. Among the most notable were the highly acclaimed arrest, extradition, and trial of Colombian drug lord Carlos Lehder; the detention and subsequent bribed release of another major Colombian trafficker, Jorge Luis Ochoa; the indictment of Panamanian strongman Manuel Antonio Noriega in U.S. federal court and his prolonged defiance of Washington; the "deportation-kidnapping" of Honduran cocaine boss, Juan Ramón Mata Ballesteros, and the ensuing anti-American riots in Honduras; the cold-blooded assassination of the Colombian attorney general, Carlos Mauro Hoyos, and hundreds of other Colombian government officials, judges, and political leaders by drug-syndicated consortium hit men; widely circulated rumors concerning Contra, Cuban, and Nicaraguan involvement in the trade; and repeated allegations of high-level drug corruption among Mexican, Caribbean, and Central and South American government officials.[2]

Electoral rhetoric and press coverage unquestionably sensationalized the drug question during the 1980s. But the "hype" also reflected growing preoccupation in the United States with the heavy economic and social costs of expanding drug abuse at home and the intensifying challenges to U.S. interests abroad. By 1989 substance abuse in the U.S. work force (including both illegal drugs and alcohol) cost the U.S. economy an estimated $200 billion annually in lost production and productivity, job- and transportation-related accidents, and health care. Meanwhile, the enormous profits derived from the illicit trade fueled the growth of violent criminal organizations whose economic resources, political influence, and firepower gave them the wherewithal to destabilize, to intimidate, or, in some cases, to manipulate various national governments in the region.

Rising concern in the 1980s over the economic and social consequences of the drug "plague" at home and the growing power of the international drug rings abroad drove both the U.S. executive branch and Congress to regard narcotics trafficking as a national security problem. This perspective was strengthened by the fact that virtually all of the marijuana and cocaine and 40 percent of the heroin smuggled into the United States annually was cultivated and processed in Latin America and the Caribbean.

President Ronald Reagan declared "war" on drugs in February 1982 and pledged his administration to the task of curtailing America's burgeoning drug consumption. To accomplish this urgent national security objective, the federal government rapidly increased the resources available for antidrug efforts both at home and abroad, reaching $6.3 billion in fiscal year (FY) 1989. Strongly backing the president's war on drugs, bipartisan majorities in Congress enacted tougher drug legislation, broadened the U.S. military's role in the fight, funded intensified interdiction efforts at U.S. borders and overseas, and expanded U.S. antinarcotics initiatives in foreign source and transit countries.[3] Over the course of Reagan's tenure, Washington consistently demonstrated its preference for supply-side over demand-side strategies via its allocation of an average of 70 percent of authorized funds to supply-oriented—versus only 30 percent for demand-oriented—programs.

Realism and Supply-Side Strategies

The underlying consensus on supply-side strategies in Washington's design and implementation of the war on drugs during the 1980s flowed directly from the core assumptions and internal logic of "realist" analyses of the international system—and of the U.S. role within it—widely accepted by U.S. foreign policy elites from both parties.[4] At base, the realist paradigm posits an international system in which (1) nation-states are the key actors in international politics, (2) state policy-making elites (as rational actors) design and implement foreign policy, (3) national security interests always rank highest on national foreign policy agendas, and (4) threats to national security emanating from the international system warrant the use of the full range of national power resources (including force) to obtain desired responses from hostile or uncooperative nation-states: "self-help" is both a right and the ultimate recourse of every sovereign nation in defense of its national interests and security.

Parting from the premise that the international system is inherently anarchic and conflictual, the realists contended that hegemonic powers, such as the United States, had to accept responsibility for enforcing the international "rules of the game" and preserving order or run the risk that the international system might lapse into instability and interstate warfare. From this perspective, the United

States not only had the right, but also the duty, to use its dominant leadership position and superior power capabilities to persuade or compel subordinate states to cooperate on issues such as the war on drugs, for failure to do so could endanger U.S. national security and, ultimately, the stability of the international system as a whole. Adoption of the realist interpretation, in effect, inexorably led to the supply-side strategy and unilateral escalation tactics advocated by President Reagan during the 1980s as central components of the U.S. antidrug campaign.

Realist analyses unquestionably inspired the successive antinarcotics bills passed by Congress during the 1980s. The new laws explicitly sought to provide the economic resources, personnel, administrative structures, and policy guidelines whose absence, insufficiency, or ambiguity their supporters believed had hobbled the Reagan administration's ability to carry out the war on drugs effectively. Notwithstanding Washington's perennial optimism, however, none of the various legislative initiatives approved over the decade were efficacious in resolving the nation's drug problems.

A serious flaw in the realist paradigm is the overly simplistic assumption that nation-states are always the primary actors in international politics, including the arena of international drug trafficking.[5] In fact, multiple subnational and transnational actors are involved in this international industry, most of whom operate outside, if not in direct defiance, of national authorities throughout the hemisphere. It is simply unrealistic to expect effective implementation of antinarcotics policies from many Latin American countries whose weak governments do not control their entire national territory; they do not have the power or resources to rein in, much less totally suppress, the well-financed, heavily armed, and ruthless drug mafias operating in their midst, no matter how insistent or painful U.S. efforts to persuade or punish become. In the real world, neither the U.S. government nor any of its Latin American counterparts has demonstrated the will or capacity needed to prevent the rise and consolidation of criminal drug enterprises (like the Medellín Cartel in Colombia or the Cosa Nostra in the United States) or to permanently disrupt their operations and profits once they have taken root. If the relatively powerful U.S. government has failed to destroy New York's famous "five families" despite a decades-long campaign to do so, can the comparatively much weaker governments of, for example, Colombia or Mexico be expected to do better?

Assertion of state control over the multiple transnational actors directly or indirectly involved in U.S.–Latin American drug trafficking networks is equally problematic in most cases. A variety of private, multinational, and commercial banks, as well as other international financial institutions, engage in illicit money-laundering activities, which few, if any, Latin American governments are equipped to regulate effectively. Similarly, state monitoring and law enforcement capabilities in most areas are generally insufficient to suppress the unauthorized importation of chemical precursors employed in cocaine-processing laboratories. In fact, even though U.S. businesses have supplied perhaps 90 percent of these inputs, until the enactment of the 1988 antidrug law, not even the U.S. government had seriously attempted to regulate the export of these basic chemical products. To believe that the institutionally weakened, financially strapped governments of Latin America and the Caribbean will be in a position to gain or maintain absolute control over these actors within the next decade is out of touch with reality. To sanction them for failing to do so is both hypocritical and counterproductive in the long run. By and large, Latin American governments do not merit sanctions; they need consistent and sustained help to strengthen state institutions and regulatory capabilities and to provide alternative economic opportunities for their populations.

In general, the realists' state-primacy assumption ignores, or gravely underestimates, the relative autonomy of the international market forces involved in the drug trade and the concomitant capacity of the drug traffickers to circumvent, adapt to, or defy state efforts to regulate or eradicate their illicit multimillion dollar industry. As long as the U.S. and other developed country markets for drugs remain profitable, suppliers will be motivated to find innovative ways to produce and smuggle narcotics to meet that demand and will be able to marshal the resources required to override whatever enforcement schemes Latin American states undertake.

The debt crisis and severe economic contractions that wracked most Latin American economies during the 1980s further complicated the situation by undermining state authority and reducing the monies available to implement antidrug programs. At the same time, the booming drug trade created employment opportunities and earned scarce foreign exchange in otherwise stagnant or declining national economies, thereby increasing the relative financial and political clout of the drug barons vis-à-vis traditional political and economic elites.

Equally revealing, even where U.S. interdiction efforts had positive results—as, for example, in reducing the flow of marijuana smuggled into the United States from Mexico during the 1970s—alternative sources of supply and transshipment quickly emerged to meet continuing demand. In practice, the decline in Mexican marijuana production was offset by a parallel boom in marijuana exports from Colombia. The subsequent success of the South Florida Task Force's mid-1980s interdiction campaign against marijuana and cocaine traffic from Colombia to Florida, in turn, stimulated a resurgence of Mexican marijuana cultivation and smuggling, along with a dispersion and proliferation of alternate smuggling routes through Mexico, Central America, the Caribbean, and the Pacific.

Meanwhile, behind the new nontariff barriers created by Washington's intensified drug interdiction and overseas eradication programs, the profitability of domestic marijuana cultivation rose exponentially, thus providing additional incentives for U.S. producers to enter the market. Whereas in the early 1970s domestic U.S. cultivation accounted for only 1–2 percent of the marijuana trade, by 1989 U.S. growers were harvesting an estimated 4.5 thousand metric tons annually and had captured some 25 percent of total U.S. demand. To Washington's chagrin, a considerable portion of the expanding domestic crop was cultivated on public lands (forests, parks, wilderness areas, and so forth) nominally controlled by federal or state authorities. Furthermore, over the late 1970s innovative U.S. producers developed more potent, hybrid strains of cannabis, such as the now-famous *sinsemilla* variety grown in Hawaii and California, which more than doubled the potency of the average marijuana cigarette smoked by consumers in many parts of the United States.

Modification of the realists' state-primacy assumption to incorporate relevant subnational and transnational actors and market forces into the analysis in no way implies that nation-states are unimportant actors in international politics, even in the global drug trade. It means simply that state-state relations must be located and analyzed in the broader world economic and political contexts within which they take place. At the policy level, it means that to be credible and effective, U.S. narcotics control efforts abroad must be designed and carried out on the basis of more sophisticated assessments of the structure and dynamics of the international political economy of the drug trade and the extent and limits of individual Latin American governments' economic, technical, and enforcement capabilities vis-à-vis international drug trafficking organizations.

A second distortion or oversimplification present in the realist paradigm lies in its assumption that Latin American governing elites select and execute foreign policies intended to advance perfectly delineated and widely accepted national interests. In fact, national policymakers in several countries of the region must routinely operate without the luxury of fully elaborated conceptual schemes that define and prioritize their nations' vital interests. Furthermore, they often must cope with fragile political systems of tenuous legitimacy where viable consensus on basic national interests is difficult to attain. Under such conditions, the conduct of foreign policy is commonly reduced to little more than frustrating, ad hoc exercises in damage control involving painful choices and sometimes unpopular trade-offs among suboptimal alternatives that, however resolved, probably will exacerbate domestic tensions and further erode national consensus rather than enhance state authority.

In many respects, Colombian policymakers in the 1980s confronted precisely such a "devil's dilemma" with regard to the issue of extradition of Colombian traffickers for prosecution in U.S. courts. On the one hand, the Colombian judicial system was manifestly incapable of bringing the country's most powerful drug lords to justice and U.S. pressures to extradite (often accompanied by implicit or explicit threats of sanctions) were intense. On the other hand, compliance aroused strong nationalist opposition, undercut system legitimacy, and provoked murderous reprisals against government officials by drug traffickers. Caught in these treacherous crosscurrents, Colombia's policymakers first refused to extradite, then yielded to U.S. pressures, subsequently procrastinated in the face of a withering campaign of mafia violence and intimidation, and then backed away from further compliance for more than two years only to renew it again after August 18, 1989, in the wake of a dramatic upsurge of narcoviolence capped by the assassination of a leading Liberal presidential candidate, Senator Luis Carlos Galán.

A third faulty realist premise is that the U.S. foreign policy agenda (not to mention those of Latin American nation-states) is characterized by a clear hierarchy or prioritization of issues in which drug trafficking, because of its security implications, ranks at the top. In practice, the United States has a range of interests in Latin America; these often inhibited or diluted Washington's commitment to combating international drug trafficking during the 1980s. Among the most obvious of these competing foreign policy objectives are anticommunism, regime stabilization, economic growth, and foreign debt repayment. Confronted with the need to balance these and other often-contradictory priorities against the war on international drug trafficking, the Reagan administration repeatedly found it prudent to de-emphasize the U.S. antidrug campaign, at least temporarily, to avoid critical setbacks on other fronts.

Predictably, the White House was in such instances harshly denounced for failing to pressure source and transit countries more vigorously. In the context of expanding interdependence and its attendant tensions, however, such trade-offs are inescapable facts of life; to ignore them altogether would be myopic and possibly counterproductive. As the major power in hemispheric affairs, the United States inevitably includes in its foreign policy agenda a range of interests that cannot always or easily be reconciled. But U.S. overseas antidrug policies have been driven more by short-run domestic political criteria, partisan posturing, and electoral cycles than by reasoned calculations of the costs and benefits for U.S. national interests abroad in the long term. To overcome this built-in feature of U.S. pluralist politics, U.S. foreign policy architects must consider how pursuit of specific goals will affect other objectives, build public and congressional support around balanced and viable strategies, and strive to minimize unproductive actions and unintended consequences.

A final misleading realist assumption is that the use of unilateral force or self-help—including retaliation and sanctions as well as direct intervention—are appropriate and potentially efficient policy instruments in the U.S. war on drugs abroad. In practice, several factors combined to reduce or negate the effectiveness of such policies in the 1980s. First, as noted above, many Latin American states were incapable of controlling their national territory or the powerful criminal drug organizations active within their boundaries; unilateral U.S. efforts to pressure them to do more or to castigate them for not doing enough did not and could not alter this reality.

Second, given the extensive U.S. economic and politico-strategic interests in most Latin American source and transit countries, threats of sanctions may inflict too much damage on other important U.S. interests. Mexico provides an excellent case in point. Despite deep dissatisfaction in the Reagan administration and in the U.S. Congress with Mexico's efforts to rein in drug trafficking, the U.S. executive branch consistently refused to decertify or directly sanction the Mexican government on grounds that such measures would reduce rather than improve cooperation with Mexico on drug issues and endanger other American goals in the process.

Extensive U.S.-Mexican interdependence seriously constrained Washington's ability to bring the full range of its overall power capabilities to bear against Mexico, and thus to compel fuller cooperation or compliance, for to do so inevitably would injure U.S. interests as well. Moreover, the outpouring of Mexican nationalism and anti-U.S. sentiment along with the legacy of tensions and frictions in U.S.-Mexican relations indicated that the costs of unilateral actions could not be valued in dollar terms alone.

The assumption that the U.S. armed forces could—if so ordered—interdict drug smuggling efficiently also reflected the realists' consistent overestimation of the efficacy of force as an instrument of policy. In fact, the U.S. military had neither the equipment nor the technical training required to undertake drug interdiction successfully. Despite the use of war analogies and the invocation of national security threats, the war on drugs is qualitatively different from the conventional wars that the U.S. military trained for traditionally. Drug trafficking does not involve the incursion into U.S. territory of large groups of easily detectable, hostile forces. On the contrary, drug smuggling is by definition a clandestine activity undertaken by individuals or small groups with the express intention of penetrating U.S. borders unseen and then disappearing without a trace. Air force combat planes, naval warships, and army or marine fighting units were never intended to fight this type of enemy; nor was military radar designed to detect smugglers. Moreover, given the country's status as one of the preeminent trading nations in the world, the almost infinitely variable channels of entry available to traffickers, and the huge profits to be derived from drug trafficking, interdiction efforts— whether carried out by the military or any other U.S. agency—are inherently incapable of seizing more than a small percentage of the total flow of illicit drugs brought into the United States. Ironically, unless the nation's borders can be "sealed" completely, U.S. interdiction programs will at most marginally raise the cost of smuggling activities, thus increasing the profit incentives for other traffickers.

Realism and Reality

As the Reagan administration and the U.S. Congress became progressively "tougher" with Latin American and Caribbean governments in the 1980s, U.S. "drug warriors" did register some victories. Cocaine seizures, for example, rose from just 2 tons in 1981 to 27 tons in 1986, while local and state enforcement agencies also increased confiscations. In May 1987, the Drug Enforcement Administration (DEA) completed a three-year undercover drug enforcement operation— the largest such initiative in federal drug enforcement history; dubbed Operation Pisces, this effort led to the confiscation of over 19,000 pounds of cocaine worth some $270 million at U.S. wholesale prices. Similarly, Operation Alliance—a multi-agency task force created in 1986 to curtail the flow of drugs across the U.S.-Mexican border—reported that seizures of marijuana in FY 1987 doubled those of FY 1986, while cocaine confiscations rose 400 percent. Arrests on drug charges also increased steeply and average prison sentences became significantly longer during the 1980s.[6]

War proclamations, bigger budgets, and more seizures, arrests, and convictions notwithstanding, at the end of President Reagan's watch, the U.S. government was still losing the war on virtually every front. Illicit drugs of all types—especially marijuana, cocaine, and heroin—were more readily available and generally cheaper in the United States in 1989 than they had been at the outset of the Reagan presidency in 1981. Drug use and abuse in U.S. society had increased dramatically over the 1980s and the U.S. drug market remained the biggest and most lucrative in the world. Drug-related crimes and violence had reached epidemic proportions in many U.S. cities, greatly exacerbated by the rapid spread of crack. The national public health system proved unable to cope with the surging demand for treatment and rehabilitation. Law enforcement agencies were overworked, underfunded, often outgunned, increasingly demoralized, and plagued with corruption. The nation's courts and prisons were overwhelmed by the influx of drug-related arrests, trials, and convictions. At the same time, the expanding economic and political power of the drug traffickers threatened, or already had compromised, the institutional integrity and political stability of several Latin American governments, thereby endangering important U.S. interests in the hemisphere. In addition, as a result of U.S. pressure on Latin leaders to "do more" to cooperate with the United States in the war on drugs, violent reprisals directed against government officials and public figures had intensified significantly, placing in doubt the survival of civilian, democratic regimes in various countries of the region.

Drugs and National Security: The Latin American Perspective

By the mid-1980s, political leaders and administration officials from Mexico to the Andean republics had gradually come to the conclusion that their state security was seriously threatened by the drug problem. To understand the forces behind this conceptual shift, it is necessary to examine how and why it occurred and who was responsible for it, as well as the scope and content of the new national security interpretation of the narcotics issue among the different governments of the region.

At least three factors converged to produce this "late" recognition of the drug problem as a national security priority for most Latin American states.[7] First, the initial position embraced by most Latin American and Caribbean leaders had held that it was largely an American problem, thus justifying a passive approach to it on their part and leaving them vulnerable to the unchecked growth of drug abuse and powerful trafficking organizations in their own countries. On the one hand, they had argued that the insatiable U.S. appetite for drugs was the driving force behind the narcotics trade. On the other hand, they observed that the bulk of drug profits was realized (and invested) in the U.S. economy, which made the United States the key player in the international political economy of drug trafficking. In short, because the United States was seen as both the major consumer and the financial epicenter of this illegal industry, they concluded that the solution to the drug problem would have to come from Washington. Independent of the conceptual and empirical merits of this analysis, its unintended consequence was to give the U.S. government virtually complete autonomy in the formulation and implementation of policies, strategies, and tactics to deal with the drug issue. While at the political-diplomatic level such an approach may have appeared plausible and defensible, at the strategic level it proved to be a serious (and ultimately costly) mistake, as it excluded Latin America almost entirely from the search for positive answers to the drug question.

Second, Latin America's self-defeating indifference gave the United States free rein to proceed unilaterally to produce a self-serving diagnosis of the drug problem couched in realist premises and to carry out a strategy to combat narcotics trafficking that ignored many of the central concerns of Latin Americans. For Washington, the origins of the drug problem were to be found on the supply side—in Latin America and Caribbean centers of cultivation, processing, and transshipment (diagnosis)—while the most appropriate policies for combating the trade were seen to be suppression at the source (strategy). In accord with this interpretation, after the inauguration of President Reagan in 1981, U.S. pressures on Latin America increased both quantitatively and qualitatively. The very language of Reagan's war on drugs symbolically captured this tendency in U.S. antidrug policies; the same rhetoric has been invoked by the Bush administration.

In many senses there is a historical parallel between the current antidrug crusade and the traditional anticommunism that dominated the U.S.–Latin American agenda in the post–World War II period. The "enemy" (now drugs rather than communism) has infiltrated the hemisphere. Because "coexistence" is impossible (and immoral), it is essential to act aggressively to curtail the international drug trade; to achieve this end, the governments of the region should accept and internalize the U.S. hard-line approach and implement it voluntarily or they can "justifiably" be compelled to do so involuntarily.

Third, as U.S. pressures on Latin America to cooperate more fully rose steadily over the decade, few if any Latin American nation-states devised their own alternative strategies to confront the drug issue. This absence of coherent, feasible, and broadly accepted solutions of Latin American origin, combined with the lack of sufficient state resources and the prevailing attitudes of permissiveness or social tolerance toward the narcotics business rooted in the economic benefits it generated, provided fertile ground for the expansion of the drug industry and the criminal rings that manage it. Moreover, virtually all Latin American countries placed other vital interests above the war on drugs as the key priorities of their domestic and foreign policy agendas (for instance, debt, economic growth, poverty, unemployment, income distribution, political violence, and democratic consolidation).[8]

Finally, both the intensification of drug-related violence precipitated by fuller Latin American compliance with U.S. antinarcotics policies and the need to safeguard national autonomy and sovereignty against U.S. pressures and reprisals for noncompliance raised the drug problem to the status of a serious national security issue for many Latin American governments.

Threat and Transformation

A series of important symbolic events in both the United States and Latin America catalyzed the transformation of Latin American thinking on the narcotics question in the mid-1980s. First, the rhetoric of the war on drugs was formalized in April 1986, when President Reagan issued National Security Decision Directive 221 stating that drug trafficking constituted a lethal threat to U.S. security interests and authorizing an expanded role for the U.S. military in the antinarcotics fight. Second, the decision to move ahead with Operation Blast Furnace in Bolivia in July 1986, with the direct involvement of American troops, signaled that the U.S. government was increasingly disposed to militarize the fight against drugs in Latin America. Third, the emphasis on repression, criminalization, and penalization contained in the 1986 antidrug legislation passed by the U.S. Congress highlighted the trend toward escalation in the war on the international narcotics trade.

In effect, the crystallization of a national security perspective on the drug problem in Washington left the governments in the hemisphere little option but to accept the U.S. lead.[9]

In Latin America, the predominance of the hard-line stance in U.S. policy-making circles became, in and of itself, a major source of national insecurity for the governing elites of the region. In effect, compliance with the U.S. national security approach pushed some Latin American states to take up front-line positions in the war on drugs. Their intensification of narcotics control efforts, in turn, unleashed an unprecedented spiral of narcoviolence against the state and of state counter-violence against the *narcos*. The negative economic and social consequences of the international narcotics trade alone had not elevated the drug issue to the rank of a national security problem. But the rising levels of violence generated by both the progressive militarization of the U.S. antinarcotics strategy in Latin America and the bloody responses of the drug traffickers—along with accompanying paramili-tary and guerrilla conflicts—set in motion a wave of drug-related crime and terrorism that directly threatened state security, most dramatically in Colombia and Peru.

As the prime front-line state, Colombia provides the most compelling, although certainly not the only, example of this security dilemma in Latin America. Drug-related violence had certainly spread in Colombia prior to the classification of narcotics as a state security issue. But because most of this violence had taken place among rival criminal smuggling gangs, or had been directed against the legal left-wing opposition (for instance, the Unión Patriótica—UP) and popular organiza-tions, the stability of the Colombian government had not been seriously jeopar-dized. Once *narcoviolencia*—spurred in part by Colombia's extradition of traf-fickers to the United States—targeted state officials and prominent public figures, however, it became far more menacing to regime stability.[10] In a similar vein, the increased involvement of the Shining Path (Sendero Luminoso) guerrillas in the drug trade in the Alto Huallaga valley in the mid-1980s provides a second example of the dangers to state security emanating from the domestic ramifications of international drug trafficking.[11]

The alternative outcome—where instead of pursuing the fight against drug traffickers, government officials cooperated with them—was initially less violent, but ultimately no less threatening to both societal and state security. In cases such as the García Meza narcomilitary coup in Bolivia, the Namphy-Paul corrupt military clique in Haiti, or Noriega's military-run money-laundering and smug-gling schemes in Panama, state institutions and democratic processes were sub-verted to the detriment of their nations' entire populations. Second-line states such as Bolivia, Jamaica, and Mexico—major source countries that did not suffer extensive drug violence in the 1980s—were nevertheless beset by increasing corruption and criminality that endangered state security at least indirectly and raised fears that they might be subjected to narcoviolence in the future.[12] This combination of present and potential dangers, along with growing U.S. pressures, prompted them to define the drug problem as a national security issue. Although more removed from drug corruption and violence, third-line states like Argentina, Brazil, Ecuador, Venezuela, and many Caribbean and Central American nations were also motivated to adopt, partially or totally, national security interpretations of the drug problem as preemptive measures to forestall possible "Colombianization."[13]

The vacuum left by the failure of Latin American and Caribbean states to develop their own alternative national and international strategies for resolving the drug question allowed this space to be filled by U.S. policies and the bellicose logic implicit in them by default. In this context, the militarization of the war on drugs was not a plot hatched on the seventh floor of the State Department, in the White House, or at the desks of DEA and CIA officials. Rather, the emphasis on force and repression was a natural outgrowth of the realist punitive-military thrust and led spontaneously to the conceptualization of the drug issue as a national security threat. In essence, by the mid-1980s Latin Americans had internalized—although not without resistance and contradictions—the U.S. diagnosis of the drug problem. Latin America's rhetorical assertion of limited responsibility deepened even further Latin American dependency on and subordination to the U.S. government's views of the drug phenomenon and its policy recommendations.

Conceptual Consensus and the Imposition of an Antidrug National Security Regime

Although a combination of elements lay behind the contradictory convergence in U.S. and Latin American governing circles regarding the threat to national security presented by the international drug business, it is nonetheless important to recognize that this tenuous conceptual consensus did not imply full agreement on the most appropriate and effective steps for combating the hemispheric narcotics trade or its specific domestic consequences within each country affected by it. Instead, it simply shifted the arena of disagreements from the conceptual-definitional level to that of strategies and tactics.

At base, the U.S. insistence on the application of supply-side approaches and military escalation called upon the "source" and "transit" nations in Latin America and the Caribbean to bear the heaviest share of the costs in the fight against drugs. U.S. authorities relied on economic incentives and sanctions, political-diplomatic pressures and reprisals, and occasional resorts to direct military intervention (or the more subtle threat of force) to extract fuller cooperation from Latin American and Caribbean governments. In short, realist U.S. policymakers invoked American superior power resources to impose what may be labeled as an "antidrug national security" regime on the nations of the hemisphere, despite the often-bitter criticisms voiced by political leaders throughout the region. Following Stephen Krasner, the term *regime* is defined here as "sets of implicit or explicit principles, norms, rules, and decision-making procedures around which actors' expectations converge in a given area of international relations."[14] An "imposed" regime refers to one that lacks legitimacy, credibility, and symmetry. A regime lacks legitimacy when the nations that are expected to observe the "rules of the game" established by the hegemonic power do not accept them as binding and try to avoid or circumvent the policy prescriptions and obligations laid down. A regime lacks credibility when the strategies and tactics proffered are not seen to be, at least potentially, efficacious in achieving the goals or objectives posited. A regime lacks symmetry when the costs and benefits of maintaining it are not viewed as fairly distributed among the parties involved.

Despite the emergence of a general consensus around the notion that international drug trafficking is a security threat for most, if not all, of the nations in the hemisphere, there is ample evidence that U.S. efforts to impose an antidrug national security regime throughout the 1980s failed to fulfill the three basic requirements—legitimacy, credibility, and symmetry—needed for effective institutionalization. In 1990 the regime was not perceived as legitimate in much of Latin America and the Caribbean because the roles assigned to the various participating nations had not emerged from collective negotiations and agreements and because the policy priorities that flowed from it were seen to be the product of unilateral decisions by U.S. policymakers. It was not perceived as credible because the fundamental thrust of the U.S. antinarcotics strategy focused mainly on stopping drugs at their source in Latin America and the Caribbean while doing little to address demand in the United States or to control the export of chemical inputs, conventional arms trafficking, or money-laundering operations. It was not perceived as symmetrical because it did not allocate equitably the burdens involved in enforcing the rules of the game, especially in terms of the human, institutional, and economic costs incurred by Latin American and Caribbean nations vis-à-vis those borne by the United States.

Although the necessity for the construction of such a national security regime emerged naturally from the realist paradigm that undergirded U.S. global narcotics control policies in the 1980s, the critical flaws inherent in the realist interpretation of the international political economy of drugs, along with the limits on U.S. power capabilities deriving from expanded Latin American–U.S. interdependence, undercut the viability and effectiveness of this imposed regime. Perhaps the key reason that this failed regime has been maintained despite its shortcomings is that the U.S. government has been in a position to punish (or threaten to punish) any nation-state that unilaterally sought to abandon it. A major danger implicit in the continuation of an imposed regime in this fashion is that it will encourage a "free-rider" syndrome in which, under compulsion, resentful Latin American and Caribbean states nominally adhere to the "letter of the law" while constantly threatening to withdraw the regime.

To create the conditions for a consensual regime, it is essential that the U.S. administration first develop an alternative analysis of the international political economy of drugs that takes into account the complex interdependent nature of the transnational narcotics business. The roots of drug trafficking and consumption go deep into the economic, social, and political structures of both North American and Latin American societies. Replacement of the inadequate realist paradigm with a political economy perspective would require that both the demand and supply facets of the drug problem be addressed simultaneously. The huge profits that stimulate production and trafficking and fuel the violence and criminality associated with drug dealing must be eliminated or at least reduced significantly. Otherwise, the logic of supply and demand within the interdependent international economy will inevitably reproduce the conditions that perpetuate drug trafficking, while stacking the deck against efforts by state authorities—in developing and developed nations alike—to rein in the industry.[15]

Second, the U.S. government must accept the need to establish cooperative, multilateral decision-making mechanisms in order to obtain a workable, consensus-based regime. There will undoubtedly be glitches, frustrations, and backsliding in these attempts, but over the long run, a consensual approach to the international drug trade provides the only realistic hope for a concerted solution. A corollary to this transition from unilateralism to multilateralism is the need to undertake long-term institution-building efforts both nationally and internationally to improve regulatory and legal capabilities throughout the hemisphere. To be sustainable, such institution-building tasks will have to be coupled with renewed economic growth in the region. To generate the political will and economic wherewithal necessary to get institution-building processes under way, alternative economic opportunities for the hundreds of thousands reliant on the drug industry in Latin America and the Caribbean are indispensable: compensatory flows of foreign exchange earnings for drug-dependent national economies and higher levels of resources for financially strapped governments will have to be found, including first and foremost a creative debt-relief initiative. The previous experiences of military-dominated governments in countries like Bolivia, Haiti, and Panama reveal the dangers in reliance on military rather than civilian institutions.

Third, to cope with the complex phenomena of demand and supply, the U.S. government must seek to delink national security from the larger set of issues—

medical, health-related, social, economic, legal, political, environmental, and diplomatic—that are present within the multifaceted drug problem: there is not "one" problem but many. The narrow national security view limits the options and reduces the flexibility available to government authorities in the United States, Latin America, and the Caribbean to deal with the broad spectrum of issues they face. To construct a viable, consensual regime, U.S. policymakers must move beyond the mechanical and simplistic identification of narcotics as exclusively a security question and confront the difficult and expensive tasks involved in institutionalizing an international drug regime that addresses the priorities of other nations along with those of the United States.

From Reagan to Bush: Continuity and Failure

Although the Reagan administration and its domestic critics frequently differed on specific tactics during the 1980s, the general rationale of U.S. legislation in the drug area consistently reflected a broad consensus between the presidency and Congress that Washington could and should escalate the war effort on all fronts: harsher penalties for both consumption and trafficking; more resources, manpower, and equipment to combat traffickers; tougher law enforcement and interdiction programs domestically and internationally; and intensified political-diplomatic pressures on (or sanctions against) uncooperative source and transit country governments. There was also agreement that the U.S. armed forces and their counterparts in trafficking countries could and should assume key roles in the antidrug battles.

There were, of course, skeptics in the United States and abroad who did not share the dominant, optimistic conviction that the "solution" to America's drug epidemic lay in further escalation of the war on drugs. Among them were civil libertarians, proponents of legalization or decriminalization, and dissidents (including many Latin American leaders) who asserted that demand rather than supply-side policies and programs should be given priority. However, the hard-liners constituted the majority in the U.S. Congress and their get-tougher attitudes dictated the pace and direction of the escalation of the war on drugs during Reagan's two terms.

Hard-liner dominance in this issue area was evident in U.S. budgetary specifications contained in the Anti-Drug Act of 1986. Of the unprecedented $3.9 billion authorized by the U.S. Congress for the antinarcotics effort in FY 1987, three-quarters were earmarked for expanded law enforcement, interdiction, and eradication/substitution programs (supply) versus approximately one-quarter for education, prevention, treatment, and rehabilitation (demand). In effect, the 1986 legislation maintained the same ratio between supply and demand strategies that the Reagan administration had established at the outset of the war on drugs.

In late October 1988, visibly frustrated by the lack of tangible progress in curbing drug production, trafficking, consumption, and related violence—and faced with intense public pressure to "do something" about the U.S. "drug plague" in advance of the November 1988 presidential election—the U.S. Congress enacted a major new antidrug law: the Anti-Drug Abuse Act of 1988. While retaining the traditional emphasis on supply-side strategies typical of previous U.S. narcotics legislation, the 1988 law focused more explicitly on the demand side of the equation, earmarking 50 percent of federal funding in FY 1989 for domestic demand control and enforcement programs and projecting an increase to 60 percent (demand) versus 40 percent (supply) in FY 1990 and subsequent years.[16]

This shift was not merely cosmetic nor simply a function of political posturing and election-year politicking, although those features were certainly present; it reflected deep disillusionment in the U.S. Congress with the ineffectual supply-side orientation of U.S. antidrug policies during the 1980s. In short, by late 1988 majorities in both houses of Congress had concluded that the current strategies and tactics were simply not getting the job done: the shift was driven by failure.

The heightened priority assigned to demand-side measures in the 1988 law suggested that a conceptual transition away from supply-side policies might be under way in Washington when President Bush assumed office in January 1989. The transition was, however, at best partial and incomplete. The 1988 law did not abandon supply-oriented programs; rather, it renewed or even increased authorized federal funding for these efforts while simultaneously opening a second front directed at demand reduction in the United States.

The Bush administration's record on resource allocations between demand and supply over the first two years in office continued to reflect a higher emphasis on supply control and interdiction than on demand reduction. In addition, beginning with his antidrugs rhetoric during the 1988 presidential campaign, through his inauguration promise that "this scourge will end" and the September 5, 1989, presentation of the new National Drug Strategy prepared by "Drug Czar" William Bennett, right up to the U.S. invasion of Panama on December 20, 1989, President Bush consistently escalated his war of words against drug use and trafficking, thereby raising public expectations of a quick fix to many of the most noxious aspects of the drug question. At the same time, his tough language resonated throughout Latin America and the Caribbean, increasing fears of growing unilateralism in U.S. narcotics control programs abroad.

The Bush administration also steadily expanded the involvement of the U.S. military in the war on drugs at home while stepping up pressure on Latin American governments to assign a greater role to their own armed forces in combating drug trafficking. The extent to which the Bush White House sought broader U.S. military participation in the domestic drug fight was clearly in evidence during Secretary of Defense Richard Cheney's September 19, 1989, statement indicating that "detecting and countering the production and trafficking of illegal drugs is a high-priority, national security mission" for the Pentagon.[17] During 1989–90, funding for the military's antidrug activities was increased substantially and its role was widened: for example, U.S. Navy cooperation with the U.S. Coast Guard in interdiction programs on the high seas, U.S. National Guard participation in patrol activities on the U.S.-Mexican border, U.S. Air Force collaboration with U.S. Customs in aerial surveillance, the military intervention in Panama to oust General Noriega, and the ill-fated deployment of the U.S. fleet off the Colombian coast without Bogotá's permission. Other signs of militarization were found in the construction of Vietnam-style fire bases for DEA operations in Peru's Alto Huallaga valley, Bennett's repeated suggestions that U.S. troops— Green Berets—might be sent to the Andean coca-producing countries, the use of sophisticated intelligence surveillance satellites over Mexican territory without informing the Mexican government, and the frequent reiteration of U.S. interest in the creation of an international strike force despite its open rejection by virtually all Latin American leaders.

The emphasis on militarization in the Bush administration's international drug policies was nowhere more evident than in the highly publicized "Andean Strategy" announced in September 1989.[18] In the first phase of this initiative—the $65 million emergency aid package sent to Colombia in late September—the U.S. government delivered primarily conventional military equipment, even though the Barco administration had requested intelligence-gathering devices and technical assistance for the severely debilitated Colombian judicial system. The second phase— the budgetary proposal of $261 million for Bolivia, Colombia, and Peru, during the first year of the Andean Strategy—contemplated almost exclusively military and police aid. Likewise, the overall Andean plan's projected expenditures of $2.2 billion over the next five fiscal years (1991–95) also emphasized military assistance over funding for development, health, and social issues and institution building.

At the February 15, 1990, Cartagena Summit attended by President George Bush, Colombia's Virgilio Barco, Peru's Alán García, and Bolivia's Jaime Paz Zamora, Bush diplomatically downplayed the military dimensions of U.S. strategy to avoid serious controversy at the meeting while admitting that U.S. demand was a basic factor in the booming international drug trade. Within a few weeks, however, the cordiality and optimism observed at this historic and symbolically important summit began to fade when the U.S. Navy seized two Colombian freighters within the two-hundred-mile international limit without the previous approval of the Colombian authorities.[19]

Conclusion

The decade of the 1980s witnessed intense pressure on the part of the U.S. government to install an antidrug national security regime in the hemisphere. These efforts failed because Washington did not establish a legitimate, credible, and symmetrical framework capable of coping with the multiple problems presented by international drug production, smuggling, and use.

Notwithstanding some hopeful signs in the 1988 U.S. antinarcotics legislation and in the Bush administration's greater focus on demand-side issues, however, in practice U.S. policy priorities and actions during the first two years of the Bush presidency constituted a reaffirmation of the traditional realist-security approach with its concomitant emphasis on militarization of U.S. antinarcotics policies at home and abroad. In our view, such attempts to return to the flawed strategies and tactics of the past decade are doomed to failure. Only by modifying both American conceptual premises and postulates (from realism to an interdependent political economy framework) and strategy (from militaristic unilateralism to multilateral and cooperative initiatives) will it be possible for the nations of the hemisphere, in the North and South alike, to make real progress in the fight against drugs. By progress, we do not mean total victory or a drug-free society, but rather movement toward the more modest and realistic goal of effective containment of the negative economic, social, and political consequences of the U.S.–Latin American drug trade in all its dimensions.

From this perspective, rather than evaluating the Bush administration and the governments of Latin America and the Caribbean on whether or not they are capable of "winning" the war on drugs outright or ending this "scourge" once and for all, the standards that should be used to judge governmental performance should be more discrete and practical:

1. In the 1990s, will the political leaders of the hemisphere be able to get away from the counterproductive cycles of rhetorical denunciations and tensions that characterized U.S.–Latin American narcodiplomacy during the 1980s?

2. Will they be able to institutionalize multilateral cooperation?

3. Will they be able to sustain coordinated policy-making and implementation structures to confront the intricate and interconnected dimensions of the hemisphere's narcotics problems? In other words, will they be able to forge a new consensus-based international narcotics regime?

4. Will Washington prove willing and able to dedicate the leadership and resources required to reduce domestic drug consumption and related vio-

lence; to address the questions of money laundering, export of chemical precursors, arms, and mercenaries; and to avoid unilateral pressure and use of military force?

5. Will the Latin American and Caribbean governments prove willing and able to restore the integrity of their legal systems, to administer justice fairly and effectively within their own national territories, to strengthen civilian control over military and police units, to minimize human rights abuses and institutional corruption, to wean their economies from drug dependency and promote healthy new poles of growth and job creation, and to deal with their own growing internal demand for drugs?

6. Will the international community be willing to commit the resources and manpower or to provide the technical assistance so desperately needed in Latin America and the Caribbean?

7. Will Europe, the former Soviet Union, and other industrialized nations undertake the preemptive domestic measures necessary to curtail the future growth of drug consumption and abuse in their societies?

If President Bush and his counterparts in Latin America and beyond make even modest progress on these fronts during the early 1990s, they will have traveled a long way down the road toward the creation of a more functional and less conflictual international regime. Failure to institutionalize such a regime in the medium run, in contrast, will raise the specter of a resurgence of the costly and negative tensions, problems, and mutual recriminations of the past decade.

Notes

1. On the explosion of the "drug problem" in the United States over the 1980s, see Musto, *American Disease*; Trebach, *Great Drug War*; and Wisotsky, *Beyond the War on Drugs*.

2. On drug trafficking and the war on drugs in Latin America, see Bagley, *Assessing the Americas' War on Drugs*; Lee, *White Labyrinth*; MacDonald, *Dancing on a Volcano*; and Walker, *Drug Control*.

3. On the rising militarization of drug control policies, see Mabry, *Latin American Narcotics Trade*; Jonathan Marshall, *Drug Wars*; and Blachman and Sharpe, "War on Drugs."

4. Major works on realist theory include Morgenthau, *Politics among Nations*; Waltz, *Theory of International Politics*; and Tucker, *Inequality of Nations*.

5. This discussion draws on the arguments presented in Bagley, "U.S. Foreign Policy and the War on Drugs."

6. See The White House, *National Drug Control Strategy*, September 1989 and January 1990.

7. The arguments presented here draw from Tokatlian, "Drogas y relaciones América Latina-Estados Unidos" and "Drogas y seguridad nacional."

8. See García-Sayán, *Coca*; Bagley, "Colombia and the War on Drugs"; and Andreas et al., "Dead-end Drug Wars."

9. See Washington Office on Latin America, *Clear and Present Dangers*, and Bagley, "Myths of Militarization."

10. On drug trafficking in Colombia, see Tokatlian and Bagley, *Economía y política del narcotráfico*, and Arrieta et al., *Narcotráfico en Colombia*.

11. On drug trafficking in Peru, see Morales, *Cocaine*, and Tarazona-Sevillano, *Sendero Luminoso*.

12. On Mexico, for example, see González and Tienda, *Drug Connection*.

13. On Ecuador, for example, see Bagley, Bonilla, and Páez, *La economía política del narcotráfico*.

14. Krasner, "Structural Causes and Regime Consequences," p. 2.

15. Major works on interdependence theory include Hoffman, *Primacy or World Order*; Keohane, *After Hegemony*; Keohane and Nye, *Power and Interdependence*; and Morse, *Modernization*.

16. For an analysis of recent legislation on U.S. budgetary allocations for international narcotics control, see Perl, "The U.S. Congress, International Narcotics Policy" and "International Aspects of U.S. Drug Control Efforts."

17. Cheney, "D.O.D.," p. 3.

18. See, in particular, U.S. Congress, Senate, "Andean Strategy."

19. On the Cartagena Summit and the controversial question of militarizing the war on drugs, see Andrew Rosenthal, "President May Revive Plan for U.S. Ships Off Colombia," *New York Times*, February 14, 1990, and Tokatlian, "Será un fiasco la cumbre?," *Semana*, February 6–13, 1990. On February 26–27, 1992, in San Antonio, Tex., George Bush hosted an expanded version of the first regional antidrug presidential summit held in Cartagena on February 15, 1990. In addition to the four countries at Cartagena—Bolivia, Colombia, Peru, and the United States—Ecuador, Mexico, and Venezuela attended the meeting in Texas. As at the previous gathering, the Bush administration's attempts in San Antonio to obtain greater cooperation in the war on drugs were largely unsuccessful. Indeed, nothing thus far demonstrates that it is likely that a credible, legitimate, and symmetrical international regime to deal with the multifaceted problems derived from drug demand and supply will be constructed in the region.

Steven E. Sanderson

Chapter Ten · POLICIES WITHOUT POLITICS:

. ENVIRONMENTAL AFFAIRS

· IN OECD–LATIN AMERICAN

· RELATIONS IN THE 1990S

T he rediscovery of environmental politics in Latin America does not do justice to the importance of natural resources to the region's history.[1] From the first European steps into the new world, dominion over the natural resources of Latin America shaped colonial economic policy. After independence, fledgling national economies progressed according to their natural resource endowments, from the resurgence of mining and the settlement of new lands for export agriculture to the pursuit of oil in the first decades of this century. Now, as the century closes, Latin America is in the grip of debt crisis, and natural resources reappear on center stage as *materia prima* for politicians and international economic experts seeking to reform Latin America and "trade away" the debt.

The single most striking difference in the region's environmental politics in the 1990s is a concern for the conservation of resources as a first-order political priority. Critics of past development successfully have indicted the sacrifice of biological diversity, environmental public goods, and rural welfare as unacceptable costs of exploiting nature for trade and development. They focus on the effect of external pressure on natural resource exploitation, as well as the deficiencies of national development strategies vis-à-vis the long-term sustainability of a country's natural resource base.

As the 1990s begin, virtually every institution with an international mandate claims a role in "correcting" environmental abuses in Latin America and other parts of the Third World. The World Bank puts environmental limits on the economic development projects it supports, as it tries to "strike a balance" between environment and development.[2] The United Nations Conference on Trade and Development has developed an International Tropical Timber Agreement, a forty-four-nation International Tropical Timber Organization (ITTO), and a putative commitment to sustainable forest use. The European Parliament has declared its intention to tax timber exports from tropical countries that do not exploit their forest resources in "sustainable ways."[3] The heads of the United Nations, the International Monetary Fund (IMF), and the World Bank have met with the World Commission on Environment and Development (Brundtland Commission) in Norway in the first summit of transnational actors concerned with the environment.[4] To great fanfare, Brazil was named to host the United Nations Conference on Environment and Development in 1992, popularly known as "The Earth Summit." Throughout the region, nongovernmental organizations militate at the international, national, and local levels.

The environmental bandwagon is more crowded by the day, but its focus is hazy and its politics are deficient. Those same institutions claiming responsibility for environment, development, and international economic stability emit confusing and contradictory signals. Then-World Bank President Barber Conable—along with much of the Organization for Economic Cooperation and Development (OECD) community—encouraged Latin America to trade more to relieve poverty and to protect the environment, though many at the same time argued that increased trade based on specialization is irrelevant (or damaging) to poverty alleviation, and that more trade would increase resource exploitation.[5] Despite its newfound environmental virtue, the World Bank's policy-based lending is inattentive to such a prospect and favors (indeed, mandates) economic development through privatization and specialization through comparative advantage.

The General Agreement on Tariffs and Trade (GATT) has given mixed signals on tropical products trade, by seeking an accord liberalizing developed-country imports in the ongoing Uruguay Round,[6] while the European Economic Community (EEC) threatens to tax virtually all tropical timber imports and the United States insists on linking tropical products trade to the general agricultural trade agenda.[7] Meanwhile, the OECD countries that threaten to engage in punitive sanctions continue their own wasteful subsidies to agriculture and energy—at an estimated cost of $300 billion per year.[8] In 1991 GATT further confused the trade-environment connection by ruling that U.S. interdiction of dolphin-unsafe tuna exports from Mexico, Venezuela, and several other countries violated GATT and could not be permitted to stand.

The World Commission on Environment and Development, whose volume *Our Common Future* is the baseline "sustainable development" document for the international community, argued that the debt crisis is the most critical *international* pressure point forcing overexploitation of natural resources in high-debt countries. Naturally, it advocated debt reduction as the first priority of the international system, which has been echoed in the more recent prescriptive volume *Beyond Interdependence*.[9] In Latin American domestic politics, governments are divided over external stabilization, domestic structural adjustment, and poverty alleviation. Politicians from Mexico to Brazil profess their interest in sustainable development and the conservation of nature, but not at the expense of economic growth. They grouse publicly about the hypocrisy of the OECD and voice concern that international pressure will force them to become hothouses for the rich ecotourist.

This is hardly a complete sketch of the environmental legacy of the 1980s, but it does capture key elements in the debate and highlights some critical deficiencies. This chapter argues that the critique of trade, debt, and development, which underlies proposed international remedies for environmental abuse, is based on durable myths and unsubstantiated surmise about the relationship of the international system to environmental and economic sustainability. Further, international actors have ignored the role of political structure and process in the environmental debate, in favor of a policy approach. Because global environmental policies have failed to link policy recommendations to the structure and limits of politics at the international level, and because those policies have been guided by a number of disturbing fallacies, the prospect for the 1990s is a continuation of the legacy of "unintended consequences" that have degraded so much of the region's biota already.

Specifically, environmental policies proposed for Latin America have searched for a nonexistent smoking gun, a straightforward cause of environmental deterioration that is susceptible to cure through good policy. Naturally, attention focuses on the forces that usually receive blame for Latin America's ills: the state, the debt crisis, and poverty. Reformists assume that debt relief, progressive incomes policies, agrarian reform, and privatization will generate environmental dividends. The thesis of this essay is that none of these assumptions is based on adequate data or on critical examination of the relationship between policy and the political structures and coalitions required to implement them. Nor do these questions receive attention that is methodologically adequate to include the complex interrelationship among OECD development and trade policy and the future of resource conservation and use in Latin America. Policymakers proceed with programs in the absence of convincing evidence that what they are proposing either makes sense or makes a difference, or, in fact, is based on a convincing set of assumptions about human behavior. The prescriptions offered are often laced with "policy" platitudes that hide the revolutionary political changes required to meet the requirements of a politics of sustainability. The result is a useless and often harmful policy mishmash that shortchanges the global dimensions of environmental politics.

This does not mean simply that "the whole world suffers," but that the policy approach to environmental politics in the 1990s is ineffectual because of its apolitical aspirations. For reasons of efficacy as well as normative concern, the primary level of analysis for Latin American environmental politics should be global. The main focus should be on creating political conditions that might change the styles of development and trade at fault in current environmental degradation. To the extent that poverty alleviation and other social policies are involved, some decision making at the national level is important. But the clear implication of this chapter is that radically different approaches to environmental politics in the 1990s must go beyond Latin American national systems and U.S.– Latin American relations, to include the entire OECD and the international political system proper. This is especially true in light of issues in the global commons—ozone shield depletion, global warming, and marine fisheries depletion, among others—that show local ecological change to be only a part of global environmental transformation, of a kind never seen before in human history.[10] The conclusions are extreme, but certainly less so than the prospect of continued complicity in the environmentally destructive dynamics of past decades.

The External Connection

Many indictments of natural resource depredation in Latin America argue that there is a direct relationship between trade (especially under conditions of debt pressure) and resource depletion,[11] and that public development incentives are *perverse* insofar as they produce negative long-term consequences for natural resources.[12] Included are varying degrees of concern for the policies of multilateral development assistance institutions in natural resource depletion, especially the World Bank.[13] Critiques of the international system and of the public sector both maintain that debt relief and the retirement of the state from resource-based economic activities will enhance the work of conservation and the prospect of development. The external sector is linked directly to domestic resource allocation under the stress of debt and external payment problems, which permits the categorical assertion that macroeconomic changes induced by the debt crisis cause an intensification of natural resource exploitation for trade.

At first blush, there is strong intuitive ground to suspect that deforestation, poaching, animal smuggling, and high-impact frontier settlement all respond to external economic shock. Anecdotal evidence seems endless. The collapse of the mining industry in Bolivia creates new forces demanding agrarian reform from the government, which may affect fragile tropical lowlands.[14] The external sector crisis in Peru results in more exploitation of coastal lowlands, accompanied by a halt in agrarian reform and the destruction of cooperatives.[15] Export promotion in agriculture changes the cropping, credit, and microecological management strategies of smallholders and *ejidatarios* in rain-fed Mexico. Export promotion may also extend to the ignoble overexploitation of game animals and aggravated abuse of CITES species, as well as threaten traditional communities where commercial incursions change lives built around natural resources.[16] The debt crisis in Ecuador is associated with greater incentives to expand shrimp cultivation for export, resulting in the degradation of mangrove nurseries and postlarval "seed" along the coast. And population pressures created by regressive income policies and skewed industrial development in the center-south of Brazil provoke the federal government to intensify settlement of the Amazon frontier, resulting in the accelerated deforestation of the Western Amazon, especially Rondônia and Acre.[17]

Indebted Latin American governments have devalued local currencies to stimulate exports and bring their external payments into balance. This makes the exploitation of tradeables in resources more likely and encourages foreign direct investment, at least in the abstract. Devaluation also makes foreign imports more expensive and encourages import substitution in resource-based products. That forced change in relative prices is often reinforced by domestic import restrictions, sometimes without regard to real costs.

International economists, looking at a Latin American scene characterized by long years of high inflation, huge public sector deficits, warped exchange rates, domestic price distortions, balance of payments deficits, and high debt, recommend economic stabilization and adjustment,[18] followed by trade liberalization to remove the state from center stage and bring the national economy back into equilibrium. Argentina, Chile, Mexico, and Uruguay typically are cited as examples, with Chile and now Mexico the main "success stories."[19] Success is defined as finding through structural adjustment a free economic base for the efficient exploitation of natural resources in a trade-based economy.

Development and resource economists are less immediately concerned with the external sector but still argue against perverse government incentives favoring resource overexploitation, though long-term resource conservation goals often run up against the exigencies of short-term exploitation in an inflationary economy. Multilateral developmentalists often recommend a sectoral approach, which cleans out the distortions of subsidized agriculture or energy to increase productivity and to "get prices right."[20] Technological optimists argue on behalf of using more trade to streamline technology transfer to the Third World, which would purportedly make Third World agriculture and industry less wasteful.[21]

To the limited extent such recommendations are implemented, increased debt pressure creates policy preferences that open the economy relative to previous periods. Pressure on the trade balance leads trading nations to favor the production of goods in which they have a comparative advantage. In much of Latin America, this means land and natural resources.[22] Unfortunately, efforts to increase trade along the lines of comparative advantage can result not only in the socially undesirable redistribution of land-based resources upward, but also in "negative environmental externalities": environmental degradation.

Efforts to protect the environment can change the comparative advantage of a country in a given commodity.[23] Thus, Ecuador's exploitation of Amazonian oil reserves results in rain forest destruction, a negative domestic externality. A conservation tax on the exploitation of that oil changes the comparative advantage of Ecuador in crude petroleum trade. Brazil's decision to use native forests to fuel pig iron mills lowers the cost of steel production by shunting the economic burden of energy to a "noneconomic" resource, the forest. Energy subsidies in Mexican petroleum make agricultural products and manufactures more competitive internationally, leading U.S. competitors to call for countervailing duties against "natural resource subsidies" in those countries.[24]

High-debt nations lose control of exports in this scenario. If the producer country is competing with others for trade and private investment, taxing production runs the risk of losing investment or diminishing competitiveness by altering comparative advantage.[25] And if the consumers of environmentally high-impact goods are outside the country, there is no way for the producer to tax consumption to pay for environmental costs (as happens with domestic gasoline taxes, for example). The potential for taxation rests with the consumer, so political power is lost to the producer. And though developed-country policy analysts wax poetic about the "global agenda" in resource management, that agenda rarely takes up the role of highly manipulated demand in the OECD countries, as well as global prices set by tariffs, nontariff barriers, "voluntary trade agreements," and subsidies.

Greater trade in resources leads to unwanted side effects over which the exporting country has little control, including the import of international environmental problems and the loss of control over the resource costs of production. To the extent that specialization in trade involves substituting Latin American agricultural production for OECD production (in soya, for example), the environmental costs of that production are imported to the producing country (and in the case of Brazil, exported to the resource frontier). In this connection, Latin America may be the next candidate for the critique applied to the United States and Europe for "exporting topsoil" (or rain forest) through productionist farm policies. Although the current economic crisis makes predictions the domain of the foolhardy, at least one study indicates that coming decades may find Brazil sawing down its tropical forests for domestic pig iron production while becoming a large exporter of eucalyptus to the developed world.[26]

To the extent that Latin American growth and economic development are tied to the external sector, there is a direct relationship between biological resource use and external shocks. Thus, the future of resource politics is to some degree a function of external debt and payments, the trade balance, foreign direct investment, and the like. Advocates of debt relief aver that the greater the economic insulation from the external sector, the less is the tendency to overexploit the natural resource base of the country. One would expect that if the international trade system is the source of increased rates of resource exploitation, those countries more open and vulnerable to trade are more likely to show increases in resource exploitation in times of increased external sector pressure. The greater the economic "turn inward," the greater is the resistance to externally imposed resource overuse. These hypotheses are consistent politically with the history of post–World War II Latin American developmentalism.

Unfortunately, they do not hold up.[27] Brazil, the most insulated country of Latin America by measures of economic openness, trade partner concentration, and industrial diversity, is certainly among the most visible environmental abusers. Mexico was at its most "extractive" during the oil boom, when it was least under pressure of external trade and payments. So while a country's insulation from external pressures may be some complex function of national industrial transformation, that should not lead us to assume that inward development somehow answers the resource question; it simply shifts the ground. In the late twentieth century, it is not the destination or the demand for the product that makes the difference. The internationalization of productive technologies has made it possible for all the countries in the world to share in environmental destruction, whether they trade or not.

One of the most persuasive connections among trade, development, and environmental degradation is the historical link between export enclaves, industrial transformation, and developed-country demand. From the colonial system to the new international division of labor, the shape of trade and industrialization has been guided by the mold of developed-country trade partners, then multinational corporations and their local counterparts. In general, the environmental performance of Latin America cannot be expected to outshine parent production systems in the developed world. Paper mills and lumber industries have all of the deficiencies of their forebears, often with few of the environmental safeguards imposed lately by developed-country governments. From commercial fishing to mechanized agriculture, the technologies of production come largely from developed world research and development, where their environmental record is poor. If the innovation rents or product life-cycle theories of direct foreign investment have any merit, there may be a significant lag between developed-country technology and exports to less-developed-country (LDC) partner producers. Set as they are in fragile lands and tropical settings, such industrial models as the great Ford and Jari experiments in the Amazon show the disastrous ecological and economic limits of cross-national economic transplants.[28] This is explicitly recognized in the proposals for "fast-track" North-South technology transfer in the Earth Summit agenda. Under such proposals, LDCs would be able to leapfrog from dirty, primitive industrial technologies to cleaner, modern, and more efficient technologies, financed by an international fund (which has yet to find backers).

The role of consuming nations in the rate and character of exploitation is also crucial. The community of nongovernmental organizations (NGOs) has shown convincingly that Japanese or European wood consumption is responsible for great devastation in Malaysia, the Philippines, and Brazil.[29] A recent survey of forest products trade in Latin America remarks on overcutting and "mining" commercial timber but says nothing about consumer responsibility for such devastation.[30] It is more likely to see a developed-country critique of global warming pointed toward rain forest burning in Brazil than to hydrocarbon consumption in the United States, as recent campaign statements in the U.S. presidential primaries have shown. Similarly, Japan may find it more convenient to invest huge sums in "sustainable forest production" in fragile areas than to address the excessive use of tropical wood imports or to trouble itself with the demands of long-term research into the meaning of sustainable yield production forestry in the Western Amazon forest.[31]

On the other hand, the connection with developed-world overconsumption is a dangerous one, mainly for the excesses and stereotypes it creates. One of the most oversimplified arguments maintains that the rain forest is being carved up for hamburger meat production exported to fast-food purveyors in the United States. The argument contends that McDonald's, Burger King, Wendy's, and others are supporting deforestation to provide low-quality lean beef for American consumers. It undoubtedly helps that junk food is vulnerable to cultural criticism on several other grounds, but, in light of its frank irrelevance to deforestation in Brazil and its marginal connection with Central America and Mexico, the contention needs to be qualified greatly.[32] Such dramatic images as the "hamburger rain forest" fail to make clear the role of Latin American development itself. And such stereotypes can be taken to awful extremes, as in the case of U.S. Senator Albert Gore's accusation in the 1990–91 Persian Gulf crisis that Brazil was exporting beef from the Amazon to Iraq.[33]

Such images of OECD country gluttony also foster another false generalization: that if developed-country consumption of ecologically sensitive products were to diminish, the problem of resource overuse in Latin America would diminish in corresponding fashion. This leads in two directions: constraints on trade from Latin America and debt relief to alleviate pressures on Latin America's external sector, thereby reducing resource exploitation.

Advocates of debt relief, whatever their political virtues, are not on strong environmental ground. Recently, an article suggested a direct relationship between the log of deforestation and debt.[34] But the relationship between external pressure and resource use *for production* to pay the debt is not so simple. The correlation between external debt and deforestation would presumably be reflected in increases in forestry consumption or export figures, which has not consistently been the case in the high-debt countries. If forest-based products including those processed domestically are considered, the result is similar. Latin America has not increased its output of forest-based wood products in a secular way over the debt crisis. This is not to say that the relationship between debt and deforestation does not exist; it is simply not reflected in a straightforward association.

Moreover, for the region as a whole, agricultural, forest, and fisheries exports have exceeded 1980 levels only once during the years since. For the principal exporting countries of Latin America, aggregate exports in each of these natural resource-based activities have not increased consistently in the years since the onset of the debt crisis. In general, Latin American primary sector production and exports have declined in importance over the past two decades, even during the period of the debt crisis. Particularly interesting in that decline is the reduction in the significance of agricultural exports in Brazil and Mexico, which together represent about half of the region's agricultural gross domestic product (GDP).[35] Also interesting is the drastic move away from tin in Bolivia and copper in Chile, subject to the above qualifications.

The assumption that Latin American countries are trading their way out of external crisis by pumping up primary sector exports also ignores the traditional problems of such export expansion in the region: inelasticities of supply and demand, developed-world price setting, changes in domestic rates of consumption, and so on. In fact, the expected increases in Latin American openness do not occur over the debt crisis. Changes in trade performance mainly come from imports, which are reduced throughout the region. Likewise, the role of agriculture, forestry, hunting, and fishing has continued its long-term postwar decline in regional GDP, which counters the thesis that the debt is being paid with increased resource exploitation. Of the countries traditionally most dependent on those activities, none is a significant trader in the region (the first is Colombia, the ninth most important trader by value in the region). Even among the most trade-dependent, there is no secular evidence of increasing importance in the production of primary goods in the period of the debt crisis.[36]

The pressure of debt is reflected in the general trend toward trade surpluses after 1982 when most countries had lived with deficits for much of the postwar period. In those economies with the fewest alternatives (that is, those that did not industrialize early), the crisis must favor exports of primary resource-based tradeables; whether they are traditional or nontraditional does not matter. In a limited, resource-exporting economy, such as Ecuador, oil exports increase even in the face of declining prices. In Bolivia, until 1985, tin was mined for export, even at a loss. And in the Caribbean, sugar exports remain the backbone of the region's economy, even as many nations try to diversify their export bills in agriculture. Because export receipts typically depend on a few key commodities, and because prices are made elsewhere, there is little flexibility in these economies. When prices go up, output must increase for foreign exchange. When prices decline, production must go up as well to make up for poor prices. This extraordinary vulnerability is compounded by the relative inflexibility of domestic production, so that output does not respond well to increased demand.

But that does not mean that resource degradation for production accelerates because of the external pressure of the debt. The fragmentary evidence suggests a politically important alternative explanation. If we look at the resource-based production and trade from Latin America over the past *two* decades, and not merely over the debt crisis, we see that there are substantial increases in production and export of primary commodities in the 1970s, after the first oil shock. In the period following 1982, in contrast, resource exploitation reflected in production and exports is reduced or stays roughly constant.

There are several possible reasons for this apparent anomaly, including the limited ability of Latin American countries to respond in production to pressures from the outside, the lack of expanding markets in consuming countries, the poor price performance of the goods in which Latin American countries traditionally trade, and so on. Another answer to this dynamic may be found in the character of the domestic adjustment process in the 1970s, compared with the 1980s. In the period following the oil crisis of 1973, Latin American governments had available large, attractive loans for infrastructure development and subsidized investment. The domestic adjustment process in oil importers involved increasing exports to balance trade and generate the foreign exchange necessary to absorb increasing energy costs. In the case of Brazil, this adjustment was complicated further by massive investments in the domestic sugar, nuclear, and hydroelectric development plans, which were direct responses to the national energy crisis. Moreover, Brazil accelerated agricultural modernization and development in the center-south to compete more effectively in international markets in feed grains, poultry, citrus, and other products.

Data from the period show another interesting trend that does not continue after 1982. Gross investment continues to be strong, as does apparent domestic consumption. Through external debt, the 1970s afforded Argentina, Brazil, Mexico, and others the possibility of undertaking domestic adjustment without the horrendous recessions, economic hardships, and disinvestment that stalked the

1980s. Whereas the 1970s offered Latin American borrowers the opportunity to weather the economic difficulties of the period and attract new money, the 1980s did not generate new capital for investment. Domestic consumption has declined, even to the point that some of the countries with the fastest growing populations in the region are expecting declines in food requirements. If external shock is the prime cause, domestic adjustment with growth may be the intervening variable. (This is also consistent with Brazil's experience in the 1980s with a heterodox shock, emphasizing rapid domestic growth and export promotion.)

The evidence suggests that resource-based output increases are more a product of the 1970s than the 1980s, except perhaps in the cases of heterodox shocks that intend to conduct stabilization without recession. The hypotheses here are that domestic adjustment in favor of domestic resource industries provokes that change in output, and that decreases in consumption and investment in the 1980s meant that such rapacious growth was denied.[37] In any event, if external pressure results in increased natural resource exploitation as a function of domestic adjustment experience, it may be that the lack of new capital in the debt crisis has actually kept a lid on the "demand side" of resource depredations characteristic of the 1970s.

On the import side, there is more interesting evidence, some of which does support a direct relationship between debt and resource exploitation. Regionally, there is a decline in both volume and value of agricultural imports since 1980, and particularly since 1984. This import contraction is not justified by economic performance in the importing countries, but it is part of the artificially high barriers to imports imposed by governments adjusting externally to the debt crisis. Measured by value, the decline has been marked, dropping from $143.7 million in 1980 to $97.7 million in 1987.[38]

If imports have declined and exports have not, either domestic production is substituting for previous imports or demand is being suppressed through the price and distribution mechanisms. It is significant, then, that the regional decline in cereal imports has not been made up in domestic production. Per capita consumption of agricultural commodities has declined, as would be expected from the impact of stabilization programs on incomes. In Mexico, the drop is radical, reflecting the "demand management side" of former President Miguel de la Madrid's misnamed Programa Nacional de Alimentación and the further contraction of wages under the administration of Carlos Salinas de Gortari.[39] The gruesome portrait that appears involves the suppression of necessary demand for purposes of stabilization, with a dubious side effect of resource conservation through privation.

Nevertheless, the index of agricultural production in the region has gone up in the same period,[40] suggesting that there is import substitution in agriculture even though demand management may reduce overall consumption levels. In this case, the effect of debt relief is not apparent without stipulating the trade arrangements and wages that go with the debt relief.

The Politics of Redistribution

Latin American resource exploitation is fashioned by designers of primary sector modernization, based on the model of the developed countries. In Latin America, however, the productive modernization of rural resource exploitation has been wrapped in the cloak of "the social question." The premise is that high rates of resource exploitation are necessary to modernize the countryside and its poor residents. In quest of economic transformation, primary sector modernization for export is key.

In its most spectacular manifestations, this has led Latin American nations to accept environmental degradation as a necessary cost of development, declaring environmental consciousness to be a luxury of the developed world far removed from the harsh necessities of economic progress. This accounts for Brazil's rather infamous remarks at the 1972 Stockholm conference.[41] But Brazil's resistance to the idea of becoming a developed-world nature park is a result of a logic and a style of development that came from the North, emphasizing economic modernization to maximize the national product.[42] Using a favorite metaphor of trade negotiators, economic progress is like riding a bicycle: forward momentum is essential, lest the rider fall off. Questions are asked less often about the bicycle's course and the long-term prognosis of the rider. The long-term costs of economic growth under current technologies and social systems may mean that for the sake of staying on the bicycle, the cyclist pedals over a cliff.

The entire trade- and market-based approach to increased resource degradation misses a particularly horrifying—and likely—possibility: that, however great the direct exploitation of resources for production, significantly greater deforestation, erosion, water contamination, and other practices are taking place without any measurable reflection in output. This is the real political point behind the Ayres connection of debt to deforestation. If the full impact on domestic resources of external debt is so great and deep as to escape reflection in the market, then both macropolitical strategies to enhance the wage share of national income or market approaches to getting prices right are woefully inadequate to the role of the poor in resource degradation.

To date, whether demand is managed by government and market working together to get prices right, or through effective import substitution in agriculture, the resource impact is to put more pressure on the agricultural frontier and to aggravate, rather than to address, the social question in the countryside. As has been shown throughout the world, there is a consistent and devastating relationship between deteriorating incomes among the poorest and resource degradation. To the extent that the rural poor no longer can sustain basic consumption needs through traditional low-output farming, they are pressed to intensify production on marginal holdings, overstressing their land. Expansion of the agricultural frontier for import substitution tends to dispossess small- and even medium-sized farmers and certainly displaces landless workers in the short term.[43] Pushed off their lands, small farmers retreat to farm hillsides.[44] Forced out of their regular labor markets by agricultural modernization, the growing numbers of rural poor become "informal sector" workers in the countryside, farming ditches, squatting, taking off game and fuelwood, "mining" the margins of the rural economy. If the prospect of debt-induced overproduction of natural resources is grim, how much grimmer is the idea that much of resource degradation goes on with no productive dividend other than the social reproduction of utter misery.

Back to the market, Malcolm Gillis and Robert Repetto, Jeffrey A. McNeely, Hans Binswanger, Dennis Mahar, and others argue that perverse incentives for domestic agricultural development relate directly to deforestation and overexploitation of natural resources. That much is clear. However, those authors, along with the World Bank, argue that the removal of such perverse incentives would enhance the environment, an argument not well supported by the evidence of their studies and not particularly well grounded in what is known about the market and development.[45]

Import substitution in agriculture (ISA) alone may be the worst possible choice, degrading the environment without being linked to the welfare of the poorest rural dweller. ISA without redistribution generally requires either an expansion of the agricultural frontier or an intensification and modernization of agricultural methods. The agricultural frontier is often expanded artificially to include lands previously thought to be unfit for agricultural use. Classic examples include the semi-arid north of Mexico, where agricultural modernization and the green revolution were driven by overuse of groundwater; the high plains of Texas, a frontier whose exploitation in the 1960s and 1970s revolutionized cattle feeding in the United States and now has been shown to have depleted the Ogallala acquifer; the tropical lowlands of Central America, which were turned to banana cultivation in the first decades of this century; and, of course, the Amazon forest, which has been thought to be the "breadbasket of Latin America" by academics and policymakers devoted to import substitution in agriculture.[46] If ISA means intensifying production and letting the market manage demand without redistributive policies, it is a double-edged threat to the environment: forcing an accelerated marginalization of the rural poor and intensifying the use of already-scarce resources. The same logic may be applied to export substitution in agriculture, as in the case of Chilean table grapes or Mexican winter vegetables.

As to the prospect of including the poor in ISA, Clifford Geertz observed a generation ago that agricultural modernization is much more viable in good land than in bad. The prospect of intensifying swidden agriculture offers mainly environmental degradation. One might add now that the modernization of agriculture even on good land has been undertaken using energy-intensive, ecologically irresponsible practices that bring into question the long-term value of production increases altogether, regardless of the quality of the land. The politics of ISA with coherent, responsible social policy are much more radical.

The Role of the Public Sector

Often the state is blamed for environmental abuses, but external sector imbalances and domestic development imperatives have been mighty forces compelling intervention in resource-based economic activities. In any event, the poor performance of the public sector in its stewardship of natural resources and the new enthusiasm for the minimalist state encourage analysts to assume (or hope for) an environmental dividend from destatization.

Defending the state in Latin America verges on the impossible. It is difficult to conceive of less environmentally sensitive policies than took place under the aegis of the Mexican oil monopoly PEMEX or official colonization programs in the Brazilian Amazon. If it is arguably more utopian to expect the private sector to treat the environment with sustainability in mind than it is the state,[47] we must be careful and complete in the treatment of public sector failures in the resource area and the degree to which they are structurally imposed. Those reasons are largely political, and they have not been joined by those who defend the privatization of environmental regulation *or* those who seek to use the state for progressive ends.

The model of the Latin American resource-exploiting government in crisis is deceptively straightforward: faced with external sector problems,[48] the threat of domestic recession under orthodox stabilization, and internal social pressures, Latin American politicians expand agriculture, forestry, and other natural resource industries. In quest of domestic development and export promotion, the resource frontier is pushed back, at the expense of both local peoples and the environment.

Typically, this "solution" involves heavy public spending, intended to reduce the domestic political impact of economic change and to stimulate domestic investment in priority activities. The program fails, however, because the social impact of frontier expansion is often regressive, the environmental costs are politically unsustainable, the fiscal wherewithal is lacking, and the export impact is disappointing. The archetype is Brazil, a country with a high-capacity, intrusive state, aggressive responses to external shock, and a broad resource frontier.[49] Often the state is seen to be callous and arrogant, as well as incompetent. Faced with the problems of "spontaneous colonization," it turns its weapons on the poor colonist; in the Ecuadorean Amazon, oil interests and the state connive to turn oil-rich national parks into armed compounds where Conoco and Texaco may trespass but *colonos* are turned away.

The central problem of the state, though, does not depend on villainy or virtue. The state is not inimical per se to the objectives of conservation and development, but the politics of natural resource exploitation do reflect the distribution of wealth in the national economy and the architecture of political power in government. It would be extraordinary to think that all publics would be served equally by the preservation of public goods, or that gains from conservation would benefit society in just ways. A more realistic, albeit less appealing, proposition is that the benefits from natural resource exploitation or conservation will reflect the structure of power in society, and that the political strength of the poor will determine to a great extent whether the state acts in their interests. As Fernando Henrique Cardoso has argued, if the state itself is an entrepreneur and defender of entrepreneurial interests, there is little prospect that, in the absence of radical change, the state will turn its power to the advantage of the voiceless.[50] Never mind, for the moment, the unsettling prospect that a redistributive radicalism also might be inattentive to the "green agenda."

If the base of political power in a Latin American society reflects the tremendous economic and social inequality pervading the region, there is little reason to expect the state to act progressively. It is clear that the public sector in Latin America as presently constituted cannot be expected to challenge environmental degradation without substantial political change; and that such change must lead in the direction of more successful attention to "the social question," especially in the countryside. Once the "poverty push" of environmental degradation is addressed, the empowered poor would presumably have to face a similar set of political issues trading off short-term economic values against longer-term environmental sustainability.

Under whatever scenario, for either development or sustainability issues to be addressed, public policy has to concern itself with "intertemporal externalities" (that is, the impact of resource exploitation over generations), as well as the social question. In neither of these areas has Latin America been even marginally successful.

Because of a general lack of confidence in the state, policy analysts have looked to the private sector for answers and focused on the market as a better allocator of values in society. But even the most generous interpretation cannot dispel the reality of unequal distribution of wealth and power in the marketplace and the absence of a market-based mandate to guard the commonweal. The market is constitutionally unable to attend to the social consequences of environmental degradation, or to prevent them through its own actions. The objective of national economic growth is the maximization of production, just as the purpose of free trade is the global maximization of production. The private sector in Latin America has steadfastly militated against state intervention for social redistribution, counting instead on the virtues of the marketplace to allocate economic resources more efficiently. There is little evidence of concern in this logic for the long-term externalities of economic growth, whether it be in Brazilian export agriculture, Mexican chemicals, or Ecuadorean oil. The entrepreneurial state Cardoso described is politically bankrupt, but that does not offer absolution to the private sector.

These points, when matched with the historical responsibility of the public economy for natural resources and resource-based industries, lead to the central *political* point of the trade-development-resource exploitation nexus: that the public sector, not the marketplace, is uniquely endowed to treat questions of intertemporal sustainability on behalf of society in general, but that the public sector, reflecting as it does the skewed (and generally unaccountable) outcome of political conflict and negotiation, is poorly constituted to represent the interests of the poor or to challenge the logic of maximizing natural resource exploitation in the short term. In other words, a market-based approach to environmental responsibility is misplaced, but the state shows little capacity to accept or impose its environmental mandate. The current international situation weakens it even further.

Whatever their potential, neither the private sector's calculus of short-term gain nor the state's imperatives for social change and economic growth has included full-fledged consideration of the question of resource sustainability. Indeed, because the Latin American state embraces short-term economic growth and development goals, because the public economy is responsible for much of the resource base of the nation, and because external shocks exert extraordinary pressure on vulnerable Latin American governments, the logic of government policy toward natural resources conflicts with the fiduciary responsibility of the public sector over the nation's public goods.

The Political Gap in Current Thinking

Approaches to Latin American environmental concerns are explicitly political: they address the state, the international order, incomes policies, and the very control of economic property in society. In view of the clearly political character of these questions, the absence of political analysis in conservation and development literature is inexplicable. The scholarly bibliography on resource management questions is almost completely without reference to politics.[51] In a recent series of monographs on environmental questions sponsored by the World Bank Environment Department, authors concerned themselves with such explicitly political topics as resource sustainability, discounting, frontier colonization, deforestation, property rights, and the like. One even proposed future policy research priorities to contain deforestation.[52] None focused on the intrinsically political character of the issues at hand. None brought the tools of political science to bear on the questions of the environment. The research and political recommendations were framed in terms of "policy," not politics, evincing a conspicuous reluctance on the part of economists and ecologists to treat the question of political mission in the relationship between social and environmental change. In fact, if theory follows historical experience, the *politics* of sustainability are central to the creative implementation of the social change necessary to avoid disastrous environmental consequences.

More broadly, a great deal of environmental literature comes from a public policy approach that revolves around rationality and efficiency, without equally important attention to individual and institutional bases of political power. These assumptions of rationality and unconcern for power and "noneconomic" values sometimes reach shocking heights. Individualist political economy leaves to the state only the provision of public goods and the control of externalities. Pierre R. Crosson and Norman J. Rosenberg remark, for example, that public sector regulation is required only when people must be forced to act against their own economic self-interest: "This is true by definition; no regulations are needed to get people to act in the direction of economic self-interest."[53]

Compared with the risks of doing nothing, the dangers of proceeding with policy recommendations without adequate basic research are generally understated. The political and ecological blunders made in the name of expeditious policy should inspire more caution.[54] Seminomadic herdsmen have found themselves victimized by economically "rational" herd-building strategies, which often conflict with the sustainable management of fragile lands. Developers in Brazil assumed that eucalyptus plantations in the Amazon would provide charcoal for the pig iron plants associated with the gigantic Carajás iron ore project. Yet, after several years of effort, dissembling, and failure, authorities resorted to plans to cut natural forest to provide the estimated 2.4 million metric tons of charcoal each year for Grande Carajás.[55] Now, the Japanese, under cover of ITTO, are proposing a "sustainable forest production program" in the Western Amazon without having undertaken necessary research to determine the meaning of sustainability in that fragile and contested area.[56]

Proceeding with assumptions about conservation and development politics without recognizing the political tasks and costs implied is even more dangerous. To the extent such strategies foreshorten the necessary political changes required to effect sustainable development dynamics, they must fail. Perhaps more insidiously in the short term, the "policy-based approach" threatens to foreclose political options that promise better environmental and development performance in the future.

Implications for the International System

The institutions of the international system have undertaken consideration of "the environmental question" with the same doubtful enthusiasm that they have addressed "the social question" throughout the postwar period. The origins of that lack of energy probably stem from the complexity of the problems and the radical potential they reveal, even on first approach. If the sketch of argument and evidence in this chapter is correct, however, a number of important dimensions must be added to the environmental debate in the 1990s. I have chosen only five from a long list to offer as an exceedingly compressed prolegomenon to that debate.

Trade and Debt

1. The debate over free trade in agriculture (which encompasses agriculture, fishery, and forestry products) is only partially joined and ignores the environmental and social implications of OECD negotiations over the future of the international agricultural system.

The current system falls short on several dimensions. First and most obvious is the relationship between OECD agricultural subsidies and Latin American commodity output and trade. A recent OECD publication on agricultural policy and trade shows the horrendous complexity of OECD country agricultural policies and their differential impact on agricultural trade with other nations.[57] Several conclusions affect the discussion here. First, the agricultural policies of the European Economic Community and the United States affect world prices and markets of basic grains, one important denominator of resource exploitation and social policy in Latin America. Second, the ways in which the OECD does affect those markets are complicated and contradictory, so that simple free trade and subsidy elimination may not have desirable effects in Latin America. So, for example, dairy supports may bolster the international price of feed grains, among which is maize, which competes with Mexican domestic production. The greater the tendency of

Mexico to depend on the market to determine maize imports versus domestic production, the greater the threat of cheap maize to domestic campesinos.[58] Because domestic maize is a key to the campesino wage, the effect of free trade and low prices correlates with rural poverty and environmental abuse.[59]

Other examples are equally complex, and all are beyond the scope of this chapter. The point here is that the current GATT discussions about the future of agricultural subsidies, not the Latin American or Third World or even OECD environmental agenda, are driving the international system's approach to farm policy. The Uruguay Round's approach to agriculture has been exclusively producer-directed (the main actors have been the Cairns Group of agricultural producer countries, the United States, and the EEC) and has not undertaken the question of environmental impact. Brazil, as one of the principals in the debate, has a significant voice in the discussions, despite the fact that its agricultural development policies have forced the resettlement of entire populations onto fragile lands.

2. There is no obvious environmental dividend from debt relief, and virtually none of the debt debate at the international level addresses the potentially devastating environmental lessons of the past.

The plea for debt relief as a beginning solution to resource degradation problems is issued without apparent consideration of the potential misuse of a "development dividend" from debt forgiveness to undermine the environment in the future. It may be that such a dividend would combine with inattention to the absolutely poor, for whom such polemical pleas are usually made. It may well be that in the larger countries, debt relief will trigger the same kind of mindless developmentalism that was associated with the acceleration of frontier expansion and resource degradation that took place in the 1970s. It is perfectly reasonable to expect, for example, that debt relief under currently possible populist coalitions would ignore the poor altogether, in favor of addressing general consumption issues for frustrated middle-class voters among the traditional bases of power. Perhaps one of the most negative prospects for the environment would be a traditional populist in office with a nationalist redistributive mandate based on higher levels of consumption for traditional supporters of populism, the urban working class and middle sectors.

But does this mean that environmentalists should militate against debt relief? No. It means that an environmental dividend from debt relief requires an approach that incorporates a radical reapprehension of the relationship among international system, national state, and domestic political organization. The international system of nation-states must understand its own role in the destruction of the environment, in both rich and poor countries. Individual governments must militate in international organizations to link economic policy-making to the environment at every level. So, the Bank of International Settlements, the Paris Club, the Group of Seven, the United Nations Conference on Trade and Development (UNCTAD) and GATT, the World Bank, and the IMF are all required to undertake fundamental rethinking to make their policies consistent with good environmental outcomes in the Third World. The closed-system approach is inadequate for the environmental agenda in an era of global economic integration. Popular developed-country portrayals of irresponsible Latin American governments or individuals destroying the rain forest are vivid, but ridiculously incomplete images of the environmental relationship between North and South.

Redistribution and Growth

3. Economic growth without significant change in the technology, resource demands, and distribution of its benefits is virtually guaranteed to continue the environmental damage now under way.

This simple statement presents politically the most difficult and elusive dilemma facing Latin American environmental politics. First, without reasonable rates of economic growth and adequate performance in external accounts, Latin America is headed toward a decade of continued consumption of the resource frontier—through import substitution in energy and agriculture—and the deepening privation of the rural poor. Even with economic growth, however, the structure and character of production that led to the most palpable acceleration of environmental abuse in the 1970s are still in place. To the extent that economic growth depends on further international economic integration, the pace and style of environmental abuse are set outside the country. But the internationalization of production in the postwar period has precluded a "turn inward" to escape the dictates of the international system. To the extent that Latin American economies have internalized northern means of production, internally driven economic growth is little different than externally linked growth. The open ground between the economic nationalist and the internationalist has disappeared, at least as far as the environment is concerned.

Second, if environmental progress without growth is impossible, according to the immiserization and environmental abuse thesis, economic growth without redistribution simply accelerates resource consumption, without addressing— and perhaps worsening—immiserization. But if redistribution is undertaken as it has been in the past, there is no obvious environmental dividend. *Nor is there a long-term social benefit, given the permanent relationship between the poor and their resource base.* Redistribution must focus, as Phillip Fearnside has argued, on areas creating surplus populations that migrate to the resource frontier.[60] Likewise, it must embrace a different, economically competitive set of production principles that are more conservationist and take as its resource base the richest—not the poorest—land in the country. In other words, if agrarian reform is the watchword of environmentalist rural policy, it must be the most radical and thoroughgoing agrarian reform in the history of Latin America. Any other kind is simple self-delusion.

The Public Sector

4. Only public sector institutions can effect such economic changes, but then only after having undergone internal structural and political changes to divest themselves of their rapacious, ineffectual record, and to change the social basis on which state performance depends.

The great burden falling on Latin American nations involves the radical reconstruction of the social basis of power and the governmental purpose to which it is put in environmental affairs. Returning to Cardoso's argument earlier in this essay, the state cannot be expected to behave responsibly if it is not constructed on a social basis that demands it. A first step in making public power more broadly based is to insist on governmental transparency in environmental affairs. The governments of Brazil, Ecuador, Mexico, and others make decisions affecting the future of their nations with almost no institutionalized public debate. The contest over alternative decisions is made *in camera*, and, as Brazil has shown, the transition to civilian rule is no guarantor of democratic process. Unrestricted public access to state decision making has the prospect of transforming what is possible in environmental abuse.

More substantially, the state has to stand apart from the economic interests most abusive of the environment. To the extent that the state itself has been responsible, and current austerity is crippling that destructive capability, the contraction of public power is a positive change. But internally, the economic sources of public power must be changed to incorporate *in the first instance* those most affected by environmental abuse and those most disadvantaged by the current way of conducting economic affairs at the national level. This implies no less than some kind of left, bottom-up, redistributive eco-populism, in which the developed world is invested politically. This runs so contrary to the temper of the times that it seems hard to imagine the political leadership or coalitions that might make it possible. Nevertheless, the logic of policy recommendations in Latin American environmental affairs points in such a direction, and to ignore it is disingenuous.

External shock in the 1980s has meant reduced state capacity. What does this imply? If the state is the developmentalist enemy of the environment, clearly its prostration in the debt crisis has some positive aspects. But long before its capacity to ruin the environment is reduced, the state abandons "the social question," breaking the last tie of development concern for the poorest of the poor. Will the market embrace them? Is not the prospect of the progressive public economy the only redoubt of those advocating "adjustment with a human face?"[61] Lower state capacity also means lower levels of environmental monitoring, opening even the modest enforcement gates that do exist. In the 1980s, when lower levels of state monitoring and enforcement were matched by poor economic performance that pressured the poor, public lands were invaded. And the market did nothing to distribute economic growth in such a way as to soften pressure on fragile resources.

Financial Responsibility and the International System

5. *The financial wherewithal to support environmental improvement in Latin America must come overwhelmingly from developed-country consumers and must be generated and dispensed with political conditions that guarantee effective disbursement but do not compromise its radical political agenda.*

In recent negotiations between the EEC and the ACP (African, Caribbean, and Pacific) country beneficiaries of the Lomé agreements, the European Economic Community suggested that it was continuing its plans for single-market integration in 1992, but EEC countries argued over whether banana and sugar producers hurt by such plans should benefit from increased development assistance to substitute for disappearing preferential trade or from simple competition in a freer trade environment.[62] The unwillingness of key countries in the West, among them Great Britain, the United States, and West Germany, to consider increased development assistance—much less direct transfers of pollution taxes or other fiscal wherewithal unconnected to their own realist political advantages—is evidence of the political risk avoidance characteristic of the North.

For developed-world politicians it would be more convenient to push the financial burden for environmental responsibility back onto Latin America, as if the egregious offenses against the rain forest or acquifers were the province of the poor countries. In view of the fiscal retrenchment of the United States and Britain, the focus on single-market integration and fiscal rationality in the EEC, and the immense new burden facing Germany as East-West integration proceeds, it is unlikely that much money will be forthcoming from the OECD for Latin American environmental purposes. Thus, the multilateral system—the World Bank and its regional affiliates, the IMF, the OECD Development Assistance Committee, the Commonwealth Equity Fund, and so forth—are the last resort of fiscally strapped petitioners looking for ways to grow economically.

In their detachment from narrow national agendas, the multilateral institutions are properly suited to the task. But in their devotion to economic models of the

North, their aversion to the state, and their lack of commitment to the kind of revolutionary political change suggested here, they are weak advocates of the environmental agenda. And if the politics of the environment are left to transnational actors, who will account for the U.S. government's reaction to radical redistribution in Latin America? Or who will monitor the environmental impact of bilateral (U.S.-Mexico), trilateral (Argentina, Brazil, Uruguay), or "minilateral" (Europe-Lomé) agreements? Where will the multilateral consensus come from, if not from the nations comprising the system that now scramble to export their environmental problems to others?

All of these questions are contingent on a great deal of political organization and rethinking, and on specific country-based research that is far from complete. But the point of this chapter has been the inadequacy of the policy-based approach when the policies recommended and the outcomes desired demand such drastic political change. Only through the blindest faith in policy incrementalism can the political changes demanded by inter-American environmental affairs be ignored.

Notes

Portions of this argument and greater empirical detail can be found in Steven Sanderson, *The Politics of Trade in Latin American Development* (Stanford: Stanford University Press, 1992).

1. See Pinto's lament in "Comments."

2. See World Bank, *Striking a Balance*. A newer and regionally more interesting statement can be found in Latin American and Caribbean Commission on Development and Environment, *Our Own Agenda*.

3. This measure, not surprisingly, promises to mean the end of international tropical timber trade for the short term, as ITTO estimates that only 0.15 percent of tropical timber enterprises are sustainable. For details of the EEC position, see reports of the November meeting of the EEC Environment Directorate, esp. Reuters, November 19, 1989.

4. The meeting came only one month after the Toronto Economic Summit proclaimed the danger of debt, environmental destruction, and poverty to the world community. Norwegian Prime Minister Gro Harlem Brundtland, chair of the World Commission on Environment and Development, was the host.

5. For a characteristic statement, see Carlson, "Monetary Talks End," or Conable's speech to the GATT mid-term review in Montreal, December 6, 1988, reported in the *International Trade Reporter* of that date. For a fuller critique of the trade connection to the environment, see Sanderson, *Politics of Trade*, chap. 3.

6. In fact, a framework accord was announced at the Montreal mid-term review in December 1988. By mid-1989, however, LDCs were again voicing their unhappiness at the lack of progress on a tropical products accord. See Sanderson, "With Exception of U.S.," p. 1586, and "Third World Accuses Developed Nations," p. 813.

7. For the EEC threat, see Reuters, November 19, 1989. Environmentalists hope to get such restrictions imposed through ITTO.

8. Based on MacNeill, "Strategies," p. 159. This issue of the *Scientific American* was devoted humbly to "managing planet earth."

9. MacNeill, Winsemius, and Yakushiji, *Beyond Interdependence.*

10. Holling, "Resilience of Terrestrial Ecosystems."

11. This argument often focuses on export crops, viz., Bramble, "Debt Crisis"; for a summary and critique, see Repetto, *Economic Policy*, p. 6. The classic exposition of the connection between debt and resource degradation is found in the World Commission on Environment and Development, *Our Common Future*, pp. 74ff.

12. McNeely, *Economics and Biological Diversity*, pp. 44ff.

13. A direct relationship between the debt crisis and accelerated resource depletion through trade, or between resource depletion and privatization, would signify a straightforward indictment of the World Bank's policy-based lending to LDCs, the IMF stabilization agreements with high-debt countries, and the entire trade policy architecture of the United States. Worse yet, it would question the validity of the World Bank's newly found environmental virtue, which is the calling card of World Bank policy reform in the late 1980s. For a glossy statement of the bank's approach to these questions, see World Bank, *Striking a Balance.*

14. For provocative surveys of some of these issues, see Library of Congress, *Draft Environmental Report on Peru*, and Freeman, *Bolivia*. The U.S. Agency for International Development (USAID) has contracted a number of these studies for AID countries in Latin America; the studies provide survey material on questions of environment and development.

15. See the chapter on Peru in Thiesenhusen, *Searching for Agrarian Reform*. Neither the environmental nor the labor market consequences of *parcelación* is clear at this point.

16. CITES = Convention on International Trade in Endangered Species of Flora and Fauna. See, for example, Nietschmann, "Cultural Context of Sea Turtle Subsistence Hunting."

17. For the debt crisis in Ecuador, see Iversen and Jory, "Shrimp Culture"; Terchunian, "Mangrove Mapping"; Siddall, Atchue, and Murray, "Mariculture Development"; and various issues of the *Marine Fisheries Review*. The trend toward more intensive resource exploitation of the western Amazon has generated a controversial Brazilian government agreement with ITTO. The agreement emphasizes "sustainable" production in tropical rain forests and is financed by the Japanese, the largest tropical timber importers in the world. The Japanese are hardly known for conserving Asian rain forests. See ITTO, "Integration of Forest-based Development." Of course, in view of the accession to power of the Collor government and the naming of José Lutzenberger to the directorship of the Environmental Protection Institute (IBAMA), the future of this agreement may be in question.

18. Stabilization is a multifaceted concept, but in the Latin American context it generally refers to policies geared to balancing external accounts or attacking the rate of inflation.

19. See, for example, Corbo and de Melo, "Lessons."

20. As has been observed, "getting prices right is not the end of development, but getting them wrong often is." See Streeten, "Development Dichotomies."

21. MacNeill, "Strategies," p. 162.

22. The emphasis here is on *relative* factor abundance. For most of the region, little is abundant except in relation to the general scarcity of capital and technology.

23. This argument has been used to suggest that environmental controls chase corporations offshore. The evidence of studies to date, according to Segerson, "Natural Resource Concepts," is that such costs are insufficient to scare away domestic production.

24. Trade retaliation against countries offering "upstream subsidies" to production was narrowly averted in both the Trade Act of 1985 and the Omnibus Trade and Competitiveness Act of 1988. The U.S. Congress especially favored such retaliation as a protectionist measure against Mexican exports to the United States. Brazilian subsidies in steel were also the target of this proposed legislation.

25. It has been argued convincingly, however, that increased environmental regulation has not caused U.S. firms to move offshore. It is not clear that this is true in Latin America, but given the multiple reasons for foreign direct investment in a country, an argument can be made that increased environmental costs at the margin will not dissuade investors. A stronger argument could be made that once costs are sunk into production, greater environmental restrictions can be imposed without inordinate fear of losing investment. This, too, ignores the political impact of direct investment and its influence on such decision making.

26. According to a consulting report prepared for Forestry Canada by Woodbridge, Reed, and Associates, Brazil will see 1985's industrial hardwood timber supply of 35 million soar to 76 million by the year 2000 (about 32.2 billion board feet). Brazilian plantation hardwood, along with Chilean softwood, will dominate Latin American exports to the world. See Forestry Canada, "Sun Will Not 'Set,'" pp. 23ff. This conclusion is highly speculative, given the state of the Brazilian economy and the controversy surrounding both pig iron and timber exports. But there is little reason to assume that Brazil will categorically reject such a future—or control it, for that matter.

27. For a more complete exposition of the empirical evidence behind this conclusion, see Sanderson, *Politics of Trade*, chaps. 2–3, and Capistrano and Sanderson, "Tyranny of the External."

28. How ingenuous, then, is the observation of MacNeill that accelerated technology transfer is a likely source of environmental improvement, or of Crosson and Rosenberg that agricultural technologies for sustainability depend mainly on farmer adoption. For the latter, see Crosson and Rosenberg, "Strategies for Agriculture."

29. See Nectoux and Dudley, *Europe*.

30. Laarman, Schreuder, and Anderson, *Overview of Forest Products Trade*.

31. McNeely (*Economics and Biological Diversity*, pp. 189–90), along with many other ecologists, apparently accepts the good-faith claims of ITTO, though the emphasis of the Brazilian agreement is production and the Japanese track record in Southeast Asia is not a happy one. See World Wide Fund for Nature, "Tropical Forest Conservation." For evidence of the limits of scientific knowledge on these questions, see Budowski, "Is Sustainable Harvest Possible?."

32. An evocative portrayal of this "hamburger connection" can be found in the European film *Jungleburger*, as well as in articles such as Matteucci, "Is the Rainforest Worth Seven Hundred Million Hamburgers?"; Nations and Komer, "Rainforests"; and Uhl and Parker, "Is a Quarter-Pound Hamburger Worth a Half-Ton of Rain Forest?." For a strong critique, see Browder, "Social Costs." For a more complete treatment of U.S. markets for manufacture quality beef, see Jarvis, *Livestock Development*, and Sanderson, *Transformation of Mexican Agriculture*.

33. U.S. Congress, Joint Economic Committee, "U.S. Policy on High Technology Exports."

34. Ayres, "Debt-for-Equity Swaps."

35. Inter-American Development Bank, *Economic and Social Progress*, p. 27.

36. Among the large traders (Argentina, Brazil, Chile, Colombia, Peru, and Mexico), the

evidence is mixed. In Chile, the increase is pronounced, thanks to growth in agriculture. In Brazil, 1987 was a critical year, as it followed on the domestic overconsumption of the Cruzado Plan in 1986. In Argentina and Mexico, there are modest increases in nonmineral primary output; in Colombia, there is modest decline. In Ecuador, along with Bolivia, the most open, primary-commodity-dependent countries of South America, output does go up.

37. That does not mean that similar levels of investment and consumption would necessarily generate the same kind of performance now as occurred in the 1970s. For one thing, the international climate is vastly different.

38. Inter-American Development Bank, *Economic and Social Progress*.

39. For further details, see Goodman et al., *Mexican Agricultural Policies*.

40. Capistrano and Sanderson, "Tyranny of the External."

41. This was hardly a slip. Again in 1989, at a meeting considering the prospect of debt-for-nature swaps as a way of combining tropical conservation with external adjustment, the Brazilian minister of interior suggested that the problem of deforestation and resource degradation was a product of debt pressure and in any event was more the responsibility of the rich, consuming nations than the burden of Brazil. See Ayres, "Debt-for-Equity Swaps."

42. See Sunkel, "Interaction between Styles."

43. See Gerardo Otero's thesis of the "disappearing middle" in "Agrarian Reform."

44. The implications of increased pressures on steep-slope agriculture are alarming. In some countries of Latin America (Colombia, El Salvador, Guatemala, Haiti, and Peru), half or more of the agricultural population already works the steep slopes. In Mexico, the estimate is 45 percent of the agricultural population. The environmental and productive contributions of these farmers are complex. See Posner and McPherson, "Agriculture on the Steep Slopes."

45. On the other side of the political fence, Susannah Hecht and Alexander Cockburn (*Fate of the Forest*) criticize that position by offering a graph that ostensibly shows little association between public rural credit and deforestation. Their analysis is partial, however, and does not account for the possibility of time lags in the impact of credit on deforestation.

46. For the effects of ISA in the semi-arid north of Mexico, see Hewitt de Alcantara, *Socioeconomic Consequences*, and Sanderson, *Agrarian Populism* and *Transformation of Mexican Agriculture*. Exploitation of the high plains of Texas generated a debate in the Carter administration called the "structure of agriculture" controversy; for an illuminating document from that debate, see Bergland, *Time to Choose*. For ISA in the tropical lowlands of Central America, see Bulmer-Thomas, *Political Economy*. The durability of the "breadbasket" myth is remarkable. For a recent academic example, see Hall, "Agrarian Crisis." Even though Hall provides a cogent critique of Brazilian government plans for agricultural development, he concludes by advocating appropriate technologies to exploit the floodplains of Amazonia, a long-standing ambition of the government that has been criticized roundly in the central Amazon.

47. This does not intend to suggest that civil society in general does not have an important role. In fact, in Latin America, "nongovernmental organizations" of various stripes have been principals in the evolution of such concerns as sustainability and biological diversity.

48. This is not restricted to the debt crisis. One of the foremost stimuli to resource depredation in the 1970s was the series of oil shocks from 1973 to 1979.

49. Binswanger, "Fiscal and Legal Incentives"; Mahar, *Government Policies*. For a more general theoretical and empirical treatment across continents, see Gillis and Repetto, *Public Policies*.

50. Cardoso, "Development and the Environment," p. 127.

51. McNeely's *Economics and Biological Diversity* offers recommendations for policy incentives without treating the political process at all. For the merits and shortcomings of this approach, see also Repetto, "Needed" and "Creating Incentives."

52. Spears, *Containing Tropical Deforestation*.

53. Crosson and Rosenberg, "Strategies for Agriculture," p. 135.

54. It is perhaps too generous to characterize these moves as mistakes, as a great deal of deception and unconcern for available knowledge has been documented in government policies for development in fragile areas.

55. This means the use of an estimated 10.4 million metric tons of dry wood annually, or an equivalent of a 620-story building with a base of 100 meters square. Fearnside, "Charcoal of Carajás." See also Fearnside and Rankin, "Jari and Carajás."

56. A particularly telling criticism of the concept of sustainable resource use is found in O'Riordan, "Politics of Sustainability." His argument is that sustainable resource use allows developers to tag whatever activity they want to pursue with the sustainable descriptor to absolve themselves of environmental criticism. The lack of clear definition to the concept allows that liberty. For sharp criticism of the misuse of "sustainability" and "forest management" concepts in Brazil, see Fearnside, "Forest Management."

57. OECD, *National Policies*.

58. For more analysis, now somewhat dated, see Sanderson, "Mexican Agricultural Politics."

59. Partly based on this role of maize, David Barkin has proposed a "war economy" approach to development in Mexico. The vanguard of the war effort is the agricultural economy, based on increases in farm income through price supports and the elimination of trade in basic grains. See Barkin, "Resolving the Dilemma" and, more recently, *Distorted Development*.

60. Fearnside, "Ecological Analysis," p. 290.

61. Viz., Cornia, Jolly, and Stewart, *Adjustment with a Human Face*.

62. See *Euromoney*, October 1989.

· *Robert L. Bach*

Chapter Eleven · HEMISPHERIC MIGRATION

. IN THE 1990S

The history of the Western Hemisphere is a tale of migration. Indigenous peoples of the hemisphere have been able to survive the conquest, colonization, and capitalist development that has repopulated the region over the last five hundred years. But they have done so as moss clinging to the growth of giant pines. Today, even the last descendants of the great Mayan civilizations join the northward trek to urban centers.[1] There they huddle among the skyscrapers of Los Angeles, Houston, and Miami, a displaced people's army.

Migration displays the legacy of primal forces of hemispheric formation and transformation: conquest, colonization, slavery, liberation, decolonization and state formation, plantations and capitalist agriculture, war, revolution, and dramatically unequal wages. The post–World War II years comprise a critical moment of this hemispheric history. Its primary features—agricultural expansion, debt, decolonization, market integration, and revolution—have been developmental in the sense that they expanded upon and reproduced the unequal, colonial structure of hemispheric relations. They have also been transformative. Just as the world the slaveholders made was equally created by slaves,[2] migrants to new areas of the region have not simply succumbed to the culture of their wage masters. They have remade their own cultures and those of others.

The 1990s may be another time of dramatic changes in the migratory patterns of the Western Hemisphere. Since World War II, the rise of U.S. hegemonic power in the region has served as an unparalleled draw on the hemisphere's resources, including its capital and labor, brains and brawn. Global economic and political changes, however, are challenging the capacity and willingness of the United States to maintain this role in the region. The 1990s will reveal the legacy of decades of entrenched migratory flows that have surrendered to capital's insatiable demand for low-waged labor. It has already recomposed the demography of local labor markets. Before the next century, the full impact will be realized in the schools, communities, churches, and consciousness of the American people.

This chapter focuses primarily on migration flows destined for the United States and their connection with U.S.–Latin American interstate relations. To provide a demographic and geographic backdrop for this analysis, the essay opens with a brief description of significant migration patterns in the Western Hemisphere during the last four decades. The discussion then turns to the formation of a U.S.-centered inter-American system within which migration policies serve as instruments of U.S. national security interests, highlighting three specific concerns: the integration of a regional labor market, the effects of U.S. domestic politics on immigration policies and interstate relations, and the role of refugee policies in U.S. political decision making. Finally, each of these themes are carried into the 1990s for the purpose of identifying the potential sources of change in migration policies and patterns as a result of challenges to the existing inter-American system. Explored are the potential consequences of dramatic changes in both the economic position of the United States and the political fortunes of socialist regimes, current issues involved in U.S. domestic political reform, and the increasing role of human rights in the conduct of U.S. foreign policy.

Regional Migrations

The combination of economic and political changes since the 1940s has probably changed the scale of hemispheric migration more than any period since slave emancipation.[3] In many countries of the Caribbean, roughly 10 percent of the population has moved abroad, first to the respective colonial metropole, then to the United States. For many, migration has become a way of life, an ever-present alternative to conditions in the home country.[4]

During this half century, regional migration was marked by several patterns. Origins and destinations multiplied, a stair-step process of movement developed throughout the region, and long-established flows of labor between contiguous countries intensified. In short, as the regional migratory system expanded, it also deepened, creating more numerous and more diverse flows.

Large-scale migration from countries of the Western Hemisphere is relatively new.[5] Until the post–World War II period, migrants originated primarily from outside the hemisphere. Migrating into the region, their destinations were Argentina, Brazil, Canada, the United States, and Venezuela. The exception was the Caribbean. Plantation production and large-scale construction projects such as the Panama Canal have long distributed workers among the region's various countries.

As hemispheric migration expanded after World War II, several countries became the source of multiple outflows. Colombia exported migrants to Ecuador, Panama, the United States, and Venezuela. Within Central America, Salvadorans moved as settlers and laborers and, later, as exiles from political and military strife. In the 1960s, Bolivia and Paraguay were primary sources of flows to Argentina; by the 1970s, Chileans and Uruguayans had joined them. Only a downturn in the Argentine economy in the 1980s slowed the various movements around the Southern Cone.[6]

The primary example of labor flow intensification has been the movement of Mexicans to the United States. This flow, which is deeply rooted in a tradition of labor exchange, has expanded both in volume and in diversity of origin and destination. With each passing year, new Mexican villages become part of the migratory labor stream to the United States. A similar cross-border labor circulation has intensified between Colombia and Venezuela. Although cyclical fluctuations have been common, Colombians move with relative ease across Venezuela's western border, facilitated by extensive road networks and cultural similarities. The Dominican migration to the United States is yet another example. Although it began only in the early 1960s, it has now also become entrenched and self-reproducing. Along with Mexico, the Dominican Republic is one of the largest contributors of immigrants to the United States.

The regional pattern of migration is also shaped by the labor demands of pockets of export production and processing. The most familiar are the notorious labor supply problems associated with sugarcane. For example, Haitians move to sugar-producing areas of the Dominican Republic, where employment conditions and standards of living are subhuman. In the last decades, the emergence of export-processing zones has also begun to influence labor force behavior and migratory movements. These "modern" export sectors share characteristics with their traditional forerunners. They often generate migration to relatively isolated sectors that have little direct connection with the local labor force.

Although direct movements from poorest to richest countries occur, the primary pattern has a stair-step quality. The poorest states send migrants to the less poor nations, which in turn export their citizens to the advanced countries. For example, Haitians move to the Dominican Republic, while Dominicans move to New York City. This hierarchy of movements has long characterized the regional system of migration. Within a country, rural workers leave for intermediate-sized cities, while urban residents move to larger cities or abroad.[7]

The migrants who follow these stair steps comprise four groups. The first and most prevalent are the unskilled and semiskilled workers who circulate temporarily across contiguous borders or move permanently. Most are young men and women who work in low-paying jobs. Historically, many left agricultural origins. Now more depart from service sectors of major cities.

The other three groups are much smaller. Different class origins of refugee flows form two groups. The most familiar includes members of the privileged classes whose economic or political fortunes were ruined by regime changes. A second group contains rural families, often women and children, from countries like El Salvador and Guatemala. Military attacks against rebel groups are the immediate cause of many of these dislocations, but the underlying conflicts over land reform and political representation make such outflows endemic. The fourth and final group consists of highly skilled technicians and professionals who climb the regional stair steps to career advancement and relocation in the United States.

After a half century of these flows, there is little mystery about the large-scale structural forces that underlie regional migration. At this point in world history, the market has touched all parts of the region and now has become the basis for inequality among states.[8] During the 1970s and 1980s, a wholesale leap in world capital accumulation was accompanied by the restructuring of both the organiza-tion of production and its geographic location. A new geography of capital accumulation emerged, defined by regional linkages among migratory flows. Origins and destinations were paired through long historical connections and reproduced social networks.[9]

A social organization of migration also appeared involving transnational net-works based on family, friendship, and community relations. These networks formed a "complex web of social roles and interpersonal relationships" across time and space that served as conduits of information and financial assistance. Through them, households became linked to the demands of the international market. In turn, these demands reorganized the involvement of individual members of the household. One consequence of this household reorganization has been a sus-tained increase in the participation of women in the migratory flows.[10]

If there is any mystery left in this analysis, it exists in determining which political and economic relations are likely to change the organization of the migration in the next decades. The safest prediction of future trends is simple reproduction—that is, patterns will remain the way they are. Yet change is occurring throughout the region on a large scale. Sources of conflict, tension, and change are built into the existing structure of the regional political and economic framework—the inter-American system.

Migration and the Inter-American System

The structure of regional migration lies in U.S. political and economic power. U.S. hegemonic control over regional flows is now fully rooted in the strength of market demand, reproduced through family reunification and the social values attached to immigration in the United States. Market demand for low-wage labor started first in the fields, moved to industries, and today is located primarily in the service sector. Increasingly, this demand seeks people with skills.

Regional Strategies and Conflicts

The multilateral and bilateral political relations that comprise the inter-American system protect market exchanges. They also undergird the regional economic structure, providing a political framework for regional immigration. This framework establishes a direct relationship between migration flows and two aims of national security that the United States pursues through the inter-American system: (1) economic assistance to fight poverty and the "root causes" of social and political unrest, and (2) direct political and military intervention to contain resistance from groups opposed to U.S. interests.[11] President John F. Kennedy expressed these twin pillars of the inter-American system as follows:

> These are the many fronts of the Alliance for Progress. The conduct of those fronts, the steady conquest of the surely yielding enemies of misery and hopelessness, hunger and injustice is the central task for the Americas in our time.

> We must honor our commitment to the peaceful settlement of disputes, the principle of collective action, and the strengthening of the Inter-American system. We must also continue to invite and urge the participation of other Western nations in development programs, and the United States will continue to urge upon its allies the necessity of expanding the markets for Latin American products. But just as we have friends abroad, we also have enemies. Communism is struggling to subvert and destroy the process of democratic development, to extend its rule to other nations of this hemisphere. If the Alliance is to succeed, we must continue to support measures to halt communist infiltration and subversion, and to assist governments menaced from abroad. The American States must be ready to come to the aid of any government requesting aid to prevent a take-over linked to the policies of foreign communism rather than to an internal desire for change. My own country is prepared to do this.[12]

U.S. migration policies have grown out of this broad national security framework and, in turn, have been used as instruments in its defense. Regional labor migration has developed into a basic form of economic assistance. Exports of labor have become a "Latin American product" for which the United States has opened access to its own "market." The United States developed this approach first in relation to Puerto Rico and the program of economic assistance called Operation

Bootstrap. Later it extended the strategy to the Dominican Republic and Jamaica. More recently, it has reinforced the connection as part of the Caribbean Basin Initiative and aid to Central America. During the 1980s, when the United States created and then confronted its own budget deficit, labor migration served as a direct form of "foreign aid" and represented a fundamental part of the U.S. regional commitment to economic growth.

Formation of the inter-American system in the 1960s was not limited to economic assistance and labor flows, however. In President Kennedy's description of friends and enemies in the region, Cuba and the image of exile came to represent the antithesis of partnership, economic cooperation, and labor migration. He observed that "no sense of confidence, of optimism in the future of the Hemisphere as a whole, can conceal our feelings at the self-inflicted exile of Cuba from the society of American Republics."[13]

Those nations, like Cuba, that opposed U.S. dominance within the inter-American system have been met with economic isolation—embargo—and political opposition. After a period of open military opposition to Cuba, U.S. containment strategies translated into political exclusion and ideological resistance. In turn, isolation and containment became the context for the U.S. refugee policy. Cuba thus became the regional model of a "totalitarian" government whose repressive practices could be used to warn other Latin American countries about the consequences of challenge and opposition. Those who left Cuba were viewed as escapees; their flight attested to the superior life-style achieved in cooperation with the United States.

For decades the United States has used its control over travel visas to regulate the levels of legal immigration. In the 1960s U.S. policy on travel made explicit its connection with larger strategic interests in the region. In one memorandum, White House Chief of Staff McGeorge Bundy wrote: "The key to the problem [of growing Soviet military influence] is to build up the will and capabilities of the Latin American countries to counter the threat. Our efforts in the field of controlling travel between Latin America and Cuba are important."[14]

Twenty years later, U.S. strategic policy returned to the use of migration as an essential tool in the defense of the inter-American system. U.S. policy toward the Nicaraguan contras was both a military, counterinsurgency program and a migration strategy. In the 1960s, President Kennedy had defined U.S. aims in these circumstances as follows: "We in this Hemisphere must also use every resource at our command to prevent the establishment of another Cuba in this Hemisphere, for if there is one principle which has run through the long history of this Hemisphere it is our common determination to prevent the rule of foreign systems or nations in the Americas."[15]

For several years after the Cuban Revolution, the U.S. National Security Council worked to prevent an exodus of people from the island in order to maintain internal opposition. The alternative was to foster an outflow in hopes of depriving the new regime of essential professional and skilled labor. Arguments against encouraging an outflow won the U.S. policy debate until it became clear that the Cuban Revolution had become fully institutionalized.

U.S. policy toward the contras repeated almost exactly the earlier strategy employed against Cuba. In Nicaragua, the course of events has led to a much different outcome. In the beginning, the United States again resisted assisting a large-scale outflow from Nicaragua in order to encourage the opposition. The contras became the internal "freedom fighters," aided and led by exiled leaders based in Miami. Support for contra base camps across the border in Honduras also kept these potential "refugees" close to or engaged in the military action. Leaders in exile were publicly welcomed to the United States. But the middle- and working-class outflow seeped quietly into the Miami area. The United States was prepared for a large-scale exodus from Nicaragua only if its initial policy of destabilization of the Sandinista Front had ended in a Cuban-like failure.

This overall strategic use of migration policies is best illustrated by the U.S. response to pairs of states during periods of conflict. In the 1960s differential use of migration policies in Cuba and the Dominican Republic helped to demonstrate the value of economic and political cooperation. In the 1980s contrasting policies toward migration from Nicaragua, on the one hand, and El Salvador, Guatemala, and Honduras, on the other, reinforced the dispersal of military aid, among other signs of assistance and opposition. Despite widespread political violence in the latter three countries, the United States only rarely recognized the legitimacy of claims that human rights had been violated. In the case of both Cuba and Nicaragua, however, the United States maintained a vigilant watch on political abuses, often using refugees to testify to repressive conditions.

Domestic Reforms and Conflict

The structure of the inter-American system and its connection with migration is not limited solely to foreign policy and national security. As Christopher Mitchell has pointed out, domestic immigration laws and policies have a serious impact in the international arena.[16] The unilateral impact of U.S. domestic reforms on relations with the hemisphere reveals the extent of its regional hegemony. As the saying goes, when the U.S. economy sneezes, the Caribbean and Latin America catch a cold. U.S. immigration reforms during the 1960s fundamentally restructured labor and refugee flows in the region. This had several consequences for the relationship between migration and U.S. foreign policy. It also set the stage for the political struggle and reform that appears to be emerging in the 1990s.

The most important reforms of the 1960s included the termination of the national origins system for admitting immigrants, a dramatic increase in the number and proportion of people migrating from the Caribbean and Latin American to the United States, and transformation of the labor flow from Mexico. In particular, the U.S. government terminated the legalized system of Mexican migrant labor recruitment for U.S. agriculture. As a result, the flow was restructured and a majority of Mexicans began migrating as undocumented workers.

The link between domestic reforms and foreign policy interests was initially organized in the 1960s around civil rights. Although successive U.S. administrations long argued against continuation of the Mexican bracero program and the restrictions of the National Origins Quota Act of 1952, it was not until these efforts were connected with large-scale domestic reforms that the reformers prevailed in Congress.

The connection began in agriculture, where mechanization and labor displacement worsened conditions among the rural population, especially among migrant farm workers. Beginning with the Eisenhower administration, the U.S. Department of Labor moved to alleviate the worst conditions of native-born and resident farm laborers. The AFL-CIO supported these measures by attacking the Mexican migrant labor system in the United States as a form of "imported colonialism." Other major trade unions and various religious and community groups joined the opposition to imported foreign workers. But reform attempts in the 1950s failed miserably. With the passage of the Civil Rights Act of 1964, however, the attack on the farm worker program was finally won.

The link between civil rights struggles and immigration also led to the Immigration and Nationality Act of 1965. Reform grew out of the obvious incongruity between a nationwide movement for civil rights and a biased immigration law that favored white northern Europeans. At the time, the *Washington Post* editorialized that "once the civil rights bill is enacted into law, immigration policy should be high on the congressional agenda. Discrimination on grounds of race and origin is as un-American at the country's gates as it is inside them."[17]

Perhaps the most important immigration reform during this time was the acceptance of family reunification as the cornerstone of U.S. immigration policy. It also was a product of the civil rights connection. Family reunification had been proposed on many occasions as a basis for selecting immigrants to the United States and defeated each time. Only in 1965, when work and national origins were virtually eliminated as selection criteria did family reunification emerge as the universal rule for deciding who should be allowed to settle in the United States. Restructuring the legal immigration system to emphasize family reunion had a significant impact on the composition of migratory flows and continues to serve as a fundamental principle within the immigration debate.

These reforms, of course, did not resolve many of the deep tensions that existed because of attempts by states to regulate entrenched labor flows. Without a legalized Mexican farm worker system, agricultural interest groups continued to argue for government help in stabilizing the domestic farm labor market. Control of access to appropriate labor supplies was clearly on their minds and would remain a viable political force into the 1990s. The termination of the legal contract worker program also did not effectively block U.S. growers' access to the Mexican labor supply. Rather, it made it "run silent" for years—until its illegality became a pervasive public issue.

The antidiscrimination, civil rights fervor of the domestic political battle complemented some foreign policy objectives. But it greatly complicated others, especially those related to Latin America. For example, the most important foreign policy interests in the 1965 Immigration and Nationality Act involved the Pacific Rim. The State Department tied concerns about discrimination in the United States to its desire to "open up" immigration opportunities from what was then called the "Asian and Pacific Triangle." Secretary of State Dean Rusk testified before Congress that the racial ancestry or national origins feature of the existing law was indefensible from a foreign policy point of view because it represented overt statutory discrimination against more than one-half of the world's population.

Domestic and foreign policy interests collided, however, when applied to Latin America and the Caribbean. In opening immigration to the Pacific, the 1965 amendments restricted the flow from Mexico and from the Western Hemisphere generally. As a result, the State Department argued against hemispheric quotas as a threat to "Pan-Americanism." State pressed Congress to "recognize the common bond uniting the Americas by exempting from any quota restrictions those immigrants who were born in independent countries of the Western Hemisphere."[18]

Domestic reforms threatened more directly the national security interests that connected immigration and foreign policy. In the immediate aftermath of U.S. military intervention in the Dominican Republic, the administrator of the Bureau of Security and Consular Affairs warned the secretary of state and the attorney general against supporting the new immigration law: "Particularly in view of the Dominican situation," he said, "imposition of an over-all ceiling [on immigration] at this time would confound our problems with our Latin American neighbors."[19]

The Department of State also faced problems with Mexico. The strength of domestic reform pressures made the termination of the Mexican contract labor program a virtual unilateral decision. A National Security Council memorandum warned that "Mexico already feels that recent U.S. actions (termination of the Migrant Labor Agreement, lower cotton prices, limitations on duty-free goods) have seriously damaged its economy. Any new blow could put serious strains on our relations."[20]

The regional framework for migration established and consolidated in the 1960s remained intact throughout the 1970s and 1980s. In the last decade, however, there have been initial cracks and even moments of crisis. Still, the overall structural and institutional connections between defense of the inter-American system and responses to migration remain the dominant features of the regional migratory system. The potential for more fundamental change in the 1990s lies with broader systemic forces that alter the political and economic calculations on which the regional national security doctrine was constructed and that led to the widespread social reforms of the 1960s.

Beyond Hegemony

The period of sustained economic growth and U.S. political hegemony achieved in the hemisphere after World War II may have reached its zenith. Already, new, diverse migration patterns hint at changing power relations in the region. Democratization in the Southern Cone may have unleashed unparalleled and certainly unanticipated massive return migration to places such as Paraguay. At the same time, new poles of capital accumulation have rearranged some pairings of origins and destinations.

The emergence of Japan as a core area in the world economy has initiated a small flow of migrant workers from Latin America. A large influx of Asian-based capital into the continent may accelerate changes in labor conditions and outflows. Japan has even agreed to provide substantial funds for restoration of the Panamanian economy. New areas, such as Brazil, are also becoming countries of incipient, large-scale outflows to the United States.

The three primary sources of potential change in the migration patterns of the 1990s are derived from the same processes that shaped the post–World War II regional framework. These are regional economic integration, domestic U.S. political struggles, and political changes that dramatically challenge conceptions of persecution and the definition of a refugee. But transformation of the regional framework for migration will not result from any one of these processes alone. Rather, they represent elements in the encompassing inter-American system rooted in U.S. hegemony. Only deep changes in this larger structure will restructure regional migration patterns.

Regional Integration

The grip of hegemonic rule has eliminated alternatives for migrants and potential migrants in their communities of origin. Entire Mexican communities, for instance, have come to depend on access to the U.S. labor market for survival. Such strong ties lead many to doubt that this situation will change. Yet long-standing labor flows have reached the level where continuation without change is no longer possible.

Restructuring involves carving out new areas of capital accumulation within and against political boundaries. New regional growth poles represent recombinations of capital and labor that challenge the political framework underlying the hemispheric migration pattern. In particular, the Mexican flow is headed for full integration of a cross-national labor zone that is forcing the United States to search for new political relations to manage it. According to one journalist, "Mexico is home to 77 million people and a work force expanding by 1 million a year. It is the source of most of the legal and illegal immigration to the U.S. And it is tied, increasingly, by language, custom, and family to the estimated 18 million Hispanics in the United States. The futures of the U.S. and Mexican economies appear inextricably linked."[21]

The political challenge represented here is emerging in serious bilateral and multilateral discussions of free trade agreements with Mexico. Similar pressures have already led the United States into a free trade agreement with Canada. Increasingly, discussions of trade and migration move toward images of a North American common market. On a global level, this movement toward integration matches similar trends in Europe and East Asia. Restructuring of the global economy is creating new zones of capital accumulation. An integrated European economy after 1992 may form one global growth pole; a North American common market could form another.

Perhaps more important than these global trends, however, is the realization that a "free trade zone" and a transnational labor market are forming within the social, personal, and psychological lives of the migrants themselves. Complete integration eliminates not only economic but also cultural alternatives. According to recent research in Mexican villages, total market integration has become a cultural pattern, involving "attitudinal orientations, socialization processes, and social structures (including transnational social networks)" that grow out of the international migratory experience. Wayne Cornelius notes the development of a "migrant syndrome" that "encourages, validates and facilitates participation in the migration movement."[22] In his words:

> Migration to the United States becomes a complete substitute for local economic activity—a solution to one's economic problems that is considerably easier and less risky than starting a business in the home community, or investing in agricultural infrastructure, or organizing a production cooperative. It is also difficult to become concerned about the lack of public services,

unpaved roads, or other deficiencies of the home community, when one spends most of his time in the United States; so there is little civic spirit, and no collective efforts to secure public goods.[23]

Complete integration also means that migration no longer is necessarily driven by economic necessity alone. The 1990s should witness an ever-increasing shift from narrow economic motivations to those involving larger social processes—family reunification, network formation, and cultural integration—as well.

The complex motivations for migration lead many observers to comment on the difficulty of nations (especially the United States) to impose their political will on the integrated social field that forms the free labor zone. To a large extent, these observers are correct. But transformation of the flow will more likely occur because the state will act to foster and facilitate the integration rather than impede it. The assumption of many of these observers is that the state opposes increased migration of workers. In fact, the primary political groups supporting economic growth and immigration reform are the same groups that support increased international labor circulation and the further removal of government regulations for economic enterprise.

The sources of transformation also lie in the integrating processes themselves. For example, Douglas S. Massey has argued that the older migratory networks have "matured" to a point where they can no longer reproduce themselves demographically.[24] Several of these social networks also have overextended themselves. Like any market, periods of sustained expansion are often followed by "shakeouts" that trim the number of participants. Faced with some difficulties, it may be increasingly harder for social networks to bear the cost of reproducing successively larger waves.[25] Finally, complete market integration eliminates possible strategies for combining sources of wage and nonwage income in order to protect households during cyclical economic downturns.

The potential changes for full-scale integration may seem far off. Historically, however, similar changes have occurred in Puerto Rico, where efforts and pressures to achieve a fully integrated labor flow have been unhampered by problems of citizenship and international borders. The changing motivations of Dominican immigrants may also indicate the transformation of the flow from an economic venture to the reproduction of more complex social relations.[26]

Domestic Reforms

U.S. domestic reforms in the 1990s will also have a profound impact on international labor flows. For instance, to the extent that the new immigration law—the Immigration Reform and Control Act of 1986 (IRCA)—works, it may significantly limit the flow of Mexican workers. Of course, many observers believe that the law will not work. The Bilateral Commission on the Future of United States–Mexican Relations, for example, concluded that "Simpson-Rodino (IRCA) is not likely to stem the tide of undocumented migration. The Law relies to a substantial degree on voluntary compliance by employers."[27] Observers generally believe that the strength of market forces underlying labor migrations is resistant to state intervention.

In the context of regional restructuring, however, IRCA may be more a policy for the 1990s and beyond than an attempt to resolve a crisis of past illegal immigration. IRCA has several provisions—each of which is much more workable than its restrictive penalties on employers for hiring undocumented aliens—that will stabilize the immigrant labor supply on which important sectors of the southwestern economy have come to rely. These include a legalization program that has enabled over three million workers and their families to become permanent residents of the United States. It also includes a Special Agricultural Workers (SAWs) program to stabilize the immigrant farm labor supply and provide a mechanism for replenishing the supply if needed.

The strongest political forces in the current debate are those that support expanded levels of immigration. It is better if these new immigrants come legally, but illegal, low-wage labor will continue to be tolerated because it is needed.[28] In a strange twist of political irony, this free market position is also supported by many human rights and immigration activists who fear that the United States is heading down the path of restrictionism.

Unlike the domestic reforms of the 1960s, the context of the 1990s involves deep rollbacks in the civil rights gains of the last few decades and a general political weakness of the coalition that fought for and achieved earlier reforms. In many ways, the Special Agricultural Workers program under IRCA and legal immigration reforms recently proposed in Congress are also rolling back the gains made in the 1960s.[29]

Like the domestic reforms of the 1960s, these new laws will have an impact on foreign relations. Anticipating that the new law would be seen as a unilateral U.S. action, Congress established through IRCA a commission to investigate the relationship between migration and economic development, especially in Mexico.[30] The series of research reports produced by this commission supports the widespread perception that market integration is increasing migration throughout the region. To the extent that recent U.S. immigration reforms increase immigration, their effect on foreign policy may be the opposite of what has been predicted. Increased market integration means the sending country's loss of control over its own labor supply. Although political tensions may increase as sending and receiving countries need to negotiate the rules of labor exchanges, the demand for labor inside the United States will continue to dominate attempts to regulate the flow of immigrant workers.

The restructuring of the U.S. economy has also shifted the demand for immigrant labor. Increasingly, U.S. capital seeks skilled labor. For example, every proposal for reform of the legal immigration system contains a substantial revision of the number of immigrants and regulations associated with gaining access to skilled labor. It is widely anticipated that the sources of these skilled technicians will be Europe and Asia, not Latin America. As a result, U.S. domestic immigration reforms may become more restrictionist toward Latin American immigration in exchange for easier access to skilled workers.

Refugees

The reorganization of global capitalist accumulation involves challenges to countries and reassertion of national and group-based rights to an extent not witnessed since the interwar period. Since the mid-1970s, there has been a qualitative leap in massive refugee flows throughout the world, including areas not previously known for large-scale, politically based movements. For the first time, for instance, a large number of refugees have appeared in the Southern Cone.[31] Violence of all sorts, rather than mere economics or politics, has become the primary motive behind refugeelike emigration.[32] The increasing complexity of motivations, experiences, and, especially, class origins of migrants has made it very difficult to draw meaningful distinctions between labor and refugee flows. The scale of the problem has also brought in new institutional actors, primarily the United Nations, and given legitimacy to broader definitions of refugees and human rights.

These new definitions have deeply challenged U.S. migration and national security policy in the hemisphere and directly signaled a crisis of U.S. hegemony. The Mariel and Haitian flows in the early 1980s were the first signs of this crisis. As noted earlier, however, U.S. success in Nicaragua and El Salvador reasserted the basic regional strategy. Still, understanding the nature of violence in the region will serve as a point of political struggle in the 1990s. Such violence has extensive implications for the inter-American system and the U.S. domestic reform movement. In fact, human rights issues focused around Central American concerns have already come to rival civil rights as the principle for immigration reform in the 1990s.

The specific points of change and contest in this political realm involve the character of reform within the socialist countries, the future of Cuba, and the extent of violence and rebellion in Central America. Clearly, the most profound political change in the 1990s involves the historic reshaping of socialist regimes. These changes have had both direct and indirect effects on the political framework for migration in the Western Hemisphere. In particular, they have radically altered the empirical reference for both policy and legal responses of the United States and the international community to refugeelike situations. A National Security Council memo of the late 1980s highlighted the problem for the United States:

. . . the issues which result from the current opportunity for sizable numbers of Soviet citizens to leave the Soviet Union and our desire to facilitate that exit has competed with our need to uniformly apply our immigration laws. . . . Further, it is apparent that changes inside the Soviet Union may be underway which could significantly impact our immigration policies. Accordingly, the NSC, in conjunction with the State and Justice Departments, should immediately undertake appropriate studies of possible immigration trends from the Soviet Union and communist countries and how the United States and the western world should respond.[33]

Dramatic changes in the Soviet Union and Eastern Europe have turned the attention of the world once again to Europe as the center of change in the definition of a refugee and human rights. Since the October Revolution of 1917 and especially since the tragedy of displaced persons during both world wars, conditions in Europe have dominated definitions of refugees, persecution, the relationship between the individual and the state, and human rights generally.

Although the debate has occurred in international arenas such as the United Nations, refugees in different parts of the world have not been treated equally. In the past half century, this inequality has created problems. The difficulties and strains of most refugee situations, and the targets of most refugee policies, are deeply embedded in North-South relations. Eurocentric definitions have proven inadequate. During the last decades these differences have been highlighted by efforts of the Organization of African Unity (OAU) and Organization of American States (OAS) to redefine the concept of a refugee to fit more closely regional conditions and the history of political oppression in these areas.

These North-South differences have created problems for U.S. policy. In both the OAU and OAS definitions, specific reference has been made to the role that outside aggression has played in creating the political conditions that have led to exile outflows. Especially in Latin America and Central America, the United States has been the primary outside aggressor. In fact, both definitions challenge the doctrinal linkage in U.S. policy between the primacy of national security concerns and differential migration policies. Both challenge the right of the United States to define the legitimacy of political views and opposition in the region, turning instead to more universalistic traditions independent of nation-state interests.

The challenge of the increasing diversity and complexity of refugeelike migrations is demonstrated by efforts to expand the definition of political persecution and to devise new reasons for accepting special groups of refugees. In the United States, for instance, the Supreme Court's Cardoza-Fonseca ruling embraced an expanded definition of "reasonable fear of persecution." Perhaps more dramatic, however, have been the National Security Council's attempts to devise a broad category of "expectation of admission" as grounds for accepting new groups of refugees.[34] Although the strategy was justified on grounds of persecution in the Soviet Union, it more accurately reflects an attempt to continue a foreign policy–based refugee policy and to circumvent the challenge of applying international standards of human rights to all groups equally.

These global challenges are clearly the reasons for historical change. But the most immediate and profound basis of transformation of the migration pattern and U.S. regional policy in the 1990s lies only ninety miles south of Miami. What would the U.S. policy toward Latin America, particularly its refugee policy, look like if Cuba was no longer an antagonist? U.S. policy toward Cuba is the cornerstone of the regional strategy—evidence that it is the sting of the stick that makes the carrot tasty. The recent collapse of the Soviet Union, Eastern Europe, and Sandinista-controlled Nicaragua makes it likely, if not certain, that Cuba will have to come to new terms with the United States in one way or another.

Although often overlooked, migration has long been the primary barometer of Cuban-U.S. relations and a window on internal conditions in Cuba. Predictions of a collapse of the Revolution are rampant, but the migration experience suggests an alternative future. Cuba may already have had the internal crisis that leads to large-scale outmigration, such as that witnessed in East Germany in December 1989. While the U.S. Immigration and Naturalization Service plans for a new influx to Miami, there is already in place a mechanism for normal emigration from Cuba. This agreement emerged from the Mariel crisis in 1980 as a recognition by both Cuba and the United States that turmoil was counterproductive for both countries. The agreement establishes a basis for negotiated settlements and provides an outlet for a crisis.

At present, however, the United States, not Cuba, is resisting use of the migration agreement to its fullest advantage. Instead, the United States employs a contradictory migration policy toward Cuba. In signing the Mariel migration agreement, it has publicly recognized that it is possible to return people to Cuba without fear of persecution. The United States has also worked to install a normal processing capacity at the Interests Section in Havana. Nearly three thousand Cubans are migrating under the normal system annually. Yet the U.S. government maintains a policy that grants political asylum to anyone who leaves Cuba by boat and makes it to Miami. Boat departures are on the increase. Currently, they run at about forty a month, and most of the immigrants do not qualify for admission under the normal preference categories used by the United States for all other countries.

Cuba is well on its way to achieving a social process of normalized emigration that resembles those in other nations of the Caribbean. Even in the midst of the Mariel crisis, this process had already begun. The characteristics and determinants of the outflow throughout the 1980s reflected systemic changes in socialist economic and political development and underdevelopment.[35] The question now is whether the United States can live up to the new arrangement. So far, the answer is no. Clearly, the normal agreement is inconsistent with the U.S. national security doctrine that considers Cuba to be the isolated, excluded pariah of the region. U.S. ability to adhere to the normalized migration agreement is simply a test of the extent to which U.S. immigration policy depends on the broader framework.

The political battle over the origins and definition of a refugee is also being waged within the United States. In particular, the concentration of Central Americans and undocumented immigrants in the Southwest has produced intense political struggles that are now working their way through the U.S. court system. In recent years, the Ninth Circuit Court, with jurisdiction over California and other high-immigration states, has been involved in a continuous dialogue with the Board of Immigration Appeals over rulings related to this issue. The landmark case, Cardoza-Fonseca, grew out of the debate on the meaning of persecution in Central America. The Supreme Court upheld that the "asylum statute was [based on a] 'well-founded fear' of persecution, a standard distinctly different and more generous than the 'clear probability' standard of proof that had been imposed by the administrative immigration authorities."[36]

According to a recent study, however, the Board of Immigration has denied asylum claims by narrowing the concept of persecution and political opinion. In cases involving Central Americans, for example, it has made restrictive judgments about political opinion. In Salvadoran cases especially, decisions have been based on the presumption that certain arrests have been within the legitimate sphere of government action. But in cases involving obvious opponents to the U.S. foreign policy, the board has ruled that the governments lacked legitimacy and therefore those arrested or threatened with arrest had a legitimate fear of persecution.[37]

The Ninth Circuit Court has overturned some of these decisions and focused on the "realities of political conflicts and politically-motivated persecution in Central American and Caribbean nations."[38] Broader legal interpretations of forms of political persecution are also developing in Canada; they signal a change in jurisprudence that may have a significant impact on U.S. policy in Central America.

Beyond the specific terms of the legal debate, however, the content of these arguments highlights a changing political debate. It calls for increased judicial involvement in migration policy and represents a deeper struggle against the older national security framework. The political struggle reveals the emergence of a new immigration reform coalition, but with a very different context and perception of the issues that underlie migration than that represented in the 1960s. The new reform movement focuses on individual defense rather than broad social struggles, and much of its interest is in foreign—not domestic—affairs. This orientation will undoubtedly leave a different stamp on immigration reform in the 1990s.

Conclusion

With the political transformation of Europe and the challenge of economic competition with Japan, the primary question of the 1990s may be, Is the Third World relevant? The Panamanian invasion, Nicaraguan elections, and the anticipated collapse of Cuba, rather than stimulating interest, may have simply eliminated problems that historically have brought attention to the region. Certainly, the continuance of U.S. hegemony in Latin America is not sufficiently in question to generate interest at the highest levels of policy-making. Nevertheless, the 1990s promise to be a period of reformulation of fundamental principles in which Latin America, and the Third World generally, should be central.

One of the problems with the current debate on immigration policies, especially in terms of changing migration patterns, is the overconfidence, even analytic smugness, that exists in many economic forecasts. Undoubtedly, intensification of the unfettered rule of capital and the marketplace limits realistic discussion of alternatives. But the declaration by some that nations and organized political power are irrelevant misses the fundamental ways in which the economy is organized institutionally through nations. These observers look to countries to restrict the reorganization of accumulation in the region. In contrast, the future will be a scramble to redefine the political relations—multilateral, bilateral, and domestic—that will facilitate and protect the emerging patterns of world accumulation in the twenty-first century. The 1990s will be a period of search for those new political relations.

Rather than nations acting to restrict hemispheric economic relations, opposition, conflict, and, therefore, transformation are more likely to come from the people, those groups and classes that will be fighting to maintain control over a cultural sphere that will appear to be under assault. Increasing integration and standardization will spawn alternatives rooted in separation, cultural differentiation, and group identities. Migration is one of the primary forces in the region and the world that embodies this fundamental contradiction between integration and differentiation. As such, it will continue to reveal both the legacy of previous developments and the twists and turns involved in remaking the regional political economy.

The response to new migration patterns will vary greatly. Canada has already declared itself an official multicultural state and now struggles with unanticipated complications caused by the diversities of contemporary immigration. The United

States has its own trajectory. How it handles social and cultural change in the 1990s and beyond, however, will depend on its capacity to forge a new political framework in the region. The hope is that this new framework will recognize that national security in the contemporary world can no longer afford to exclude any nation or people.

Notes

1. See Rodriguez, "Mayan Migration to Houston."
2. The reference here, of course, is to Genovese, *The World the Slaveholders Made*.
3. For a comparison of historic periods of migration in the Caribbean, see Dawn Marshall, "History of West Indian Migrations."
4. See, for example, Bach, "Caribbean Migration to the United States."
5. For a discussion of some of these themes, see Bach, "Emigration from the Spanish-Speaking Caribbean," and Balan, "International Migration."
6. Balan, "International Migration."
7. See Salt, "Comparative Overview."
8. Zolberg, "The New Waves."
9. Portes and Walton, *Labor, Class*.
10. Massey, *Return to Aztlan*; Boyd, "Family and Personal Networks" (quotation); Hareven, "Family History at the Crossroads," cited in Boyd, ibid.; Fernandez-Kelly, *For We Are Sold*. See also Bach and Schraml, "Migration, Crisis"; Pessar, "Role of Gender."
11. Schoultz, *National Security*.
12. This section is based on Bach, "Immigration and U.S. Foreign Policy in Latin America and the Caribbean," from which the Kennedy quotation was taken.
13. Speech to the Inter-American Press Association, Miami Beach, Fla., May 5, 1962, as quoted in Bach, "Immigration and U.S. Foreign Policy in Latin America and the Caribbean."
14. McGeorge Bundy, Memorandum of a meeting with President Johnson, December 17, 1963, White House Central Files, Papers of President Lyndon Johnson, as quoted in Bach, "Immigration and U.S. Foreign Policy in Latin America and the Caribbean."
15. Speech to the Inter-American Press Association, Miami Beach, Fla., May 5, 1962, as quoted in Bach, "Immigration and U.S. Foreign Policy in Latin America and the Caribbean."
16. Mitchell, "International Migration."
17. "Whom We Shall Welcome" (editorial), *Washington Post*, April 16, 1964, p. C10.
18. Unsigned memorandum to President Johnson, May 8, 1965, White House Central Files, Papers of President Lyndon Johnson, as quoted in Bach, "Immigration and U.S. Foreign Policy in Latin America and the Caribbean."
19. Memorandum, May 20, 1965, White House Central Files, Papers of President Lyndon Johnson, as quoted in Bach, "Immigration and U.S. Foreign Policy in Latin America and the Caribbean."
20. Undated memorandum, State Department to Walt Rostow, White House Central Files, Papers of President Lyndon Johnson, as quoted in Bach, "Immigration and U.S. Foreign Policy in Latin America and the Caribbean."
21. Yemma, "Mexicans Ponder."

22. Cornelius, *Labor Migration*, p. 76 (first quotation); Reichert, "Migrant Syndrome," p. 61 (second quotation). See also Cornelius, *Labor Migration*.

23. Cornelius, *Labor Migration*, p. 77.

24. Massey, "Economic Development," pp. 408–9.

25. For some preliminary evidence, see Bach and Brill, *Shifting the Burden*.

26. See Grasmuck and Pessar, *Between Two Islands*, chap. 7, 1990.

27. Bilateral Commission on the Future of United States–Mexican Relations, *Challenge of Interdependence*, p. 104.

28. For a review of some of these issues, see Bach and Meissner, "America's Economy in the 1990s."

29. For a discussion of the political principles underscored by the debate about IRCA, see Bach and Meissner, "Employer Sanctions."

30. Working Paper Series, Commission for the Study of International Migration and Cooperative Development, Washington, D.C., n.d.

31. See Zolberg, "The New Waves," p. 414.

32. See Zolberg, Suhrke, and Aguayo, *Escape from Violence*.

33. Memorandum from Edwin Meese III, Attorney General, to Lt. General Colin Powell, Assistant to the President for National Security Affairs, The White House, August 4, 1988, pp. 2–3.

34. "Expectation of admission" was used by the National Security Council and the U.S. Department of Justice to justify the use of parole in the case of the greatly increased number of Soviets allowed to leave their country. Although there is no question that U.S. foreign policy has created such an expectation among, in particular, Soviet Jews, the concept is so imprecise—and the use of support for emigration as a tool of U.S. foreign policy so pervasive—that it accurately describes refugee and family reunification situations around the world.

35. See Bach, "Emigration and Socialist Construction."

36. Anker and Blum, "New Trends in Asylum Jurisprudence."

37. See ibid., pp. 67–82.

38. Blum, "The Ninth Circuit."

·
·
·
·
· BIBLIOGRAPHY
·
·
·
·
·

Newspapers and Magazines

Capítulos del SELA
CEPAL News
Economist
Euromoney
Financial Times
Informe Latinoamericano (London)
International Herald Tribune (Paris)
Latin American Newsletters
Miami Herald
New York Times
Reuters
Semana
Wall Street Journal

Books, Articles, and Other Materials

Abente, Diego. "The Military in Paraguay and the Prospects for Democratization." Paper presented to American Political Science Association, Washington, D.C., September 1988.

Abrams, Elliot. "Looking South: The U.S. and Latin America in the 1990s." Remarks to the Hudson Institute National Policy Forum, Washington, D.C., September 18, 1990.

Abreu, M. P. "Developing Countries and the Uruguay Round of Trade Negotiations." *Proceedings of the World Bank Annual Conference on Development Economics, 1989.* Washington, D.C.: World Bank, 1990.

Abreu, M. P., and Fritsch, W. "Latin American and Caribbean Countries in the World Trade System: Past Problems and Future Prospects." North-South Roundtable, London, 1987. Mimeo.

Adair, Major Rod. "Civil-Military Relations in Honduras." Manuscript, n.d.

Agüero, Felipe. "The Military and the Limits to Democratization in South America." Manuscript, 1989.

———. "The Military in Processes of Political Democratization in South America and

Southern Europe: Outcomes and Initial Conditions." Paper presented at the 15th International Congress of the Latin American Studies Association, Miami, December 1989.

————. "The Military and Democracy in Venezuela." In *The Military and Democracy: The Future of Civil-Military Relations in Latin America*, edited by Louis Goodman, Johanna Mendelson, and Juan Rial, pp. 257–75. Lexington, Mass.: Lexington Books, 1990.

Aguilera, Gabriel. "The Development of Military Autonomy and Corporateness in Central America." In *Democracy Under Siege*, edited by Augusto Varas, pp. 163–87. New York: Greenwood Press, 1989.

————. "The Armed Forces, Democracy, and Transition in Central America." In *The Military and Democracy: The Future of Civil-Military Relations in Latin America*, edited by Louis Goodman, Johanna Mendelson, and Juan Rial, pp. 23–28. Lexington, Mass.: Lexington Books, 1990.

Ameringer, Charles. *Don Pepe*. Albuquerque: University of New Mexico Press, 1978.

Anderson, Stephen J. "Las visiones japonesas de América Latina en la Cuenca del Pacífico." In *El mundo en transición y América Latina*, edited by Carlos Portales, pp. 185–221. Buenos Aires: GEL, 1989.

Andreas, Peter R.; Bertram, Eva C.; Blachman, Morris J.; and Sharpe, Kenneth E. "Dead-end Drug Wars." *Foreign Policy*, no. 85 (Winter 1991–92): 106–28.

Anker, Deborah, and Blum, Carolyn Patty. "New Trends in Asylum Jurisprudence: The Aftermath of the U.S. Supreme Court Decision in INS v. Cardoza-Fonseca." *International Journal of Refugee Law* 1, no. 1 (January 1989): 67–68.

Armanet, Pilar, ed. *América Latina en la cuenca del Pacífico: Perspectivas y dimensiones de la cooperación*. Santiago: Institute of International Studies, University of Chile, 1987.

"Aronson Pledges to Push Democracy," *Miami Herald*, June 16, 1989.

Arrieta, Carlos G.; Orjuela, Luis J.; Sarmiento, Eduardo; and Tokatlian, Juan G. *Narcotráfico en Colombia*. Bogotá: Ediciones Uniandes/Tercer Mundo Editores, 1990.

Ashby, Joe C. *Organized Labor and the Mexican Revolution under Cárdenas*. Chapel Hill: University of North Carolina Press, 1967.

Aspen Institute, "State Crimes: Punishment or Pardon." Conference Report, March 1989.

Atkins, G. Pope. *Latin America in the International Political System*. 2d rev. ed. Boulder, Colo.: Westview Press, 1989.

Ayala, José, and Durán, Clemente Ruiz. "Development and Crisis in Mexico: A Structuralist Approach." In *Latin American Political Economy: Financial Crisis and Political Change*, edited by Jonathan Hartlyn and Samuel A. Morley, pp. 243–64. Boulder, Colo.: Westview Press, 1986.

Ayón, David R., and Anzaldua Montoya, Ricardo. "Latinos and U.S. Policy toward Latin America." In *Latin America and Caribbean Contemporary Record*, edited by Abraham F. Lowenthal, pp. A126–42. Vol. 5, 1985–86. New York: Holmes and Meier, 1988.

Ayres, José Marcio. "Debt-for-Equity Swaps and the Conservation of Tropical Rain Forests." *Tree* 4, no. 11 (November 1989): 331–35.

Bach, Robert L. "Emigration from the Spanish-Speaking Caribbean." In *U.S. Immigration and Refugee Policy: Global and Domestic Issues*, edited by Mary M. Kritz, pp. 133–54. Lexington, Mass.: D. C. Heath, 1983.

————. "Emigration and Socialist Construction: Lessons from Mariel." *Cuban Studies* 15, no. 2 (1985): 19–36.

————. "Caribbean Migration to the United States: Causes and Consequences." *Migration Today*, 1987.

————. "Immigration and U.S. Foreign Policy in Latin America and the Caribbean." In *Immigration and U.S. Foreign Policy*, edited by Robert W. Tucker, Charles B. Keely, and Linda Wrigley, pp. 123–49. Boulder, Colo.: Westview Press, 1990.

Bach, Robert L., and Brill, Howard. *Shifting the Burden: The Effects of IRCA on Labor Markets in the United States*. Final Report to the U.S. Department of Labor. Washington, D.C.: GPO, May 1990.

Bach, Robert L., and Meissner, Doris. "America's Economy in the 1990s: What Role Should Immigration Play?" Occasional Paper Series No. 1, Carnegie Endowment for International Peace, December 1989.

————. "Employer Sanctions Three Years Later." Occasional Paper Series No. 2, Carnegie Endowment for International Peace, April 1990.

Bach, Robert L., and Schraml, Lisa A. "Migration, Crisis, and Theoretical Conflict." *International Migration Review* 16, no. 2 (Summer 1982): 320–41.

Baghwati, J. *The World Trading System at Risk*. Princeton, N.J.: Princeton University Press, 1990.

Bagley, Bruce M., guest ed. *Assessing the Americas' War on Drugs*. Special Issue, *Journal of Interamerican Studies and World Affairs* 30, nos. 2–3 (Summer–Fall 1988).

————. "U.S. Foreign Policy and the War on Drugs: Analysis of a Policy Failure." In *Assessing the Americas' War on Drugs*, edited by Bagley, pp. 189–212.

————. "Colombia and the War on Drugs." *Foreign Affairs* 67, no. 1 (Fall 1988): 70–92.

————. "Myths of Militarization: The Role of the Military in the War on Drugs in the Americas." In *North-South Center Drug Trafficking in the Americas Series*, no. 1 (1991): 1–37.

————. *Myths of Militarization: The Role of the Military in the War on Drugs in the Americas*. Miami: North-South Center, 1991.

Bagley, Bruce M.; Bonilla, Adrián; and Páez, Alexei, eds. *La economía política del narcotráfico: El caso ecuatoriano*. Quito: FLACSO/North-South Center, 1991.

Bagley, Bruce M., and Tokatlian, Juan G., eds. *Economía y política del narcotráfico*. Bogotá: Ediciones Uniandes, 1990.

Baker, Caler. "U.S. Lacks Cohesive Third World Conflict Policy." *Defense News*, December 11, 1989.

Baker, James A., III. "Latin America and the U.S.: A New Partnership." *Current Policy*, no. 1160 (March 30, 1989).

Balán, Jorge. "International Migration in Latin America: Trends and Consequences." In *International Migration Today: Trends and Prospects*, edited by Reginald T. Appleyard, pp. 210–63. Paris: UNESCO, 1988.

Baldwin, Robert E. "U.S. Trade Policy: Recent Changes and Future U.S. Interests." *American Economic Association Papers and Proceedings* 79, no. 2 (May 1989): 128–32.

Baloyra, Enrique. "Negotiating War in El Salvador: The Politics of Endgame." *Journal of Interamerican Studies and World Affairs* 28 (Spring 1986): 123–48.

————. "Democracy Despite Development." *World Affairs* 150, no. 2 (Fall 1987): 86–89.

————. "Public Opinion about Military Coups and Democratic Consolidation in Venezuela." In *Democracy in Latin America: Colombia and Venezuela*, edited by Donald Herman, pp. 210–14. New York: Praeger Publishers, 1988.

Barkin, David. "Resolving the Dilemma of the Internationalization of Mexican Agriculture." Paper presented at the 15th International Congress of the Latin American Studies Association, Miami, December 1989.

————. *Distorted Development: Mexico in the World Economy*. Boulder, Colo.: Westview Press, 1990.

Barrios, Raúl. "The Armed Forces and Democratization in Bolivia, 1982–1986." In *Democracy Under Siege*, edited by Augusto Varas, pp. 189–203. New York: Greenwood Press, 1989.

Barros, Alexandre. "The Brazilian Military in the Late 1980s and Early 1990s: Is the Risk of Intervention Gone?" In *The Military and Democracy: The Future of Civil-Military Relations in Latin America*, edited by Louis Goodman, Johanna Mendelson, and Juan Rial, pp. 177–87. Lexington, Mass.: Lexington Books, 1990.

Barros, R. "The Left and Democracy: Recent Debates in Latin America." *Telos* (Summer 1986).

Bell, J. P. *Crisis in Costa Rica*. Austin: University of Texas Press, 1971.

Bergland, Robert. *A Time to Choose*. Washington, D.C.: USDA, 1979.

Bilateral Commission on the Future of United States–Mexican Relations. *The Challenge of Interdependence: Mexico and the United States*. Lanham, Md.: University Press of America, 1989.

Binswanger, Hans. "Fiscal and Legal Incentives with Environmental Effects on the Brazilian Amazon." *World Bank Report* 69 (1987): 71–86.

Blachman, Morris J., and Sharpe, Kenneth E. "The War on Drugs: American Democracy under Assault." *World Policy Journal* 7, no. 1 (Winter 1989–90): 135–67.

Blasier, Cole. "Moscow's Retreat from Cuba." *Problems of Communism* (November–December 1991): 91–99.

Blum, Carolyn Patty. "The Ninth Circuit and the Protection of Asylum Seekers since the Passage of the Refugee Act of 1980." 23 *San Diego Law Review* 327 (1986).

Bodenheimer, Thomas S., and Gould, Robert. "U.S. Military Doctrines and Their Relation to Foreign Policy." In *Hemispheric Security and U.S. Policy in Latin America*, edited by Augusto Varas, pp. 7–32. Boulder, Colo.: Westview Press, 1989.

Borón, Atilio. "Authoritarian Ideological Traditions and Transition towards Democracy in Argentina." Columbia University Papers on Latin America, no. 8, 1989.

————. "Relaciones internacionales de Argentina: Las desventuras del 'Idealismo Periférico.'" *América Latina/Internacional* (July–September 1991): 431–39.

Bosworth, Barry P., and Lawrence, Robert Z. "America's Global Role: From Dominance to Interdependence." In *Setting National Priorities: Policy for the Nineties*, edited by Henry J. Aaron, pp. 29–52. Washington, D.C.: Brookings Institution, 1990.

Bourque, Susan, and Warren, Kay. "Democracy without Peace: The Cultural Politics of Terror in Peru." *Latin American Research Review* 24, no. 1 (1989): 7–34.

Bouvier, Virginia. "Decline of the Dictator: Paraguay at a Crossroads." Washington Office on Latin America, July 1988.

Bouzas, Robert. "A US-MERCOSUR Free-Trade Area: A Preliminary Assessment." *Documentos e informes de investigación* (Buenos Aires: FLACSO), no. 123 (1991): 1–39.

Boyd, Monica. "Family and Personal Networks in International Migration: Recent Developments and New Agenda." *International Migration Review* 23, no. 3 (Fall 1989): 638–70.

Bramble, Barbara. "The Debt Crisis: The Opportunities." *Ecologist* 17, nos. 4–5 (1987): 192–99.

Braudel, Fernand. *The Perspective of the World: Civilization and Capitalism, 15th–18th Century.* Vol. 3. New York: Harper and Row, 1984.

Brigagao, Clovis. "The Institutional System and the Management of the Crisis." In *Latin America: Peace, Democratization, and Economic Crisis,* edited by José Silva Michelena, 151–57. Tokyo: United Nations University and Zed Books, 1988.

Briones, Alvaro. "El tercer mundo en la perspectiva latinoamericana." *Estudios Internacionales* (Santiago), 19. no. 75 (July–September 1986): 335–70.

Browder, John O. "The Social Costs of Rain Forest Destruction: A Critique and Economic Analysis of the 'Hamburger Debate.'" *Interciencia* 13, no. 3 (May–June 1988): 115–20.

Brown, Ralph S. *Loyalty and Security.* New Haven: Yale University Press, 1958.

Budowski, Gerardo. "Is Sustainable Harvest Possible in the Tropics?" *American Forests* (November–December 1988): 34–81.

Bull, Hedley. *The Anarchical Society: A Study of Order in World Politics.* New York: Columbia University Press, 1977.

Bulmer-Thomas, Victor. *The Political Economy of Central America since 1920.* Cambridge: Cambridge University Press, 1988.

Bush, George. "Commitment to Democracy and Economic Progress in Latin America." *Current Policy,* no. 1168, May 2, 1989.

———. "Security Strategy for the 1990s." *Current Policy,* no. 1178, May 24, 1989.

———. "Enterprise for the Americas Initiative." *Current Policy,* no. 1288, June 27, 1990.

Bustamante, Fernando. "Fuerzas armadas en Ecuador: ¿Puede institucionalizarse la subordinación al poder civil?" In *Democracia y fuerzas armadas en Sudamérica,* edited by Fernando Bustamante et al., pp. 129–60. Quito: CORDES, 1988.

———. "The Armed Forces of Colombia and Ecuador in Comparative Perspective." In *Democracy Under Siege,* edited by Augusto Varas, pp. 17–34. New York: Greenwood Press, 1989.

Bustamante, Fernando; Buzeta, Oscar; Cavagnari Filho, Geraldo Lesbat; Fitch, J. Samuel; Moneta, Carlos Juan; Montserrat, Marcelo; Morales Bermúdez, Francísco; and Müller Rojas, Alberto. *Democracia y fuerzas armadas en Sudamérica.* Quito: CORDES, 1988.

Caffrey, Dennis. "The Inter-American Military System: Rhetoric vs. Reality." In *Security in the Americas,* edited by Georges Fauriol, pp. 39–59. Washington, D.C.: National Defense University Press, 1989.

Canadian Department of Forestry. "Sun Will Not 'Set' on Forest Industry in Next 20 Years." *Forest Industries* 116, no. 10 (October 1989).

Canak, William. "Debt, Austerity, and Latin America in the New International Division of Labor." In *Lost Promises: Debt, Austerity, and Development in Latin America,* edited by William Canak, pp. 9–30. Boulder, Colo.: Westview Press, 1989.

Canavan, Terence C. "The Threat to the International Banking System." In *Latin America's Debt Crisis: Adjusting to the Past or Planning for the Future?,* edited by Robert Pastor, pp. 53–60. Boulder, Colo.: Lynne Rienner, 1987.

Capistrano, Ana Doris, and Sanderson, Steven E. "The Tyranny of the External: Debt, Trade, and Resource Use in Latin America." Paper presented at the 16th International Congress of the Latin American Studies Association, Crystal City, Va., April 1991.

Cardoso, Fernando Henríque. "Associated-Dependent Development: Theoretical and Practical Implications." In *Authoritarian Brazil: Origins, Policies and Future,* edited by Alfred Stepan, pp. 142–76. New Haven: Yale University Press, 1973.

———. "Development and the Environment: The Brazilian Case." *CEPAL Review* 12 (December 1980): 111–28.

———. "Entrepreneurs and the Transition Process." In *Transitions from Authoritarian Rule: Comparative Perspectives*, edited by Guillermo O'Donnell, Philippe Schmitter, and Laurence Whitehead, pp. 137–53. Baltimore: Johns Hopkins University Press, 1986.

Carlson, Alver. "Monetary Talks End with Call for Freer Trade to Ease Poverty." *Reuters Business Report*, September 29, 1988.

Castañeda, Jorge. "The Mexican Perspective." In *Limits to Friendship*, edited by Robert A. Pastor and Jorge Castañeda, pp. 217–41. New York: Alfred A. Knopf, 1988.

———. "Latin America and the End of the Cold War." *World Policy Journal* (Summer 1990): 469–92.

Catterberg, Edgardo. "La consolidación de la democracia en Argentina y el sistema de partidos políticos, 1983–1989." Paper presented at the 15th International Congress of the Latin American Studies Association, Miami, December 1989.

Cavagnari Filho, Geraldo Lesbat. "Autonomía militar y construcción del poder." In *Democracia y fuerzas armadas en Sudamérica*, edited by Fernando Bustamante et al., pp. 47–89. Quito: CORDES, 1988.

Cavarozzi, Marcelo, and Grossi, María. "From Democratic Reinvention to Political Decline and Hyperinflation (The Argentina of Alfonsín)." Paper presented at the 15th International Congress of the Latin American Studies Association, Miami, December 1989.

CEPAL. *Estudio económico de América Latina*. Santiago: Publicaciones de Naciones Unidas, 1991.

Chancellor, John. *Peril and Promise: A Commentary on America*. New York: Harper and Row, 1990.

Cheney, Dick. "D.O.D. and Its Role in the War against Drugs." *Defense* (November–December 1989): 2–7.

Chernick, Marc. "Negotiations and Armed Conflict: The Colombian Peace Process (1982–1986)." Columbia University Papers on Latin America, no. 1, August 1988.

Child, Jack. "Geopolitical Thinking in Latin America." *Latin American Research Review* 14, no. 2 (1979): 89–111.

———. *Unequal Alliance: The Inter-American Military System, 1938–1978*. Boulder, Colo.: Westview Press, 1980.

———. "Inter-State Conflict in Latin America in the 1980s." In *The Dynamics of Latin American Foreign Policies*, edited by Elizabeth G. Ferris and Jennie K. Lincoln, pp. 21–35. Boulder, Colo.: Westview Press, 1981.

———. "The Inter-American Military System and the Latin American Democracies." Paper prepared for Inter-American Dialogue, August 1987.

———. "Geopolitical Thinking." In *The Military and Democracy: The Future of Civil-Military Relations in Latin America*, edited by Louis Goodman, Johanna Mendelson, and Juan Rial, pp. 143–64. Lexington, Mass.: Lexington Books, 1990.

Cohen, Roger. "Shift in U.S. Policy on Latin America Decreases Likelihood of Military Coups," *Wall Street Journal*, May 4, 1989.

Collier, Ruth Berins, and Collier, David. *Shaping the Political Arena: Critical Junctures, the Labor Movement, and Regime Dynamics in Latin America*. Princeton: Princeton University Press, 1991.

Commission for the Study of International Migration and Cooperative Economic Development. "Report of the Commission for the Study of International Migration and Cooperative Economic Development." Washington, D.C.: GPO, 1990.

Conable, Barber B. Speech to the GATT midterm review, Montreal, December 6, 1988. Reported in the *International Trade Reporter*, December 6, 1988.

CONADEP, *Nunca Más: Informe de la Comisión Nacional sobre la Desaparición de Personas*. Buenos Aires: Editorial Universitaria de Buenos Aires, 1985.

Conaghan, Catherine. "Politicians against Parties: Electoralism and the New Economic Fatalism in Ecuador." *Dialogues*. Occasional Paper Series, Florida International University, Miami, 1988.

———. "Dreams of Orthodoxy, Tales of Heterodoxy: León Febres Cordero and Economic Policy-Making in Ecuador, 1984–88." Paper presented at the 15th International Congress of the Latin American Studies Association, Miami, December 1989.

———. "Ecuador: The Politics of Locos." *Hemisphere* 1, no. 2 (Winter 1989): 13–15.

Conaghan, Catherine; Malloy, James; and Abugattas, Luis. "Business and the 'Boys': The Politics of Neoliberalism in the Central Andes." *Latin American Research Review* 25, no. 2 (1990): 3–30.

Connolly, Charles R. "Foreign Aid for the 1990s: Democracy." *Christian Science Monitor*, July 13, 1989.

Constable, Pamela, and Valenzuela, Arturo. *A Nation of Enemies: Chile Under Pinochet*. New York: Norton, 1991.

Corbo, Vittorio, and de Melo, Jaime. "Lessons from the Southern Cone Policy Reforms." *World Bank Research Observer* 2, no. 2 (July 1987): 111–42.

Cornelius, Wayne A. *Labor Migration to the United States: Development Outcomes and Alternatives in Mexican Sending Communities*. Final Report to the Commission for the Study of International Migration and Cooperative Economic Development. Center for U.S.–Mexican Studies, University of California, San Diego, March 1990.

Cornia, Giovanni Andrea, Jolly, Richard; and Stewart, Frances, eds. *Adjustment with a Human Face: Protecting the Vulnerable and Promoting Growth*. New York: Oxford University Press, 1987.

Crahan, Margaret. "National Security Ideology and Human Rights." In *Human Rights and Basic Needs in Latin America*, edited by Margaret Crahan, pp. 100–127. Washington, D.C.: Georgetown University Press, 1982.

Craig, Gordon A., and George, Alexander L. *Force and Statecraft: Diplomatic Problems of Our Time*. New York: Oxford University Press, 1983.

Crosson, Pierre R., and Rosenberg, Norman J. "Strategies for Agriculture." *Scientific American* (September 1989): 128–35.

Dam, K. W. *The GATT: Law and the International Economic Organization*. Chicago: University of Chicago Press, 1970.

Dassin, Joan, ed. *Torture in Brazil: A Report by the Archdiocese of São Paulo*. Translated by Jaime Wright. New York: Vintage Books, 1986.

Debray, Régis. *Strategy for Revolution*. New York: Monthly Review Press, 1971.

Degregori, Carlos Iván. "The Origins and Logic of Shining Path: Two Views: Return to the Past." In *The Shining Path of Peru*, edited by David Scott Palmer, pp. 33–44. New York: St. Martin's Press, 1992.

de Soto, Hernando. *The Other Path: The Invisible Revolution in the Third World*. New York: Harper and Row, 1989.

Diamond, Larry; Linz, Juan; and Lipset, Seymour Martin, eds. *Democracy in Developing Countries: Latin America*. Vol. 4. Boulder, Colo.: Lynne Rienner, 1989.

Diamond, Larry; Lipset, Seymour Martin; and Linz, Juan. "Building and Sustaining Democratic Government in Developing Countries: Some Tentative Findings." *World Affairs* 150, no. 1 (Summer 1987): 11–15.

Díaz Alejandro, Carlos F. *Essays on the Economic History of the Argentine Republic*. New Haven: Yale University Press, 1970.

Domínguez, Jorge I. "The Nature and Uses of the Soviet-Cuban Connection." In *The USSR and Latin America*, edited by Eusebio Mujal-León, pp. 159–82. Boston: Unwin and Hyman, 1989.

Domínguez, Virginia R., and Domínguez, Jorge I. "The Caribbean: Its Implications for the United States." Headline Series Pamphlet No. 253, Foreign Policy Association, February 1981.

Dornbusch, R. "Policy Options for Freer Trade: The Case for Bilateralism." In *An American Trade Strategy: Options for the 1990s*, edited by R. Lawrence and C. Schultze, pp. 106–41. Washington, D.C.: Brookings Institution, 1990.

Drake, Paul. "Debt and Democracy in Latin America, 1920s–1980s." In *Debt and Democracy in Latin America*, edited by Barbara Stallings and Robert Kaufman, pp. 53–56. Boulder, Colo.: Westview Press, 1989.

Drekonja, Gerhard, and Tokatlian, Juan G., eds. *Teoría y práctica de la política exterior latinoamericana*. Bogotá: CEREC/CEI, University of Los Andes, 1983.

Dresser, Denise. "Exporting Conflict: Transboundary Consequences of Mexican Politics." In *The California-Mexico Connection*, edited by Abraham F. Lowenthal and Katrina Burgess. Forthcoming.

Durand, Francisco. "La nueva derecha peruana: Orígenes y dilemas." *Estudios Sociólogicos* 8, no. 23 (1990): 372.

El-Agraa, E. *The Theory and Measurement of International Economic Integration*. New York: St. Martin's Press, 1989.

Escudé, Carlos. "La política exterior de Menem y su sustento teórico implícito." *América Latina/Internacional* (Buenos Aires: FLACSO) (January–March 1991): 394–406.

Fagen, Richard. *Forging Peace: The Challenge of Central America*. New York: Blackwell, 1987.

Fajnzylber, Fernando. "Democratization, Endogenous Modernization, and Integration: Strategic Choices for Latin America and Economic Relations with the United States." In *The United States and Latin America in the 1980s: Contending Perspectives on a Decade of Crisis*, edited by Kevin J. Middlebrook and Carlos Rico, pp. 131–60. Pittsburgh, Pa.: University of Pittsburgh Press, 1986.

Falcoff, Mark. "A Look at Latin America." In *Sea-Changes: American Foreign Policy in a World Transformed*, edited by Nicholas X. Rizopoulos, pp. 71–83. New York: Council on Foreign Relations Press, 1990.

Fáunde-Ledesma, Héctor. "The Inter-American System: Its Framework for Conflict Resolution." In *Latin America: Peace, Democratization, and Economic Crisis*, edited by José Silva Michelena, pp. 168–86. Tokyo: United Nations University and Zed Books, 1988.

Fauriol, Georges A. *The Third Century: U.S. Latin American Policy Choices for the 1990s*. Washington, D.C.: Center for Strategic and International Studies, 1988.

———. "The Shadow of Latin American Affairs." *Foreign Affairs* (America and the World, 1989–90): 116–34.

Fearnside, Phillip. "An Ecological Analysis of Predominant Land Uses in the Brazilian Amazon." *Environmentalist* 8, no. 4 (1988): 14–31.

———. "The Charcoal of Carajás: A Threat to the Forests of Brazil's Eastern Amazon Region." *Ambio* 18, no. 2 (1989): 141–43.

————. "Forest Management in Amazonia: The Need for New Criteria in Evaluating Development Options." *Forest Ecology and Management* 27 (1989): 61–79.

Fearnside, Philip, and Rankin, J. R. "Jari and Carajás: The Uncertain Future of Large Silvicultural Plantations in the Amazon." *Interciencia* 7 (1982): 326–28.

Feinberg, Richard E. "Latin American Debt: Renegotiating the Adjustment Burden." In *Development and External Debt in Latin America: Bases for a New Consensus*, edited by Richard E. Feinberg and Ricardo Ffrench-Davis, pp. 52–76. Notre Dame, Ind.: University of Notre Dame Press, 1988.

————. "Bush's Enterprising Initiative." *Hemisphere* 3, no. 1 (Fall 1990): 10–11.

Ferguson, Yale. "Cooperation in Latin America: The Politics of Regional Integration." In *The Dynamics of Latin American Foreign Policies*, edited by Jennie K. Lincoln and Elizabeth G. Ferris, pp. 37–55. Boulder, Colo.: Westview Press, 1984.

Fernández-Kelly, Patricia. *For We Are Sold: I and My People*. Albany: State University of New York Press, 1983.

Ferris, Elizabeth G., and Lincoln, Jennie K. *Latin American Foreign Policies: Global and Regional Dimensions*. Boulder, Colo.: Westview Press, 1981.

Finger, J. Michael. "Ideas Count, Words Inform." In *Issues in World Trade Policy*, edited by R. Snape, pp. 257–80. New York: St. Martin Press, 1986.

Fishlow, Albert. "The Latin American State." *Journal of Economic Perspectives* 4 (Summer 1990): 61–74.

Fitch, J. Samuel. "United States Human Rights Policy in Latin America under Carter and Reagan." In *Latin American and Caribbean Contemporary Record*, vol. 2, edited by Jack Hopkins, pp. 65–76. New York: Holmes and Meier, 1982–83.

————. "Inter-American Military Relations: Past, Present, and Future." Paper presented at a conference on "The United States and Latin America: The Next Decade," FLACSO, Santiago, June 1989.

————. "Military Professionalism, National Security, and Democracy: Lessons from the Latin American Experience." *Pacific Focus* 4, no. 2 (Fall 1989): 126–33.

Fitch, J. Samuel, and Fontana, Andrés. "Military Policy and Democratic Consolidation in Latin America." Paper presented at the World Congress of the International Sociological Association, Madrid, July 9, 1990.

Fontana, Andrés. "La política militar en un contexto de transición: Argentina, 1983–1989." Paper presented at the CEDES–Schell Center for Human Rights conference on "Transición a la democracia en Argentina," Yale University, March 1990.

Fox, Jonathan. "Toward Democracy in Mexico?" *Hemisphere* 1, no. 2 (1989): 40–43.

Foxley, Alejandro. *Latin American Experiments in Neoconservative Economics*. Berkeley: University of California Press, 1983.

Fraga, Rosendo. "Permanente inestabilidad: Frágiles relaciones cívico-militares en Argentina." Paper presented at workshop on "Civil-Military Relations: Toward the Year 2000." American University and PEITHO, Washington, D.C., April 1991.

Freeman, Peter H. *Bolivia: State of the Environment and Natural Resources*. McLean, Va.: JRB Associates, 1980.

Frieden, Jeffry. *Debt, Development, and Democracy: Modern Political Economy in Latin America, 1965–85*. Princeton, N.J.: Princeton University Press, 1991.

Fritsch, Winston. "Latin America's Export-Growth Imperative in the 1980s: Can the United States Help Achieve It?" In *The United States and Latin America in the 1980s: Contending Perspectives on a Decade of Crisis*, edited by Kevin J. Middlebrook and Carlos Rico, pp. 231–60. Pittsburgh, Pa.: University of Pittsburgh Press, 1986.

————. "The New Minilateralism and Developing Countries." In *Free Trade Areas and U.S. Trade Policy*, edited by Jeffrey J. Schott, pp. 337–52. Washington, D.C.: Institute for International Economics, 1989.

————. "O Plano Bush e o interesse nacional." In *Brasil em mudança*, edited by João Paulo dos Reis Velloso, pp. 29–48. São Paulo: Nobel, 1991.

Frohmann, Alicia. *Puentes sobre la turbulencia: la concertación política latinomericana en los 80*. Santiago: FLACSO, 1990.

Fruhling, Hugo. "Justicia y violación de derechos humanos en Chile." Centro de Estudios del Desarrollo, materiales para discusión (Center for Studies on Development, Materials for Discussion) no. 220, Santiago, November 1988.

Gamba, Virginia. "Missions and Strategy: The Argentine Example." In *The Military and Democracy: The Future of Civil-Military Relations in Latin America*, edited by Louis Goodman, Johanna Mendelson, and Juan Rial, pp. 165–76. Lexington, Mass.: Lexington Books, 1990.

Gantenbein, James W. *The Evolution of Our Latin American Policy: A Documentary Record*. New York: Columbia University Press, 1950.

Garcia, Jose. "The Crisis in Paraguay." Paper presented at the 14th International Congress of the Latin American Studies Association, New Orleans, March 1988.

García, Robert. "Guatemala under Cerezo: A Democratic Opening." *SAIS Review* 6 (Summer–Fall 1986): 69–92.

García-Sayán, Diego, ed. *Democracia y violencia en el Perú*. Lima: CEPEI, 1988.

————, ed. *Coca, cocaína y narcotráfico: Laberinto en los Andes* (Lima: Comisión Andina de Juristas, 1989).

Garzón Valdés, Ernesto. "The Argentine Military and Democracy." Manuscript.

Geertz, Clifford. *Agricultural Involution*. Berkeley: University of California Press, 1963.

Genovese, Eugene. *The World the Slaveholders Made: Two Essays in Interpretation*. New York: Pantheon Books, 1969.

Gereffi, Gary. "New Patterns of Industrial Integration in the World Economy: Evidence from Latin America and East Asia." Paper prepared for Inter-American Dialogue workshop on "The Changing Global Context for U.S.–Latin American Relations," Airlie House, Warrenton, Va., May 23–25, 1990.

Gergen, David. "How Is America Changing? American Leadership: The Challenges Back Home." *Adelphi Paper* no. 256 (London: International Institute of Strategic Studies, 1990).

Ghai, D., and Hewitt de Alcántara, C. "The Crisis of the 1980s in Sub-Saharan Africa, Latin America, and the Caribbean: Economic Impact, Social Change, and Political Implications." *Development and Change* 21, no. 3 (1990): 389–426.

Gibson, Edward. "Democracy and the New Electoral Right in Argentina." *Journal of Interamerican Studies and World Affairs* 32, no. 3 (Fall 1990): 177–228.

Gibson, James L. "Political Intolerance and Political Repression during the McCarthy Red Scare." *American Political Science Review* 82 (June 1988): 511–29.

Gil, Federico G. *The Political System of Chile*. Boston: Houghton Mifflin, 1966.

Gillespie, Charles. "Praetorianism versus Party Systems: Prospects for Democratic Consolidation in the Southern Cone and Brazil." Paper presented to the International Political Science Association, Washington, D.C., 1988.

————. "The Reconsolidation of Democracy in Uruguay: Politics as Usual or Learning from Mistakes." Paper presented at the 15th International Congress of the Latin American Studies Association, Miami, December 1989.

Gillis, Malcolm, and Repetto, Robert, eds. *Public Policies and the Misuse of Forest Resources*. Cambridge: Cambridge University Press, 1988.

Gleijeses, Piero. "The Decay of Democracy in Argentina." *Current History* (January 1988): 5–8, 43.

———. *Shattered Hope*. Princeton, N.J.: Princeton University Press, 1991.

Goncalves, R., and de Castro, J. A. "El proteccionismo de los países industrializados y las exportaciones de la América Latina." *El Trimestre Económico* 56, no. 222 (April–June 1989): 443–69.

González, Guadalupe, and Tienda, Marta, eds. *The Drug Connection in U.S.-Mexican Relations*. San Diego: Center for U.S.–Mexican Studies, University of California, San Diego, 1989.

Goodman, Louis W.; Sanderson, Steven E.; Shwedel, Kenneth; and Haber, Paul L. *Mexican Agricultural Policies and the Forces That Shape Them*. Washington, D.C.: Woodrow Wilson International Center for Scholars, 1985.

Goodman, Louis, and Mendelson, Johanna. "The Threat of New Missions: Latin American Militaries and the Drug War." In *The Military and Democracy: The Future of Civil-Military Relations in Latin America*, edited by Louis Goodman, Johanna Mendelson, and Juan Rial, pp. 189–95. Lexington, Mass.: Lexington Books, 1990.

Grabendorff, Wolf. "Interstate Conflict Behavior and Regional Potential for Conflict in Latin America." Working Papers, no. 116, Latin American Program, The Wilson Center, Washington, D.C., 1982.

———. "The Central American Crisis: Is There a Role for Western Europe?" *Millennium Journal of International Studies* (London) 13, no. 2 (Summer 1984): 203–17.

Grasmuck, Sherri, and Pessar, Patricia. *Between Two Islands: Dominican International Migration*. Berkeley: University of California Press, 1991.

Graziano, Frank. "Messianism and Atrocity: The Eschatology of the Argentine 'Dirty War.'" Paper presented at the 15th International Congress of the Latin American Studies Association, Miami, December 1989.

Grieco, Joseph M. *Cooperation among Nations: Europe, America, and Non-Tariff Barriers to Trade*. Ithaca, N.Y.: Cornell University Press, 1990.

Grinols, E. "Procedural Protectionism: The American Trade Bill and the New Interventionist Mode." *Weltwirtschaftliches Archiv* 125, no. 3 (1989): 501–747.

Guedes da Costa, Thomaz. "Bases da postura dos paises sudamericanos para a decada de noventa." Paper presented at a conference on "The United States and Latin America: The Next Decade," FLACSO, Santiago, June 1989.

Guimaraes, Roberto. "Brasil vuelve al banquillo: La ecopolítica de la destrucción en la Amazonía." *Síntesis* (Madrid), no. 12 (September–December 1990): 173–84.

Hakim, Peter, and Lowenthal, Abraham F. "Latin America's Fragile Democracies." *Journal of Democracy* 2, no. 3 (Summer 1991): 16–29.

Halberstam, David. *The Next Century*. New York: William Morrow, 1991.

Hall, Anthony. "Agrarian Crisis in Brazilian Amazonia: The Grande Carajás Programme." *Journal of Development Studies* 23 (July 1987): 522–52.

Hamilton, C., and Whalley, J. "A View from the Developed World." In *Dealing with the North*, edited by J. Whalley, pp. 5–83. CSIER Research Monograph. London, Ontario: University of Western Ontario, 1987.

Hamilton, Nora. *The Limits of State Autonomy: Post-Revolutionary Mexico*. Princeton, N.Y.: Princeton University Press, 1982.

Handelman, Howard, and Baer, Werner. "Introduction: The Economic and Political Costs of Austerity." In *Paying the Costs of Austerity in Latin America*, edited by Howard Handelman and Werner Baer, pp. 1–17. Boulder, Colo.: Westview Press, 1989.

Handy, Jim. "Resurgent Democracy and the Guatemalan Military." *Journal of Latin American Studies* 18 (November 1986): 383–409.

Hareven, Tamara. "Family History at the Crossroads." *Journal of Family History* 12, no. 1–3 (1987): ix–xxiii.

Harrison, Lawrence. *Underdevelopment Is a State of Mind*. Lanham, Md.: University Press of America, 1985.

Hart, M. *A North American Free Trade Agreement: The Strategic Implications for Canada*. Ottawa: Institute for Research in Public Policy, 1990.

Hartlyn, Jonathan. *The Politics of Coalition Rule in Colombia*. Cambridge: Cambridge University Press, 1988.

Hayes, Margaret Daly. *Latin America and the U.S. National Interest: A Basis for U.S. Foreign Policy*. Boulder, Colo.: Westview Press, 1984.

———. "The U.S. and Latin America: A Lost Decade?" *Foreign Affairs* 57 (1988–89): 180–98.

Hecht, Susannah, and Cockburn, Alexander. *The Fate of the Forest: Developers, Destroyers, and Defenders of the Amazon*. London: Verso, 1989.

Heine, Jorge. "De la Negligencia Benigna a la Doctrina Bush? Estados Unidos y América Latina en 1989." In *El desafío de los 90s: anuario de políticas exteriores latinoamericanas, 1989–1990*, edited by Heraldo Muñoz, pp. 335–44.

Hellman, Ronald G., and Rosenbaum, H. Jon, eds. *Latin America: The Search for a New International Role*. New York: Wiley, 1975.

Hewitt de Alcantara, Cynthia. *Socioeconomic Consequences of the Green Revolution*. Geneva: UNRISD, 1976.

Hirschman, Albert O. "The Political Economy of Latin American Development: Seven Exercises in Retrospection." *Latin American Research Review* 22, no. 3 (1987): 7–36.

Hirst, Mónica. "El programa de integración y cooperación Argentina-Brasil: Los nuevos horizontes de vinculación económica y complementación industrial." *Serie de documentos e informes de investigación* (Buenos Aires: FLACSO), no. 81 (September 1989): 23–48.

———. "Reflexiones para un análisis político de MERCOSUR." FLACSO, Buenos Aires, November 1991.

———, ed., *Continuidad y cambio en las relaciones América Latina y Estados Unidos*. Buenos Aires: GEL, 1987.

Hoffman, Stanley. *Primacy or World Order*. New York: McGraw-Hill, 1978.

Holling, C. S. "The Resilience of Terrestrial Ecosystems: Local Surprise and Global Change." In *Sustainable Development of the Biosphere*, edited by W. C. Clark and R. E. Munn, pp. 292–317. Cambridge: Cambridge University Press, 1986.

Holmes, H. Allen. "FY 1990 Security Assistance Program." *Current Policy*, no. 1159, March 8, 1989.

Hurrell, Andrew. "Latin America and the New World Order: The Mirage of a Hemispheric Regional Bloc." Paper prepared for the World Congress of the International Political Science Association, Buenos Aires, July 21–25, 1991.

Immerman, Richard H. *The CIA in Guatemala: The Foreign Policy of Intervention*. Austin: University of Texas Press, 1982.

Insulza, José Miguel. "Europa, Centroamérica y la Alianza Atlántica." *Síntesis* (Madrid), no. 4 (January–April 1988): 264–79.

———. "Los temas estratégicos en las relaciones entre Europa y América Latina." Paper presented to Panel for European Studies at 10th Annual Meeting of RIAL Program, Montevideo, October 1988.

———. "Estados Unidos y la nueva realidad internacional: Límites y desafíos." In *El Mundo en Transición y América Latina*, edited by Carlos Portales, pp. 85–130. Buenos Aires: GEL, 1989.

Inter-American Development Bank. *Economic and Social Progress in Latin America: 1989 Report*. Washington, D.C.: IDB, 1989.

———. *The IDB*. Washington, D.C.: January–February 1991. Pamphlet.

Inter-American Dialogue. *The Americas in a New World: The 1990 Report of the Inter-American Dialogue*. Washington, D.C., 1990.

———. *The Changing Global Context for U.S.–Latin American Relations*. Papers prepared for a workshop of the Inter-American Dialogue, Aspen Institute, May 23–25, 1990.

International Commission for Central American Recovery and Development, *The Report of the International Commission for Central American Recovery and Development: Poverty, Conflict, and Hope*. Durham: Duke University Press, 1989.

International Monetary Fund. *Direction of Trade Statistics Yearbook*. Washington, D.C.: IMF, 1990.

International Tropical Timber Organization (ITTO). "Integration of Forest-Based Development in the Western Amazon—Phase I—Forest Management to Promote Policies for Sustainable Production." Project Document 24/88, n.d. Typescript.

IRELA. *El Grupo de los Ocho: ¿Un nuevo interlocutor regional en América Latina?* Madrid: IRELA Dossiers no. 17, 1989.

———. *Europe and Latin America in the 1990s: Towards a New Relationship?* Madrid: IRELA Dossiers no. 20, 1989.

———. *A New Attempt at Regional Integration: The Southern Cone Common Market*. Madrid: IRELA Dossiers no. 30, 1991.

Isaacs, Anita. "The Obstacles to Democratic Consolidation in Ecuador." Paper presented at the 15th International Congress of the Latin American Studies Association, Miami, December 1989.

ITTO. Project Document. "Integration of Forest-based Development in the Western Amazon: Phase I, Forest Management to Promote Policies for Sustainable Production." Prepared by Brazilian Agency for Cooperation, 1988.

Iversen, Edwin S., and Jory, Darryl E. "Shrimp Culture in Ecuador: Farmers without Seed." *Sea Frontiers, Sea Secrets* 32, no. 6 (November–December 1986): 442–53.

Jackson, J. *The World Trading System: Law and Policy of International Economic Relations*. Cambridge, Mass.: MIT Press, 1989.

Jaguaribe, Helio. "América Latina dentro del contexto internacional de la actualidad." *Revista Mexicana de Sociología* (Mexico) 51, no. 3 (July–September 1989): 55–73.

Jarvis, Lovell. *Livestock Development in Latin America*. Washington, D.C.: World Bank, 1987.

Jonas, Susanne. "Contradictions of Guatemala's Political Opening." In *Democracy in Latin*

America: Visions and Realities, edited by Susanne Jonas and Nancy Stein, pp. 65–84. New York: Bergin and Garvey Publishers, 1990.

Karl, Terry L. "Imposing Consent? Electoralism vs. Democratization in El Salvador." In *Elections and Democratization in Latin America, 1980–1985*, edited by Paul Drake and Eduardo Silva, pp. 9–36. San Diego: University of California, San Diego, 1986.

———. "Central America at the End of the Cold War." Paper presented at the conference on Superpower Conflict and Cooperation, University of California, Berkeley, October 4–6, 1990.

Kaufman, Robert. *The Politics of Debt in Argentina, Brazil, and Mexico*. Berkeley: Institute of International Studies, University of California, 1988.

———. "Economic Orthodoxy and Political Change in Mexico: The Stabilization and Adjustment Policies of the de la Madrid Administration." In *Debt and Democracy in Latin America*, edited by Barbara Stallings and Robert Kaufman, pp. 109–26. Boulder, Colo.: Westview Press, 1989.

Kelly, Philip, and Child, Jack, eds. *Geopolitics of the Southern Cone and Antarctica*. Boulder, Colo.: Lynne Rienner, 1988.

Kennan, George. "The Future of U.S.-Soviet Relations." Statement for presentation to the U.S. Congress, Senate, Committee on Foreign Relations, 101st Cong., 1st sess., April 4, 1989.

———. "An Irreversibly Changed Europe, Now to Be Redesigned," *International Herald Tribune*, November 14, 1989.

Kennedy, Paul. "Can the U.S. Remain Number One?" *New York Review of Books*, March 16, 1989.

Keohane, Robert O. *After Hegemony: Cooperation and Discord in the World Political Economy*. Princeton, N.J.: Princeton University Press, 1984.

Keohane, Robert, and Nye, Joseph S. *Power and Interdependence*. Boston: Little, Brown, 1977.

Kirkpatrick, Jeane. "Dictatorships and Double Standards." In *Human Rights and U.S. Human Rights Policy*, edited by Howard J. Wiarda, pp. 21–28. Washington, D.C.: American Enterprise Institute, 1982.

Kornblith, Miriam. "Deuda y democracia en Venezuela: Los sucesos del 27 y 28 de febrero de 1989." Paper presented at the 15th International Congress of the Latin American Studies Association, Miami, December 1989.

Krasner, Stephen D. "Structural Causes and Regime Consequences: Regimes as Intervening Variables." In *International Regimes*, edited by Stephen D. Krasner, pp. 1–22. Ithaca, N.Y.: Cornell University Press, 1983.

———. *Structural Conflict: The Third World against Global Liberalism*. Berkeley: University of California Press, 1985.

Krueger, Anne O. "The Case for Free Trade." In *An American Trade Strategy: Options for the 1990s*, edited by Robert Z. Lawrence and Charles L. Schultze, pp. 68–105. Washington, D.C.: Brookings Institution, 1990.

Kuczynski, Pedro-Pablo. *Latin American Debt*. Baltimore: Johns Hopkins University Press, 1988.

Laarman, Jan G.; Schreuder, Gerard F.; and Anderson, Erick T. *An Overview of Forest Products Trade in Latin America and the Caribbean Basin: Forestry Private Enterprise Initiative (FPEI)*. Working Paper no. 21. Durham, N.C.: FPEI, June 1987.

Laird, Sam, and Sapir, André. "Preferencias arancelarias." In *La Ronda Uruguay: Manual para las negociaciones comerciales multilaterales*, edited by J. Michael Finger and Andrzej Olechowski, pp. 96–103. Washington, D.C.: Banco Mundial, 1987.

Laird, Sam, and Yeats, Alexander. "Trends in Non-Tariff Barriers of Developed Countries, 1966–1986." *Weltwirtschaftliches Archiv* 126, no. 2 (1990): 299–325.

Lamounier, Bolivar. "Challenges to Democratic Consolidation in Brazil." Paper presented to American Political Science Association, Washington, D.C., September 1988.

Landau, George; Feo, Julio; and Hosono, Akio. *Latin America at a Crossroads: The Challenge to the Trilateral Countries: A Report to the Trilateral Commission.* New York: Trilateral Commission, August 1990.

Latin American and Caribbean Commission on Development and Environment. *Our Own Agenda.* Washington, D.C.: Inter-American Development Bank and United Nations Development Programme, 1990.

"Latin American Perceptions on the Pacific Basin." *Serie de Publicaciones Especiales del Instituto de Estudios Internacionales de la Universidad de Chile*, no. 63 (1985).

Lawrence, Robert Z., and Schultze, Charles L. *An American Trade Strategy: Options for the 1990s.* Washington, D.C.: Brookings Institution, 1990.

Lee, Rensselaer W., III. *The White Labyrinth: Cocaine and Political Power.* New Brunswick, N.J.: Transaction, 1989.

Leopold, Richard W. *The Growth of American Foreign Policy.* New York: Alfred A. Knopf, 1962.

Lessard Donald L., and Williamson, John. *Capital Flight and Third World Debt.* Washington, D.C.: Institute for International Economics, 1987.

Levine, R. M. *The Vargas Regime: The Critical Years, 1934–1938.* N.Y.: Columbia University Press, 1970.

Lezcano, Carlos María. "El régimen militar de Alfredo Stroessner: Fuerzas armadas y política en el Paraguay (1954–1989)." *Documento de trabajo* no. 1, Grupo de Ciencias Sociales (Social Sciences Group), Asunción (May 1989).

Library of Congress. Science and Technology Division. *Draft Environmental Report on Peru* (Washington, D.C.: Department of State, 1979). Typescript.

López, Ernesto. *Seguridad nacional y sedición militar.* Buenos Aires: Ed. Legasa, 1987.

Lowenthal, Abraham F. "Ending the Hegemonic Presumption: The United States and Latin America." *Foreign Affairs* 55 (Autumn 1976): 199–213.

———. "The United States and South America." *Current History* 87, no. 525 (January 1988): 1–4.

———. *Partners in Conflict: The United States and Latin America in the 1990s.* Rev. ed. Baltimore: Johns Hopkins University Press, 1990.

———. "Rediscovering Latin America." *Foreign Affairs* (Fall 1990): 27–41.

———. "Learning from History." In *Exporting Democracy: The United States and Latin America, Themes and Issues*, edited by Abraham Lowenthal, pp. 383–405. Baltimore: Johns Hopkins University Press, 1991.

———. "The United States in a Fast-Changing World." Remarks prepared for dedication of Hesburgh Center for International Studies, Notre Dame University, September 13, 1991.

Lowenthal, Abraham F., and Burgess, Katrina, eds. *The California-Mexico Connection.* Stanford, Calif.: Stanford University Press. Forthcoming, 1993.

Lowenthal, Abraham F., and Treverton, Gregory F. "The Making of U.S. Policies toward Latin America: Some Speculative Propositions." Working Paper No. 4, Latin American

Program, Woodrow Wilson International Center for Scholars, Washington, D.C., 1977.

Mabry, Donald J., ed. *The Latin American Narcotics Trade and U.S. National Security*. New York: Greenwood Press, 1988.

McCann, Frank. "Modernizing Authoritarian Rule and the Brazilian Military, 1964–1985." Manuscript.

McClintock, Cynthia. "The APRA Government and the Peruvian Military, 1985–1987." Paper presented at conference on "APRA as Party and Government." University of California at San Diego, March 1988.

———. "The War on Drugs: The Peruvian Case." *Journal of Interamerican Studies and World Affairs* 30 (Summer–Fall 1988): 127–42.

———. "The Prospects for Democratic Consolidation in a 'Least Likely' Case: Peru." *Comparative Politics* 21, no. 2 (1989): 127–48.

MacDonald, Scott B. *Dancing on a Volcano: The Latin American Drug Trade*. New York: Praeger, 1988.

———. *Mountain High, White Avalanche: Cocaine and Power in the Andean States and Panama*. New York: Praeger, 1989.

McNeely, Jeffrey A. *Economics and Biological Diversity: Developing and Using Economic Incentives to Conserve Biological Resources*. Gland, Switzerland: IUCN, 1988.

MacNeill, Jim. "Strategies for Sustainable Economic Development." *Scientific American* (September 1989): 154–65.

MacNeill, Jim; Winsemius, Pieter; and Yakushiji, Taizo. *Beyond Interdependence: The Meshing of the World's Economy and the Earth's Ecology*. New York: Oxford University Press, 1991.

McNeil, Josephine Buckley. "La cara cambiante de la hegemonía: El Fondo Nacional para la Democracia." *Cono Sur* (July–August 1990): 6–10.

Mahar, Dennis. *Government Policies and Deforestation in Brazil's Amazon Region*. Washington, D.C.: World Bank, 1989.

Maingot, Anthony. "Problems of a Transition to Democracy in Haiti." Paper presented to Royal Institute of International Affairs, London, April 1988.

Mainwaring, Scott. "The Transition to Democracy in Brazil." *Journal of Interamerican Studies and World Affairs* 28 (Spring 1986): 149–79.

———. "Institutional Dilemmas of Multiparty Presidential Democracy: The Case of Brazil." Paper presented at the 15th International Congress of the Latin American Studies Association, Miami, December 1989.

Mainwaring, Scott; O'Donnell, Guillermo; and Valenzuela, J. Samuel. *The New Democracies in Latin America: Problems of Transition and Consolidation*. Notre Dame, Ind.: University of Notre Dame Press, 1991.

Maira, Luis, ed. *El sistema internacional y América Latina: ¿Una nueva era de hegemonía norteamericana?* Buenos Aires: GEL-RIAL, 1986.

Mallin, Jall, ed. *"Che" Guevara on Revolution*. N.Y.: Dell Publishing Company, 1969.

Manning, Bayless. "The Congress, the Executive, and Intermestic Affairs: Three Proposals." *Foreign Affairs* (January 1977): 306–24.

Mansilla, H. C. F. "Latin America in the Third World: The Search for a New Identity, the Acceptance of Old Concepts." *Ibero-Amerikanisches Archiv* (Berlin) 11, no. 2 (1985): 171–91.

Marcella, Gabriel. "Latin American Military Participation in the Democratic Process." In

Security in the Americas, edited by Georges Fauriol, pp. 261–83. Washington, D.C.: National Defense University Press, 1989.

Marcella, Gabriel, and Woerner, General Fred. "Strategic Vision and Opportunity: The United States and Latin America in the 1990s." Paper prepared for National Defense University symposium on "Evolving U.S. Strategy for Latin America and the Caribbean," November 16–18, 1990.

Mármora, Leopoldo. "Integración argentino-brasileña: Peligros, posibilidades y costos." *Opciones* (Santiago), no. 12 (September–December 1987): 43–67.

Marshall, Dawn. "A History of West Indian Migrations: Overseas Opportunities and 'Safety-Valve' Policies." In *The Caribbean Exodus*, edited by Barry B. Levine, pp. 15–31. New York: Praeger, 1987.

Marshall, Jonathan. *Drug Wars: Corruption, Counterinsurgency, and Covert Operations in the Third World*. Forestville, Calif.: Cohen and Cohen, 1991.

Martz, John. *Politics and Petroleum in Ecuador*. New Brunswick, N.J.: Transaction Books, 1987.

Massey, Douglas S. *Return to Aztlan: The Social Process of International Migration from Western Mexico*. Berkeley: University of California Press, 1987.

———. "Economic Development and International Migration in Comparative Perspective." *Population and Development Review* 14, no. 3 (September 1988): 383–414.

Matsushita, Hiroshi. "La política japonesa hacia América Latina en la década de 1980: Discrepancia y colaboración con los Estados Unidos." Paper presented at the 15th International Congress of the Latin American Studies Association, Miami, December 1989.

Matteucci, Silvia Diana. "Is the Rainforest Worth Seven Hundred Million Hamburgers?" *Interciencia* 12, no. 1 (1987): 8–11.

Mauceri, Philip. "The Military, Insurgency, and Democratic Power: Peru, 1980–1988." Columbia University Papers on Latin America, no. 11, 1989.

Maxfield, Sylvia. "National Business, Debt-Led Growth and Political Transition in Latin America." In *Debt and Democracy in Latin America*, edited by Barbara Stallings and Robert Kaufman, pp. 75–90. Boulder, Colo.: Westview Press, 1989.

Mayorga, René Antonio. "Tendencias y problemas de la consolidación de la democracia en Bolivia." Paper presented at the 15th International Congress of the Latin American Studies Association, Miami, December 1989.

Mesa-Lago, Carmelo, et al. "Relaciones económicas de Cuba con la URSS y el CAME: Pasado, presente y futuro." Paper presented at second meeting of LASA Study Group on Latin America, Cuba, and the International Economy. Centro de Investigaciones de la Economía Mundial (Center of Economic Investigations), Havana, July 9–10, 1990.

Middlebrook, Kevin J., and Rico, Carlos. "The United States and Latin America in the 1980s: Change, Complexity, and Contending Perspectives." In *The United States and Latin America in the 1980s: Contending Perspectives on a Decade of Crisis*, edited by Kevin J. Middlebrook and Carlos Rico, pp. 3–57. Pittsburgh, Pa.: University of Pittsburgh Press, 1986.

Mikoyan, Sergo. "Soviet Foreign Policy and Latin America." *Washington Quarterly* (Summer 1990): 179–91.

Miller, Nicola. *Soviet Relations with Latin America, 1958–1987*. New York: Cambridge University Press, 1989.

Millett, Richard. "The Limits of Influence: The United States and the Military in Central

America and the Caribbean." In *The Military and Democracy: The Future of Civil-Military Relations in Latin America*, edited by Louis Goodman, Johanna Mendelson, and Juan Rial, pp. 123–40. Lexington, Mass.: Lexington Books, 1990.

Mitchell, Christopher. "International Migration, International Relations, and Foreign Policy." *International Migration Review* 23, no. 3 (Fall 1989): 681–708.

Molineu, Harold. *U.S. Policy toward Latin America: From Regionalism to Globalism*. Boulder, Colo.: Westview Press, 1986.

Moneta, Carlos J. *El acercamiento Argentina-Brasil: De la tensión y el conflicto a la competencia cooperativa*. Santiago: Documento de Trabajo PROSPEL no. 11, 1988.

Montgomery, Tommie Sue. "Pacts and Politics in El Salvador, 1979–1988." Paper presented at the 14th International Congress of the Latin American Studies Association, New Orleans, April 1988.

Morales, Edmundo. *Cocaine: White Gold Rush in Peru*. Tucson: University of Arizona Press, 1989.

Morales Gamboa, Abelardo. "El discreto encanto por Centroamérica en el Viejo Mundo." In *América Latina y Europa Occidental en el umbral del siglo XXI*, edited by Atilio Borón and Alberto van Klaveren. Santiago: PNUD/CEPAL, 1989.

Morgenthau, Hans J. *Politics among Nations*. New York: Alfred A. Knopf, 1948.

Morris, James. *Honduras: Caudillo Politics and Military Rulers*. Boulder, Colo.: Westview Press, 1984.

Morse, Edward L. *Modernization and the Transformation of International Relations*. New York: Free Press, 1976.

Mujal-León, Eusebio, ed. *The USSR and Latin America: A Developing Relationship*. Boston: Unwin and Hyman, 1989.

Mulford, David. "The View of the Reagan Administration: Toward Stronger World Growth." In *Latin America's Debt Crisis: Adjusting to the Past or Planning for the Future?*, edited by Robert Pastor. Boulder, Colo.: Lynne Rienner, 1987.

Muñoz, Heraldo. "Las relaciones entre Estados Unidos y América Latina bajo el gobierno de Reagan: Divergencias y ajustes parciales." *Foro Internacional* 27, no. 4 (April–June 1987): 509–15.

Muñoz, Heraldo, and Portales, Carlos. *Elusive Friendship: A Survey of U.S.-Chilean Relations*. Boulder, Colo.: Lynne Rienner, 1991.

Muñoz, Heraldo, and Tulchin, Joseph S., eds. *Latin American Nations in World Politics*. Boulder, Colo.: Westview Press, 1984.

Musto, David F. *The American Disease: Origins of Narcotic Control*. Expanded ed. New York: Oxford University Press, 1987.

National Democratic Institute for International Affairs. *Civil-Military Relations: The Argentine Experience*. Washington, D.C.: NDIIA, 1989.

Nations, James, and Komer, Daniel I. "Rainforests and the Hamburger Society." *Ecologist* 17, nos. 4–5 (1987): 161–67.

Nau, Henry R. "The NICs in a New Trade Round." In *Hard Bargaining Ahead: U.S. Trade Policy and Developing Countries*, edited by E. Preeg, pp. 63–84. New Brunswick, N.J.: Transaction Books, 1985.

———. *The Myth of America's Decline: Leading the World Economy into the 1990s*. New York: Oxford University Press, 1990.

Nectoux, Francois, and Dudley, Nigel. *Europe: A Hard Wood Story*. London: Friends of the Earth, 1987.

Nelson, Jack. "CIA Chief Warns of 'Coup Plotting' in Latin America." *Los Angeles Times*, February 9, 1989.

Nietschmann, Bernard. "The Cultural Context of Sea Turtle Subsistence Hunting in the Caribbean and Problems Caused by Commercial Exploitation." In *Biology and Conservation of Sea Turtles: Proceedings of the World Conference on Sea Turtle Conservation*, edited by Karen A. Bjorndal, pp. 439–45. Washington, D.C.: Smithsonian Institution Press, 1981.

Norden, Deborah. "Democratic Consolidation and Military Professionalism in Argentina." Paper presented at the 15th International Congress of the Latin American Studies Association, Miami, December 1989.

Nye, Joseph S., Jr. "Understanding U.S. Strength." *Foreign Policy* 72 (Fall 1988): 105–29.

————. *Bound to Lead: The Changing Nature of American Power*. New York: Basic Books, 1990.

O'Donnell, Guillermo; Schmitter, Philippe; and Whitehead, Laurence, eds. *Transitions from Authoritarian Rule: Prospects for Democracy*. Baltimore: Johns Hopkins University Press, 1986.

O'Donnell, Guillermo. *Modernization and Bureaucratic Authoritarianism: Studies in South American Politics*. Berkeley: Institute of International Studies, University of California, 1973.

————. "América Latina, Estados Unidos y democracia: Variaciones sobre un viejísimo tema." Kellogg Institute Working Paper No. 19, 1984, p. 1.

Organization for Economic Cooperation and Development, *National Policies and Agricultural Trade*. Paris: OECD, 1987.

O'Riordan, Timothy. "The Politics of Sustainability." In *Sustainable Environmental Management: Principles and Practice*, edited by R. Kerry Turner, pp. 31–49. Boulder, Colo.: Westview Press, 1988.

Orrego Vicuña, Francisco, ed. *América Latina: ¿Clase media de las naciones?* Santiago: Ed. Universitaria, 1979.

Otero, Gerardo. "Agrarian Reform in Mexico: Capitalism and the State." In *Searching for Agrarian Reform in Latin America*, edited by William C. Thiesenhusen, pp. 276–304. New York: Unwin and Hyman, 1989.

Oye, Kenneth A., ed. *Cooperation under Anarchy*. Princeton, N.J.: Princeton University Press, 1984.

Palmer, David Scott. "La actual formulación de la política exterior estadounidense hacia América Latina." *Cono Sur* 9, no. 5 (September–October 1990): 24–27.

Pang, Eul-Soo. "The Darker Side of Brazil's Democracy." *Current History* 8 (January 1988): 21–24.

Pásara, Luis, and Parodi, Jorge, eds. *Democracia, sociedad y gobierno en el Perú*. Lima: CEDYS, 1988.

Pastor, Robert A. *Condemned to Repetition: The United States and Nicaragua*. Princeton: Princeton University Press, 1987.

————. "George Bush and Latin America: The Pragmatic Style and the Regionalist Option." In *Eagle in a New World: American Grand Strategy in the Post–Cold War World*, edited by Kenneth Oye, Robert Lieber, and Donald Rothchild, pp. 361–87. Boston: Little, Brown, 1992.

————, ed. *Migration and Development in the Caribbean: The Unexplored Connection*. Boulder, Colo.: Westview Press, 1985.

————, ed. *Democracy in the Americas: Stopping the Pendulum*. New York: Holmes and Meier, 1989.

Pastor, Robert A., and Castañeda, Jorge G. *Limits to Friendship: The United States and Mexico*. New York: Alfred A. Knopf, 1988.

Pastor, Robert A., and Fletcher, Richard. "The Caribbean in the Twenty-first Century." *Foreign Affairs* (Summer 1991): 98–114.

Peeler, John. "Deepening Democracy and Democratic Consolidation in Latin America." Paper presented at the 15th International Congress of the Latin American Studies Association, Miami, December 1989.

"Pentagon Is Ordered to Set Plans for Drug Interdiction." *Wall Street Journal*, September 19, 1989.

Perelli, Carina. "The Legacies of the Transitions to Democracy in Argentina and Uruguay." In *The Military and Democracy: The Future of Civil-Military Relations in Latin America*, edited by Louis Goodman, Johanna Mendelson, and Juan Rial, pp. 39–54. Lexington, Mass.: Lexington Books, 1990.

————. "The Military's Perception of Threat in the Southern Cone of South America." In *The Military and Democracy*, edited by Goodman, Mendelson, and Rial, pp. 93–105.

————. "Amnistía sí, amnistía no, amnistía puede ser." PEITHO Working Paper, Montevideo, n.d.

Pérez López, J. "Swimming against the Tide: Implications for Cuba of Soviet and Eastern European Reforms in Foreign Economic Relations." *Journal of Interamerican Studies and World Affairs* 33, no. 2 (1991): 81–139.

Perl, Raphael F. "The U.S. Congress, International Narcotics Policy, and the Anti-Drug Abuse Act of 1988." In *Assessing the Americas' War on Drugs*, edited by Bruce M. Bagley. Special Issue, *Journal of Interamerican Studies and World Affairs* 30, nos. 2–3 (Summer–Fall 1988): 19–52.

————. "International Aspects of U.S. Drug Control Efforts." *C.R.S. Review* 10, no. 10 (November–December 1989): 43–65.

Perry, William. "In Search of a Latin American Policy: The Elusive Quest." *Washington Quarterly* 13, no. 2 (Spring 1990): 125–34.

Pessar, Patricia A. "The Role of Gender in Dominican Settlement in the United States." In *Women and Change in Latin America*, edited by June Nash and Helen Safa, pp. 273–94. South Hadley, Mass.: Bergin and Garvey.

Pierre, Andrew, ed. *Third World Instability: Central America as an European-American Issue*. New York: Council on Foreign Relations, 1985.

Pinto, Aníbal. "Comments on the Article 'The Interaction between Styles of Development and the Environment in Latin America.'" *CEPAL Review* 12 (December 1980): 51–54.

Pion-Berlin, David. "A House Divided: Segmented Professionalism and Security Ideology in the Argentine Army, 1984–1989." Paper presented at the 15th International Congress of the Latin American Studies Association, Miami, December 1989.

————. "Latin American National Security Doctrines: Hard- and Softline Themes." *Armed Forces and Society* 15, no. 3 (1989): 418.

————. "Civil-Military Relations in Democratic Argentina: An Unstable Equilibrium." Manuscript, June 1990.

Portales, Carlos. "Sudamérica: Seguridad regional y relaciones con Estados Unidos." *Documentos de trabajo*, no. 289 (Santiago: FLACSO) (1986).

————. "Democracia y derechos humanos en la política exterior del Presidente Reagan." *Estudios Internacionales* 66 (July–September 1987): 352–78.

Portes, Alejandro, and Walton, John. *Labor, Class, and the International System.* New York: Academic Press, 1981.

Posner, Joshua L., and McPherson, Malcolm F. "Agriculture on the Steep Slopes of Tropical America: Current Situation and Prospects for the Year 2000." *World Development* 10, no. 5 (1982): 341–56.

Potash, Robert. "Alfonsín and the Argentine Military." Paper presented at the 15th International Congress of the Latin American Studies Association, Miami, December 1989.

Powell, Colin. "U.S. Foreign Policy in a Time of Transition." *Current Policy*, no. 1127 (October 27, 1988).

Prebisch, Raúl. *The Economic Development of Latin America and Its Principal Determinants.* New York: United Nations, 1950.

Puig, Juan Carlos, ed. *América Latina: Políticas exteriores comparadas.* 2 vols. Buenos Aires: GEL, 1984.

Quick, Stephen A. "The International Economy and the Caribbean in the 1990s and Beyond." Paper prepared for World Peace Foundation, Boston, 1991.

Ray, Edward J. *U.S. Protectionism and the World Debt Crisis.* Westport, Conn.: Quorum Books, 1989.

Ray, Edward J., and Marvel, Howard P. "The Pattern of Protection in the Industrialized World." *Review of Economics and Statistics* 66, no. 3 (August 1984): 452–58.

Reichert, Josh. "The Migrant Syndrome: Seasonal U.S. Wage Labor and Rural Development in Central Mexico." *Human Organization* 40 (1981): 56–66.

Remmer, Karen. "Exclusionary Democracy." *Studies in Comparative International Development* 20 (Winter 1985–86): 64–85.

————. "Democracy and Economic Crisis: The Latin American Experience." *World Politics* 42 (April 1990): 315–35.

————. *Military Rule in Latin America.* Boulder, Colo.: Westview Press, 1991.

Repetto, Robert. "Creating Incentives for Sustainable Forest Development." *Ambio* 16, nos. 2–3 (1987): 94–99.

————. *Economic Policy Reform for Natural Resource Conservation.* World Bank Environment Department Working Paper No. 4, Washington, D.C.: World Bank, May 1988.

————. "Needed: New Policy Goals." *American Forests* (November–December 1988): 59–86.

Reynolds, Clark W. "Mexican-U.S. Interdependence: Economic and Social Perspectives." In *U.S.-Mexico Relations: Economic and Social Aspects,* edited by Clark W. Reynolds and Carlos Tello, pp. 21–46. Stanford, Calif.: Stanford University Press, 1983.

Rial, Juan. "The Armed Forces and Democracy: The Interests of Latin American Military Corporations in Sustaining Democratic Regimes." In *The Military and Democracy: The Future of Civil-Military Relations in Latin America,* edited by Louis Goodman, Johanna Mendelson, and Juan Rial, pp. 277–95. Lexington, Mass.: Lexington Books, 1990.

————. "The Armed Forces and the Question of Democracy in Latin America." In *The Military and Democracy,* edited by Goodman, Mendelson, and Rial, pp. 3–21.

————. "Las relaciones cívico-militares en el Uruguay tras la restauración de la democracia." Report prepared for the Inter-American Dialogue, 1988.

Rico, Carlos. "Crisis ¿y recomposición? de la hegemonía norteamericana: Algunas reflexiones en torno a la coyuntura internacional en la segunda mitad de los ochenta." In *El sistema internacional y América Latina: ¿Una nueva era de hegemonía norteamericana?*, edited by Luis Maira, pp. 38–57. Buenos Aires: GEL-RIAL, 1986.

Riquelme, Marcial Antonio. *Hacia la transición a la democracia en Paraguay*. Asunción: Editorial Histórica, 1989.

Rizzo de Oliveira, Eliézer. "O aparelho militar: Papel tutelar na Nova República." In *A tutela militar*, edited by J. Quartim de Moraes, Wilma Peres Costa, and Eliézer Rizzo de Oliveira, pp. 54–81. N.p.: Vértice, 1987.

Robinson, Linda. *Intervention or Neglect: The United States and Central America beyond the 1980s*. New York: Council on Foreign Relations, 1991.

Rock, David. *Argentina, 1516–1982: From Spanish Colonization to the Falklands War*. Berkeley: University of California Press, 1985.

Rodríguez, Nestor. "Mayan Migration to Houston: A Community of Origin Perspective." Manuscript, Department of Sociology, University of Houston, 1990.

Roett, Riordan. "Democracy and Debt in South America: A Continent's Dilemma." *Foreign Affairs: America and the World, 1983* 62, no. 3 (1984): 695–720.

———. "Latin America's Response: Excerpts from Communiqués of the Cartagena Group." In *Latin America's Debt Crisis: Adjusting to the Past or Planning for the Future?*, edited by Robert Pastor. Boulder, Colo.: Lynne Rienner, 1987.

———. "The Debt Crisis: Economics and Politics." In *United States Policy in Latin America: A Quarter Century of Crisis and Challenge, 1961–1986*, edited by John D. Martz, pp. 237–59. Lincoln: University of Nebraska Press, 1988.

———. "Latin America's Debt: Problems and Prospects." *International Journal, Canadian Institute of International Affairs* 43, no. 3 (Summer 1988): 428–45.

———. "How the 'Haves' Manage the 'Have-Nots': Latin America and the Debt Crisis." In *Debt and Democracy in Latin America*, edited by Barbara Stallings and Robert Kaufman, pp. 59–73. Boulder, Colo.: Westview Press, 1989.

Ronfeldt, David. "Patterns of Civil-Military Rule." In *Beyond Cuba: Latin America Takes Charge of Its Future*, edited by Luigi Einaudi, pp. 107–26. New York: Crane, Russak, 1974.

———. "A New Dark Age for Latin America." *Hemisphere* 2, no. 1 (Fall 1989): 34–35.

———. *U.S. Involvement in Central America: Three Views from Honduras*. Santa Monica, Calif.: RAND, 1989.

Rubio, José Luis. "La soledad de Iberoamérica." *Política y sociedad* (Madrid), no. 4 (Summer 1989): 55–63.

Rubio Correa, Marcial. "The Military in Peruvian Politics." In *Democracy Under Siege*, edited by Augusto Varas, pp. 40–44. New York: Greenwood Press, 1989.

———. "The Perception of the Subversive Threat in Peru." In *The Military and Democracy: The Future of Civil-Military Relations in Latin America*, edited by Louis Goodman, Johanna Mendelson, and Juan Rial, pp. 107–22. Lexington, Mass.: Lexington Books, 1990.

Russell, Roberto. "El idealismo periférico: Un esquema para orientar la política exterior de los países del cono sur en la posguerra fría." *América Latina/Internacional* (July–September 1991): 425–31.

Salt, John. "A Comparative Overview of International Trends and Types, 1950–80." *International Migration Review* 23, no. 3 (Fall 1989): 431–56.

Sanderson, Steven E. *Agrarian Populism and the Mexican State: The Struggle for Land in Sonora*. Berkeley: University of California Press, 1981.

———. *The Transformation of Mexican Agriculture: International Structure and the Politics of Rural Change.* Princeton, N.J.: Princeton University Press, 1986.

———. "Mexican Agricultural Politics in the Shadow of the U.S. Farm Crisis." In *The International Farm Crisis*, edited by David Goodman and Michael Redclift, pp. 205–33. London: MacMillan, 1988.

———. "With Exception of U.S., GATT Nations Approve Tropical Products Trade Accord." *International Trade Reporter* 5, no. 48, December 7, 1988.

———. "Third World Accuses Developed Nations of Delaying Action on Tropical Products." *International Trade Reporter* 6, no. 25, June 21, 1989.

———. *The Politics of Trade in Latin American Development.* Stanford, Calif.: Stanford University Press, 1992.

Sater, William F. *Chile and the United States: Empires in Conflict.* Athens, Ga.: University of Georgia Press, 1991.

Schirmer, Jennifer. "Rule of Law or Law of Rule?: Guatemalan Military Attitudes toward Law, National Security, and Human Rights." Paper presented to Northeast Council on Latin American Studies, Wellesley College, October 1988.

———. "Oficiales de la Montaña: Based on an Exclusive Interview with the Guatemalan Golpistas of May 11, 1988." *Human Rights Internet Reporter* 13, no. 1 (1989): 13–16.

Schodt, David. *Ecuador: An Andean Dilemma.* Boulder, Colo.: Westview Press, 1987.

Schott, Jeffrey J. "More Free Trade Areas?" In *Free Trade Areas and U.S. Trade Policy*, edited by Jeffrey J. Schott, pp. 1–58. Washington, D.C.: Institute for International Economics, 1989.

Schott, Jeffrey J., and Hufbauer, Gary C. "Free Trade Areas, the Enterprise for the Americas Initiative, and the Multilateral Trading System: Implications for Latin America." Paper presented at International Forum on Latin American Perspectives, Paris, November 1991.

Schoultz, Lars. *Human Rights and United States Policy toward Latin America.* Princeton, N.J.: Princeton University Press, 1981.

———. *National Security and United States Policy toward Latin America.* Princeton, N.J.: Princeton University Press, 1987.

Segerson, Kathleen. "Natural Resource Concepts in Trade Analysis." In *Agricultural Trade and Natural Resources: Discovering the Critical Linkages*, edited by John D. Sutton, pp. 9–34. Boulder, Colo.: Lynne Rienner, 1988.

SELA. "América Latina y el proteccionismo norteamericano." *Papeles del SELA* (Buenos Aires: GEL), no. 1 (1985): 1–87.

———. "The Omnibus Trade and Competitiveness Act of 1988: Its Impact on Latin America and the Caribbean." *SP/DCC.I.T.* (Caracas: SELA), no. 3 (1988): 127–255.

Servicio Paz y Justicia. *Uruguay nunca más: Informe sobre la violación a los derechos humanos (1972–1985).* Montevideo: Servicio Paz y Justicia, 1989.

Shafer, D. Michael. *Deadly Paradigms: The Failure of U.S. Counterinsurgency Policy.* Princeton: Princeton University Press, 1988.

Sharpe, Kenneth. "The Drug War: Going After Supply: A Commentary." *Journal of Interamerican Studies and World Affairs* 30, nos. 2–3 (Summer–Fall 1988): 77–85.

Siddall, Scott E.; Atchue, Joseph A., III; and Murray, Robert L., Jr. "Mariculture Development in Mangroves: A Case Study of the Philippines, Ecuador, and Panama." In *Coastal Resources Management: Development Case Studies*, edited by John R. Clark, pp. 112–71. Washington, D.C.: Research Planning Institute, Inc., for National Park Service and USAID, 1985.

Skidmore, Thomas E. *Politics in Brazil, 1930–1964*. New York: Oxford University Press, 1967.

Smith, Marcia S. "Space Policy and Funding: NASA and Civilian Space Programs." *Congressional Research Service Issue Brief*, no. IB82118, Washington, D.C., 1985 (updated July 1).

Smith, Peter H. *Argentina and the Failure of Democracy: Conflict among Political Elites, 1904–1955*. Madison: University of Wisconsin Press, 1974.

———. "Japan, Latin America, and the New International Order." Paper presented at Institute of Developing Economies, Tokyo, August 28, 1990.

Smith, William C. *Authoritarianism and the Crisis of the Argentine Political Economy*. Stanford, Calif.: Stanford University Press, 1989.

Spears, John. *Containing Tropical Deforestation: A Review of Priority Areas for Technological and Policy Research*. Environment Department Working Paper No. 10, Washington, D.C.: World Bank, October 1988.

Stallings, Barbara. *Banker to the Third World*. Berkeley: University of California Press, 1987.

———. "The Reluctant Giant: Japan and the Latin American Debt Crisis." *Journal of Latin American Studies* 22, no. 3 (February 1990): 1–30.

Stallings, Barbara, and Székely, Gabriel. "A Rising Sun in Latin America." *Hemisfile* (La Jolla, Calif.) (March 1990): 1–23.

Stanchenko, Vladimir. "The Soviet Role in Central America." *Washington Quarterly* 13 (Summer 1990): 193–202.

Steinbruner, John D. "The Prospect of Cooperative Security." In *Restructuring American Foreign Policy*, edited by John D. Steinbruner, pp. 1–11. Washington, D.C.: Brookings Institution, 1989.

Stepan, Alfred. *Rethinking Military Politics: Brazil and the Southern Cone*. Princeton, N.J.: Princeton University Press, 1988.

Streeten, Paul. "Development Dichotomies." In *Pioneers in Development*, edited by Gerald M. Meier and Dudley Seers, pp. 337–62. New York: World Bank and Oxford University Press, 1984.

Suárez Salazar, L. "Cuba: ¿Aislamiento internacional o reinserción en un mundo cambiado?" Manuscript prepared for Anuario de Políticas Exteriores Latinoamericanas (Annual Review of Latin American Foreign Policies), Nueva Sociedad/PROSPEL, Caracas, 1990–91.

Sunkel, Osvaldo. "The Interaction between Styles of Development and the Environment in Latin America." *CEPAL Review* 12 (December 1980): 15–50.

Tarazona-Sevillano, Gabriela (with John B. Reuter). *Sendero Luminoso and the Threat of Narcoterrorism*. New York: Praeger, 1990.

Terchunian, Aram. "Mangrove Mapping in Ecuador: The Impact of Shrimp Pond Construction." *Environmental Management* 10, no. 3 (1986): 345–50.

Thiesenhusen, William C., ed. *Searching for Agrarian Reform in Latin America*. New York: Unwin and Hyman, 1989.

Thorup, Cathryn L. "The Politics of Free Trade and the Dynamics of Cross-Border Coalitions in U.S.-Mexican Relations." *Columbia Journal of World Business* 26 (Summer 1991): 12–26.

Tokatlian, Juan G. "Drogas y relaciones América Latina-Estados Unidos: Reflexiones críticas." *Colombia Internacional*, no. 7 (July–September 1989).

———. "Drogas y seguridad nacional: ¿La amenaza de la intervención?" *Documentos de Trabajo, Comisión Sudamericana de Paz*, no. 1 (1990): 103–42.

Tokatlian, Juan G., and Bagley, Bruce M., comps. *Economía y política del narcotráfico*. Bogotá: Ediciones Uninandes/C.E.I./C.E.R.E.C., 1990.

Tomassini, Luciano, ed. *El diálogo Norte-Sur: Una perspectiva latinoamericana*. Buenos Aires: Editorial de Belgrano, 1982.

———, ed. *Nuevas formas de concertación regional en América Latina*. Buenos Aires: GEL, 1990.

Torres Rivas, Edelberto. *Centroamérica: La democracia posible*. San José, Costa Rica: Epoca, 1987.

Trebach, Arnold S. *The Great Drug War*. New York: Macmillan, 1987.

Trebat, Thomas J. "Mexican Foreign Debt: Old Lessons, New Possibilities." In *Mexico and the United States: Managing the Relationship*, edited by Riordan Roett, pp. 71–86. Boulder, Colo.: Westview Press, 1988.

Treverton, Gregory F. *Latin America in World Politics: The Next Decade*. Adelphi Papers, no. 137. London: International Institute for Stategic Studies, 1977.

Tucker, Robert W. *The Inequality of Nations*. New York: Basic Books, 1977.

Tussie, D. "The Developing Countries and the Uruguay Round: The Balance So Far and the Dilemmas Ahead." Buenos Aires: FLACSO, 1991. Mimeo.

Uhl, Christopher, and Parker, Geoffrey. "Is a Quarter-Pound Hamburger Worth a Half-Ton of Rain Forest?" *Interciencia* 11, no. 5 (1986): 17–24.

UNCTAD Trade and Development Report. Ginebra, 1985.

United Nations. "Report of the Independent Commission on Disarmament and Security." New York, 1983.

United Nations Development Programme. *Human Development Report*. New York: Oxford University Press, 1991.

United Nations Economic Commission for Latin America. *Economic Bulletin for Latin America*. Vol. 5, 1960.

United Nations Economic Commission for Latin America and the Caribbean. *Changing Production Patterns with Social Equity*. Santiago, 1990.

———. *Preliminary Overview of the Economy of Latin America and the Caribbean, 1990*. Santiago, 1990.

U.S. Bureau of the Census. *Historical Statistics of the United States: Colonial Times to 1970*. Vol. 2. Washington, D.C.: GPO, 1975.

———. *Statistical Abstract of the United States*. Washington, D.C.: GPO, 1990.

U.S. Congress. Joint Economic Committee. Subcommittee on Science and Technology Hearings. "U.S. Policy on High Technology Exports to Developing Countries and Whether They Effectively Serve U.S. Foreign Policy, National Security, and Economic Objectives." September 21, 1990. Transcript.

U.S. Congress. Senate. Committee on Armed Services. "Andean Strategy." In *The Andean Drug Strategy and the Role of the U.S. Military*. Washington, D.C.: GPO, 1990.

———. Committee on Governmental Affairs, Permanent Subcommittee on Investigations. *Cocaine Production, Eradication, and the Environment: Policy, Impact, and Options*. Washington, D.C.: GPO, July 1990.

U.S. Department of Commerce, *U.S. Foreign Trade Highlights, 1988*. Washington, D.C.: GPO, 1989.

———. *U.S. Foreign Trade Highlights, 1989*. Washington, D.C.: GPO, 1990.

U.S. Department of Energy. Office of Oil and Gas, Energy Information Administration. *Petroleum Supply Monthly*. Washington, D.C.: Energy Information Administration, January 1991.

U.S. Department of State. *Environmental Report on Peru.* Washington, D.C.: Department of State, 1979. Typescript.

U.S. International Trade Commission. "The Likely Impact on the United States of a Free Trade Agreement with Mexico." In *USITC Publication 2353.* Washington, D.C.: USITC, 1990.

Vacs, Aldo. "Crisis, Reform, and Accommodation: The Impact of Soviet Perestroika on Argentina and Brazil." Paper presented at the 16th International Congress of the Latin American Studies Association, Washington, D.C., April 4–6, 1991.

Valkenier, Elizabeth Kridl. "*Glasnost* and *Perestroika* in Soviet-Third World Economic Relations." *Harriman Institute Forum,* October 1991.

Vandenberg, Arthur H., Jr., ed. *The Private Papers of Senator Vandenberg.* Boston: Houghton Mifflin, 1952.

van Klaveren, Alberto. "Enfoques alternativos para el estudio del autoritarismo en América Latina." *Revista de Estudios Políticos* (Madrid), no. 51 (May–June 1986): 23–52.

————. "Las nuevas formas de concertación política en América Latina." *Estudios Internacionales* (Santiago) 17, no. 68 (October–December 1987): 513–36.

————. "Las relaciones de los países latinoamericanos con Estados Unidos: Un ejercicio comparativo." In *Continuidad y cambio en las relaciones América Latina y Estados Unidos,* edited by Mónica Hirst, pp. 323–53. Buenos Aires: GEL, 1987.

————. "Latin America and Europe in the 1990s." Paper prepared for Inter-American Dialogue, June 1991.

————. "Europa Occidental y América Latina: Hacia un encuentro largamente esperado." In *Las relaciones Europa-América Latina ante la nueva administración estadounidense* (provisional title). Madrid: Ed. Cultura Hispánica. Forthcoming.

Varas, Augusto. "Soviet–Latin American Relations under U.S. Regional Hegemony." In *Soviet–Latin American Relations in the 1980s,* edited by Augusto Varas, pp. 13–80. Boulder, Colo.: Westview Press, 1987.

————. "The Chilean Military at the Crossroad: Politicization or Professionalization." Paper presented to Inter-University Seminar on Armed Forces and Society, Baltimore, October 1989.

————. "Democratization and Military Reform in Argentina." In *Democracy Under Siege: New Military Power in Latin America,* edited by Augusto Varas, pp. 47–64. New York: Greenwood Press, 1989.

————. "Military Autonomy and Democracy in Latin America." In *Democracy Under Siege,* edited by Varas, pp. 6–12.

————. "Civil-Military Relations in a Democratic Framework." In *The Military and Democracy: The Future of Civil-Military Relations in Latin America,* edited by Louis Goodman, Johanna Mendelson, and Juan Rial, pp. 200–218. Lexington, Mass.: Lexington Books, 1990.

————, ed. *América Latina y la Unión Soviética: Una nueva relación.* Buenos Aires: GEL/FLACSO, 1987.

————, ed. *Hemispheric Security and U.S. Policy in Latin America.* Boulder, Colo.: Westview Press, 1989.

Vernon, Raymond. "Critical Factors in Latin American Economic Relations." Paper prepared for Inter-American Dialogue workshop on "The Changing Global Context for U.S.–Latin American Relations," Airlie House, Warrenton, Va., May 23–25, 1990.

Waciuma, Wanjohi. *United States–Latin American Relations: A Study of the Evolution of the*

Doctrine of Non-Intervention in the Inter-American System. Ann Arbor, Mich.: University Microfilms, 1971.

Walker, William O., III. *Drug Control in the Americas.* Albuquerque: University of New Mexico Press, 1989.

Waltz, Kenneth N. *Theory of International Politics.* Reading, Mass.: Addison-Wesley, 1979.

Washington Office on Latin America. "The Killing Fields of Peru." *Latin America Update* 15, no. 6 (1990): 1, 5.

———. *Clear and Present Dangers: The U.S. Military and the War on Drugs in the Andes.* Washington, D.C.: WOLA, 1991.

Watanabe, Akio. "Latin America in Japan's Foreign Policy." Unpublished ms., University of Tokyo, 1990.

Weinstein, Martin. *Uruguay: Democracy at the Crossroads.* Boulder, Colo.: Westview Press, 1988.

Weekly Compilation of Presidential Documents 25. December 25, 1989: 1974–84. Washington, D.C.: GPO.

Weekly Compilation of Presidential Documents 19. October 31, 1983: 1497–1502. Washington, D.C.: GPO.

Weschler, Lawrence. *A Miracle, A Universe: Settling Accounts with Torturers.* New York: Pantheon Books, 1990.

Whitehead, Laurence. "Debt, Diversification, and Dependency: Latin America's International Political Relations." In *The United States and Latin America in the 1980s: Contending Perspectives on a Decade of Crisis,* edited by Kevin J. Middlebrook and Carlos Rico, pp. 87–130. Pittsburgh, Pa.: University of Pittsburgh Press, 1986.

The White House. *National Drug Control Strategy* (September 1989). Washington, D.C.: GPO, 1989.

———. *National Drug Control Strategy* (January 1990). Washington, D.C.: GPO, 1990.

Wiarda, Howard J. "Corporatism and Development in the Iberic-Latin World: Persistent Strains and New Variations." In *The New Corporatism: Social-Political Structures in the Iberian World,* edited by Fredrick B. Pike and Thomas Stritch, pp. 3–33. Notre Dame, Ind.: University of Notre Dame Press, 1974.

———. Introduction to *Politics and Social Change in Latin America: The Distinct Tradition,* edited by Howard J. Wiarda, pp. 3–22. Amherst: University of Massachusetts Press, 1974.

———. *The Democratic Revolution in Latin America: History, Politics, and U.S. Policy.* New York: Holmes and Meier, 1990.

———. "United States Strategic Policy in Latin America in the Post–Cold War Era." Paper prepared for National Defense University Symposium, Washington, D.C., November 15–16, 1990.

Weintraub, Sidney. *A Marriage of Convenience: Relations between Mexico and the United States.* New York: Oxford University Press, 1990.

Wiesner, Eduardo. "The State of the Debt Crisis: Benefits and Costs." In *Latin America's Debt Crisis: Adjusting to the Past or Planning for the Future?,* edited by Robert Pastor, pp. 25–32. Boulder, Colo.: Lynne Rienner, 1987.

Williamson, John. *The Progress of Policy Reform in Latin America.* Washington, D.C.: Institute for International Economics, January 1990.

———, ed. *Latin American Adjustment: How Much Has Really Happened?* Washington, D.C.: Institute for International Economics, April 1990.

Williamson, Richard S. "Toward the Twenty-first Century: The Future for Multilateral Diplomacy." *Department of State Bulletin.* Vol. 88, no. 2141, p. 54.

Wilson, Larman. "Military Rule and the Hopes for Democracy in Haiti: The Limits of U.S. Policy." Paper presented to the 15th International Congress of the Latin American Studies Association, Miami, December 1989.

Wise, Carol. "Political Responses to the Debt Crisis." Columbia University Papers on Latin America, no. 2, 1988.

———. "In Search of Markets: Latin America's State-Led Dilemma." Paper, 1992.

Wisotsky, Steven. *Beyond the War on Drugs.* New York: Prometheus Books, 1980.

Wood, Bryce. *The Dismantling of the Good Neighbor Policy.* Austin: University of Texas Press, 1985.

World Bank. *Striking a Balance: The Environmental Challenge of Development.* Washington, D.C.: World Bank, 1989.

World Commission on Environment and Development (Brundtland Commission). *Our Common Future.* New York: Oxford University Press, 1987.

World Wide Fund for Nature. "Tropical Forest Conservation and the ITTA [International Tropical Timber Agreement]." WWF Position Paper, Spring 1987. Typescript.

Woy-Hazleton, Sandra, and Hazleton, William. "Political Violence and the Future of Peruvian Democracy." Paper presented to the 15th International Congress of the Latin American Studies Association, Miami, December 1989.

Wynia, Gary. "The Peronists Triumph in Argentina." *Current History* (January 1990): 13–16, 34–35.

Yemma, John. "Mexicans Ponder Their Increasing Economic Ties with 'El Norte.'" *Christian Science Monitor*, September 3, 1985.

Yurrita, Alfonso. "The Transition from Military to Civilian Rule in Guatemala." In *The Military and Democracy: The Future of Civil-Military Relations in Latin America*, edited by Louis Goodman, Johanna Mendelson, and Juan Rial, pp 75–90. Lexington, Mass.: Lexington Books, 1990.

Zagorski, Paul. "The Brazilian Military under the 'New Republic.'" *Review of Latin American Studies* 1, no. 2 (1988): 45–64.

———. "The 'South Atlantic Zone of Peace' and the Future of the Argentine and Brazilian Armed Forces." Paper presented to Inter-University Seminar on Armed Forces and Society, Baltimore, October 1989.

Zirker, Daniel. "Democracy and the Military in Brazil: Elite Accommodation in Cases of Torture." *Armed Forces and Society* 14 (Summer 1988): 587–605.

Zolberg, Aristide R. "The New Waves: Migration Theory for a Changing World." *International Migration Review* 23, no. 3 (Fall 1989): 403–30.

Zolberg, Aristide R.; Suhrke, Astri; and Aguayo, Sergio. *Escape from Violence: Conflict and the Refugee Crisis in the Developing World.* New York: Oxford University Press, 1989.

· CONTRIBUTORS

Robert L. Bach is Associate Professor of Sociology at the State University of New York at Binghamton. He is also Director of the Institute for Research on Multiculturalism and International Labor and a Senior Research Associate with the Carnegie Endowment for International Peace. His publications include *Latin Journey: Mexican and Cuban Immigrants in the United States* (1985); "Settlement Policies in the United States," in James Jupp and Gary Freeman, eds., *Australia and U.S. Immigration Policies* (1992); and *Changing Relations: Newcomers and Established Residents in U.S. Communities* (1992).

Bruce M. Bagley is Associate Dean of the Graduate School of International Studies (GSIS) at the University of Miami and Director of Inter-American Studies at GSIS and of the North/South Center Drug Trafficking Task Force. Among his recent publications are *En busca de la seguridad perdida: aproximaciones a la seguridad nacional mexicana*, coedited with Sergio Aguayo Quezada (1990); *Economía política del narcotráfico en el Ecuador*, coedited with Adrián Bonilla and Alexei Páez (1991); and *Myths of Militarization: The Role of the Military in the War on Drugs in the Americas* (1991).

Roberto Bouzas is Research Fellow at the Latin American Faculty of Social Sciences (FLACSO), Argentina, and at the National Council for Scientific and Technical Research (CONICET). His recent publications include *El desafío de la incertidumbre: Informe sobre la economía mundial: Perspectiva latinoamérica* (1988), *De espaldas a la prosperidad: América Latina y economía* (1989), and *Conversión de deuda externa y financiación del desarrollo en América Latina* (1990).

Marcelo Cavarozzi is Professor and Research Fellow at the Latin American Faculty of the Social Sciences, Mexico, a Researcher at CEDES-CONICET in Argentina, and a Visiting Fellow at the Overseas Development Council in Washington, D.C. His recent publications include *Muerte y resurrección: Los partidos políticos en el autoritarismo y las transiciones en el Cono Sur*, coedited with Manuel Antonio Garretón (1989), and "Patterns of Elite Negotiation and Confrontation in Chile and Argentina," in John Higley and Richard Gunther, eds., *Elites and Democratic Consolidation in Latin America and Southern Europe* (1992).

Rosario Espinal is Assistant Professor of Sociology at Temple University in Philadelphia. Her publications include *Democracia y autoritarismo en la política dominicana* (1987);

"Unlikely Transitions to Uncertain Regimes?: Democracy without Compromise in the Dominican Republic and Ecuador," with Catherine Conaghan, *Journal of Latin American Studies* (1990); and "Between Authoritarianism and Crisis-Prone Democracy: The Dominican Republic after Trujillo," in Colin Clarke, ed., *Society and Politics in the Caribbean* (1991).

J. Samuel Fitch is Associate Professor of Political Science at the University of Colorado at Boulder. He has received research and travel grants from the American Philosophical Society, the U.S. Institute of Peace, and the National Science Foundation. His publications include *Armies and Politics in Latin America*, coedited with Abraham F. Lowenthal (1986); *The Military Coup d'Etat as a Political Process* (1977); and various articles and essays on the political role of the Latin American militaries.

Jonathan Hartlyn is Associate Professor of Political Science at the University of North Carolina at Chapel Hill. His publications include *Latin American Political Economy*, coedited with Samuel A. Morley (1986); *The Politics of Coalition Rule in Colombia* (1988); and "The Dominican Republic: Problems and Prospects," in Jorge Domínguez, Robert Pastor, and Deslisle Worrell, eds., *The Caribbean Prepares for the Twenty-first Century* (1992).

Abraham F. Lowenthal has been Professor of International Relations at the University of Southern California in Los Angeles, since 1984. From 1982 to 1991, he was the founding executive director of the Inter-American Dialogue in Washington, D.C.; previously he was the founding director of the Latin American Program at the Woodrow Wilson Center. His many publications include *The Dominican Intervention* (1972), *Partners in Conflict: The United States and Latin America in the 1990s* (1990), seven edited volumes, and numerous articles, including five in *Foreign Affairs* and five in *Foreign Policy*.

Riordan Roett is Sarita and Don Johnston Professor and Director of the Latin American Studies Program at the Johns Hopkins Nitze School of Advanced International Studies in Washington, D.C. His publications include *Latin America, Western Europe, and the U.S.: Reevaluating the Atlantic Triangle* (1985), *Mexico's External Relations in the 1990s* (1991), and *Paraguay: The Personalistic Legacy* (1991). The fourth edition of his book, *Brazil: Politics in a Patrimonial Society*, was published in late 1992.

Steven E. Sanderson is Professor of Political Science and Director of the Tropical Conservation and Development Program at the University of Florida. He has studied the agrarian question, natural resource politics, and the impact of the international system on rural poverty in Latin America. He has lived and worked in Brazil and Mexico. He is the author of *Agrarian Populism and the Mexican State: The Struggle for Land in Sonora* (1981), *The Transformation of Mexican Agriculture: International Structure and the Politics of Rural Change* (1986), and, most recently, *The Politics of Trade in Latin American Development* (1992).

Lars Schoultz is William Rand Kenan, Jr., Professor of Political Science and Director of the Institute of Latin American Studies at the University of North Carolina at Chapel Hill. He is the author of *Human Rights and United States Policy toward Latin America* (1981) and *National Security and United States Policy toward Latin America* (1987).

Juan Tokatlian is Director of the Centro de Estudios Internacionales (Center for International Studies) at the Universidad de Los Andes (Bogotá, Colombia). His most recent publications include *Política exterior colombiana: De la subordinación a la autonomía?*, written with Rodrigo Pardo (1988); *Economía y política del narcotráfico*, coedited with Bruce M. Bagley (1990); *Narcotráfico en Colombia*, written with Carlos Arrieta, Luis J. Orjuela, and Eduardo Sarmiento (1990); and *Medio ambiente y relaciones internacionales*, edited with Ernesto Guhl (1992).

Alberto van Klaveren is Academic Director of the Asociación de Investigación y Especialización sobre Temas Iberoamericanos (AIETI) in Madrid and adviser to the Chilean Ministry of Foreign Affairs. He was previously Associate Director of the Instituto de Estudios Internacionales of the Universidad de Chile and the Institute for European–Latin American Relations (IRELA) in Madrid. His publications include *La detente y las crisis planetarias* (1976); *Democratización y política exterior en América Latina*, coedited with Dieter Nohlen and Mario Fernández (1992); and numerous articles and book chapters on Latin American international relations.

Augusto Varas is Senior Fellow and Coordinator of the International Studies and Security Area at the Latin American Faculty of Social Sciences (FLACSO), Chile. His many publications include *Democracy under Siege: New Military Power in Latin America* (1989), *Hemispheric Security and U.S. Policy in Latin America* (editor) (1989), and *From Komintern to Perestroika: Latin America and the Soviet Union* (1991).

· INDEX